The Full-Knowing Reader

The Full-Knowing Reader

Allusion and the Power of the Reader

in the Western Literary Tradition

Joseph Pucci

Yale University Press

New Haven and London

Portions of Chapter 6 were first published as articles and are reprinted here by kind permission of the editors of *Arethusa* and *Classical World.*

Set in Adobe Garamond and Stone Sans types by The Composing Room of Michigan, Inc.
Printed in the United States of America.

Library of Congress Cataloging-in-Publication Data
Pucci, Joseph Michael, 1957–
    The full-knowing reader : allusion and the power of the reader in
the western literary tradition / Joseph Pucci.
        p.   cm.
    Includes bibliographical references and index.
    ISBN 0-300-07152-3 (alk. paper)
    1. Allusions in literature.   2. Literature—History and criticism.
3. Reader-response criticism.   I. Title.
PN43.P83   1998
809—dc21   97-18238
                                                              CIP

A catalogue record for this book is available from the British Library.

10 9 8 7 6 5 4 3 2 1

Contents

Preface

The verse oft, with allusion, as supposing a full-knowing reader, lets slip.
—Michael Drayton, *Poly-olbion, or a Chronological History of Great Britain* (1612)

I believe that literary artists (as opposed to philosophers, historians, sociologists, psychologists, and the like) write in discrete, rhetorically laden ways, creating for their readers tangible (real) worlds fashioned of and by and in and for the mind (imagination). I believe also that literary artists expect and, indeed, require their readers to construct mental as well as spiritual and emotional worlds quite apart from the everyday worlds in which they, and their readers, at other times live. I believe that the processes invoked in this construction, as in the creative process that gives rise to it, are at once pleasurable, innate, instinctive, and grounded in the beauty of verbal sound and imaginative vision. And I believe that all of what I have just described, taken in some combination, is the essence of what used to be called (and what I still call) literature.

But I hear now (and listen) to other voices championing a cultural turn in literary study, telling me that the "sonnets on the beauty of the forest make a new kind of sense next to the language of timber legislation, and advertisements by timber and environmental lobbies are best understood in terms of their reliance on complex narratives of progress and conservation."[1] And now I hear, too, that the term *literature* itself will no longer do (I hear it is a bourgeois invention) and that what I thought was literature is really just one sort of discursive exercise, one kind of cultural production or species of social practice. Yet if I can somehow subscribe to an interest in this "new kind of sense," still my interest has not been translated into belief, for I don't happen to believe that it is the best sense to be gotten where literature is concerned.

To be sure, the cultural turn in literary study has demonstrated the truth that Poststructuralism (via Structuralism) taught so well: that writing, because it is rhetorical in nature, cannot be neatly categorized as "factual" or "nonfactual." In a sense, all writing, from a *formal* point of view, is "nonfactual." This means that the formal qualities of, say, a newspaper article or a work of historical prose are open to the same sorts of readerly scrutiny because there is a rhetoric of journalism as there is a rhetoric of philosophy, or of history, and so forth. There is a certain logic, therefore, in reading different kinds of writing together or, at the least, in taking down the barriers that once separated them—barriers based squarely on rhetorical grounds.

But rhetoric is only half of the issue, for form is not a measure of function. It may well be that Marx or Hegel or Nietzsche or a newspaper reporter uses rhetorical principles to buttress his or her account of philosophical truth or historical explanation or everyday events. But that fact does not mean that Marx or Hegel or Nietzsche or the reporter take us to the same place *with* their rhetoric—take us, say, to the space of Dickens, or Thackery, or Austen. They are all of them part of a cultural fabric, they are all practitioners of writing, but the *reading* they demand is *different*. And herein lies the importance of the term *literature,* for as a literary work of art takes us somewhere apart from our own world (that is, our own lived-in-the-moment world) and as it does so in a carefully wrought way, it also demands something vigorous and unique of its readers. Nowhere are this vigor and this uniqueness more apparent than in the literary allusion. This is a book about how allusion demands, and in demanding creates, a special kind of reader, who is empowered at the expense of the author to make a literary work mean.

1. F. Lentricchia and T. McLaughlin, eds., *Critical Terms for Literary Study,* 2d ed. (Chicago, 1995), ix.

I take the organizing figure of my study, the "full-knowing reader," from a quotation of Michael Drayton's written in the seventeenth century. The quotation, as old as it is, speaks to several fundamental points that help to frame the competencies of the full-knowing reader. Drayton's quotation focuses attention in turn on the allusive text, the allusive reader, and the reading performed by that reader. Drayton is clear in the ways he assigns the power of allusive meaning to the work being read, not to the author who wrote it. It is, after all, the "verse let[ting] slip" here. Drayton also privileges the reader in the process of unraveling allusive meaning and in the function of that meaning. This is not a uniformly accessible meaning, for only a full-knowing reader can have it, that is, a reader who spies the allusion and constructs a meaning for it. The reading constructed by the full-knowing reader is also formulated in a peculiar space, not entirely textual, not entirely mental, but curiously both, for the process of letting "slip" is a function both of the text's ability to reveal heretofore "hidden" parts of itself and of the reader's power both to recognize and to make coherent what was formerly hidden.

Full-knowledge in my reckoning does not correspond to a complete knowledge of all that the allusion can mean, nor even a privileged, superior reading. Indeed, it represents less the competencies of the reader of the allusion at all, and more readily highlights the contingency, but also the gusto, the power, the purity of the moment in which the allusion's meaning is constructed, its limitlessness, the burgeoning of potential meanings, all playing for attention. My claim is that the peculiar situation in which the allusion is read allows for the "fullness" of this readerly bounty to accrue and, moreover, validates each meaning reached by the full-knowing reader—at least provisionally.

But allusion also represents a violent textuality in which a playing (*ludere*) to or toward (*ad*) meaning complicates the ways in which the literary work would seem to function. This violence, which I qualify by the neologism "attextuality," is destructive of much that Western readers hold dear. One cannot remain a student of attextuality and harbor illusions about the closed system of a literary work, about the unilateral power of authorial intent, or about the ability of language to mean concretely, unproblematically, and without ambiguity.

Yet the reality of attextuality does not consign readers to the gloom of textual nihilism. Much of the literary activity of the latter half of this century has championed the evanescence of the written word, its deceptive nature, has regaled the tissues of meanings that herald the demise of linguistic meaning in general or the relativism of language's signification. And the ludic quality of allusive meaning, the ways in which the reader is invited into the construction of allusive meaning, speaks powerfully to the ways in which linguistic meaning is not entirely verbal or textual, but is, or can become, dialogical, imaginative, of the moment. At the same time that allusion points to these qualities of literary activity, however, it also highlights by its very violence what is stable in writing. The very fact that an allusion can be seen to stand apart from the literary work in which it is found affirms the abiding quality, the stability, of that work.

And that is an important point to consider, for those who study literature need to keep always before them the object of their scrutiny: the verbal work itself, and put to the side (though not out of view) the methodologies of philosophy, psychology, sociology, and history, as well as the burdensome architecture of over wrought theories. When those are set in proper relationship to the literary work itself, the demands required of it become clearer—and those demands help us to understand what is unique about literature and to articulate a methodology, a set of disciplinary protocols. This study is about one such protocol, the kind of reading occasioned by allusion. But it also is a study written in affirmation of the literary work for its own sake, as a vehicle of well-wrought imaginings that teach us about experience from the inside out. That is, after all, what imagination offers us. It is also what literature's students seem so easily to have forgotten in their rush to make literature good for every other discipline but their own. It is what allusion compels us most vigorously to remember.

This study first took shape as a dissertation for a Ph.D. in comparative literature at the University of Chicago, and I would be an ungrateful student not to thank my teachers, Françoise Meltzer, František Svejkovský, and Winthrop Wetherbee. Much of the initial rewriting took place while I held a joint appointment in Classics and Honors at the University of Kentucky, and there I was fortunate to have Hubert Martin, Jane Phillips, Robert Rabel, and Louis Swift as my first colleagues. To them, and to Sharon Gill, Mary Ann Cooper, and my students at Kentucky, go warm thanks.

What follows was brought into final shape at Brown, and I am under deep obligations to my colleagues in Classics for affording me an enviable place to teach and write. No less are my debts to my medievalist colleagues, especially Sheila Bonde, who read an earlier draft, and James McIlwain, who spent nearly all of a snowy New England day going over points of style and argumentation. Research support from Brown enabled me to hire assistants at various stages, and it is a particular pleasure to thank Megan Kim, Jesse Soodalter, and Evan Serton for their work. William F. Wyatt, Jr., arranged for a partial subvention to bring the book to publication, for which I owe thanks also to Provost James Pomerantz. Ruthann Whitten and Carole Cramer have offered all manner of practical and logistical support in their respective roles as administrators of Classics and of medieval studies, but so too has their friendship sustained me over the years. Sarah Spence was a careful reader of much of what follows, but I hope she knows how indebted I am to her important studies of ancient and medieval rhetoric and of medieval corporality. I don't believe there is a more learned or humane editor in academic publishing than Harry Haskell, and I will always be in his debt. Marty Secker and Linda Margolis were there at the start and remain with me, as does P. H. L.—*animae pars meae*—who started it all twenty years ago (*quo vadis?*). To my parents and to Joey and Kitty go my first, last, and best thanks, for every reason that they know and all that I cannot say.

Michael Putnam spent much time correcting and improving an earlier version of what follows, even though he was burdened with administrative, teaching, and publishing duties. His devotion to my work is unmerited. I hope he will feel himself in the company of the man to whom this book is dedicated and without whose trust and devotion so much would be different in my life.

Introduction

The premises of this study are three: first, that allusion is an essential literary figure, rctrievable in roughly the same form and performing roughly the same functions in Homer as in hip-hop; second, that the most important feature of this essentialism is a powerful reader, possessed of discrete and unique competencies; and third, that a sensitivity to this reader and her competencies is fundamental to an understanding of allusion historically in the Western literary tradition. Because these premises are contentious, especially given the current state of literary study, a word or two is in order about each of them.

To assert the essentialism of allusion is, I am aware, to cut against the grain of much current thinking about literature; I reveal this tendency even in my use of the term *literature*. My claim here, however, is circumscribed. In speaking of the allusion's essentialism I mean only to stress my belief that allusion is possessed of a unique and consistent identity, retrievable down through time, on the model of other rhetorical figures, such as metaphor, simile, or allegory.[1] I can-

1. See, for example, P. Ricoeur, *La Métaphor vive* (Paris, 1975), and S. Sacks, ed., *On Metaphor* (Chicago, 1978).

not investigate a topic situated in the past without first accounting for its stability in this way. At the same time, I make no broader claims about literary works, for I do not feel it incumbent upon me to construct a complete system of literary meaning. My focus here is on allusion and my claims for essentialism begin and end with allusion.

I hasten to add that my essentialism is not based on preconceived notions about allusion. On the contrary, I arrived at my conclusions after inquiring for half a decade into the ways Western littérateurs had approached allusion, both as a form of literary expression and as an object of literary study. Their collective voices pointed the way toward an abiding form for allusion founded in a powerful reader—hence my second claim in this study. I had no idea I would make such a claim when I began this project; indeed, initially I focused on the allusive author. My concern with authorial power, I now know, was grounded in contemporary assumptions about allusion inherited from the New Criticism, rather than in a tradition retrievable from the career of allusion prior to the twentieth century. I was able to get beyond this presupposition, in any case, only because of my determination to solve two key puzzles about allusion that could not be pursued from a contemporary perspective: to explain the lack of a term for allusion in antiquity and to make sense of ancient rhetoric's silence with respect to allusion.

I set out to find in ancient rhetoric the term that had for so long evaded critics, convinced that others had simply not seen what I hoped to find. In returning to ancient rhetoric for descriptions of allusive function, however, I discovered a body of evidence that soon led me down an unanticipated path of inquiry. Ancient rhetoric, though fundamentally silent about allusion, did seem carefully to consider the dynamics of allusive reading in its discussion of the so-called forceful style, given the Greek name δεινότης. It was not so much that δεινότης and allusion were equivalent terms, for clearly they were not. Yet there were enough affinities between it and allusion to make me ponder the category further. In turn, I began examining how the adjective δεινός was used in Greek literary culture (it being the derivative source of δεινότης) and I discovered that Greek literary artists (especially the dramatists) regularly used δεινός to talk about a powerful reader or audience. Plato proved the currency of this usage when he carefully qualified writing as δεινός in the *Phaedrus* precisely because of the demands it made of readers. In short, the histories of δεινότης and δεινός revealed a tension in the Greek literary tradition between authorial intent and readerly understanding. I had been searching for a term for allusion in ancient rhetoric. I discovered instead something equally important: a hermeneutical dynamic, problematized by Greek littérateurs and codified by Greek rhetoricians, in which the reader was empowered at the expense of the author.

Antique rhetoric had not supplied an answer to my two key puzzles, but it offered something more profound by considering a powerful audience or reader in the context of rhetorical persuasion. Moreover, the way antique rhetoric framed its discussion was important, for it called the sort of style that negotiated the tension between authorial and readerly power by a name (δεινότης) already associated in Greek literature with that selfsame tension (δεινός). At this point, however, I did not yet have a sense that allusion in antiquity was closely associated with this tension. That conclusion arose later, after I had undertaken to locate and analyze *descriptions* of allusion in ancient literature. I had begun this line of inquiry because it seemed to me inadequate to claim that a given line of ancient writing was allusive, lacking hard evidence suggesting how such an allusion might have functioned (if at all) in antiquity. Absent this evidence, after all, one might easily read back into ancient texts a modern notion of allusion that had no currency in the ancient tradition. The danger of anachronism was especially high, too, since there was no term for allusion in antiquity. A control in the ancient evidence itself was needed.

I found just such a control in a cohort of passages from Terence, Aristophanes, Varro, and Virgil, which described the process by which older literary language was used in a newer work of verbal art. More important than the similarity of these descriptions, however, was the conformity of their authors' vocabulary. Consistently, these writers used images of textual movement, implantation, and cutting to describe what seemed to be allusion. But at the same time that they seemed to be describing allusion in terms of shared language between two texts, these authors also were consistent in the ways they lavished attention onto the reader, receiver, or audience involved in the hermeneutic dynamic they were sketching. In doing so, they made clear that a powerful reader—the δεινός reader of Greek rhetoric—was essential to the antique notion of allusion.

Nonetheless, the two puzzles remained unsolved: I still could not say why there was no term for allusion in antiquity, nor why ancient rhetoric ignored allusion. I did possess a cohort of terms used by antique littérateurs to talk about allusion. But I wondered why antiquity was so circumspect about allusion—at least until the late antique period, when the term *allusio* and a concept of allusive function suddenly emerge in the evidence. That sudden emergence remained mysterious until I read Sarah Spence's treatment of Christian rhetoric in her important book on ancient and medieval hermeneutics. In particular, Spence's analysis of Augustine's rhetorical model helped me to understand the part played by late antiquity in the development of allusion, for her analysis rightly emphasized the importance of a powerful reader as the crucial figure of Christian rhetoric, a reader ennobled by Christian *caritas* to make any text read in the best way.[2] Suddenly, the break in antiquity's silence made good sense. It occurred only after Christian rhetoric made a powerful reader the centerpiece of its rhetorical program. Allusion became a legitimated rhetorical figure in the Western literary tradition, in other words, only after the key ingredient in its function, a powerful reader, was itself made the focal point of Western hermeneutical practice.

With this discovery, the career of allusion down to the Middle Ages made much better sense. There were two lines of ascent running from the Christian legitimation of a powerful reader. One line led back to δεινότης in ancient rhetoric, which focused on readerly power, while the other led back to ancient littérateurs, who described allusion in consistent ways and always within the context of readerly power. Both lines of ascent met in Christian rhetoric, specifically in the Augustinian model of Christian reading, where a powerful reader was codified into a coherent rhetorical system.

The function of this system is the backdrop, then, of my third premise, that one needs to concentrate on the powers required of the reader in order to understand allusion down through time. In pursuing this premise, I am aware of arguing against some of the strongest traditions of modern thinking about allusion, which have stressed the intentionality of the allusive author. But, as I will argue, there are good reasons to privilege the reader in the function of the allusion, most notably the fact that the reader is called upon to perform unique tasks.

In what follows, then, I have not aimed to tell the history of allusion, nor aimed much at originality in describing the ways in which allusion seems to function. I have chosen rather to focus on what seem to me to be the essential qualities of the allusion, to suggest the importance of those qualities down through time, and to exemplify those qualities in a series of readings of ancient, medieval, and modern texts. I have put to the side permanently any hope of discovering an ancient term for allusion—for I now know there is no single way of designating allusion in antiquity. But I hope in what follows to point to a

---

2. S. Spence, *Rhetorics of Reason and Desire: Vergil, Augustine, and the Troubadours* (Ithaca, 1988), esp. pp. 98–101.

discrete body of terms, images, and motifs that were deployed consistently in antiquity to talk about allusion; I hope also to highlight some of the qualities that antiquity considered important in the allusion, which are fundamental to the establishment of allusion as a concept and a term in the early Middle Ages—indeed, in the Western literary tradition as a whole.

When I first began reading about allusion from the perspective of my modern colleagues in the mid-1980s, I recall spying in a note in some article that a certain author (the name escapes me now) would soon bring out a "new book on allusion." Since the article I was reading was published in the late 1970s, my heart began to race. Was there really a book on allusion? Were some of the questions I had been asking for so long already answered, if only provisionally? Would I, at long last, find the road map for which I had been searching, some path down which I could travel? I searched—in vain—for that book for several years. As far as I know it was never published. I now understand the obstacles my colleague must have faced in attempting to write that book. Allusion is everywhere, and nowhere, in the Western literary tradition; it is part of the ingrained critical imagination in the West, so much so that it is hard to know precisely where, or how, to begin to talk about it. I often think that the best-laid plans of my colleague of the 1970s went awry not for lack of talent or skill, but only because of the daunting nature of the topic. The problem is not one of seeing only the trees at the expense of the forest, for that implies some higher, retrievable ground of vision. With allusion, the problem is to know which of the hundreds of forests to enter, and to determine in them those trees whose fruit is best to taste. And so I realize that what follows is not all that can be said about allusion. But it is a start and, I hope, a useful road map for future students of allusion—of which I remain one.

Abbreviations

Except where noted, all translations are my own.

AJP	*American Journal of Philology*
Battaglia	S. Battaglia, ed., *Grande dizionario della lingua italiana* (Turin, 1961)
Blaise	A. Blaise and H. Chirat, eds., *Dictionnaire latin-français des auteurs chrétiens* (Paris, 1954)
Brockhauswahrig	*Brockhauswahrig deutsches Wörterbuch* (Wiesbaden, 1980)
Conte	G. B. Conte, *The Rhetoric of Imitation: Genre and Poetic Memory in Virgil and Other Latin Poets,* Trans. C. P. Segal (Ithaca, 1986)
DHLE	J. Casares, V. G. de Diego, and R. L. Melgar, eds., *Diccionario histórico de la lengua Española* (Madrid, 1981)
Grand Larousse	L. Guilbert, R. Lagane, and G. Niobey, eds., *Grand Larousse de la langue française* (Paris, 1971)
Harari	J. V. Harari, ed., *Textual Strategies: Perspectives in Post-Structuralist Criticism* (Ithaca, 1979)
HSCP	*Harvard Studies in Classical Philology*

Imbs	P. Imbs, ed., *Trésor de la langue française: Dictionnaire de la langue du XIXe et du XXe siècle* (1789–1960) (Paris, 1971)
Littré	E. Littré, ed., *Dictionnaire de la langue française* (Paris, 1956)
LS	C. Lewis and C. Short, eds., *A Latin Dictionary* (Oxford, 1879)
LSJ	H. G. Liddell, R. Scott, and H. S. Jones, eds., *A Greek-English Lexicon*, 9th ed. (Oxford, 1940)
Mitt. Wört	O. Prinz, ed., *Mittellateinisches Wörterbuch bis zum ausgehenden 13. Jahrhundert* (Munich, 1967)
MLWL	R. E. Latham, ed., *Revised Medieval Latin Word List from British and Irish Sources* (Oxford, 1965)
Niermeyer	J. F. Niermeyer, ed., *Mediae Latinitatis Lexicon Minus* (Leiden, 1993)
OED	*Oxford English Dictionary* (Oxford, 1933)
Pasco	A. Pasco, *Allusion: A Literary Graft* (Toronto, 1994)
Petròcchi	P. Petròcchi, ed., *Nuovo Dizionario universale della lingua italiana* (Milan, 1931)
PMLA	*Proceedings of the Modern Language Association*
PL	J. P. Migne, ed., *Patrologia Cursus Completus, Series Latina* (Paris, 1844–56)
Sleumer	A. Sleumer, ed., *Kirchenlateinisches Wörterbuch* (Hildesheim, 1990)
TAPA	*Transactions of the American Philological Association*
TLL	*Thesaurus Linguae Latinae* (Leipzig, 1905)
Wörterbuch	*Duden: Das große Wörterbuch der deutschen Sprache* (Mannheim, 1978)

Part One **The Modern Context**

Chapter 1 Contemporary Versions of Allusion

[The allusion is a] tacit reference to another literary work, to another art, to history, to contemporary figures, or the like. Allusion may be used merely to display knowledge, as in some Alexandrian and medieval poems; to appeal to a reader or audience sharing some experience or knowledge with the writer; or to enrich a poem by incorporating further meaning.
—*The Princeton Encyclopedia of Poetry and Poetics* (1965)

Should we not therefore . . . attempt to renew the study of poetry by returning yet again to fundamentals? No poem has sources and no poem merely alludes to another. Poems are written by men, and not by anonymous Splendors.
—Harold Bloom, *The Anxiety of Influence: A Theory of Poetry* (1973)

The term *intertextuality* designates this transposition of one (or several) sign system(s) in another; but since this term has been frequently understood in the banal sense of "source criticism," we now prefer in its place the term *transposition.*
—Julia Kristeva, *La Révolution du langage poétique; l'avant-garde à la fin du XIXe siècle: Lautréamont et Mallarmé* (1974)

[The allusion is a] poet's deliberate incorporation of identifiable elements from other sources, preceding or contemporaneous, textual or

extratextual. Allusion may be used merely to display knowledge, as in some Alexandrian poems; to appeal to those sharing experience or knowledge with the poet; or to enrich a poem by incorporating further meaning.
—*The New Princeton Encyclopedia of Poetry and Poetics* (1993)

There ought to be something troubling about the fact that two distinct versions of allusion exist in old and new editions of *The Princeton Encyclopedia of Poetry and Poetics.*[1] Then, too, there ought to be cause for confusion when one realizes that the two theories most closely associated with allusion in contemporary criticism—Harold Bloom's "anxiety of influence" and the idea of "intertextuality" invented by Julia Kristeva—are not, by their authors' own admission, theories of allusion at all. Given its universal presence in literary works and its close scrutiny by innumerable critics, one expects to recover in the Western literary tradition a straightforward notion of the allusion's form and function.[2] But allusion has never invited consistency of conception or critical consensus.[3]

1. I use the terms *allusion, allusiveness,* and *literary allusion* interchangeably to designate literary borrowing, by which I mean the use in a newer literary work of older material from a prior literary work. Other terms have been suggested—*echo, reminiscence, quotation, imitation, intertext,* etc.—but only *allusion* has been used consistently in the Western tradition to designate this phenomenon. This consistency is reflected in western terminology itself: the Latin *allusio* is the root of the English *allusion* and the Romance forms *allusion, alusión, allusione,* while the German compound *Anspielung* (*An* + *Spiel*) is a literal rendering of the Latin *ad* + *ludere*.

2. For a sense of the number of works, see C. Perri et al., comps., "Allusion Studies: An International Annotated Bibliography, 1921–1977," *Style* 13 (1979), pp. 178–225; and, for works since the mid-1970s, U. J. Hebel, comp., *Intertextuality, Allusion, and Quotation: An International Bibliography of Critical Studies* (New York, 1989).

3. I do not mean to single out the *Princeton Encyclopedia;* there are as many versions of allusion as authors willing to articulate them; see, for example, P. Fontanier, *Les Figures du discours* (Paris, 1835; rpt. 1977), p. 125: "L'Allusion, qu'il ne faut pas confondre avec l'Allegorie, quoiqu'on distingue des allégories allusives, consiste à faire sentir le rapport d'une chose qu'on dit avec une autre qu'on ne dit pas, et donc ce rapport même réveille l'idée"; Littré, p. 339, s.v. *allusion:* "figure de rhétorique consistant à dire une chose qui fait penser à une autre"; H. Morier, ed., *Dictionnaire de poétique et de rhétorique* (Paris, 1961; rev. ed., 1981), p. 86, s.v. *allusion:* "Figure consistant à dire une chose avec l'intention d'en faire entendre une autre," and also pp. 86–96; G. Genette, *Palimpsestes: La Littérature au second degré* (Paris, 1982), distinguishes among citation, plagiarism, allusion, and intertextuality (p. 8); in *Figures II* (Paris, 1969), trans. A. Sheridan as *Figures of Literary Discourse* (New York, 1982), Genette proposes that "in its more canonical form, allusion consists in the borrowing of one or several elements of the allusive discourse from the material of the situation alluded to" (p. 271); H. Meyer, *Das Zitat in der Erzählkunst,* trans. T. and Y.

Critics have always felt justified in choosing and defining their own terms.[4] One finds instead a complex history.

Some of that complexity is apparent in the more recent *Princeton* version of allusion. This variant begins by appealing to a general notion to which no right-minded student of literature would take exception, namely, that allusion is about literary borrowing ("incorporation of. . . elements from other sources"), a claim whose roots stretch back to the Latin Middle Ages.[5] Of less venerable provenance are this version's subsequent claims: that the allusion represents an intentional act on the part of the author ("a poet's deliberate incorporation") and that it is, or can be, composed of a diversity of materials ("preceding or contemporaneous, textual or extratextual")—views owed to contemporary debates on the status of the author and on the ways in which literary texts are constituted. These debates, which tend to frame allusion against the scrim of the author or of the culture in which it is produced, are evinced from another angle in the effects this version claims for the allusion ("to display knowledge, to appeal to those sharing experience or knowledge, to enrich a poem"), revealing assumptions in Western notions of interpretation (only recently challenged) that accentuate the role of the author and/or the power of the dominant culture.

The earlier *Princeton* version of allusion has a somewhat different, but no less useful, story to tell, revealing a pedigree that reaches back nearly five hundred years in the Western literary tradition. The idea of literary borrowing is downplayed in this version (presumably it can be taken for granted) but the pride of place accorded to the referentiality of the allusion ("the allusion is a tacit reference . . .") links this version to a notion current in the West since the sixteenth century that conceives of the allusion as a species of reference.[6] The

---

Ziolkowski as *The Poetics of Quotation in the European Novel* (Princeton, 1968), pp. 7–9; R. D. Schier, "Büchner und Trakl: Zum Problem der Anspielungen im Werk Trakls," *PMLA* 87 (1972), pp. 1052–64.

4. I owe these words to E. Finkelpearl, "Psyche, Aeneas, and an Ass," *TAPA* 120 (1990), p. 334.

5. Blaise, p. 54, s.v. *adludere; MLWL*, p. 15, s.v. *allusio; Mitt. Wört.*, pp. 484–85, s.v. *alludere;* Niermeyer, p. 35, s.v. *allusio;* Sleumer, p. 98, s.v. *allusio; TLL*, vol. 1, fasc. 8, p. 1700, s.v. *allusio;* one might even begin the accounting of this tradition with Cassiodorus, *Exp. Psalm., Praef.* 17.26–28.

6. Battaglia, p. 341, s.v. *allusione; Brockhauswahrig*, p. 261, s.v. *Anspielung; DHLE*, p. 653, s.v. *alusión*, 3, 5; *Grand Larousse*, p. 129, s.v. *allusion;* Imbs, p. 597, s.v. *allusion*, A; Littré, p. 117, s.v. *allusion; OED*, p. 242, s.v. *allusion*, 3, 4; Petròcchi, p. 77, s.v. *allusione; Wörterbuch*, pp. 159–60, s.v. *Anspielung.*

intentional author is still in view here, revealed in the purposes put to the allusion (". . . may be used to display knowledge . . ."), while the passive reader is implied in these same purposes, much as in the later version. But a prominent difference between this version and its newer counterpart appears in this version's opening line, where allusion is described as covert ("[a] tacit reference"), reflecting assumptions in place in Western thinking about allusion for several centuries.[7] The covert quality of the allusion has been erased in the later *Princeton* version, but the notion that the allusion is overt is not nearly as common as the idea that it is somehow obscure or hidden.

Some common ground emerges from both versions. In particular, the ideas that the allusion is (1) a species of reference that (2) refers, covertly or not, by (3) borrowing, are part of the immutable fabric of Western conceptualizing about allusion. One would be hard pressed to find a literary critic of any stripe who would contest these notions as working premises, even if some would dispute their cogency. On two key points, authorial power and allusive significa-tion, however, these versions—far from registering the *opinio communis*—suggest a disagreement in contemporary criticism at the most basic level. The newer version stresses the role of the author as a figure who intends the allusion in order to control tradition, demonstrate learning, or embellish meaning in his use of older literary material and whose intentions presuppose a model reader who is up to the literary, cultural, and aesthetic demands of the author.[8] The older version, by distinction, highlights the allusion's freedom from authorial control (the author is mentioned only once in this version, nine words from its conclusion), stressing instead the allusion's ability to signify broadly and widely (". . . reference to another literary work . . . another art . . . to history . . .") on a grid of cultural interchanges whose patterns, forms, and outcomes are varied.[9] As the *Princeton* versions demonstrate, this disagreement is profound enough to have effected a revision of the very definition of allusion within the space of thirty years. Thus the tasks for this chapter are to trace the development of an intellectual dynamic powerful enough to achieve this revision, and then to

7. Battaglia, p. 341, s.v. *allusione; Brockhauswahrig,* p. 261, s.v. *Anspielung; DHLE,* pp. 653–654, s.v. *alusión,* 3c, 6b; *Grand Larousse,* p. 129, s.v. *allusion;* Littré, p. 117, s.v. *allusion; OED,* p. 242, s.v. *allusion,* 3; Petròcchi, p. 77, s.v. *allusione.*

8. See most recently for this approach Pasco, p. 76, e.g., on T. S. Eliot; the author is never far from view, even if Pasco downplays authorial power.

9. See most recently for this approach R. R. M. Wasserman, "Mario Vargas Llosa, Euclides da Cunha, and the Strategy of Intertextuality," *PMLA* 108 (1993), pp. 460–73.

situate the contemporary versions of allusion that emerge in their larger critical and historical context.

THE ALLUSION AND THE AUTHOR

The rescue of the author from the critical margins in the more recent *Princeton* version of allusion is owed in part to the currency of critical movements—New Historicism, culture studies, for example—willing to assign a function to the author in their analyses of the cultural settings in which literary meaning is produced.[10] At the same time, the return of the author in this version reminds allusion's students of how natural it seems to conceive of the practice of allusion as an intentional act on the part of a willful author, highlighting the easy shorthand we employ ("Eliot alludes to Donne . . .") to explain a manifold and complex phenomenon. It was not today's critical fashion, however, but the rise of the New Criticism nearly seventy years ago that inaugurated and sustained this shorthand.

It is easy to forget that the very idea of scrutinizing a literary work as a form unto itself was out of vogue before the New Criticism reoriented critical sensibilities, balancing Romanticism's interest in authorial biography with its own commitment to the literary work as an object worthy of study. The author did not fall from view in the paradigm put forward by the New Critics—quite the contrary—but the equation was changed.[11] Where Romanticism had adduced

10. New Historicism has found a place for the author in the production of cultural materials, especially to the extent that the author can be shown to be, in Foucault's terms, a luxury behind which social and cultural power resides. This is an improved position for the author, whose rejection by the Structuralists marked a turning point in Western critical habits of reading. For the general lines of the New Historicism see H. A. Veeser, ed., *The New Historicism* (New York, 1989), or his *The New Historicism Reader* (New York, 1994); see also J. R. de J. Jackson, *Historical Criticism and the Meaning of Texts* (London, 1989). The author appears in culture studies most often as the articulator of oppression, division, as a subject working against the power of the dominant culture(s), and, most radically, as the purveyor of cultural materials of enormous linguistic, ethnic, and racial variety. On culture studies in general, see V. B. Leitch, *Cultural Criticism, Literary Theory, Poststructuralism* (New York, 1992).

11. I use the term *New Criticism* to designate the enormous body of critical work produced after the 1920s in England and the United States, in which formal qualities of language, rhetoric, and semantics were analyzed in the production of interpretations of literary works. The history of New Criticism has yet to be written and it is by no means a term

literary works to buttress fanciful accounts of authorial feeling and sentiment, New Critics now advanced the same works as the primary object of scrutiny.[12] The author reappeared not as a character animated by the literary work but as an intentional, willful artist. Moreover, because it was a criticism of close reading which stressed the relationship of semantics and rhetoric to the larger artistic aims of theme and intent, the rise of the New Criticism had a salutary effect on allusion, awakening an interest in it for its own sake, as an important mechanism by which an author might fashion his literary art. By insisting that the literary work was worthy of close scrutiny, therefore, and by instantiating the power of the author as the producer of the literary work, the New Criticism melded the allusion and the author in the minds of several generations of critics.

It is difficult to retrieve from the mass of New Critical writing the development of this melding. Its origins may be owed to T. S. Eliot's claim that the truly new literary artist had to engage the materials of his (literary) culture boldly, strategically.[13] And clearly its development was not hindered by the articula-

---

that designates unproblematically a monolithic movement or critical approach. Yet now, from a longer view, it is clear that, their disagreements aside, New Critics were united in their belief in the accessibility of the literary work through close analyses of its constitutive parts. To the general exclusion of all else, they focused on the work itself. They believed in the unity of the work and of its objective status. Often enough, they downplayed the role and function of the author—yet the author regularly appears in their interpretations as a shorthand for the work itself and so, like it or not, the New Critics affirmed a criticism of authorial power, especially, as we will see below, where allusion is concerned. On the New Criticism in general, see M. Beardsley, *Aesthetics from Classical Greece to the Present: A Short History* (University, Ala., 1975), pp. 365–70 and (though he caricatures the New Criticism somewhat) J. Culler, *The Pursuit of Signs: Semiotics, Literature, Deconstruction* (Ithaca and London, 1981), pp. 3–17.

12. I designate by the term *Romanticism* the criticism of the late nineteenth century that stressed authorial genius, imagination, and the sensibilities of the author as a personality. A classic study of this kind is J. L. Lowes, *The Road to Xanadu: A Study in the Ways of the Imagination* (Boston and New York, 1927).

13. In "Tradition and the Individual Talent," Eliot argued that the "truly new" work of art could take its place among the body of world literature only by insinuating itself into the texture of it verbally. In Eliot's rendition, "tradition" became an abstraction for allusive function, since the easiest way for Eliot's "truly new" artist to achieve such an insinuation, to "alter the existing order," was to allude to the earlier works that constituted "tradition" in the first place. For critics raised on the poetics of Eliot's formulation, tradition and allusion were easily melded and the identity of the alluding author closely linked to the function of allusion itself.

tion of the so-called intentional fallacy, which warned against an overreliance on the critic's ability to get at the author's motivations in estimations of literary art.[14] Whatever its informing principles were, however, there can be no gain-saying the dominance of the author in the work done on allusion in the heyday of the New Criticism. One finds in the standard bibliography on allusion for this period literally hundreds of works sustained by an unwavering faith in a strong author, controlling, intending, manipulating the allusion.[15] Reuben Brower's book on Pope and Dryden, published in 1959, is exemplary as a measure of this belief in the author's power.[16] Brower articulated the aims of the allusion's New Critical students in his insistent elevation of allusion to parity with other modes of literary discourse, such as metaphor, allegory, and simile, and in his use of allusion as the overarching category of analysis in his treatment of the poetry of Alexander Pope (one of the first critics to do this in a substantive, book-length study). Yet, despite the fact that the term *allusion* appears both in the title of his work and in several chapter headings, Brower felt no need to define allusion or discuss what the term might mean—precisely because the allusion meant whatever the author made of it.[17]

14. See W. K. Wimsatt and M. Beardsley, "The Intentional Fallacy," *Sewanee Review* 54 (1946), pp. 468–88. This manifesto against authorial power points up the variety of critical postures collected under the rubric "New Criticism." But Wimsatt and Beardsley did not deny an important role to the author; indeed, their formulation of the fallaciousness of authorial intent was an attempt to limit the power of the author, who was, when they wrote, asserting a strong hegemony over much New Critical writing.

15. See, e.g., Perri et al., "Allusion Studies: An International Annotated Bibliography," pp. 178–225.

16. R. A. Brower, *Alexander Pope: The Poetry of Allusion* (Oxford, 1959).

17. See the following articles, written under the influence of New Criticism also: S. Bergsten, "Illusive Allusions: Some Reflections on the Critical Approach to the Poetry of T. S. Eliot," *Orbis Litterarum: Revue internationale d'études littéraires* 14 (1959), pp. 9–18; K. Malkoff, "Allusion as Irony: Pound's Use of Dante in 'Hugh Selwyn Mauberley,'" *Minnesota Review* 7 (1967), pp. 81–88; W. F. Hall, "Hawthorne, Shakespeare and Tess: Hardy's Use of Allusion and Reference," *English Studies* 52 (1971), pp. 533–42; G. Defaux, "Sur des Vers de Virgile: Alissa et le mythe gidien du bonheur," *La Revue des lettres modernes* 9 (1972), pp. 97–121; A. H. Pasco, "A Study of Allusion: Barbey's Stendahl in 'Le Rideau cramoisi,'" *PMLA* 88 (1973), pp. 461–71; I. J. Driscoll, "Visual Allusion in the Work of Théophile Gauthier," *French Studies* 27 (1973), pp. 418–28; M. Donker, "'The Waste Land' and the *Aeneid*," *PMLA* 89 (1974), pp. 164–73; K. H. Macfarlane, "Baudelaire's Revaluation of the Classical Allusion," *Studies in Romanticism* 15 (1976), pp. 423–44; and these books, among many others that could be cited: R. G. Noyes, *The Thespian Mirror: Shakespeare in the Eighteenth-Century Novel* (Providence, 1953) and also

This was not the view the New Critics initially held of allusion. The earliest of them had seen in allusion a discrete literary form with set properties and functions.[18] But that view developed over time into something more severe, with the lines between authorial power and allusive form blurred. Having been trained to associate the allusion with that power exclusively, the New Critics eventually were unable (or unwilling) to reassert the boundaries between the allusion's form and an author's deployment of it. Allusion existed for them as something shaped strictly by an author's individual usage. To say more about allusion—to analyze its form, to articulate its function—was impossible because the allusion changed with each author's deployment of it. The New Critics came to the conclusion, therefore, that there were as many kinds of allusion as allusive authors. Most of them, if asked, would have "defined" allusion along the lines set down by Davis Harding in 1962 in his study of Milton: "The allusion is a protean device, and may appear now in one guise, now in another, ranging all the way from the borrowed incident or the direct quotation to the subtlest variations on old words, cadences, or rhythms. But in whatever shape it appears, with the good poet its purpose is seldom merely decorative. By means of it, he is able to convey to the reader an idea or an emotion which he could not convey in any other fashion without some kind of loss."[19]

This strain of New Critical thinking held sway down to the end of the 1960s, when Structuralism began to expose the slippage between the desires of the reader of the allusion and the kind of authorial power of which Harding speaks—warning critics away from the seductive but false security of the author's power. This warning sent shock waves through the ranks of the allusion's New Critical students. Their response was to search for a champion to articulate a case they had for forty years considered self-evident. They lacked such a figure until Harold Bloom published *The Anxiety of Influence,* in 1973.

Not that Bloom meant to make their case. There is no small irony in the fact

his *The Neglected Muse: Restoration and Eighteenth-Century Tragedy in the Novel (1740–1780)* (Providence, 1958); R. M. Adams, *Surface and Symbol: The Consistency of James Joyce's " Ulysses"* (Oxford, 1962); K. L. Moler, *Janes Austen's Art of Allusion* (Lincoln, Neb., 1968); R. Cohen, *Literary References and Their Effect Upon Characterization in the Novels of Richardson* (Bangor, Me., 1970).

18. See, for example, E. Colby, *The Echo-Device in Literature* (New York, 1920); O. C. Johnson, "Allusion and Style," in *Fred Newton Scott Papers* (New York, 1929), pp. 189–98; E. E. Kellett, *Literary Quotation and Allusion* (New York, 1933).

19. D. P. Harding, *The Club of Hercules: Studies in the Classical Background of "Paradise Lost,"* Illinois Studies in Language and Literature 50 (Urbana, 1962), p. 1.

that when they found themselves under siege, the New Critics pilfered a theory of literature written squarely in the Romantic tradition—the very tradition to which the New Criticism had itself laid siege fifty years before. The Structural attack on the New Criticism, however, was much more pointed than the New Critical rejection of Romanticism, for while there was much common ground between the views of the New Critics and those of the Romantics whom they helped to discredit, no such affiliation was possible with the Structuralists. By the time *The Anxiety of Influence* appeared, virtually every position staked out by the New Critics was under attack. Most notably for students of allusion, the Structuralists rejected the New Critical acceptance of authorial power, banning the author to the critical margins as a luxury no longer affordable, and declaring the very idea of authorship to be a subterfuge used merely, and dishonestly, to authenticate readerly desire.[20] By 1973, the author had been replaced in Structuralist criticism by an interest in larger concerns: language, system, and cultural codes.

Bloom brooked no talk of cultural codes, signification, *langue,* or *parole* in *The Anxiety of Influence*. Indeed, to read Bloom's manifesto of antithetical criticism is to return to some of the best strains of Romantic criticism, for his notion of the anxious poet battling a strong precursor employs a methodology in which literary works are used to embellish the life—in this case the psychological life—of the literary artist.[21] Everyone is familiar with Bloom's artist, who suffers in competition with a strong "precursor" and attempts to outdo him by (mis)reading and (mis)appropriating his words. These attempts, as the scenario goes, make all the difference, for the projected success of every literary work hinges on the author's ability to navigate the mazes of his precursor's works. Brought low by feelings of inferiority and disability, the truly original literary artist asserts his power despite these handicaps, and avows his own might against the overweening vigor of the precursor. He does this, ultimately, by reading his precursor's work and making that work, presumably at any cost, part of his own newer creation.

It is remarkable, given its author's clear disdain for allusion ("no poem has sources and no poem merely alludes to another.") that *The Anxiety of Influence* should have become so quickly, and remained so steadfastly, associated with

20. Articulated famously by M. Foucault, "What Is An Author?" in Harari, pp. 141–60.
21. *The Anxiety of Influence* is the most famous of four books—Bloom's tetralogy of antithetical criticism—of which the others are *A Map of Misreading* (New York, 1975), *Kabbalah and Criticism* (New York, 1975), and *Poetry and Repression: Revisionism from Blake to Stevens* (New Haven, 1976).

allusion.[22] This particular act of critical legerdemain confirms as nothing else could, however, the dire situation in which the New Criticism found itself by the early 1970s. The New Critics had banked on the Author. It was impossible even to begin to apprehend their critical output absent the notion of this figure. To remove him—or to suggest his instability—was to raise thorny problems and complicate a heretofore tidy critical scene. When they encountered Harold Bloom, then, the New Critics found a thinker clearly on their side (Bloom wrote his tetrarchy of antithetical criticism in response to the excesses of Structuralism in general) who also seemed to be talking about allusion. There were, to be sure, many obscure passages in Bloom's work, requiring much effort of the reader, but when one got beyond the work's opacity, Bloom's notion of influence seemed remarkably familiar—almost like a manifesto of the powerful allusive author, the self-same author that the New Critics had been championing for forty years. It was of little consequence that Bloom was not talking about allusion, that he rarely analyzed shared language, that he regularly disdained allusion in his work.[23] What mattered were the exigencies of the moment: in the face of Structuralism's threat, students of allusion raised on the New Criti-

22. On the ease with which Bloom's theory became synonymous with allusion, see J. K. Chandler, "Romantic Allusiveness," *Critical Inquiry* 8 (1982), esp. pp. 461–63 and nn. 1 and 2. See also M. Wood, review of *A Map of Misreading, New York Review of Books,* 17 April 1975, p. 18 on the reception of Bloom's tetralogy of antithetical criticism as part of a project centered on allusion. See also most recently Conte, p. 27 and n. 8; and Pasco, p. 3.

23. Even if Bloom had not explicitly dissociated his work from allusion, it would still be patent that his project is much more broadly conceived. His close readings, though they entertain the ways in which poets influence each other, are rarely concerned with shared language. For example, in his reading of Wallace Stevens's "The Owl in the Sarcophagus," Bloom claims that Walt Whitman's "The Sleepers" is important. Where Whitman identifies night and the mother with good death, so Bloom's argument runs, Stevens establishes an identity between good death and the larger maternal vision, opposed to night because she contains all the memorable evidence of change, or what we have seen in our long day, though she has transformed the seen into knowledge (see *The Anxiety of Influence,* pp. 66–69; see also Bloom's discussion of Stevens's relationship with Emerson and Whitman in *Poetry and Repression,* pp. 267–93). But in Bloom's analysis there is no verbal evidence—borrowed language, the sine qua non of allusion—only vague intimations of shared ideas and temperaments, of similar symbols, themes, images that somehow make these two poems akin. This mode of criticism is powerful and worthy, to be sure, but it is obviously not a criticism of allusion. Nor, as Bloom makes clear in *The Anxiety of Influence,* was it ever meant to be. On Bloom as a thinker, see P. De Bolla, *Harold Bloom: Towards Historical Rhetorics* (London and New York, 1988).

cism needed a champion and they found—or, better to say, made—in Bloom the champion they required.

They might not have needed him. Much of the critical project of Structuralism, but without the aim of discrediting New Criticism, had been adumbrated nearly thirty years earlier in Italy by Giorgio Pasquali, whose suggestive paper "Arte allusiva" analyzed allusion in relation to authorial power.[24] Pasquali was not a New Critic in the technical sense, since he stood outside the sphere of Anglo-American criticism, but he was one intellectually, sharing with the New Critics fundamental premises, most notably a sensitivity to borrowed words, images, and language, which could possibly link literary works. The New Criticism had arrived at these premises by focusing on the work of art as a discrete form worthy of study unto itself. Pasquali's interest arose initially from his classical training, which included the search for *loci similes* in ancient works of literary art. Pasquali had already published in 1920 an important book on the *loci similes* in the poetry of Horace, foreshadowing the method announced two decades later in "Arte allusiva."[25]

In the intervening space of time, Pasquali had grown familiar with the interpretive practices of Romance philology, which stressed close readings on the model of *explication de texte,* a model of reading akin to that practiced by the New Critics. Armed with this new model—unknown to classical philology at the time—Pasquali was able to exploit the interpretive potential of *loci similes,* which now became, in his parlance, "allusions." The change in terminology was not incidental. Where before Pasquali had seen in *loci similes* only sterile and isolated instances of literary borrowing, now he saw the cultural constituents of literary texts, the ways in which texts were composed of authorial, readerly, and cultural materials. The relatedness of literary materials, what would later be called by Structuralists the "intertextuality" of literary production, led Pasquali to believe that literary art could not be understood outside of its wider cultural space and, more specifically, that a literary work's best identity could be retrieved only by paying careful attention to the allusions that embodied its cultural setting. The New Critics had focused primarily on the author's manipulation of allusion. Pasquali emphasized also the ways in which allusion pointed to a fixed cultural inheritance—what would become in Structural parlance the cultural "code." In so doing he refused simply to take for granted the power of the author, opting instead to place the author and the author's art

24. Originally published in *Italia che scrive* 11–12 (1942), pp. 185–87, and reprinted in *Stravaganze quatre e supreme* (Venice, 1951), pp. 11–20.
25. G. Pasquali, *Orazio lirico: Studi* (Florence, 1920).

in a wider context—a practice it would take students of allusion another thirty years to perfect, and then from outside the bounds of the New Criticism.

THE ALLUSION AND THE SIGN

Had the New Critics been willing to engage their Structuralist colleagues in a debate about allusion, the lines that quickly developed into opposing camps might not have arisen, or, at the least, been so starkly drawn. That debate might have sounded much like Pasquali's discussion of allusive artistry, with its emphases on the author and on the wider cultural grid in which the literary work is produced. But the New Critics were not reconciliators (nor were the Structuralists), and they chose to forge ahead in spite of (and without regard to) Structuralism, hardening their views. For its part, Structuralism proceeded with its critique of the New Criticism and eventually produced an influential and sophisticated body of work on allusion.

Unlike their New Critical colleagues, the allusion's Structuralist students paid close attention to the form, function, and status of allusion as a discrete literary form. They refused to take for granted received notions that relied on intuition or vague assertions of the allusion's protean qualities, and focused instead on the ways in which the allusion was part of a larger system of signification that included all manner of cultural material. Their focus was abetted in the late 1960s when Julia Kristeva (in her Structuralist phase) invented a new term, *l'intertextualité*, precisely to designate this connectedness among and between cultural materials.[26]

Kristeva's contribution to the Structuralist debate was not as a student of allusion. In her view, "texts" were not exclusively (nor even primarily) literary in nature, but rather were any of the materials of culture which, like literary works, required reading in order to be understood. Literary works were introduced into, and analyzed through, *l'intertextualité* only insofar as they were part of the grab-bag of cultural material, and they were "intertextual" not because they were allusive but because they bore a fundamental relationship to other texts on the cultural grid. Kristeva did not mean the term *intertextuality* to

26. The term first appeared in "Le Mot, le dialogue, et le roman," in *Séméiotiké: Recherches pour une sémanalyse* (Paris, 1969), pp. 82–112; trans. in L. S. Roudiez, ed., and T. Gora, A. Jardine, and L. S. Roudiez, trans., Julia Kristeva, *Desire in Language: A Semiotic Approach to Literature and Art* (New York, 1980), pp. 64–91; and repr. also in T. Moi, ed., *The Kristeva Reader* (New York, 1986), pp. 34–61.

designate allusion, nor did it ever function as a term for allusion in any of her writing—quite the contrary.[27]

Unfortunately, she introduced the term at just that moment when her Structuralist colleagues—having determined that *allusion* would no longer do—began to search for a term to replace it. *L'intertextualité* seemed to the Structuralists just the term they required. Apart from its novelty was the added attraction of its (etymological) suitability, for in one compound word was contained (seemingly) a literal description of the allusion. But it was not just the Structuralists who took the term to heart. By the end of the 1970s, "intertextuality" had become synonymous with "allusion," and in some corners even replaced it. By the 1980s, everyone from New Critics to the emerging Poststructuralists used it.[28]

Few people remembered what the term had originally meant, and fewer still could recall why the term had been purloined. Much like the New Critical pilfering of Harold Bloom's theory of influence, however, the theft of Kristeva's term measured a critical determination—this time from the Structuralist side of the equation—to assert identity and claim interpretive prerogatives. While clearly in agreement with those prerogatives, Kristeva nonetheless abandoned her term in 1974 to the critical crowd, choosing a new term (*transposition*) to replace it. Yet the term remains, nearly a quarter of a century later, an important part of the fabric of contemporary terminology, used indiscriminately by students of allusion of every stripe and critical inclination.

One of the chief reasons that the term was so easily purloined—even in the face of its inventor's objections—was the easy shorthand it offered students of allusion. Intertextuality, after all, sounded very much like a literal description of allusion. But that shorthand did not do justice to the complexity or, indeed, the fundamental thrust of the Structuralist engagement of allusion. "Inter" and "text" might sound as if they were another way of designating allusion, but they were, in Kristeva's usage, broad terms suggestive of the overarching interplay of all cultural materials. The "intertext" that became allusion, by distinction, was simply a literary text that happened to come into contact with, or contain a

27. The term, as L. Roudiez has rightly noted, "met with immediate success" but has been generally "misunderstood," being "much abused on both sides of the Atlantic." It has nothing to do with "influence . . . or with the sources of a literary work." Rather, it involves the "components of a textual system." See his introduction to *Desire in Language*, p. 15.

28. Conte, p. 29, accepts the term but qualifies it (see n. 11); see also Genette, *Palimpsestes*, pp. 15–17, for a fuller discussion of the meanings and mutations of the term.

piece of, another literary text. Most of all, there was no sense in the pilfered term of the larger Structural concern with signification. But in no other area did the Structuralists strike out more boldly in fresh directions.

Literary Structuralism arose in the merging of linguistic and anthropological methodologies that privileged the sign as the normative object of analysis.[29] It was, therefore, a movement especially open to allusion, since allusion had always been considered a species of reference, a discrete way of signifying something. Unlike the New Critics, moreover, the Structuralists saw in allusion a discrete literary form functioning apart from authorial intention and control. In the place of the author, the Structuralists offered the system of signification, and the allusion became at once more complex and more distanced from any controls external to language's signifying power.

In 1976 Ziva Ben-Porat's article "The Poetics of Literary Allusion" advanced a Structural version of allusion for the first time by deploying a formal notion of allusive signification (what she called "definition") to frame specific readings of literary works.[30] To do this, she posited a "poetics" of allusion, in which allusion, like a sign, signified something larger than itself: "The literary allusion is a device for the simultaneous activation of two texts. The activation is achieved through the manipulation of a special signal: a sign (simple or complex) in a given text characterized by an additional larger 'referent.' This referent is always an independent text. The simultaneous activation of the two texts thus connected results in the formation of intertextual patterns whose nature cannot be predetermined."[31] This poetics of allusion functioned on the analogy of grammar's relationship to language. Conceiving of the allusion as a *signifiant,* whose *signifié* was revealed in the merging of two texts that are joined by one sign, Ben-Porat drew upon Sausurre's model of linguistic signification, but modified it to fit the more specific focus of allusion.[32] This modification allowed her to draw a much fuller picture of allusive function and to limit the

---

29. The development of Structuralism has been exhaustively treated from its roots in the earlier part of this century in Saussure's linguistic theory, Russian Formalism, and the Prague School, through its anthropological phase, developed in the 1950s in the work of Lévi-Strauss, down to its literary incarnations in the work of Lacan, Althusser, Kristeva, Todorov, Barthes. For a concise overview, see Harari, pp. 17–72, which treats also the analogous development of Poststructuralism from the work of Structuralism.

30. "The Poetics of Literary Allusion," *PTL: A Journal for Descriptive Poetics and Theory of Literature* 1 (1976), pp. 105–28, a summary of "The Poetics of Allusion," Ph.D. diss., University of California, Berkeley, 1974.

31. Ibid., pp. 107–8.

32. A schematic graph is used to illustrate this important point in ibid., p. 111.

intrusion of authorial power in that function. More to the point, Ben-Porat was able to make a strong claim for an empowered reader in her description of allusive function, for, in her view, the connection of two texts resulted in "intertextual patterns" whose natures varied, depending on the perspective of the reader and on the position of the reader within the "intertextual" system.

Where the allusion was concerned, that system, according to Ben-Porat, functioned in specific ways. Allusions were "actualized" first by the "recognition" of a "marker," which pointed to the "referent" (the older or prior) text. Such a recognition entailed identification of the marking element(s) as belonging to, or being closely related to, an independent referent text. The referent text was then identified. The development of context came next: there is modification of the allusion in light of the older material underlying it. The modification was the result of the interaction between two texts, and revealed the formation of "at least one intertextual pattern." Finally, the activation of the whole referent text (also called the "evoked" text by Ben-Porat) formed a "maximum intertextual pattern." This entailed a corresponding activation of the whole alluding text.[33]

Although the work of Ben-Porat did much to reveal the larger space in which the allusion functioned, subsequent work focused more closely on language in the context of that larger space. Carmela Perri's notion of allusive function,[34] for example, while also informed by a Structural paradigm, relied on the models offered in the linguistic subfields of pragmatics and semantics, and specifically the distinctions between connotative and denotative language:

> Allusion is a way of referring that takes into account and circumvents the problem of what we mean when we refer: allusion markers act like proper names in that they denote unique individuals (source texts), but they also tacitly specify the property(ies) belonging to the source text's connotation relevant to the allusion's meaning. In ordinary language reference, when we use a proper name, we cannot control the activation of its connotation; our audience, even while correctly extending the name, may apply some, or all, of the wrong attributes associated with the name for our use of it—unless we explicitly mention the relevant attributes.[35]

33. I paraphrase Ben-Porat's lengthier discussion at ibid., pp. 110–11.
34. C. Perri, "On Alluding," *Poetics* 7 (1978), pp. 289–307, a summary of "The Poetics of Dew: A Study of Milton's Sonnets," Ph.D. diss., City University of New York, 1977. Cf. her "Knowing and Playing: The Literary Text and the Trope Allusion," *American Imago* 41 (1984), pp. 117–28.
35. Perri, "On Alluding," pp. 291–92.

The allusion was unique in Perri's view because it "is a manner of signifying which includes both the unique extension (connotation) and precise aspects (denotation) of the referent's intention, without overtly mentioning this aspect(s)."[36] Perri's claim was that "allusion in literature is a manner of signifying in which some kind of marker (simple or complex, overt or covert) not only signifies un-allusively, within the imagined possible world of the alluding text, but through echo also denotes a source text and specifies some discrete, recoverable property(ies) belonging to the intention of this source text (or specifies its own property(ies) in the case of the self-echo); the property(ies) evoked modifies the alluding text, and possibly activates further, larger inter- and intra-textual patterns of properties with the consequent further modification of the alluding text."[37]

The process was eventually reduced by Perri to ten basic steps, whose details offer a unique picture of allusive function written in the Structural mold:[38]

1. The alluding author and his audience share the same language and cultural tradition.
2. The allusion-marker must occur as part of some stretch of discourse, the possible world of the alluding text, which the audience understands in a work of literature.
3. The allusion-marker has an un-allusive literal meaning within the possible world of the alluding text.
4. The allusion-marker echoes, by some technical, phonological or semantic repetition, a source text outside itself, or the marker echoes some part of the text in which it appears, previous to its occurrence.
5. The echo is sufficient to be recognized as such.
6. The author intends that the allusion-marker's echo will identify the source text for the audience.
7. The source text is possible to know for the audience.
8. Identifying the source text as the referent of the allusion-marker's echo is insufficient to make sense out of the marker.
9. This insufficiency of sense, the particular formation of the marker, i.e., what part of the source text it echoes, and the meaning of the alluding text previous to the marker's occurrence, suggest the appropriate property(ies)

36. Ibid., p. 292.
37. Ibid., p. 295.
38. Ibid., p. 300; these are modified from J. Searle's illocutionary rules for the performance of speech acts as developed in his *Speech Acts: An Essay in the Philosophy of Language* (Cambridge, 1969), pp. 12, 45, 94–96.

of the source text's intention necessary to complete the sense of the allusion-marker in its context.

10. The referent source text may, upon further consideration, provide further properties to be applied to the alluding text, or it may suggest properties of texts other than itself for application.

Throughout the 1970s, Structuralism focused on the ways in which the allusion functioned like a sign in a broad system of signification. Eventually, this emphasis gave way to a more detailed interest in the allusion as a special kind of language and, as the perspective on allusion incrementally became more language-specific, the Structural work on it became increasingly technical, as Claes Schaar's study of Milton showed. Schaar emphasized in his work the ways in which the allusion was a linguistic sign informed by its position in a "contextual" (that is, intertextual) system. He did not, to be sure, reject the principles informing the earlier studies of Perri and Ben-Porat. One finds in Schaar's analysis an expected concern for the system in which the allusion works and a belief in the synchronicity of the materials of culture informing the ways in which constituent parts of culture function and mean. But Schaar more closely focused on the fragility of the allusion's meanings—analyzing in particular the ways in which position and perspective informed the interpretive paths open to the reader of the allusion on the intertextual grid. This fresh interest in allusive "paths" led Schaar to designate allusion by a new phrase, "vertical context system,"[39] in which "the surface context—whether word, word-group or larger entity—is charged with significance by contact with the infracontext, the hidden word pattern, which bears some kind of similarity to it: stronger or weaker, but at any rate close enough to be recognized by a reader with sufficient knowledge."[40]

Reading the vertical context system involved, in Schaar's view, the recognition of the surface context which triggered a memory of the "infracontext" and the retrieval, if possible, of the context of that memory.[41] At this point the

---

39. C. Schaar, *The Full Voic'd Quire Below: Vertical Context Systems in* Paradise Lost (Lund, 1982). Cf. his *The Golden Mirror: Studies in Chaucer's Descriptive Technique and Its Literary Background* (Lund, 1955). The phrase and the architecture required to support it were first introduced in Schaar's paper "Vertical Context Systems," in H. Raingbom, ed., *Style and Text: Studies Presented to Nils Erik Enkvist* (Stockholm, 1975), pp. 146–57.

40. Schaar, *Full Voic'd Quire Below,* pp. 17–18.

41. Cf. his "Linear Sequence, Spatial Structure, Complex Sign, and Vertical Context System," *Poetics* 7 (1978), pp. 377–88, a much more accessible rendition of Schaar's vertical context system.

"signal" of the infracontext would be transformed into a sign, as surface and infracontext coalesced.[42] Eventually, different kinds of meaning were possible: "[There] . . . is the synecdochic type where infracontexts do not similarly coincide along a vertical plane, broad or narrow, with surface contexts, but extend into the periphery, moving outwards, as it were, beyond the vertical boundaries outlined by the surface contexts. They are zero parts of the vertical context systems. . . ."[43] Schaar's view of allusion was complicated, subtle, and even at times opaque in its insistence on a vocabulary that stresses system, schema, and abstract theorization. His views, in any case, represented the last gasps of Structuralism's domination of the allusion.[44] The movement's tenacity had produced a spate of critical work but, by the mid-1980s, nearly two decades after its rise, other views were asserting themselves against its hegemony.

This assertion of contrary views occurred on two fronts, the one stressing (yet again) the author, the other affirming for the first time (if only briefly) the importance of the allusion's reader—and (expectedly) both emphasizing aspects of the allusion downplayed or ignored by the Structuralists. The New Critics vetted their decades-old approach in new clothes, touting authorial influence and worrying in fresh ways over the issues of authorial intent and artistic motive. As it turned out, however, the second wave of the New Criticism worried most of all about terminology.

John Hollander's book on allusion, published in 1981, for example, sought to analyze allusion without fettering it too closely to a notion of authorial intent. To that end, Hollander decided to do away with the term *allusion* entirely, offering *echo* in its place. His claim was that allusion was a metaphor for echo but, more important, that echo, unlike allusion, was not associated with authorial intent.[45] There could be no doubting Hollander's claim that *allusion* had been for several generations closely associated with a notion of authorial intent, even if the introduction of another term was bound to cause confusion.

42. Schaar, *Full Voic'd Quire Below,* p. 18.
43. Ibid., pp. 26–27. Unfortunately, Schaar's notions verge on parody when he talks about a big screen being suspended underneath surface contexts, filtering out vast quantities of literary material floating upward from the infrastrata; or when he talks about recovering the "stuff" stuck on that screen.
44. His immediate predecessor in this regard is M. Riffaterre, *Semiotics of Poetry* (Bloomington, Ind., 1978), who conceives of allusion as an unintentional act on the part of the author, who remains in the critical discussion only because interpreters cannot otherwise account for their own readerly desires.
45. *The Figure of Echo: A Mode of Allusion in Milton and After* (Berkeley and Los Angeles, 1981).

Nor was Hollander acting unilaterally in pressing this terminological shift. Indeed, he was doing exactly what the Structuralists had done a decade earlier in asserting the merits of *intertextuality*. Hollander's aim was to affirm the novelty of his approach to literary borrowing and to forge a unique identity for it by giving it a new name.

That Hollander's aim was not achieved did not keep Richard Thomas from articulating the same goal in an article on the poetry of Virgil published in 1986—for Thomas introduced yet another term to replace allusion—but for precisely the opposite reasons Hollander had cited. Working on the Hellenism of Latin antiquity's greatest poet, Thomas had decided that *allusion* was not closely enough associated with authorial intention. Now, to be sure, by the mid-1980s, the term had been bandied about by so many critics that it was difficult to sort out its unique identity, especially since many of the studies touting the "intertextual" aspects of the allusion did in fact discount authorial intention. Thomas was not simply misconstruing the critical landscape he spied in pressing for yet another new term. All the same, one cannot discount the fact that the New Critics had used *allusion* for forty years in just the way Thomas wanted to use it.[46] The term had to go, nonetheless, in Thomas's view, because it was too "frivolous" to meet the demands of the sort of allusion practiced by Virgil. Instead, this brand of literary borrowing was called by Thomas *reference*—a term that seemed, on the one hand, to key into the Structural concern with the way the allusion referred, but which, on the other, revived yet again the New Critical insistence on an allusion intended by its author.

Old problems did not dominate the attention of all of the allusion's critics, however. At the same time that Hollander was publishing his book on allusion and echo, Poststructuralism began a vigorous assault on several of the cherished assumptions of literary Structuralism. Most notably, where the Structuralists had tended to stress the stability of the system in which cultural materials were gathered and refracted, Poststructuralists were inclined to a more pessimistic view that stressed the indeterminacy of the system by which cultural materials were parlayed. Although most Poststructural critics were averse to analyzing literary forms of any kind, owing to their belief in the fundamental instability of such forms, the allusion was fortunate to receive an acute Poststructural treatment in 1986 by Pietro Pucci. Pucci's notion of allusive function empha-

46. "Vergil's *Georgics* and the Art of Reference," *HSCP* 90 (1986), pp. 171–98; see esp. p. 172, n. 8.

sized the autonomy of the text and its ability to play with its readers. Writing of the *Odyssey*, Pucci claimed that "all the language of Homer is allusive: to different degrees, all the epic language plays constantly with references in a ludic display of intertextual noddings, winks, and gestures and, accordingly, puts itself on stage and acts out its own idiosyncrasies and preferences in a sort of narcissistic extravaganza while it says what it says. This signifying level, that of the allusive sense, is unknown to the characters, may also fully or in part escape the intentions of the poets, and constitutes an implicit addition for the reader to decode in order to interpret the text. What we call literature is nothing else."[47]

Pucci's claims took the allusion far afield from the grid of Structuralism's system, replacing it with a ludic landscape that privileged the continual movement of literary language in a series of "noddings, winks, gestures," and which disavowed the power of the author to control that movement, whose intentions, in any case, were unknown "fully or in part" to the author himself. In place of system and of author, however, Pucci offered a special sort of reader, possessed of certain key competencies that enabled him to "decode" the allusion, to play with it, in order for interpretation to occur.

Ironically, in making the case for a strong reader in the allusion's function, the Poststructuralists returned to a position staked out by a small cohort of New Critics in the waning years of the 1960s. In a little-known article, "The Limits of Allusion in 'The Rape of the Lock,'" published in 1966, Earl Wasserman had written that allusion "ought to be defined broadly enough to include a creative act by the reader. For it suggests that the reader is not only to appreciate the poet's invention in finding appropriate allusions but is actively invited by them to exercise . . . his own invention by contemplating the relevances of the entire allusive context and its received interpretation."[48] These were radical words at the time. It had never occurred to the New Critics (of which Wasserman was one) to make so open a place for the reader in the function of the allusion. This is not to say that the New Critics had denied a role to the reader in their work—quite the contrary. But that role was passive. In the New Critical view, literary meaning was elicited in an author's use of language, not a reader's response to

47. P. Pucci, *Odysseus Polutropos: Intertextual Readings in the "Odyssey" of Homer* (Ithaca and London, 1986), p. 240.
48. E. Wasserman, "The Limits of Allusion in 'The Rape of the Lock,'" *Journal of Germanic and English Philology* 65 (1966), pp. 443–44. Some incisive comments about the idea of allusion in New Criticism, including a discussion of the passage cited here by Wasserman, is in Chandler, "Romantic Allusiveness," pp. 462–64.

that usage. The reader was more or less a decoder of data, a transcriber of production, not a producer of meaning. Wasserman's claim for the reader's role in the production of allusive meaning suggested the growing influence of the Structural critique of the New Criticism, a critique then ascendant on the critical scene.

There was merit in bringing to the attention of critics the undervalued role of the reader in the construction of allusive meaning, as Pucci's book vigorously did. That attention, however, was overshadowed by the appearance, in 1986, of a translation into English of Gian Biagio Conte's work on allusion, originally published in Italy as two separate books in the 1970s.[49] The wide access accorded to Conte's work spoke to the durability of allusion as an artistic tool and critical topic, but the popular reception of *The Rhetoric of Imitation* was also a measure of the insinuation of Structuralism into mainstream thinking about literary activity. Conte was able to speak to an audience raised on many of the most important principles of his work. Thus, to the extent that he represented a novel approach to allusion, he also affirmed the fuller measure of Structuralism's hegemony in Western critical discourse. He seemed fresh, in other words, but not radical.

Conte shifted the focus of debates about allusion back to questions privileged by Structuralism, but reformulated them in important ways, for his work was less proscribed by the rigid categories of pragmatics, semantics, or signification and more focused on allusion as a construct of poetic "memory," retrievable, as Pasquali had suggested, through careful attention to the cultural material inscribed in it. Nor was Conte extreme in the venue he privileged for the retrieval of these bundles of cultural material. On the contrary, he conceived of this retrieval as a project favoring neither an all-powerful author, system, or reader. Instead, for him, a balance existed between reader and author within the system in which the allusion functioned. Indeed, this balance was of the essence, for the allusion occurred, in Conte's view, only "if a sympathetic vibration [could] be set up between the poet's and the reader's memories when these [were] directed to a source already stored in both."[50] In Conte's view, summarized in a descriptive introduction written for the English translation of his work, the most important feature of allusive function was its ability to "dislodge" an older meaning and to make it function in a strange, new sense, a

49. *Memoria dei poeti e sistema letterario: Catullo, Virgilio, Ovidio, Lucano* (Turin, 1974); *Il Genere e i suoi confini: Cinque Studi sulla poesia di Virgilio* (Turin, 1980), published, with some deletions, as Conte, to which the following notes refer, unless otherwise specified.

50. Conte, p. 35.

process framed by a sign system, manipulated by an author, and appropriately received by a reader:

> Allusion, I suggest, functions like the trope of classical rhetoric. A rhetorical trope is usually defined as the figure created by dislodging of a term from its old sense and its previous usage and by transferring to a new, improper, or "strange" sense and usage. The gap between the letter and the sense in figuration is the same as the gap produced between the immediate, surface meaning of the word or phrase in the text and the thought evoked by the allusion. The effect could also be described as a tension between the literal and the figurative meaning, between the "verbum proprium" and the "improprium." In both allusion and the trope, the poetic dimension is created by the simultaneous presence of two different realities whose competition with one another produces a single more complex reality. Such literary allusion produces the simultaneous coexistence of both a denotative and connotative semiotic.[51]

Conte's debt to Structuralism was patent in his use of a linguistic model in which the allusion produced "the simultaneous coexistence of . . . a denotative and connotative [sign]." The theoretical underpinnings of this sign were also owed to a Structural distinction between language "made to be consumed" and language "made to recycled."[52] In the allusion, comprised of "recycled" language, the normal denotative function informing everyday discourse gave way to a connotative level, where a double referent, pointing both to itself and outside of itself, allowed for the allusion's meaning.[53] Conte's Structural debts were also made clear in his analysis of linguistic action within the allusion. In offering typologies of allusion, for example, Conte framed his discussion in terms of metaphoric (or connotative) and surface (or denotative) levels of discourse. No matter what the type, there was always a tension between the world of the text and the world evoked in the allusion, between surface and deeper layers of meaning, between denotation and connotation.

But Conte modified the underlying Structuralism of his approach by insisting that the allusion acted fundamentally like the trope of classical rhetoric. By this he meant that the allusion elicited a meaning appropriate to its obvious context (the *verbum proprium*), but that it also contained an inappropriate, alternate meaning, arising in the deeper layers of language (the *verbum impro-*

---

51. Ibid., pp. 23–24.
52. Ibid., pp. 18–20. Conte uses H. Lausberg's distinctions of *Verbrauchsrede* (language made to be consumed) and *Wiedergebrauchsrede* (language made to recycled), articulated in "Rhetorik und Dichtung" in *Der Deutschunterricht* (Stuttgart, 1967), pp. 47–56.
53. A good discussion of this aspect of Conte's project is A. L. Johnson, "Allusion in Poetry," *PTL: A Journal for Descriptive Poetics and Theory of Literature* 1 (1976), pp. 580–86.

prium). A tension was created between the literal and the figurative levels of meaning, which in turn created the "poetic dimension" of the allusion by adducing the "presence of two different realities whose competition . . . produc[ed] a single more complex reality."[54] Eventually, the text was empowered to "predict the moves of others," because "generating a text [meant] activating a strategy that predicts" those moves.[55] Clearly this empowered text was an authorial and a readerly construct. Yet Conte himself put to the side any analysis of authorial intention or readerly desire, choosing instead to focus intently on the system in which allusion functioned while not denying a role to the author and the reader in that system's best functioning.

Conte's work, especially because of its eclecticism and balance, dominated allusion studies down to the mid-1990s. But one finds in the most recent thinking about allusion not so much an approach born of eclecticism as traces of prior debates adorning fresh utterances and seemingly novel perspectives. In Alan Pasco's recent book on allusion, for example, familiar names and terms— Kristeva, Structuralism, Bloom, *reader, intertextuality*—crowd the first page.[56] The aim of this new accounting of an old form, however, is fundamentally New Critical in nature: to make sense of one literary text that has, owing to shared language, reminded the reader of an earlier literary text.[57] Typologies loom large in this accounting of the allusion, calling to mind the Structural inclination to categorize by kind and type within the grid of the allusion's system. But the author is everywhere the controlling principle of this book's readings, and the words of T. S. Eliot—praising the retrievable intent and motive of the author—are cited approvingly at the conclusion of one chapter.[58]

In the same way, much recent work on intertextuality deploys the term to distinguish work on culture, gender, and power from the more traditional work of critics who use the term *allusion* to talk about an intentional, authorially motivated work of literary art. The difference now, however, is that this new cohort of critics seems to possess a more sophisticated sense of the complexity of intertextuality. It is not, for example, as Renata Wasserman makes clear in a recent article, simply a fancier, newer term for allusion, but rather an instance in which literary texts "connect with other . . . texts, with nonliterary texts, and with broadly conceived cultural contexts. It comprises a historical component

54. Conte, p. 24.
55. Ibid., p. 30.
56. Pasco, p. 1.
57. Ibid., p. 21.
58. Ibid., p. 76.

. . . between new cultural productions and earlier ones."[59] One is reminded in this description of the affinities of this view to Julia Kristeva's notion of *l'inter-textualité*. Yet, in Wasserman's own work, one is called up short in the concluding pages of her analysis by the intrusion of the author's intentions, whose desires eventually subsume the clearly articulated functions of the intertextual system that inform much of the earlier sections of her work. Despite a sensitivity to the latest trends in literary and critical theorizing in the recent work of Wasserman and Pasco, students of allusion (Wasserman and Pasco included) continue to rehearse old critical battles over the author or the sign, pointing up the critical stalemate that animates current thinking about allusion.

This stalemate is curious, given the enormous strides of perspective and sophistication that have informed studies of allusion in this century. It is all too easy to forget, for example, that before the New Criticism there was little accounting for allusion in literary studies. It was the New Critics' focused attention on the literary work that legitimated allusion as an object worthy of study, even if, as the Structuralists later demonstrated, that legitimation was too heavily dependent on the fictions of the author. In redressing the imbalance between work and author, however, the Structuralists did much more than reorient critical perspectives from author to work. They also offered a fresh model by which to understand how the allusion (indeed, how all of literature) "meant," and in making students ponder the "meaning of meaning," they sensitized them also to the implicit power of the reader to produce meaning. Especially on this last point, the time seems right to pursue work in which the competencies and qualities of the reader can somehow be brought into better balance with the role of the author and function of the system in which the allusion subsists and is produced. My work on allusion takes shape in the context of this proposed balance. My claim in what follows is that the allusion demands a special sort of reader (the full-knowing reader)—who is just as busy as the author of the literary work and, so I hope to suggest, just as powerful.

59. See Wasserman, "Mario Vargas Llosa, Euclides da Cunha, and the Strategy of Intertextuality," p. 460.

Chapter 2 The Full-Knowing Reader:

A New Version of Allusion

. . . a bracelet of white hair about the bone. . . .
—John Donne, "The Relic"

Arms that are braceleted and white and bare,
but in the lamplight downed by light brown hair.
—T. S. Eliot, "The Love Song of J. Alfred Prufrock"

When readers spy the famous allusion to John Donne's "The Relic" in
T. S. Eliot's "The Love Song of J. Alfred Prufrock"—a model allusion
to which I will refer throughout this chapter[1]—they can agree (regardless of critical stripe) as to why this is an allusion: Eliot's phrase
"arms that are braceleted and white and bare" is an instance of borrowed material that refers (covertly or not, in some fashion) to
Donne's line "a bracelet of white hair about the bone." The question
taken up by this chapter—much harder to answer—asks how this is
an allusion. The previous chapter summarized contemporary answers

1. Z. Ben-Porat, "The Poetics of Literary Allusion," *PTL: A Journal for Descriptive
Poetics and Theory of Literature* 1 (1976), pp. 118–21, discusses this allusion.

to this question. In this chapter I venture my own answer. I take cognizance of prior work on allusion, acknowledging the lessons of authorial power taught by the New Critics, while recognizing, as the Structuralists have made clear, that this power is configured in a larger system of cultural production. Yet my answer is not as unilateral in its affiliations. I do not grant to the author as much power as the New Critics did, nor do I believe as completely as the Structuralists in the stability of the sign system. Indeed, in studying the ways in which the allusion would seem best to function, the lessons that have loomed largest have been those taught in the Poststructural critique of formalist approaches to literary study. Those lessons have placed a premium on the constructed quality of literary interpretation, as they have made clearer the subjectivity involved in literary reading.[2]

While I hope to make a place in this chapter for the author and for the system in which literary activity subsists, I will argue that (1) the allusion exploits the constructed, arbitrary quality of literary reading, drawing specifically on the power of the reader to configure meaning in relation to his desires, as (2) the power of the author to intend meaning and the power of language to mean in a set, stable, referential field evanesces. My work emphasizes the necessity of the subjective, contingent qualities of allusive meaning, and the ways in which the allusion exploits as it fosters these qualities in its function. Needless to say, the importance I attach to reading means that the reader is the crucial component in the best function of allusion. My claim is that the allusion demands, and in demanding creates, a powerful reader—whom I call, for reasons outlined below, the Full-Knowing Reader.[3]

2. The bibliography on Postmodernism is enormous; two works that I have found useful are J.-F. Lyotard, *The Postmodern Condition: A Report on Knowledge,* trans. G. Bennington and B. Massumi (Minneapolis, 1984), and F. Jameson, *Postmodernism, or, The Cultural Logic of Late Capitalism* (Durham, N.C., 1991). The Poststructural critique of Structuralism (and, by implication, New Criticism, Romanticism, and all that came before it) gave rise to the Postmodern perspective, and it is not limited to literary activity by any means. In the main, however, such a view has helped to focus more attention onto the "constructor" of human experience and onto the power of the desires that front interpretations, which turn out to be commensurate with—perhaps even superior to—those of the "creator" or the medium in which creation occurs. Applied to the realm of literary study, this assumption translates into a special place for the reader and for a renewed interest in the power that accrues to those to whom it falls to study the materials of culture.

3. I cannot review here the scholarship on reading in the past thirty years, but several works have been helpful in my own thinking. A historical accounting of the career of the reader in modern Western literature is E. Freund, *The Return of the Reader: Reader-Response*

The historical pedigree of this reader—for her lineage reaches back to Greek antiquity—will be sketched in part 2. Here I aim simply to analyze my claims for the allusion's best function while defending their cogency in the context of a powerful reader. This aim will be accomplished below through an analysis of the process of reading demanded of the allusion. I begin, however, by returning to the foundational notions of borrowing, referentiality, and coversion in order to establish more precisely the identity of these three fundaments of allusion. As it turns out, there are important divergences of conception across the critical spectrum with respect to these notions and, as a first order of business, it is important to sketch their identity more securely. The chapter concludes with a new, literary-specific definition of allusion—the first, so far as I know, of its kind—based on the analyses ventured throughout.

Criticism (London and New York, 1987), pp. 21–66 and, in a more specific context, P. J. Rabinowitz, *Before Reading: Narrative Conventions and the Politics of Interpretation* (Ithaca, 1987), esp. pp. 1–46. More theoretical is S. Fish, *Surprised by Sin: The Reader in Paradise Lost* (Berkeley, 1971); and his *Is There a Text in This Class? The Authority of Interpretive Communities* (Cambridge, Mass., 1980). Fish is criticized usefully by W. Iser, "Talk Like Whales," *Diacritics* 11 (1981), pp. 82–87 and by Eugene Goodheart, "The Text and the Interpretive Community," *Daedalus* 112 (Winter 1983), esp. pp. 215–20. Fish replies to Goodheart's criticisms in the same number of *Daedalus* ("A Reply to Eugene Goodheart," pp. 233–37). The questions put to the notion of the author by M. Foucault, "What Is An Author?" in Harari, esp. pp. 141–43, are excellent. Useful more generally is M. Charles, *Rhétorique de la lecture* (Paris, 1977) and I. C. Wimmers, *Poetics of Reading* (Princeton, 1988). More applicable to allusion specifically is U. Eco, *The Role of the Reader: Explorations in the Semiotics of Texts* (Bloomington, Ind., 1979) and the more comprehensive *Opera aperta*, trans. A. Cancogni as *The Open Work* (Cambridge, Mass., 1989), esp. pp. 1–43. Finally, *Rezeptionsästhetik*, founded in Germany by W. Iser, has mounted a vigorous critical investigation of the process of reading but would divorce reading from the effects and responses of the text that would support, for example, Charles's views, or Eco's. Iser is concerned with the presence of a model reader, who is manipulated by the text. Hans Robert Jauss has more specifically located the act of reading within a context of reception. The work of M. Riffaterre has also stressed the role of the reader, especially the act of decoding that each reader is expected to make in order to read properly. Indeed, such a stellar list of thinkers points to the fact that much of the criticism of the twentieth century is concerned with the power of the reader to work his or her magic over a text (a reading) once thought to be the sole property of the author. See W. Iser, *The Implied Reader: Patterns of Communication in Prose Fiction from Bunyan to Beckett* (Baltimore and London, 1974); *The Act of Reading: A Theory of Aesthetic Response* (Baltimore and London, 1978); H. R. Jauss, *Toward an Aesthetic of Reception*, trans. T. Bahti (Minneapolis, 1982); and M. Riffaterre, *Semiotics of Poetry* (Bloomington, Ind., 1978).

VARIATIONS ON FOUNDATIONAL THEMES

Borrowing

It is appropriate to begin an analysis of how an allusion functions by returning to the idea of borrowing, for this notion is so ingrained in the Western identity of allusion that it would be difficult to find a critic who would dispute its cogency.[4] But this seeming unanimity is deceptive. Critics have agreed upon the premise of borrowing, to be sure, but they have not agreed in their conceptualizations about it. As we will see below, some have taken the view that just about anything constitutes borrowing—the use of a name, a reference to an historical event, and so forth—while others have attempted to restrict and limit the notion, establishing guidelines based on key criteria. While taking cognizance of what others have attempted to do with respect to borrowing, I will make three claims: (1) that the borrowing involved in literary allusion always involves language shared between two literary works; (2) that this borrowing is specific and verifiable, that is, it points to a discrete moment in a prior work; and (3) that this borrowing cannot be quantified.

My first claim centers on the literary quality of allusion, and I can perhaps best defend the necessity of the claim, as well as its truth-value, by considering typological studies, for these represent the most glaring instances in which the literary quality of allusion is ignored. Such studies know no critical boundaries. Venues such as poetical encyclopedias written squarely within the New Critical tradition (Morier's *Dictionnaire*, for example) are replete with descriptions of allusive types, which tend toward broad categories ("historical" or "mythological" allusion, for example), while Structuralism has produced its own brand of typologies, such as those most recently found in the work of Gian Biagio Conte, whose categories tend to be more focused on specific instances of allusion (two of Conte's types are "integrative" or "reflective allusion," for example).[5] Whatever their scope, however, typologies jumble the materials making up the allusion with the larger contexts in which they subsist, so that, eventually,

---

4. One might begin the accounting of this tradition with Cassiodorus, *Exp. Psalm., Praef.* 17.26–28; cf. Blaise, p. 54, s.v. *adludere; MLWL,* p. 15, s.v. *allusio; Mitt. Wört.,* pp. 484–85, s.v. *alludere;* Niermeyer, p. 35, s.v. *allusio;* Sleumer, p. 98, s.v. *allusio; TLL,* vol. 1, fasc. 8, p. 1700, s.v. *allusio;* Battaglia, p. 341, s.v. *allusione; Brockhauswahrig,* p. 261, s.v. *Anspielung; DHLE,* p. 653, s.v. *alusión,* 3, 5; *Grand Larousse,* p. 129, s.v. *allusion;* Imbs, p. 597, s.v. *allusion,* A; Littré, p. 117, s.v. *allusion; OED,* p. 242, s.v. *allusion,* 3, 4; Petròcchi, p. 77, s.v. *allusione; Wörterbuch,* pp. 159–60, s.v. *Anspielung.*
5. See Conte, esp. pp. 66–70.

everything can somehow be considered allusive—not only borrowings from the plastic, visual, or musical arts, but virtually any part of the cultural fabric.[6]

Conte's typologies, for example, qualify the relationships of the alluding author to the prior text (or author) being mined for material. An integrative allusion produces, in his view, a "condensation of two voices in a single image," while a reflective allusion involves "intentional confrontation"; two items are juxtaposed and compared.[7] By distinction, historical allusion is defined in Morier's dictionary as any reference to a "trait of history," and the reference to Michelangelo in the refrain to Eliot's "Prufrock," ("In the room the women come and go / Talking of Michelangelo") would be an instance of this type. In much the same way, Morier's description of mythological allusion includes not only figures from the Greek or Roman pantheons but also references to famous mythological events and narratives.

But clearly the compass granted to the allusion in the foregoing examples is so broad or so subjective (or both) as to include potentially everything. By insisting, therefore, that allusion is a literary borrowing, that is, a borrowing comprised of language shared between two literary works, I aim to limit the otherwise wide compass often claimed for it. From my more restricted view, the naming of Michelangelo in Eliot's refrain is not allusive because it does not involve shared language. Rather, it is simply a species of reference in which a work participates in a culture by refering to materials in that culture.

6. When Conte, pp. 66–69, and esp. p. 67, for example, discusses "integrative," "reflective," or "ironic" allusion, he posits categories that preclude specific lines of interpretation that others might well care to pursue in his prized texts. He does much the same thing in his discussion of quotation (cf. pp. 59–60), in which, because "both openly acknowledge the work of another . . . no tension is established between the two texts" (p. 60). While Conte's claim about open acknowledgment is well taken, his subsequent claim that no tension is established between the texts seems to me doubtful. Similarly, when R. Thomas, "Vergil's *Georgics* and the Art of Reference," *HSCP* 90 (1986), pp. 171–98, finds in Virgil's poem a mode of allusiveness that he calls "technical reference," he limits by his terminology the function of allusion, which would seem to work beyond the rubric of reference, technical or otherwise. I would argue that categories of allusion change, depending on the reader's place in time. To posit typologies is to fetter allusion to a particular historical situation, to make one's admittedly contingent and arbitrary construction of allusive meaning the only possible meaning for allusion, to neutralize the ludic quality that makes allusion unique, and to substitute historical for readerly subjectivity. For the most recent reliance on typological analysis, see Pasco, pp. 4–6 for the categories, and any of his chapters for the typological analyses.

7. See Conte, pp. 66–67, e.g.; cf. pp. 28–31 and esp. n. 12, where Conte tries to get out of the conundrum of subjectivity implied in typologies—unsuccessfully, I think.

My second claim is that the allusion must be specific and verifiable. The need for such a claim is perhaps not self-evident, for students of allusion, regardless of critical stripe, have never been explicit about the criteria used in identifying an allusion. Davis Harding and Reuben Brower, as we have seen, would admit a wide variety of literary material—from quotations to individual words that are, in their view, loaded with allusive potential. Conte, by distinction, would admit a much smaller repertoire of verbal material that conforms carefully to certain linguistic, rhetorical, or generic rules. Whatever the criteria advanced, however, it is important to try to articulate a broad statement that can accommodate the wide space between the views represented by Brower and Harding on the one side, and Conte on the other.

This claim is perhaps best defended by returning to Eliot for a moment. In the refrain to "Prufrock," there are many who might hold that the naming of Michaelangelo is an allusion. I would argue that such a naming is patently not an allusion because Eliot does not link his poem to a specific literary moment in a prior text in which Michelangelo subsists. By distinction, when he writes "arms that are braceleted and white and bare," Eliot does link this line to a specific prior source—Donne's "The Relic"—and in a verifiable way. Close study of English poetry suggests, for example, that no other poem contains a comparable phrase. Eliot's close reading of the metaphysical poets and his reliance on them at many points in his other poems help to confirm the presence of Donne's language here. There is, by distinction, no comparable way to verify the source for Eliot's naming of Michelangelo. His name has been "written" thousands of times in countless venues.

All the same, an allusion that is specified and verified is not necessarily somehow quantifiable. It is one thing to situate an allusion discretely in a prior text, and quite another to claim that an allusion must contain a set number of words. My claim is that, provided the allusion is specific and verifiable, the quantity of words it contains is irrelevant. This means that an allusion will have manifold appearances, running the gamut from the most obvious instance in which material is quoted verbatim to the least obvious, a single word. As we will see below, it falls to the reader, not to some preordained formula, to determine what is and is not allusive.

Referentiality

In the same way that borrowing is part of the critical landscape of allusion, so too has there hardly been a time when allusion has not been conceived as a species of reference.[8] Yet wide critical agreement has not translated into consensus as to how the allusion refers. Especially since the 1970s, critics have differed widely over the dynamics of the allusion's referentiality, and the previous chapter sketched the historical context of this disagreement. New Critics claimed that the allusion referred under the aegis of a powerful author, whose control presupposed a stable referent accessible to all literary readers. It was the Structuralists, however, who expanded the conception of allusive referentiality by claiming that the allusion referred like a sign in a broad system of intertextual action.[9] Their conception of language, filtered through work in linguistics and anthropology, was at a remove from the New Critical notion, which had always privileged a stable and fixed referential system controlled by a willful author. Language was conceived by the Structuralists in a less proscribed way, as a complex system of interconnecting units controlled less by an author than by the constituent parts of the literary work itself—author, words, social and cultural constraints, and so on, which were configured in relation to each other.

Especially since allusion had long been conceived as a species of reference, it was natural that Structuralist critics such as Ziva Ben-Porat and Carmela Perri would find the allusion an inviting topic of inquiry. Ben-Porat's conception of allusion, as we have seen, centered on the notion that allusion was a sign that contained an "additional larger referent," an independent text.[10] This sign, as it turned out, referred in a special way: it signified within the referential field of the literary work in which it was situated ("Prufrock," in our example), so that the words of the allusion could be read unallusively in the work's situation of discourse. It also referred simultaneously outside of that field to a larger referen-

8. Battaglia, p. 341, s.v. *allusione; Brockhauswahrig,* p. 261, s.v. *Anspielung; DHLE,* p. 653, s.v. *alusión,* 3, 5; *Grand Larousse,* p. 129, s.v. *allusion;* Imbs, p. 597, s.v. *allusion,* A; Littré, p. 117, s.v. *allusion;* OED, p. 242, s.v. *allusion,* 3, 4; Petròcchi, p. 77, s.v. *allusione. Wörterbuch,* pp. 159–60, s.v. *Anspielung.*

9. In making this claim, most Structuralists implicitly subscribed to the linguistic theory of Ferdinand de Saussure, who argued that a word (any word), the so-called *signifiant,* was merely a collection of letters bearing no necessary relationship to the thing it signified, the *signifié.* To use Saussure's famous example, there was nothing essential about the collocation of letters and sounds in the *signifiant* "tree" (or, *arbor, arbre, Baum, albero, arbol*) that connected those letters and sounds to its *signifié,* the real tree found in nature. The connec. ion was entirely arbitrary. See C. Bally, A. Sechehaye and A. Riedlinger, eds., *Cours de ling uistique générale,* trans. W. Baskin as *Course in General Linguistics* (New York, 1959), esp. pp. 22–26.

10. See Ben-Porat, "The Poetics of Literary Allusion," esp. pp. 107–8.

tial grid—the intertextual system itself—comprised of the older work whose language formed the allusion. The allusion referred, therefore, in two discrete ways, signifying both within the work itself and outside of it.[11]

This unique, double referentiality was also important to the work of Carmela Perri, who analyzed the ways in which the allusion, though composed of two texts, was in fact a single sign that was able to refer both denotatively and connotatively. In Perri's view, the allusion denoted unallusively in the situation of discourse in which it existed, but also connoted beyond the confines of that discrete narrative situation, thus opening up the "possible world" of allusive meanings "belonging to the intention" of the text in which the allusion existed.[12] This intention was retrievable because the allusion circumvented the normal difficulties of "proper-naming." Normally, Perri asserted, "when we use a proper name, we cannot control the activation of its connotation; our audience, even while correctly extending the name, may apply some, or all, of the wrong attributes associated with the name for our use of it—unless we explicitly mention the relevant attributes."[13] The allusion alleviated this difficulty, however, because it included "both the unique extension (connotation) and precise aspects (denotation) of the referent's intention."[14]

Ben-Porat and Perri were correct to see the allusion as a unique sign possessed of a double referentiality. But, quite apart from the obvious ways in which the allusion signifies and refers in the two works which compose it, more needs to

---

11. Ben-Porat was criticized on just this score by C. Schaar, who noted that she "[leaves] out of account two important features of functioning allusions: their synthetic and kinetic character. Ben-Porat's charts endanger cohesion and petrify dynamics." The claim that formalist approaches petrify literary dynamics is, of course, not a new one. And to a certain extent it is an unfair claim, because a concern with form necessarily translates into less interest in content, that is to say, in the synthetic and kinetic quality of allusive meaning. Indeed, Ben-Porat was moving away from a tradition that had privileged content over form, or at least had used form merely as a means to embellish content. In her view, such a tradition had placed too great an emphasis on critical intuition. Yet in rejecting what she rightly saw as an excess of New Criticism, Ben-Porat turned to the equally excessive paradigm of Structural signification, with the result that her positions did not always fare well under closer scrutiny. See C. Schaar, *The Full Voic'd Quire Below: Vertical Context Systems in "Paradise Lost"* (Lund, 1982), p. 22, n. 46. A similar criticism of Structural approaches in general is made by P. Ricoeur, *Interpretation Theory: Discourse and the Surplus of Meaning* (Fort Worth, 1976), pp. 4–7.

12. C. Perri, "On Alluding," *Poetics* 7 (1978), p. 295.

13. Ibid., pp. 291–92.

14. Ibid., p. 292.

be said about the nature of allusive signification at the level in which allusive meaning is created. With Perri and Ben-Porat, I concur that the allusion signifies within the referential fields of its two constitutive works. In "Prufrock," for example, it is patent that the language of Eliot's allusion to Donne signifies normally in the situation of discourse in Eliot's poem (that is, it signifies unallusively), just as Donne's language signifies normally within its own situation of discourse in "The Relic."

But it is a different matter altogether to claim, as Perri and Ben-Porat do, that Eliot's phrase "arms that are braceleted and white and bare" signifies and refers to Donne's phrase "a bracelet of white hair about the bone." This claim seems to be true: Eliot's phrase, after all, does resemble Donne's, and the imposition of the Structural model of signification allows readers to explain how one gets safely from Eliot to Donne—and back again. But when this explanation is considered only in the context of linguistic signification, its insufficiencies are more obvious. For example, it is easy enough in Structural terms to see how Eliot's phrase functions as a sign system: words (arbitrary though they may be) signify and refer to things outside of language and are comprehended by the reader, who understands how the system works and can make appropriate connections. The phrase "arms that are braceleted and white and bare" signifies and refers to a cluster of set symbols that, when taken together, form a composite picture of a discrete situation of discourse within Eliot's poem. This much is uncontentious.

But how does one move unproblematically from the closed system of Eliot's poem to Donne's poem? That is, how does one account for the connection of Eliot's language to Donne's phrase strictly within the limits of the system of signification that animates Eliot's phrase? Ben-Porat offered no clue, finessing the problem by focusing on the ability of the allusion to activate two texts through "the manipulation of a special sign."[15] But clearly "activation" and "manipulation" were not autotelic activities engendered by and through the "ability" of language itself. Perri attempted an answer by focusing more intently on the function of the sign within the linguistic system, distinguishing, as we have seen, between connotation and denotation within the allusion's function. The sign of the allusion, in her view, was able to connect two discrete textual moments on the analogy of language's ability to denote and connote at the same time.

15. Ben-Porat, "The Poetics of Literary Allusion," pp. 107–8.

In fact, Perri played a critical shell-game in making this claim, subsuming under the veneer of linguistic function what is, in my view, the crucial component of the allusion's function, namely, the creation of the allusion in the mind of the reader. I would like to simplify the position taken up by the Structuralists over the past thirty years, if I can, and strip away the veneer of linguistic function that has grown up around the allusion since the 1970s. The Structuralists taught us in their time that language signifies in discrete, set ways. But it is equally clear now that the process of signification established by Structuralism does not account for the association of the two texts that make up the allusion from within that system of signification. That accounting can only be accomplished by the reader, who connects two discrete systems of reference in her own mind. It is at the point of mental connection that the allusion is created—and only at this point. To claim otherwise is, in my view, to replace an essentially autonomous creative act on the part of the reader with a paradigm in which that act is distorted, hidden, or subsumed.

With respect to signification, then, my claim is that the connection of the two phrases that compose the allusion can only occur in the mind of the reader, who is reminded by virtue of shared language of a connection between a later set of words and an earlier set, and who configures on his own terms the interpretive outcomes of this connection. This claim is of fundamental importance in my conception of the allusion, not least because it means that the language of the allusion makes possible but does not determine the creation, function, or conceivable interpretations of the allusion.

I will return to these points in a moment. First, however, it is important to acknowledge that my claim runs against the grain of some of the more important Structural work on allusion of the past thirty years. Conte's positions regarding the issues of signification and referentiality, for example, are in obvious opposition to my views:

> In allusion, as in metaphor, a sign that corresponds to one fact supplants the sign that corresponds to another fact, and the substitution produces a new semantic whole. The new act of signification involves the two facts but is achieved by a single sign. The synthesis of the two original semantic processes into a single sign welds the two facts together. A *single* [his emphasis] image emerges from the superimposition of the present on the absent sign; it produces a poetic denial of normal linguistic convention. The outcome of this superimposition is the "suppression" of the "proper" (expected) word. The concrete presence of the "usurping" word coupled with the "invisible" presence of the usurped word creates a new meaning.[16]

16. Conte, pp. 53–54; cf. Perri, "On Alluding," pp. 291–95.

The difficulty of this view lies in the assumptions that support it, especially the notions of semantic wholeness and the new act of signification achieved by a single sign. Ultimately, it is the co-presence of incongruities melded into consonances that creates allusive meaning: "the concrete presence of the 'usurping' word [the allusion] coupled with the 'invisible' presence of the usurped word [the text from which it comes] creates a new meaning." My claim takes up specifically the implications of this process of creating new meaning. Conte's model of creation is stable: there is a simple transferal of "one fact" supplanting "another" in the construction of allusive meaning—almost as if readers of the allusion were automatons processing bits of data. My claim focuses on this moment in the allusion's function in order to highlight its fragility, for much can go wrong in Conte's process of "transferal," and I will attend more fully to the details of this fragility below.

One finds the same concept of stability informing Carmela Perri's notion of allusion as a species of proper-naming, which she adduces in order to specify the doubly-referential character of the allusion. In proper-naming, connotation and denotation are generally at cross-purposes: an audience, even while correctly "extending the name, may apply some, or all, of the wrong attributes associated with the name for our use of it—unless we explicitly mention the relevant attributes."[17] The allusion, however, already includes "both the unique extension (connotation) and precise aspects (denotation) of the referent's intention,"[18] so that misfiring of the sort normally associated with proper-naming is not possible. For Perri, then, allusive meaning, like the process of naming, is simultaneously connotative and denotative, but the denotative level of meaning somehow inhibits the misconstrual of the intent of the allusion at the connotative level. For Conte, by distinction, allusive meaning results from an easy transferal from one to another "fact" under the controlling rubric of a single sign that refers in two ways. The transferal is neat, and the intent of the author of the literary work (as expressed by Conte) is patent. But clearly the reality of allusive function is messier than Conte or Perri would have it, precisely because the linguistic model they both employ veils the more fundamental action of the reader, who uses language's system in order to make sense of a literary work.

One can agree with Perri that the allusion's function is in some ways analogous to proper-naming.[19] But it is hard to see how the allusion "proper-names"

17. Perri, "On Alluding," p. 292.
18. Ibid.
19. Ibid., p. 290.

in a way different from proper-naming in ordinary linguistic reference, in which the audience "extends" the proper-name to some or all of the wrong attributes, "unless we explicitly mention the relevant attributes." Indeed, the allusion would seem to invite just this kind of "mistake," because the "extension" into connotative meaning (reading) is subjective and because it cannot function under the "referent's intention" (whether ascribed to an author or the text itself).

By distinction, Conte's insistence on the easy transference of references—one fact to another—under a stable system of signification ignores entirely the creative act on the part of the reader of the allusion, who must, after all, perform this transference not as an automaton but as a cognizant, judgmental intellect situated in a discrete time and place. Indeed, in describing allusive referentiality in the ways he does in the passage cited above, Conte returns to the fundamental position staked out earlier in *The Rhetoric of Imitation,* that the allusion functions like the trope of ancient rhetoric, a point whose logic further undermines his basic premise.

Normally, Conte points out, a trope is understood to symbolize the dislodging of an old meaning and the introduction of a new meaning within the same text, arising from a single word or set of words. The *verbum proprium* gives rise to the *verbum improprium,* but both function within their own language, fixed within the single text that gives rise to them.[20] But this can only be true if one believes, as Conte does, in the notion of a fixed referential system, waiting to be imposed from on high onto a reader, who is willing to be controlled somehow by a literary work. My claim about allusive referentiality argues for a less ideal situation, in which a meaning is constituted for the allusion in the mind of the reader—and quite apart from the systems of referentiality that give rise to it.

Coversion

I have claimed in the foregoing discussion only that the allusion functions fully, most completely, apart from the referentialities of both of the texts that compose it, so that to fetter it to a system of signification is to suppress what is truly unique about it. In due course I shall return to this claim. I need, however, to consider briefly the final quality of allusion treated in received opinion: coversion. Generations of its students have considered the allusion to be covert, so

20. See Conte, esp. pp. 38–39, 54–55.

much so that, as we have seen, it is a commonplace of Western conceptualizing about allusion.[21] This notion is more taken for granted than analyzed, however.

At one level, to be sure, an allusion is hidden because it does not announce itself. In "Prufrock," for example, there is no red flag in the margin of the poem to inform the reader that an allusion to Donne exists in v. 63. My claim, however, is that the allusion is overt—and then some. If one considers allusion alongside plagiarism,[22] for example, which always seeks to hide itself, then the overt quality of allusion is more obvious. After all, the allusion, unlike the stolen line, needs to be recognized in order to function. A hidden allusion is no allusion at all. With regard to allusion's coversion, therefore, a distinction can be made between function and form. Allusion is not functionally covert, because it functions only after it is recognized. It appears hidden only because it refers, as we have seen, in a way which makes it seem hidden, obscure, unlike normal referential language. Only in terms of form, therefore, is allusion covert—that is, it is not necessarily easily, or readily, identifiable. But in terms of function, allusion advertises its "otherness," demands that a reader recognize it for what it is. In this regard, allusion is the boldest and most strikingly overt part of a literary work, for the allusion does not seek, as plagiarized words do, to conceal its "otherness."

In considering the foundational themes of received opinion, I have accepted the notions that allusion is a species of reference that refers, covertly or not, by borrowing. But I have modified these notions by pressing the following claims: (1) that allusive borrowing is a literary borrowing that always involves language shared between two literary works; (2) that this borrowing is specific and verifiable; (3) that this borrowing cannot be quantified; (4) that the significating and referential qualities of the allusion are initiative, not determinative, of meaning; (5) and, finally, that the allusion is functionally overt, though to appearances formally covert. A final claim has been suggested but not examined: that the allusion functions only when it is constituted by a powerful reader outside of the specific orbits of signification and reference established by its language. The task for the remainder of this chapter is to expand upon this

21. Battaglia, p. 341, s.v. *allusione;* Brockhauswahrig, p. 261, s.v. *Anspielung; DHLE,* pp. 653–54, s.v. *alusión,* 3c, 6b; *Grand Larousse,* p. 129, s.v. *allusion;* Littré, p. 117, s.v. *allusion; OED,* p. 242, s.v. *allusion,* 3; Petròcchi, p. 77, s.v. *allusione.*

22. On plagiarism, see F. Meltzer, *Hot Property: The Stakes and Claims of Literary Originality* (Chicago, 1994). In citing my teacher's most recent book, I can thank her for discussing with me nearly a decade ago the distinctions between allusion and plagiarism.

notion of readerly power by offering a description of the figure who wields that power, the figure I call the Full-Knowing Reader.

EXPANDING ON FOUNDATIONAL NOTIONS

Intent

In assessing the cogency of the Structural model of allusion, I argued above that the process of signification privileged by Structuralism did not account for the association of the two texts that make up the allusion from within that system of signification. This led me, in turn, to argue that such an accounting could only be accomplished from outside that system, namely, by the reader, who connects two discrete systems of reference in her own mind. This point of mental connection is of the first moment in my view, for, as I suggested above, it is at this point—and only at this point—that the allusion is created. The process of creation proposed here, it should be clear, involves no unilateral activity: it is in part a function of authorial writing and in part a function of readerly desire. The shared creation of allusion thus points to its dual intentionality, wherein the author intends the potential for meaning, and the reader intends the actualization of that potential. This duality can be expressed more positively: the allusion functions in the potential for meaning made possible by an author's unmotivated placement of language, but it gains a meaning only through the reader's actualization of it.[23]

This claim can perhaps be explained more concretely by returning to "Prufrock" for a moment. As we have seen, Structural critics would locate Eliot's intent in the function of linguistic activity, arguing that his words activate a special sign that refers to Donne's poem. New Critics, by distinction, would locate intent with Eliot himself, seeing in the allusion to "The Relic" a purposeful act on the part of Eliot. I argue that Eliot "intends" the allusion to "The Relic" in "Prufrock" only inasmuch as he makes possible the creation of the

23. I argue here against the tradition of an authorially intended allusion that dominated, as we have seen, much New Critical work. See E. Wasserman, "The Limits of Allusion in *The Rape of the Lock*," *Journal of Germanic and English Philology* 65 (1966), pp. 425–44, or Perri, "On Alluding," pp. 289–307. I agree in principle with M. Riffaterre, who dissociates intent from allusion (*Semiotics of Poetry*, pp. 150–70). His position has been criticized (unsuccessfully, I think), by J. K. Chandler, "Romantic Allusiveness," *Critical Inquiry* 8 (1983), pp. 464–65, n. 11, who raises the issue of the implicit presence of an author who must "intend" for the text to be allusive. But, as I suggest here, this does not mean that the author intends the meanings of the allusion elicited by its language, only that the language itself is intentional.

allusion by the placement of words on a page, but that he does not direct or control how the allusion is created or what sorts of interpretations arise from it. Eliot's intentionality, therefore, is solely causative and unmotivated. It is not, in other words, consciously and willfully directed at a specific interpretation. Specific interpretations are only implicit in the author's intent. This does not mean that one cannot posit a specific, motivated meaning on the part of the alluding author—quite the contrary, as I will suggest in a moment. But it does mean that no specific interpretation of the allusion can be demonstrated in any convincing way to be intended by the author (as the New Critical tradition often argued). It also means that the allusion requires a reader for its activation, that it does not, like some autotelic literary device, activate its own function (as the Structuralists often seemed to believe).[24]

Reading the Allusion

I have laid much stress on the process by which two literary works are joined in the mind of the reader—who creates the allusion by associating those works mentally. But creation is only the first of several steps that lead to the articulation of meaning for the allusion. Each of these steps involves a discrete act on the part of the allusion's reader, which, when taken collectively, constitute a description of allusive reading. After the creation of the allusion, the interruption of reading occurs, occasioned by the realization that what is being read is akin to something else. In our example, the reader must think now about "The Relic" at the same time that she is reading "Prufrock." This interruption occasions, in turn, the fuller engagement of both literary works, by which the allusion is made fully to mean. This unique engagement is the expansion of reading, wherein the reader considers specific images, themes, symbols contained in both "Prufrock" and "The Relic." In "Prufrock," for example, the reader will understand the sinister and sorrowful description of a dead arm in Donne's poem and return to "Prufrock" to attempt to render the tone of this image in the context of Eliot's evocation of spiritual ennui. And certainly Eliot's poem can be used to explicate Donne's line also, for there is much to be gained

24. It is on this crucial point that Perri's arguments about intention break down, for there is no clear connection between what Perri calls the intent of the "denotation" of the allusion and the resulting "connotations" that are sanctioned by it. For that to be true, after all, one has to posit an authorial "superperson," or, to use the phrase of R. M. Adams apropos of Milton, one has to posit an author "with no sense of discrimination at all, a bibliophilic Grangousier; and then we shall have either five or six authors or a physical impossibility." See R. M. Adams, *Ikon: John Milton and the Modern Critics* (Ithaca, 1955), pp. 129–35, cited by Schaar, *Full Voic'd Quire Below,* p. 15, n. 19.

in considering how Eliot would seem to have read Donne's poem, and how that reading impinges on "Prufrock."

Eventually, the reader will come to tentative conclusions about the relationship of the two texts based on the expansion of reading, but those conclusions are only fully reached through a diversion of reading, wherein the reader turns her attention away from the language of the allusion in order to consider a panoply of potential meanings for it, some of them grounded in the language of the allusion, some of them grounded more liberally in an interpretive free for all occasioned, but not controlled, by the allusion's language. In "Prufrock," for example, the reader will come to tentative conclusions about the allusion to "The Relic," realizing, say, that both poems use the arm as a symbol of human spirituality. Yet the allusion requires a stepping away from the language of either poem, because the situations of discourse established verbally in them cannot be considered congruous—to say the least, the situations imagined for readers in both poems reveal an interpretive tension, because Eliot's arms are alive, whereas Donne's arm is dead.

The allusive reader is confronted, therefore, with dissonances that she must resolve outside of the language of the allusion, since that language is the source of the dissonance. This resolution requires, therefore, a lack of interest in the works that constitute the allusion. Eliot's arms might be rendered, for example, physically alive but symbolically dead, or Eliot's arms, which belong to women, might be seen to evoke a spiritual point about the lives these women led. Since Eliot's arms are described in great detail, a sexual sense might be read into that description, which is rendered in a specific light through the allusion to Donne. The possibilities are manifold. The point is that nothing in the situation of discourse established in "Prufrock" allows readers to consider the arms of Eliot's braceleted women as dead. That interpretive possibility arises outside of the referential situation created by Eliot's language.

Conversely, Donne's dead arm is rendered in a new light through its linkage to Eliot's poem. That arm, for example, can be seen symbolically to evoke the eternal life that love proffers or, less happily, it might be read in the context of spiritual, sexual, and psychological ennui created in Eliot's poem, the possible results of emotions too strongly felt and too long denied. The diversion of the reader's attention, then, occasions interpretive dissonance, as the reader attempts to make interpretive sense out of two discrete verbal moments with competing referentialities. This attempt at interpretive consonance is performed outside the language that comprises the allusion, in the clearing of a special space in the mind of the reader.

Allusive Space

I call this mental place where the allusion is made to mean allusive space. It is a unique space in literary reading because it exists apart from the referential and significative control of the language that gives rise to it. So, too, are the meanings that arise in it unique, because they result from an interpretive free-play on the part of the reader, as the dissonances of two discrete works are mediated in the give and take of a mental, interpretive dialogue. As it turns out, that dialogue may extend to places and topics that have nothing at all to do with the two works that constitute the allusion, whose language nonetheless occasions their articulation, if only momentarily. This dialogue ensures that the reader assumes complete interpretive power over the allusive moment—and at the expense of author, whose power evanesces. In the event, it is this assumption of power that makes the allusion's reader "full-knowing."[25] By this point it should be clear that full-knowledge in my reckoning does not correspond to a complete knowledge of all that the allusion can mean. Rather, it represents the purity of the moment in which allusive meaning is constructed, its limitlessness, the momentary burgeoning of potential meanings, all playing for attention and vying for consideration. The allusion's reader is full-knowing, therefore, because her desires are called upon fully, completely, to make the allusion mean.

It bears repeating at this point that the full-knowing reader is an active reader. Now, to be sure, all readerly models put forth an "active" reader. But the full-knowing reader is active in a unique way in that she constitutes the allusion. Constitution is perhaps an unhappy word. I use it here simply to stress the fact that allusive meanings exist only in the mind of the reader and, therefore, that in constituting an allusion, a reader adds something to the text she reads that is otherwise not there, creates something in the text that exists in it only *in potentia*. The full-knowing reader is an active reader, then, because, far from merely responding to a discrete set of symbols when she reads, as is the case with normal reading, she makes the text anew, in fresh terms, and quite apart from the referential and significative fields of normal linguistic function.

The full-knowing reader is also a reader who makes meaning. Of course, all

25. Because this reader is responsible only for the articulation of allusive meaning, we can view the competencies demanded of her in some detail. And because this reader is not a general reader, the articulation of her habits can be located outside of the disputes about reading that have dominated critical debate for the past thirty years. For the two poles of the debate, see S. Fish, "Why No One's Afraid of Wolfgang Iser," *Diacritics* 11 (1981), pp. 2–13 and W. Iser, "Talk Like Whales," ibid., pp. 82–87.

readers make language mean when they interpret it and all literary reading demands a response that calls forward the articulation of meaning through the interpretation of language. By definition, an interpretation, no matter how radical or subjective, relies on, and therefore must be limited by, the language behind it. An allusive reader makes meaning, however, beyond the level of interpreting a discrete body of words, for the language of the allusion only serves the purpose of making a reader consider two texts together that otherwise are separated verbally. Beyond that function, the meaning sanctioned by an allusion is neither controlled by, nor limited to, the language behind it. Much like the author's intent, which sanctions the potential for allusion, the language of the allusion serves to make possible an interpretation of allusion that it neither controls nor limits.

The qualifications *active* and *meaning-making* suggest the autonomy of the allusive reader, and this autonomy is also a part of the fullness of knowledge that is the hallmark of the allusion's reader. The meaning at which the full-knowing reader arrives is not the only, nor even necessarily the best, reading. All full-knowing readers know, in other words, that what they read in an allusion is only part of what is contained in it. They will see the part or parts that are theirs to see, they will participate in the dialogue that is theirs to construct, and the rest they will see dimly or not at all.[26] Theirs is a knowledge, therefore, that is full because it recognizes its own limits, realizes that it is not last, but only provisional.

Attextuality and the Attext

In arguing for a powerful reader, I have thus far put to the side the role of the author of the alluding text—T. S. Eliot in our example—for we have been considering the function of allusion on internal grounds, from the perspective of the allusion's own best function. The articulation of allusive meaning, which, so I have argued, falls to the reader's authority to pronounce, must be distinguished from the function of that meaning in the literary work as a whole in which it exists, for the allusion does exist in a work of art—and that work abides. The question that looms largest in considering how an allusion's meaning is made to operate in the verbal work of art in which it arises is to determine how and where one locates the allusion's meaning once it is articulated. The

26. I owe these words and their insight to W. R. Johnson, *The Idea of Lyric: Lyric Modes in Ancient and Modern Poetry* (Berkeley and London, 1982), ix. In citing this much-honored work, I can thank my teacher for making clear to me that allusion is abiding, essential, in literary studies and deserving of fresh attention.

answer to this question completes the several steps that comprise the reading of the allusion.

The issue at stake is one of voice. Returning to "Prufrock" for a moment, it is true that the autonomy of the full-knowing reader in the nonallusive parts of "Prufrock" is not equal to the power evinced when this reader reads an allusion. Whatever the equation of power might be in the nonallusive parts of "Prufrock," it must be granted that the full-knowing reader becomes some other kind of reader in those nonallusive moments, and, further that this reader relinquishes much of her interpretive power to the author of the text in which the allusion exists. This is due to the features of reading outlined above, which are specific to the allusion but absent from the nonallusive parts of the text. Those nonallusive parts of the text are, in turn, more securely controlled interpretively by the intention of their author. Outside of the allusion, therefore, the author reasserts interpretive control.

There is a strong logic calling for such a view, for clearly there must be some semblance of solid ground, some stable point, from which interpretation proceeds.[27] We have seen that allusion privileges free-play and takes firmest shape in the give and take of a readerly dialogue that is not beholden to the limits implied by the language behind it. In order for this readerly dialogue to mean anything, however, it must be returned to the larger context—the verbal work of art—in which it arises in order to be interpretively valuable. The allusive dialogue spoken by the full-knowing reader, then, is a speaking for the author, who, given the nature of the allusion itself, cannot speak for herself. At the same time, since the reader of the allusion is not the author of the larger text in which the allusion exists, to which it must be returned in order to harbor interpretive value, the voice of the allusion's reader disappears when the allusion is placed in the text in which it arises, where it becomes the voice of the author.

There is no contradiction, therefore, in asserting that Eliot (or any writer) "intends" for his allusion to Donne to mean such and such, because his allusion to Donne, by definition, allows the reader to make such a declaration for him. An allusion can only function as a literary phenomenon, therefore, when its

27. It would be interesting to examine the ways in which this control is reasserted, but the details of this vexed topic would take us into a discussion of theories of reading, and far beyond the scope of our present concern. The point is that the status of the reader is increased radically wherever and whenever that reader reads an allusion, and this status is achieved at the expense of the author. The fact that nonallusive parts of the literary text can be read with reference to authorial control is of secondary importance to my task here.

meanings are considered in the context of the work that gives rise to it. And since the voice of that work is its author's, any announcements of meaning are made under the authority of the author and with his voice. This does not mean that the author intends the meanings arrived at when an allusion is read, only that he is made to say them—or that they are said for him.

The etymology of allusion—*ad* plus *ludere,* literally, "a playing to or toward"—well suggests the power and authority afforded the full-knowing reader in making the allusion mean. Play is, after all, the fundamental quality of allusive space. But it is a play, as we have seen, located in a specific orbit of textualities, intents, and desires. Stock-in-trade terms such as *intertextuality* or *influence* fail to render the fullness of allusive form and function, yet, because allusion arises in language and is returned to language, to deny its essential textuality is to set the allusion afloat on a sea of endless potential meanings, to make it function like some Postmodern chimera, now here according to the whims of the reader, now gone owing to the death of the author. This will not do, because, as we have seen, the allusion begins and ends in a work written by an author; it is not some free-floating mass of literary potential, autotelically actualizing itself, but rather a discrete literary phenomenon that partakes of the intentionalities of both reader and author, a phenomenon that arises in the collusion of literary works, desires, and intents—not despite them.

I call the peculiar collusion of texts, intents, and desires resident in the allusion *attextuality,* a term that accounts both for the freedom of the allusion's function and for the fixity of the text in which the allusion subsists. The "attext," therefore (literally *ad* plus *text*),[28] expresses the peculiar form and function of the allusion by taking account of the way in which the allusion's textual (fixed) status is fundamentally (and perhaps paradoxically) provisional, by highlighting the way in which this status plays at being fixed but never truly achieves fixity.

Play is an old idea, an antique habitat of human activity, but it is of the moment for allusion, for it represents the essential activity pursued by the full-knowing reader, as it is the hallmark of attextuality. Friedrich von Schiller suggests its importance when he argues that play, which for him admits not of "everything" but only and simply of all that can be, represents the apogee of human existence, a sublime moment when oppositions dissolve and clarity,

28. Western criticism needs a new term compounded of "textuality" even less than it needs a new theory of literary meaning, but I offer this term with the hope that its precision might render allusion more accessible to critics, who have always "felt justified in choosing and defining their own terms" with respect to it.

provisional but crystalline, obtains.[29] Schiller's notion of play has an analogue in the allusion, which is, by its very nature, fleeting, precisely because it demands of its practitioner autonomy and full attention, and because it promises perfected, if provisional, moments of insight. That these moments are transitory, fleeting, is not an indication of their inconsequence, but rather, as Schiller has taught us, a measure of their sublimeness. In this regard, the good case can be made that full-knowing reading affords its practitioners a heady dose of those things that abide, authentically, in human consciousness: the verbal icon, its author, the empowered voice of a reader. That these components do abide, even if they seem not to, is registered in our ages-old fascination with them, a fascination, where allusion is concerned, as old as the Homeric inscription. If they were as ephemeral as some have argued with increasing stridency in the latter half of this century, then surely we (and they) would not be so in love after all this time with conquering them, or be so certain that we still might—a conquering best represented in the work of this chapter by the following definition of allusion: The literary allusion is the verbal moment in a subsequent text of a specific and verifiable verbal moment in a prior text, generated through the collusion of authorial and readerly intent, neither controlled nor limited by the language that constitutes it, in which a bundle of potential meanings obtains, retrievable at any given time only in part.

In its own version of literary veneration, this chapter has attempted to describe the process encapsulated in this definition. It has made claims for a powerful reader and an allusion with specific traits. These claims have been grounded carefully in the modern dialogue attending to allusion. Though many of them may appear to be new claims about allusion, they are only new versions of a cohort of ideas long associated with allusion. When the Greeks and the Romans thought about literary borrowing, for example, they seem also to have framed their concept against the competencies of a powerful reader, a tack inherited and vigorously developed by Christian littérateurs in late antiquity

---

29. F. von Schiller, *Briefe über die ästhetische Erziehung des Menschen in einer Reihe von Briefen*, trans. E. M. Wilkinson and L. A. Willoughby as *On the Aesthetic Education of Man, in a Series of Letters* (Oxford, 1967), esp. letters 12 and 15; cf. W. Kaufmann, *Hegel: A Reinterpretation* (Notre Dame, Ind., 1978), pp. 18–31 and esp. p. 28; on play in a variety of contexts, see M. I. Spariosu, *Dionysus Reborn: Play and the Aesthetic Dimension in Modern Philosophical and Scientific Discourse* (Ithaca, 1989); and also his *God of Many Names: Play, Poetry and Power in Hellenic Thought from Homer to Aristotle* (Durham, N.C., 1991); and his *Literature, Mimesis, and Play: Essays in Literary Theory* (Tübingen, 1982); and cf. J. Derrida, *Dissemination* (Chicago, 1981), pp. 156–71.

and the Middle Ages. In focusing on the reader, then, in turning to pursue historical work below, I am doing nothing more than following where the evidence leads. Here I have aimed to reorient views of allusion in the larger context of contemporary theory and criticism. In later chapters, I hope also to reorient views attending to the development of the very concept of allusion in the Western literary tradition. That development, as the next part suggests, is intimately bound to the notion of the figure whom I call the full-knowing reader, whose identity this chapter has attempted in some measure to articulate.

Part Two **The Ancient and Medieval Context**

Chapter 3 Versions of Reading

The vigorous and detailed attention evinced in contemporary think-ing about it speaks to the central place allusion has always held in the Western literary tradition. But the development of that thinking in the centuries prior to our own is less well known. Contemporary critics might easily be able to debate the status of the allusion as a sign or a construct of authorial power, but most would be hard pressed to articulate how allusion came to be a recognized and legitimate mode of literary discourse in the West. As an aspect of Western literary history, the question is important in its own right. It is germane to the present study as well because the answer, as we will see, is intimately connected to Western conceptualizing about readerly power.

Were one to attempt such an articulation on the basis of extant evidence, one could begin no sooner than the sixth century c.e., when the substantive *allusio* first designates a literary function. The term was not a new one at the time, for it appears as early as the third century c.e. in Arnobius's *Adversus Nationes*.[1] But it does not have a

1. For the first time in extant evidence, though not presumably for the first time:

literary or rhetorical connotation until Cassiodorus deploys it in his *Expositio Psalmorum* to denote a hidden level of reference.[2] Presumably Cassiodorus understood *allusio* to mean "allusion or hint," the denotation it has in subsequent evidence. And presumably, too, he had access to the verb *alludere*, which means "to allude" by the eighth century.[3] The difficulty with the extant evidence, of course, is that is does not account for the literary activity of the thirteen centuries prior to the time of Cassiodorus.

This gap is itself, however, a telling piece of evidence, suggesting that a *need* for a term for allusion *arose* in the late antique period—presumably a need that was not present in antiquity.[4] The evidence points to late antiquity, therefore, as the crucial period in which attitudes toward allusion were transformed from older, antique views. But what changed? The evidence supplied by Cassiodorus offers a large part of the answer, for when he deployed the term *allusio* in his exegetical treatise on the *Psalms,* he wrote as a Christian, producing a commentary on sacred scripture for the education of a monastic community of readers—aims antiquity would have hardly recognized or sanctioned. We might take Cassiodorus as emblematic of the sea-change in rhetorical assump-

---

"Ut si manu viperam mulceas, venenato blandiaris aut scorpio, petat illa te morsu, hic contactus aculeum figat, nihilque illa prosit adlusio" (7.23). My text is C. Marchesi, ed., *Arnobii Adversus Nationes Libri VII,* in *Corpus Scriptorum Latinorum Paravianum,* vol. 62 (Turin, 1934).

2. "In octava, parabolis et tropicis allusionibus congregatis, subsequens drama decurritur et per allegoricas similitudines omnia referuntur ad Dominum Christum" (*Praef.* 17.26–28). My text is *Magnii Aurelii Cassiodori Expositio Psalmorum,* in *Corpus Christianorum, Series Latina,* vols. 97 and 98 (Turnhout, 1958). Cassiodorus uses *allusio* in a somewhat restricted way, to qualify a discussion of literary reading. The term is used specifically to describe a style or kind of language that is obscure in the same way that a parable or a level of scriptural meaning is obscure. Cassiodorus's usage suggests that by the late sixth century *allusio* has taken on a literary connotation. One can conjecture that his deployment of the term represents a common usage in Christian exegesis that is not reflected in extant texts, for whatever reasons, until the sixth century. It seems doubtful, given his conservatism, that Cassiodorus resuscitated a word that had not been used since the third century in order to make it function in an exegetical context. It would seem more likely that he simply represents a tendency in Christian writing that has disappeared from the evidence.

3. See *Mitt. Wört.,* pp. 484–85, which does not, however, list an entry for the substantive *allusio;* cf. *MLWL,* p. 15; Blaise, p. 54; Niermeyer, p. 35.

4. It could be argued that this evidence suggests that the West may not have conceived of allusion until the sixth century c.e.—a counterintuitive position to which I will return in chapter 4.

tions in general that occurred under the influence of Christianity, and associate the specific tasks he undertakes—the production of commentaries on scripture based on his own *reading*, for purposes of guiding the *reading* of other monks—as affirmative of a new status accorded to the reader and to reading in Christian culture.

In fact, Christianity made a powerful reader the sine qua non of its rhetorical program. Cassiodorus simply reflects attitudes that had been in place for a century or more in the West when he wrote. Those attitudes mark a turning away from the more circumspect attitudes of Greek and Roman antiquity. Antiquity did not uniformly scorn reading, to be sure, but it did not, as Christianity did, accept reading—and the necessity of readerly power—as an unproblematic given. Below I will analyze in some detail the ways in which Christianity made an active, meaning-making reader the crux of its rhetorical program, thus enabling allusion, with its emphasis on a powerful reader, not long after to flourish. First, however, I need to take cognizance of Greek and Roman attitudes toward this reader, for such views stand in stark contrast to Christian attitudes, but also redound onto the ways in which antiquity conceived of allusion despite the lack of a term to designate it—as the discussion in chapter 4 will outline.

ANCIENT ATTITUDES TOWARD THE FULL-KNOWING READER

My claim is that a term for allusion arose only after literary culture in the West made a powerful reader the centerpiece of its rhetorical program. In saying this I do not mean to imply that allusion did not exist before the sixth century C.E. On the contrary, I hold that allusion was conceived before this time as a literary mode that exploited the power of the reader but that it also subsisted in a literary culture that was fundamentally hostile to that power. We can trace that hostility in various guises in antiquity, but one strain of evidence weaves its way through Plato, the Greek dramatists, and Greek rhetoric, and bears a unique witness to ancient versions of our full-knowing reader. Importantly, this strain of evidence reappears in a corroborative way, as we will see in the next chapter, in antique descriptions of allusion written by literary artists.

This strain of evidence is best traced first in Plato's *Phaedrus,* where a direct questioning of writing and, by implication, of reading occurs.[5] Plato broaches

5. My text of Plato is J. Burnet, ed., *Platonis Opera,* vol. 2 (Oxford, 1901). For a general

this topic in the form of a bromide, related by Socrates, in which the god Theuth, the proud inventor of letters (γράμματα, 274D), offers his discovery to King Thamus for approbation, commending them as a medicine for memory and wisdom (μνήμης τε γὰρ καὶ σοφίας φάρμακον ηὑρέθη; 274E). Thamus reacts to Theuth's invention with displeasure, however, arguing that letters, instead of aiding memory, will induce forgetfulness. Theuth has created, Thamus contends, a "medicine of reminding, not of memory" (οὔκουν μνήμης ἀλλὰ ὑπομνήσεως φάρμακον ηὗρες; 275A). Socrates fleshes out this line of reasoning subsequently when he chastises anyone who thinks that writing is useful unto itself (275C/D). Writing merely subverts the attempt to gain knowledge, he says, because one can only be reminded through writing of what one already knows. When Plato has Socrates go on to conclude his condemnation of writing, he says that "writing is strange" (Δεινὸν . . . ἔχει γραφή; 275D) because it harbors a unique silence (γραφή . . . πάνυ σιγᾷ. ταὐτὸν δὲ καὶ οἱ λόγοι; 275 D). Writing speaks through its readers, not to them. It invites its readers to believe that what is written bears a direct relationship to the thought (the dialogue) that gave rise to it. The key word in Plato's condemnation of writing is the adjective he uses to describe it, δεινός, "strange," "odd," "dangerous." The oddity, danger, and strangeness of letters are a function, so Plato concludes, of their ability to mean beyond the control of their users, of the insistent way they always demand, and in demanding, empower, a reader or interpreter to take the place of their author.[6]

The Greek tragedians confirm this usage, for consistently in their work they use the term δεινός to dramatize the ability of language (both spoken and written) to be strange, odd, dangerous in precisely the ways Plato feared. While Aeschylus uses δεινός mostly in the context of describing prophetic language, Sophocles and Euripides both deploy this adjective more specifically to qualify a kind of speech (and sometimes a kind of perception) that is wily, difficult to control, prone to misconstrual or misinterpretation, thus staging Plato's worst fears by demonstrating language's ability to mean beyond the control of its

---

discussion see P. Friedländer, *Plato: The Dialogues,* trans. H. Meyerhoff (Princeton, 1968), vol. 3, pp. 227–35; R. Hackforth, *Plato, Phaedrus* (Cambridge, 1972); and G. R. F. Ferrari, *Listening to the Cicadas: A Study of Plato's "Phaedrus"* (New York, 1987), esp. pp. 214–221.

6. Cf. the contrary views of R. Burger, *Plato's "Phaedrus": A Defense of a Philosophic Art of Writing* (University, Ala., 1980), esp. pp. 70–109, who sees more affirmation than I (or most) do in Plato's view of writing.

user's intent.[7] In particular, Sophocles' *Antigone* is replete with scenes in which Creon and Antigone, while both hearing and using the same words, come to different conclusions and choose opposing paths of action—words and paths described consistently as δεινός by Sophocles.[8] The *Ajax,* the *Oedipus Tyrannus,* and the *Oedipus at Colonus* also feature scenes of this kind prominently.[9] Perhaps the most committed use of the term to qualify a kind of discourse that is wily, difficult to control, prone to misinterpretation is found in Euripides' *Bacchae,* where δεινός language represents the kind of discourse available to Pentheus and Dionysus—two-sided, manipulable, easily misconstrued, a kind of language that means not what its users intend but what its hearers (and readers) desire it to mean.[10] When Greek rhetoricians working in the Hellenistic period decided to codify a kind of rhetorical style that called upon the audience's best interpretive powers in order to achieve certain oratorical ends, then, it makes every sense that they called their new "fourth" style δεινότης, the "dangerous" style.

In two discrete bodies of evidence—Plato and Greek drama—the term δεινός is uniquely associated with the attributes of a powerful reader or audience. In a third body of evidence—later Greek rhetoric—this term is resident in δεινότης, which designates the rhetorical style in which an audience or receiver is expressly invited into the making of meaning. In Greek rhetoric, therefore, δεινός is specifically associated with the power of the reader to make meaning through a subjective interpretation of language, precisely the power feared by Plato in the *Phaedrus* in his consideration of writing's δεινός quality, and precisely the dilemma of δεινός language scripted in Greek drama.

7. See Aeschylus, *Ag.* v. 1215; and on prophetic language in general, see R. W. Bushnell, *Prophesying Tragedy: Sign and Voice in Sophocles' Theban Plays* (Ithaca, 1988), pp. 43–107.
8. See *Ant.* vv. 332–75, esp. 353 ff. on δεινός speech and/or perception; see also vv. 96, 243, 408, 690, 915, 951, 959, 1046, 1091, 1096–97 on δεινός language, self-perception and misunderstanding; and on these themes in relation to δεινός in *Antigone* see also J. C. Kamerbeek, *The Plays of Sophocles* (Leiden, 1978), vol. 3, p. 73; and the comments of J. C. Hogan, *A Commentary on the Plays of Sophocles* (Carbondale, Ill., 1991), pp. 139 ff.
9. *Ajax* vv. 1066, 1124, 1126–27 and *Oed. Tyr.* vv. 316 ff., 439 on δεινός and interpretation; vv. 545, 722, 806 on δεινός speech and/or prophecy; and *Oed. Col.* v. 661 on δεινός as facile, manipulable speech.
10. Euripides, *Bacchae* v. 971 ff. esp. on δεινός and prophetic misunderstanding; *Medea* vv. 565, 585, 1243, 1294 on δεινός as clever speech; see also E. R. Dodds, *Euripides Bacchae, A Commentary* (Oxford, 1940), pp. 196–97 and on Euripides and prophetic language, Bushnell, *Prophesying Tragedy,* pp. 108–127.

Although their witnesses are important, I prefer to see Plato and the Greek dramatists as a control on the more focused discussion of readerly power in Greek rhetoric. The dramatists, after all, consider language in its totality to be δεινός, making no distinction between written and spoken forms, while Plato is concerned in the *Phaedrus* to condemn only writing, and considers reading as a secondary problem.[11] The rhetorical evidence, then, while participating in the literary culture shaped by currents beholden to Platonic notions and those espoused by the dramatists, marks the first time in Western literary culture in which versions of a powerful reader (or audience) are articulated in discrete ways. I focus, therefore, on Greek rhetoric's articulation of δεινότης, because it is the first ancient version of a full-knowing reader. I then consider later rhetorical evidence from Rome before returning to the late antique period to examine in more detail the shift of attitudes toward reading occasioned by the rise of Christianity in the West.

δεινότης: The First Ancient Version of the Full-Knowing Reader

The most committed treatment of δεινότης[12] is found in Demetrius's *On Style,* a derivative treatise that uses some 240 of its 304 sections to recapitulate

11. Plato has Socrates go on to describe the "silence" of writing and the dangers it implies in the specific context of an active, meaning-making reader (275D ff.). Writing, he says, like an orphaned child, lacks a parent—the author. The author "speaks" (or, at least, spoke) in order to articulate the words that are inscribed in writing. That authorial "speaking" is not implicit in the written word, however, because writing loses its voice once it is divorced from its author. All writing can do is repeat itself, without any possibility of authorial emendation, addition, or correction. To read an author's writing, therefore, is not to return to the truth implicit in its author's (spoken) intention, but to become, in the act of reading, the parent that writing otherwise lacks by virtue of its liberation from its author. The necessity for readers to interpret writing, as against the ability of a writer to speak for his writing each time it is read, symbolizes for Plato the fundamental danger of writing. By virtue of its "silence," its orphaned condition, writing implies a loss of authorial control over what is communicated verbally. At the same time, writing also implies the empowerment of the reader (or audience) in the making of meaning. See the discussion of these passages in Ferrari, *Listening to the Cicadas,* pp. 204–232 and Burger, *Plato's Phaedrus,* pp. 90–109.

12. δεινότης is deployed in the context of rhetoric also by Dionysius of Halicarnassus, *On Demosthenes* and *On Thucydides,* and also by "Longinus" in *On the Sublime.* Demosthenes discusses in a negative context (*De Cor.* 277) the abilities of Aeschines, whom he considers a δεινός orator. Isocrates (1.4) uses the term simply to mean "skill" in oratory. Since Demetrius's text has not been dated with certainty, it is not clear whether Demetrius, Dionysius of Halicarnassus, or "Longinus" first uses the term in a rhetorical context. All that can be said is that the term does not exist until after Aristotle, who does

positions taken by Aristotle in his *Rhetoric*.[13] The bulk of the sections of the *On Style* leads readers, therefore, to familiar places. Only in his consideration of δεινότης, which falls near the end of the final book of the treatise (5.241 ff.), does Demetrius follow a path apart from his exemplars. In these final sections, Demetrius's aim seems to be to examine an oratorical pose in which the audience is actively involved in the persuasive end, in the production of which the orator actually holds back from saying all that can be said, leaving certain appropriate connections and conclusions to the audience's confection.

Now, to be sure, some of Demetrius's treatment of δεινότης derives from prior rhetorical assumptions that privilege the orator's ability to move an audience to any persuasive end through oratorical skill. The discussion of brevity, for example, is couched in the wider claim that saying less is more forceful, while saying more loosens vehemence and ferocity (τὸ γὰρ μῆκος ἐκλύει τὴν σφοδρότητα, τὸ δὲ ἐν ὀλίγῳ πολὺ ἐμφαινόμενον δεινότερον; 241), a

---

not use it in a rhetorical sense (though he does use it, on which see this note, below). Since Demetrius's treatise, with its close recapitulation of Aristotle's rhetorical positions, is clearly post-Aristotelean, a *terminus a quo* of about 300 B.C.E. is plausible. W. Rhys Roberts dates the text down to the age of Plutarch and identifies Demetrius as the Demetrius of Tarsus mentioned by Plutarch in *On the Cessation of the Oracles* (2). His argument offers a *terminus ad quem* of c. 50 C.E., making the text roughly contemporaneous with Quintilian. See W. Rhys Roberts, ed. and trans., *Aristotle: The Poetics, "Longinus:" On the Sublime, Demetrius: On Style*, Loeb Classical Library (London and New York, 1927), p. 271 and n. a (but see now also the comments in the revision of Roberts's translation by D. C. Innes in *Poetics of Aristotle*, S. Halliwell, ed. and trans., *Longinus: On the Sublime*, W. H. Fyfe, ed. and trans., *Demetrius: On Style*, D. C. Inness, ed. and trans., Loeb Classical Library [London and New York, 1995] pp. 311 ff., the text I cite from here). Roberts also holds (p. 271) on internal evidence that the text postdates Dionysius of Halicarnassus and cannot possibly be later than Hermogenes (170 C.E.). The issue will always remain vexed. On δεινότης generally see L. Voit, *Deinotes: ein antiker Stilbegriff* (Leipzig, 1934). In any case, δεινότης is a late word and does not possess much of a history outside of rhetoric. It is used by Thucydides (3.46) to describe the force or "terror" of laws that can dominate subjugated people, but in general Thucydides employs the term (3.59; 4.10; 3.37) to mean little more than "severity." Demosthenes (*De Cor.* 18.144; 18.242) uses it simply as an expression of "cleverness" or "shrewdness." Aristotle uses it more formally in a moral context in the *Nichomachean Ethics* (1144a23) in order to posit what he calls the "faculty of cleverness." None of these examples points conclusively to a particular notion of cleverness, however. The term is used in these instances both in negative and positive ways. Indeed, Aristotle (*EN* 1144a27) uses the term in positive and negative contexts. Only Antiphon (5.5) uses the term in a negative way to designate the opposite of truth.

13. On this see Roberts, *Aristotle, "Longinus," Demetrius*, pp. 271–72.

claim that can hardly be considered novel. The example cited is the famous message of the Lacedaemonians to Philip: "Dionysius at Corinth," an exemplary passage, Demetrius explains, because, though all the necessary information is present in these three simple words, the information itself is not expressed overtly. The audience, in other words, must make appropriate connections and fill in the gaps of history and circumstance in order for the phrase to function properly. Importantly, however, and squarely within the tradition of oratorical control embodied in Aristotle's *Rhetoric,* this sort of audience response is directed by the manipulations of the orator. There is, after all, little room for interpretive license in this example.

Demetrius's treatment of symbolic expression is cast in like terms. Because the listener or reader must infer the greater meaning from the "shallows" of the symbolic statement, symbolism is an important part of δεινότης (διὸ καὶ τὰ σύμβολα ἔχει δεινότητας, ὅτι ἐμφερῆ ταῖς βραχυλογίαις· καὶ γὰρ ἐκ τοῦ βραχέως ῥηθέντος ὑπονοῆσαι τὰ πλεῖστα δεῖ; 243). In the phrase "your cicadas will chirp from the ground" (χαμόθεν οἱ τέττιγες ὑμῖν ᾄσονται), the audience, Demetrius says, must make sense of the symbolism of these words. The process of recognizing their symbolic weight lends a "more forceful" (δεινότερον) quality to what is said than if one simply said something like "your trees will be mowed down" (τὰ δένδρα ὑμῶν ἐκκοπήσεται). In both instances, Demetrius goes on to say, the point is to draw attention away from the language being used in the presentation in order to make the reader engage the topic dialogically in his or her own mind. If too much attention is lavished on the formal presentation of the symbol, then the auditor or reader will not have the appropriate response (247). Once again, however, Demetrius's examples are offered within the context of the orator's ability to restrict interpretive license. There is, after all, little that can be done with this phrase interpretively, beyond equating its words to the idea that "all your trees will be mowed down." The extent to which the audience can maneuver interpretively here is carefully proscribed by context, by the orator's strict control.

When Demetrius talks subsequently about "conciseness," or συντομία, however, he would seem to enter a persuasive world conceived in terms apart from his rhetorical predecessors. In speaking of the central place συντομία holds in δεινότης, for example, Demetrius notes that it is considered even more forceful simply to stop speaking at points (ἡ συντομία τῷ χαρακτῆρι χρήσιμον, ὥστε καὶ ἀποσιωπῆσαι πολλαχοῦ δεινότερον; 253; cf. 269). Strategic silences allow the listener or reader to make his own inferences from what has already been said and, in suiting each individual's temperaments best, allow for the most potent position to be argued, each person for himself. In this regard, obscurity (ἀσάφεια) is also praised as an important tactic in δεινότης, because the force of inferring meaning is preferable to the effects of stating something plainly (ἡ ἀσάφεια πολλαχοῦ δεινότης ἐστί· δεινότερον γὰρ τὸ ὑπονοούμενον; 254).

Demetrius's position contrasts notably with Quintilian's, whose views are a good distillation of ancient rhetorical assumptions in general. "If the material to be treated is weightier," Quintilian says in the *Institutio Oratoria,* "no ornament ought to be held back which does not obscure anything" (at si maior erit materia, nullum iis ornatum, qui modo non obscuret, subtrahendum puto; 5.14.34). Quintilian furthers this line of reasoning in his discussion of paraphrase, in which he cautions orators not to be too liberal in their use of ornament. It is not a good thing to think it "better to say a greater number of things than simply to state it" (pleraque significare melius putamus quam dicere; 8 *Praef.* 24).[14] So, too, are metaphor,[15] allegory, and riddling to be avoided, because they serve to obscure one's argument (8.6.14).[16]

Demetrius's discussion of ἀσάφεια also contrasts sharply with Aristotle's discussion of style in the *Rhetoric* (3.1.6 ff.; 1404a), which stresses clarity of approach and presentation. This emphasis is important because it allows Aristotle specifically to move to a discussion of the poets as the originators of a kind of style he would warn against. Gorgias is held out for especial scorn in this discussion, for this emotional and luxuriant exemplar is seen to be particularly loathsome to the goals of clear persuasion. If the speech, Aristotle goes on to say, does not make the meaning clear, it will not perform its proper function. Much the same point is made by Quintilian in his discussion of rhetorical imitation. He distinguishes between a poetic "making" that can involve an active meaning-maker as reader or audience, and a rhetorical "making" whose audience is more constrained in its activity (cf. 10.1.28). Quintilian's more restricted notion

14. See the similar treatment of allegory at *Inst. Or.* 8.6.51–52. My text of Quintilian is M. Winterbottom, ed., *M. Fabi Quintiliani, Institutionis Oratoriae Libri Duodecim* (Oxford, 1970).

15. See Aristotle's similar discussion of metaphor at *Rhet.* 3.2.8; 1405a; see also W. M. A. Grimaldi, ed., *Aristotle: A Commentary* (New York, 1988), and on the *Rhet.,* see G. A. Kennedy, trans., *On Rhetoric: A Theory of Civic Discourse* (New York, 1991), pp. i–xvi.

16. For the same reason, Quintilian's discussion of synecdoche (8.6.22) raises questions as to whether or not an orator ought to use this rhetorical tool except in arguments strictly related to factual presentation, that is, in situations where it can be safely controlled by the orator's manipulation of context and nuance. Metonymy (8.6.24) evokes much the same response in Quintilian's discussion, and he eventually suggests ways in which the orator might control this figure in order to ensure its most effective deployment.

of imitation involves a process of composition and reconfiguration of prior models that is carefully controlled by the orator's ability to select and glean from those models exemplary traits. This process involves the "making" of a new creation based on older models which is not tied to those older models for meaning or for sense. "Although," he says, "there can be no doubt that a large part of art inheres in imitation, . . . it is a general rule of life that we should wish to do [*facere*] what has been shown to work" (neque enim dubitari potest, quin artis pars magna contineatur imitatione . . . omnis vitae ratio sic constat, ut quae probamus in aliis facere ipsi velimus; 10.2.1–2). The process implied in *facere* is to "do" or "make" something new based on an engagement with prior models, but without the intrusion of those models into the finished product, the new work.

Demetrius's discussion of what he calls σχῆμα λόγου (veiled language; 287 ff.) is also cast in terms apart from those of his rhetorical peers.[17] He frames it by relating the story of Aristippus and Cleombrotus reported by Plato in the *Phaedo* (59C), which centers on the great philosopher's reproach of these two figures for feasting at Aegina while Socrates was imprisoned in Athens. Plato does not reproach them openly, Demetrius notes, but instead insinuates into his dialogue a question as to the whereabouts of the two men. It is eventually reported that both were at Aegina. The fact that Aegina is near Athens, and the subsequent indiscretion that both men commit in feasting at so solemn a time, instead of making the short journey to Athens, go unmentioned overtly. The audience, Demetrius says, is put in the position of making the appropriate connections and drawing correct conclusions without any explicit statement to assist them. This makes Plato's writing at this point in the *Phaedo* a prime example of δεινότης (κὰι πολὺ δεινότερος ὁ λόγος δοκεῖ τοῦ πράγματος αὐτοῦ ἐμφαίνοντος τὸ δεινόν, οὐχὶ τοῦ λέγοντος; 288).

The δεινός orator is specifically enjoined (289) to use σχῆμα λόγου in a political context, when a despot or some hard-to-handle person needs to be censured, but in such a way as to be as inoffensive as possible.[18] The orator who uses σχῆμα λόγου, however, would seem to be δεινός on several counts, not simply by virtue of practicing δεινότης. He is δεινός owing to the autonomy he grants to his audience, for there is an implicit danger involved in the grant of such autonomy. His intended meaning might—or might not—be comprehended by his audience, after all. Moreover, the stakes are higher when one uses

17. This category is translated (incorrectly) by Roberts, p. 473, as "allusion;" see also n. b.
18. F. Ahl has analyzed this necessity in later rhetoric in its political and social context for the Roman tradition in "The Art of Safe Criticism in Greece and Rome," *AJP* 105 (1985).

σχῆμα λόγου, for it is one thing to fail to persuade an audience, quite another to speak to a powerful political figure in such a way as (possibly) to invoke vehement displeasure.

The δεινός orator, then, is not simply forceful by virtue of the accomplished power of his language. Using δεινότης and being δεινός involve both what an orator does and does not do with language. Demetrius describes a situation in which political or social constraints render normal rhetorical control impossible—the orator must rely on his audience to make a point, must take a leap of faith and hope the desired persuasive end obtains. Yet, because several intended, and surely many unintended, interpretations are possible, there is danger in invoking σχῆμα λόγου. Part of δεινότης, then, entails a strategy on the part of the orator to persuade from beyond the control implicit in rhetoric's procedures; to throw the issue to the audience by taking advantage of language's ability to mean different things to different interpreters. Because the language deployed by an orator in this context is ultimately beyond the control of that orator, there is always the distinct possibility of audience misinterpretation, and such an outcome is fraught with rhetorical and personal danger. To practice δεινότης, then, implies a host of difficulties and dangers not normally admitted by rhetoricians into the oratorical dynamic.

The extent to which such a dynamic is otherwise warned against in ancient rhetoric can be gauged by returning to Quintilian, who speaks disapprovingly of an empowered audience at several points in the *Institutio,* specifically in discussions of oratory that uses language from another source. "It is considered scarcely a sign of clarity," he says, "to repeat what another had said" (parum creditur disertum quod et alius dixisset; 8 *Praef.* 24), before going on to conclude that "we derive figures and metaphors from the most corrupt poets and consider it ingenious if, in order to be understood, a genius is necessary" (A corruptissimo quoque poetarum figuras seu tralationes mutuamur, tum demum ingeniosi scilicet si ad intellegendos nos opus sit ingenio; 8 *Praef.* 25). Here Quintilian would seem to reject literary borrowing out of hand because such borrowings are obscure, and obscurity invites confusion as each audience member or reader attempts to make sense of the oration or the text. The various responses can hardly be expected to serve the aims of rhetorical persuasion, since they cannot be predicted and, hence, controlled.

Quintilian returns to this theme in a discussion of *adianoeta,* or riddles (8.2.20–21), remarking on the troublesome ways in which hidden meaning must be ferreted out of riddles, whose most bothersome quality is that they harbor a secret meaning (occultos sensus) apart from the ostensible meaning of their words (quae verbis aperta habent). Quintilian opts, expectedly, for clarity, the first ingredient of a good style (8.2.22): "if what we say is neither more or less than necessary . . . the matter will be plain and obvious to even a dull audience" (Nam si neque pauciora quam oportet neque plura neque inordinata aut indistincta dixerimus, erunt dilucida et neglegenter quoque audientibus aperta; 8.2.23). By contrast, if one does say more than what is necessary, then the audience will not follow the intended course of the argument, or worse, be left to their own devices in constructing a course of their own.

Quintilian is an exemplar of rhetorical conservatism. Late in the *Institutio Oratoria,* however, he discusses an unnamed genus of figure, whose function would seem to demand a powerful reader or audience of the sort we seek:

> And now I must come to a class of figure which is most frequent and on which I think I shall be expected to say something; the one in which we excite some suspicion that we are not saying what we want the audience to receive; but our meaning is not in this case contrary to that which we express, as with irony, but rather a hidden meaning which is left to the hearer to discover. . . . This class of figure has three uses: first, if it is unsafe to speak openly; second, if it is not proper to speak openly; third, when it is employed in order to enhance the elegance of what we say and gives greater pleasure owing to the novelty and variety it introduces than if our meaning had been expressed straightforwardly.

> (Iam enim ad id genus quod et frequentissimum est et expectari maxime credo veniendum est, in quo per quandam suspicionem quod non dicimus accipi volumus, non utique contrarium, ut in εἰρωνείᾳ sed aliud latens et auditori quasi inveniendum. . . . Eius triplex usus est: unus si dicere palam parum tutum est, alter si non decet, tertius qui venustatis modo gratia adhibetur et ipsa novitate ac varietate magis quam si relatio sit recta delectat; 9.2.65–66).

Quintilian's unnamed genus is carefully qualified. An orator does not invoke this genus if he intends to communicate the opposite of what he says (*contrarium*). Rather, the intended meaning is hidden (*latens*) from the audience and must be divined by its interpretive powers. This genus of figure, much like σχῆμα λόγου, is used in special circumstances: when it is politically unwise to speak openly, when it is unseemly, or when it is more accomplished to speak in this way. There can be little doubt that Quintilian has in mind here a meaning-making audience of the sort we seek, an audience, much like Demetrius's, whose interpretive powers are called upon to supplement the orator's own persuasive power. But given the scope of Quintilian's twelve books, the attention paid here to the sort of reader we seek is hardly noticeable, especially when one takes into account the fact that Quintilian eventually attempts to qualify his discussion of this genus by equating it with allegory.[19] Qualifications aside, no more telling an indication of the position of rhetoric toward a powerful reader can be found than in Quintilian's treatment of this genus of figure—that he refuses even to (or that does not even possess a) name.

THE LEGITIMATION OF THE FULL-KNOWING READER

Ancient rhetoric conceives of an audience or a reader empowered to make meaning apart from the control of the orator, but it does so rarely, and with much circumspection. This attitude presumably represents antique cultural norms attending to the best ways to communicate. Those norms slowly were challenged and then transformed on a large scale in the Christian era, when notions about preferred ways to communicate were revisited, resulting, so I hold, in the legitimation of allusion in the late antique period. Two writers are witnesses to this fundamental shift in greatest detail. Macrobius considers the implications of a powerful reader in his *Saturnalia,* a treatise devoted in part to analyzing the ways in which Virgil borrowed language from Homer, whereas Augustine, writing at about the same time, articulates in the *De doctrina christiana* and in the *Confessions* the importance attached by Christians to a meaning-making reader. Their respective works, though written with different aims and assumptions, nonetheless confirm the tendency on the part of late antique littérateurs to consider substantively the role and function of a powerful reader, portending the normalization of the authority of reading from Christianity's fresh purview. This privileging of reading and the new power accorded to the Christian reader are important links bridging antiquity's circumspection about, and modernity's vigorous practice of, allusion, as the remainder of this chapter will suggest.

19. Quintilian goes on to devote much space to an elaboration of this genus. As he works his way through the discussion, he seems to moderate his views, so that, at 9.2.92, for example, he comes to the conclusion that much of what he has discussed is akin to allegory. But throughout his discussion of this unnamed genus, Quintilian makes it clear that an active, meaning-making audience is required in order for this genus to function appropriately. Though he hedges his discussion by linking it subsequently to allegory, Quintilian's discussion of the unnamed genus is one of the few moments in ancient rhetoric in which the audience is invited into the construction of meaning. For a general discussion of Quintilian see G. A. Kennedy, *A New History of Classical Rhetoric* (Princeton, 1994).

Macrobius's *Saturnalia:* The First Detailed Version of the Full-Knowing Reader

When one extrapolates from Macrobius's *Saturnalia* the kind of reader he would seem to construct in his work, the similarity to our full-knowing reader is striking.[20] This conformity of competencies in large measure derives from the purposes of the *Saturnalia,* which would seem to have been composed to explicate Virgil's *Aeneid* in the light of the *Iliad* and the *Odyssey* from a formally pedagogical perspective. In pursuing what is seemingly a more formalized exercise of a kind expected of a *grammaticus,* Macrobius has occasion to draw upon the tradition of ancient commentaries perhaps best represented by Servius. His more focused attention on the use of Homeric words in the *Aeneid* also links him to an old tradition best represented by works such as Herennius's *Vitia* or Perellius Faustus's *Furta.*[21] But the *Saturnalia* is also a literary work, whose author would seem to have been conscious of issues attending to more creative goals than normally admitted in a schoolbook. In particular, the dialogue form of the *Saturnalia* affords Macrobius opportunities for creativity and invention. These talents are nowhere more in evidence than in the fifth book of the *Saturnalia,* in which Macrobius considers specific Virgilian passages in their Homeric context. The literary stakes are raised, the examination of Virgilian borrowing more committed. Here, for the first time in Western writing, a detailed version of our full-knowing reader emerges.

Modes of reading are highlighted in a variety of ways in book 5, but these procedures are advanced through a carefully wrought scene that forces the *Saturnalia*'s own readers to conjure in their minds a picture of Virgil as a reader of Greek literature. Macrobius induces this response by making Evangelus— one of the participants in the Saturnalian festivities around which the dialogue takes shape—take the incredible position of doubting whether Virgil knew any of the Greek orators ("Tunc Evangelus irridenti similis, 'bene,' inquit, 'opifici deo a rure Mantuano poetam comparas quem Graecos rhetoras, quorum fecisti mentionem, nec omnino legisse adseveraverim'"; 5.2.1).[22] After all, says Evangelus, Virgil was just a country bumpkin ("rusticis parentibus nato inter silvas et frutices educto"). The fact that Evangelus is an uninvited participant at the Saturnalian festivities does not mitigate the shock value of his declaration, which, in drawing attention both to himself as a figure and to his doubts,

---

20. R. Kaster, "Macrobius and Servius: Verecundia and the Grammarian's Function," *HSCP* 84 (1980), pp. 220–62, remains the best overall treatment of the *Saturnalia.*
21. P. V. Davies, *Macrobius: The Saturnalia* (New York, 1970), pp. 17–18, lists these works.
22. My text of Macrobius is J. Willis, ed., *Ambrosii Theodosii Macrobii Saturnalia* (Leipzig, 1963).

compels the readers of the *Saturnalia* to consider in what ways Virgil is specifically a Greek reader.

Evangelus is clearly out of place in the group assembled to celebrate the Saturnalia and his quasimocking tone (*irridenti similis*) suggests that he relishes this role.[23] But Macrobius is not simply biding his time by introducing a boor and his uneducated doubts into the *Saturnalia*'s dialogue. Indeed, Evangelus easily represents the broader attitudes of ancient culture toward the issues attending reading, writing and, in this more rarefied context, literary borrowing itself. While it is true that Evangelus's doubts center more on Virgil's learning than on his literary borrowing, the point remains that Macrobius focuses his most complete discussion of Virgilian borrowing in a debate between someone who champions the idea of Virgilian borrowings of Homer, and someone who cannot fathom that they exist at all.

These may be caricatures, but they point nonetheless to fundamental attitudes in place in the fourth and fifth centuries in the West—in those centuries when Christianity was beginning to shape normative attitudes toward reading, writing, and interpretation in fresh ways. When Macrobius goes on a few lines later to take up the issue broached by Evangelus, therefore, he is in a position to devote close attention both to literary borrowing and to our full-knowing reader. Only the most committed of discussions will dispel Evangelus's haughty proclamation. Virgil's Hellenism becomes the focal point, therefore, as a matter of necessity, calling for an attention to detail that would be unnecessary in the closed company of Macrobius's circle of littérateurs. If he is to be swayed at all, Evangelus will have to be taken by the hand and, as it were, walked through the obvious evidence of Virgil's Greek learning, an erudition made functional through literary borrowing.

Macrobius begins by having Eustathius assure Evangelus of Virgil's learning, which is, so he says, beyond the dictates of birthright or class. The proof of his learning, Eustathius continues, inheres in Virgil's borrowings from the Greeks ("non parva sunt alia quae traxit a Graecis et carmini suo tamquam illic nata conservit"; 5.2.2). The mention of these borrowings allows another participant, Praetextatus, all the excuse he needs to ask more of this topic. Eustathius now is free to begin a more detailed examination of Virgil's relationship to Homer by positing the category of borrowings that are common knowledge ("quae vulgo nota sunt"; 5.2.4)—for example, that Virgil used Theocritus, Hesiod, or even

23. Evangelus is the sort of guest who, in the midst of intelligent conversation, thinks to ask what came first, the chicken or the egg—as exactly he does at 7.16.

Pisander as his models (5.2.4). Since this sort of indebtedness is the stuff of schoolboy lessons, it requires, according to Eustathius, no explication (5.2.5). Macrobius then has Eustathius pose an artistic and aesthetic question about Virgil's reliance on Homer, asking if it can be denied that Virgil has borrowed his epic entirely from Homer ("Iam vero Aeneis ipsa nonne ab Homero sibi mutuata est errorem primum ex Odyssea, deinde ex Iliade pugnas?"; 5.2.6).

Eustathius goes on at some length to consider specific instances of Virgil's use of Homer before articulating an answer to this question, eventually asserting that all of Virgil's poem is "formed in the mirror of Homer's poem" (Homerici operis speculo formatum est; 5.2.13). While appearing to be an affirmation of the thrust of the question whose answer it forms, this response is articulated in such a way as to render the notion of borrowing in a specific way. The question that elicitied this response broached the issue of borrowing straightforwardly, as the Latin verb used there, *mutuari* ("to borrow"), attests.[24] The verb used in Eustathius's answer, however, is *formare* ("to form," "to create," "to compose").[25] Moreover, Eustathius introduces a new quality in his putative answer to the question of Virgil's indebtedness to Homer, claiming that the *Aeneid* was modeled, after the fashion of a mirror image (*speculum*), on Homer's epic cycle.

Two points are implied in this response. First, while acknowledging that Virgil is, indeed, a literary borrower, Eustathius is careful to use a verb suggestive of creation in describing Virgil's engagement of Homer. Virgilian borrowing in the *Aeneid* is cast in this response, therefore, not in the context of slavish copying—as the verb *mutuari* can imply. It is, rather, a function of *formare,* of a creative and artistic response on the part of Virgil to Homer's poetry. Perhaps more interesting in Eustathius's version of Virgil's borrowings is the presence of a full-knowing reader, whose competencies are required in order for the Homeric context of Virgil's poetry—in Eustathius's phrase, the "mirror" of Homer—to be recognized and interpreted. Lacking the sort of meaning-making reader, who connects the *Iliad,* the *Odyssey* and the *Aeneid* verbally and who articulates meanings based on those connections, the notion of a mirrored Homer falls flat. Such a reader, in Macrobius's parlance, becomes the "viewer" who spies the Virgilian image reflected in the mirror of Homer and who works interpretively in the glare of that reflection.

The function accorded to a full-knowing reader is more centrally addressed

24. LS, p. 1181, s.v. *mutuor.*
25. Cicero uses the verb only with abstract nouns, but Quintilian uses it regularly to talk about appropriate rhetorical composition (*Inst. Or.* 1.12.9; 10.7.7, e.g.; and LS, p. 769, s.v. *formo* II).

subsequently. The analysis proceeds apace under the rubric of translation, Eustathius having agreed to quote actual lines of Homer which Virgil "has translated almost word for word" (vultis me et ipsos proferre versus ad verbum paene translatos; 5.3.1). Although the point of these examples, which continue for nearly seven chapters of book 5, is to cement the notion of Homer as a mirror for Virgil, Macrobius's use of the word *translatus* implies a further specification of Virgilian borrowing that leads, eventually, to an overt recommendation of readerly power.

Macrobius uses *translatus* to describe the verses in the *Aeneid* that are reflections of Homeric poetry. An examination of these verses reveals that most of them are anything but translations in the normal sense. Most of the passages cited, for example, fail to qualify as either literal or free translations of Homer's Greek. Nor is the context of the Homeric model usually consonant with its Virgilian reflection. Sometimes Eustathius even finds lines in Virgil that were formed by combining parts of lines separated in Homer. In the ninth example cited by Eustathius at the opening of 5.3, for instance, words that link to specific moments in *Odyssey* 5 and *Iliad* 8 and 15 are shown to have been combined by Virgil at *Aeneid* 1.92, the discovery of which implies in no uncertain terms the procedures demanded of an active, meaning-making reader. Moreover, the fact that Macrobius can adduce so many examples of Homeric translation in the *Aeneid* confirms the idea that, far from desiring to hide his reliance on Homer, Virgil would seem to invite such a comparison for purposes of enriching his own poetry. The alternating lines of Latin and Greek passages set for comparison in books 3–12 of the *Saturnalia* attest to the vastness of Virgil's engagement of Homer and sanction the reader's active participation in the construction of a meaning for Virgil's "translated" lines, because such meanings can only be articulated through an assessment of the Latin "translation" rendered in the light of its Greek context. In short, the independence of Virgil's translations confirms the sense implied in Eustathius's answer to his own question, that Virgilian borrowing is unique.

The competencies of a full-knowing reader are called forth subsequently by Eustathius as an ordering principle near the end of the lengthy list of Virgilian translations of Homer. "These passages," Eustathius says, "must be left to the judgment of the reader, for it is for him to make up his own mind about the comparisons I have made"[26] (Et haec quidem iudicio legentium relinquenda sunt ut ipsi aestiment quid debeant de utriusque collatione sentire; 5.11.1). In

---

26. This emphasis on a powerful reader is sustained in the later sections of book 5.

the end, Eustathius would seem to say, the entire Virgilian project hinges on the ability of Virgil's readers to work their way through his translations, spying for themselves the reflections of Homer that form the backdrop of Virgil's poetry and that lead ultimately to a more authoritative interpretive perspective, grounded as much in readerly as in authorial power.

This acknowledgment of readerly power on the part of Eustathius comes late in the fifth book (5.13). Macrobius portrays Eustathius as a full-knowing reader at the beginning of the catalogue of Virgilian translations of Homer also. There, Avienus and Eustathius play a verbal game of cat and mouse that leads, eventually, to a full articulation of readerly power:

> "Please go on, I beg you," said Avienus, "to examine all the passages in which Virgil has drawn from Homer. What is more agreeable than to hear how the two greatest of poets say the same thing? There are three things that are judged to be equally impossible: to rob Jupiter of his thunderbolt, Hercules of his club, and Homer of a line. And even if it were possible, it would be fitting for no one but Jupiter to launch the thunderbolt, no one but Hercules to wield the oaken club, and no one but Homer to sing the songs that Homer sang. And yet Virgil has so happily translated the words of the older poet as to make them seem his own. You will then meet the wishes of us all if you share with us your knowledge of all that our poet has borrowed from yours." "Very well," said Eustathius, "give me a copy of Virgil, for by looking at individual passages in it I shall more easily recall the corresponding lines in Homer."

> ("Perge quaeso," inquit Avienus, "omnia quae Homero subtraxit investigare. Quid enim suavius quam duos praecipuos vates audire idem loquentes? Quia cum tria haec ex aequo inpossibilia iudicentur, vel Iovi fulmen vel Herculi clavam vel versum Homero subtrahere, quod etsi fieri possent, alium tamen nullum deceret vel fulmen praeter Iovem iacere, vel certare praeter Herculem robore, vel canere quod cecinit Homerus: hic oportune in opus suum quae prior vates dixerat transferendo fecit ut sua esse credantur. Ergo pro voto omnium feceris si cum hoc coetu communicata velis quaecumque vestro noster poeta mutuatus est." "Cedo igitur," Eustathius ait, "Vergilianum volumen, quia locos singulos eius inspiciens Homericorum versuum promptius admonebor . . . "; 5.3.16–17).

Eustathius's response in these lines evokes some of the specific tasks demanded of a full-knowing reader, especially the recognition of the allusion and the diversion and disinterest in reading evinced once an allusion begins to be read. He portrays himself as an active participant as he reads Virgil, considering the language of Virgil carefully and determining on his own authority what passages from Virgil link to the poetry of Homer. Interestingly, Macrobius uses the verb *mutuari* with no misgivings to describe Virgilian borrowings here because in this passage the locus of interpretive authority has already shifted from author to reader, a transference confirmed in even stronger language at 5.18.1, where Macrobius considers passages in Virgil which are "understood by no one except those who have drunk diligently of the learning of Greece" (nullis cognita sunt nisi qui Graecam doctrinam diligenter hauserunt). In these cases, as Macrobius makes clear, a reader must ferret out meaning from verbal linkages that are sometime inordinately obtuse. The authority for pursuing such readings, in any case, rests entirely with the reader, whose competencies form the basis of the interpretive project.

At the opening of book 6, Macrobius offers some larger comments about literary borrowing. He seems always at pains as he works his way into this book to contrast the sophisticated kind of interpretive responses often elicited by Virgil to something less grand. More important, perhaps, as he continues through his litany of examples, Macrobius has his latest mouthpiece, Furius Albinus, choose examples of Virgil's borrowings that highlight this loftier kind of interpretive response—examples in which the parallelism between Homer and Virgil is much less close, and in which the full powers of the reader are increasingly brought to the fore. Here, more than ever perhaps, the competencies of a full-knowing reader are implicit in the compilation of "borrowings" that Furius Albinus has gathered. More to the point, and in keeping with the subtlety always at work in the *Saturnalia,* Macrobius himself demands these competencies of his own readership, sensitizing his audience through the very experience of it to something his culture could not even name, though they seem to have recognized it (and its complexities) when they saw it. In the event, the work of Augustine ensured that Macrobius and his intellectual compatriots would be near to the last of antique littérateurs to lack a term for allusion.

Augustine and the Predominance of the Full-Knowing Reader

Though they are roughly contemporaries, there can be no connecting Augustine and Macrobius in cultural terms, for Macrobius, unlike Augustine, wrote for, and functioned in, a pagan culture. That both are concerned with active, meaning-making readers is not coincidental, however, but rather measures the necessity of such a reader in cultural terms. Macrobius's discussion is wide-ranging and leisurely, unsystematic because the cultural stakes for him were not severe. His ability to write a dialogue of the sort represented by the *Saturnalia* clearly reflects cultural shifts owed to Christianity, even if the faith informing those shifts and their wider cultural implications are not directly relevant to Macrobius. By distinction, Augustine works in the *De doctrina christiana* and in the *Confessions* to articulate for his culture a cogent notion of Christian rhetoric that brings to the fore the power and authority of the Christian reader. The stakes are high because the very premises of Christian culture, grounded in Scripture, hang in the balance.

The importance of Augustine's project is gleaned perhaps most readily in the careful way that he links his model of Christian rhetoric to the crucifixion, the defining moment of Christian theology. As I will suggest below, Augustine employs in the *De doctrina christiana* the symbol of a cut or wounded body to represent both Scripture and the *corpus Christi,* while recommending an external process of "healing" symbolic of the process of interpretation and the redemption of the body of Christ by God the Father. Beyond simply locating Christian interpretation as the provenance of an active, meaning-making reader, however, Augustine draws upon images and vocabulary that link to Macrobius's pointed discussion in *Saturnalia* 5, suggesting accepted ways of referring to a powerful reader long in place in the Western tradition.

The establishment of an active, meaning-making reader at the center of Christian culture has been analyzed by Sarah Spence[27] in a study no student of allusion can ignore. Spence is concerned in her book with pagan and Christian persuasion, and she notes that Christianity specifically transformed the figure of the classical orator into the singular figure of God, the only orator whose persuasive ends were worth following. Spence rightly asserts that *caritas* replaced the many strategies and rules that informed rhetorical training and performance, and it alone became the means by which genuine persuasion obtained. The single difficulty, if it be called this, in the Christian system inhered in the fact that God was not an accessible orator. It took hard work to hear his voice and act upon his words.

Spence's depiction of Christian rhetoric in its Augustinian context is corroborated in a variety of ways in the late antique evidence. For example, the notion of a Christian orator-God so important to Spence's argument is analyzed in several poems by Paulinus of Nola, where the rhetorical role of *caritas* is accorded a clear articulation:[28]

---

27. S. Spence, *Rhetorics of Reason and Desire: Vergil, Augustine, and the Troubadours* (Ithaca, 1988).

28. On this relationship, see C. Witke, *Numen Litterarum: The Old and the New in Latin Poetry from Constantine to Gregory the Great* (Leiden, 1971), pp. 3 ff. My text of Paulinus is W. von Hartel, ed., *Sancti Pontii Meropii Paulini Nolani Carmina,* in *Corpus Scriptorum Ecclesiasticorum Latinorum,* vol. 30 (Vienna, 1894).

Surge, igitur, cithara, et totis intendere fibris,
excita vis animae; tacito mea viscera cantu,
non tacita cordis testudine dentibis ictis
pulset amor, linguae plectro lyra personet oris. (*Carm.* 15.26–29)

(Rise, therefore, my cithara, and fill every fiber of my being with the rousing force of my own soul; let its love pulsate in my whole being through its silent song and let the lyre of my own voice pour forth music by means of the plectrum of language so that the music of my soul makes words move from my mouth.)

Non adficta canam, licet arte poematis utar.
historica narrabo fide sine fraude poetae;
absit enim famulo Christi mentita profari.
gentibus hae placeant ut falsa colentibus artes;
at nobis ars una fides et musica Christus,
qui docuit miram sibimet concurrere pacem
disparis harmoniae quondam, quam corpus in unum
contulit adsumens hominem. (*Carm.* 20.28–35)

(I will not sing of fictions like the old poets, but I can use the art of poetry nonetheless; for the fraud of the old poets is absent the servant of Christ—those frauds of art that pleased ages past that they might cultivate false poetry. For us, Christ is both faith and music, the one who taught us of the wondrous peace found deep within the souls of each of us; he offered to us a certain disparate harmony in assuming the form of man.)

Using the symbol of the cithara, the classical instrument of divinely inspired poetry, Paulinus informs his old teacher, Ausonius, that Christians have no need for classical poetry, or a classical *vates* on the model of Pindar,[29] because each Christian soul contains within it the music of God, which is a silent music contemplated in solitude ("tacito mea viscera cantu, / . . . pulset amor . . ."; *Carm.* 15.27, 29). A true Christian, Paulinus goes on to suggest, need only rely on *caritas,* represented by the music of the cithara, in order to achieve Christian wisdom. Ultimately, each soul becomes a cithara itself when the love of God is realized.[30]

Paulinus's rejection of the classical cithara and his transformation of this

29. The distinction between *vates* and *poeta* and the role of Pindar was well known to Paulinus, via the influence of his teacher Ausonius, who is one of the last literary figures in the West to move with equal ease between Latin and Greek.

30. This fundamental aspect of Paulinus's poetry is analyzed by J. Fontaine, "Les symbolismes de la cithare dans la poésie de Paulin de Nole," reprinted in *Études sur la poésie latine tardive d'Ausone à Prudence* (Paris, 1980), pp. 393–413.

important symbol has a direct bearing on developments in Christian rhetoric occurring when he wrote. Because God is the ultimate speaker or singer and because his love is the ultimate music playing within each soul, Christians have no need to center their creative energies on external, divinely inspired sources, such as a *vates*—or an orator. Instead, they need simply to listen carefully to the music innate within their own souls. When they do, they realize fully the love that will sustain them as they attain the truth they seek.

Paulinus's symbolic use of the soul as a cithara points to a revaluation accorded the role of the individual in the attainment of wisdom or truth. Classical rhetoric placed the onus of responsibility for wisdom's attainment in the perfection of an orator's innate talent and in the application of the best wisdom within the context of the orator's life. In this view, the orator, like the *vates,* led his audience to the "truth." Paulinus, on the other hand, transforms the external impetus of the orator's persuasive abilities and perfect wisdom to the figure of God, so that He directs and persuades each Christian through the soul's mediation. In this sense, the importance of individual oratorical effort in the classical model is replaced by the omnipresence of Christian *caritas,* symbolic of God and innate to each Christian soul. One must simply accept God's *caritas* to participate in his unity.[31]

Paulinus's reconfiguration attests to analogous shifts in concepts of reading (and writing) by Christian thinkers. Two features in particular conspired to lift the concept of written text to a new, privileged status. First, God was not only the first "speaker" but also the first "writer," for He handed down his law in writing and in so doing accorded to writing a status equal to speech, a status it clearly lacked in antiquity. Second, the Christian gospels, especially the gospel of John, conceived of God symbolically as logos and that conception, with implications beyond the mere connotation of "word" in Greek, nevertheless accentuated the role of God in symbolic terms as present in, and associated with, writing. Finally, Christian culture was a culture of the book. Long before Christ lived, the status of writing had been privileged in the Jewish tradition by virtue of the pervasive moral, ethical, and social influence of the Old Testament. The addition of the New Testament confirmed the status of writing in Christian culture and this remained an important reason, in Christian terms, for privileging writing over orality.

But this privileging brought with it a singular problem. Because Christianity sought to assimilate two traditions, Jewish and Christian, and because both

31. See also Paulinus, *Carm.* 20.34 ff., on the *dispars harmonia* and its implications.

traditions possessed "books" of equal stature that oftentimes conflicted with each other, Christian intellectuals found themselves in the position of having to explain how either book could be reconciled with the other. Christian rhetoric took as its basic task, therefore, to mediate the dissonant biblical texts which constituted its tradition. Accordingly, allegory was introduced early on as an interpretive strategy, whereby the dissonances of sacred texts could be mediated by playing to the different levels of meaning language could imply. This strain of Christian rhetoric was particularly strong in the early centuries of Christianity in the East, where a school of Christian Platonists writing in Greek arose at Alexandria. By the late fourth and early fifth centuries, that tradition had found an intellectual home in the Western church also, through the mediation of Ambrose and his greatest pupil, Augustine. What is striking in the rise of allegoresis in Christian rhetoric is the grounding of this approach in those qualities of language—its ability to mean different things, to be interpreted at different levels—that had been, as we have seen, marginalized by ancient rhetoric and feared by Plato.

Augustine is the most important witness in the mediation of scriptural allegoresis and exegesis, because of the prominent role played by Ambrose in his training. One can gain more than a glimpse of that role in Augustine's *Confessions,* where Ambrose is remembered in several ways that attend directly to notions of reading. Ambrose's most important role, in Augustine's view, would seem to be his work as a teacher, for much attention is devoted in the *Confessions* to the ways in which he opened up the Bible to students through the use of allegory. Before Ambrose, Augustine admits, he had been hard pressed to read the Bible, finding its simple style and often contradictory passages intellectually inaccessible and stylistically repellent.[32] But Ambrose also figures in Augustine's life as a model, someone to watch and to "read," like a passage from Scripture itself, and when Augustine describes him in the act of reading in book 6 of the *Confessions,* the exemplarism of Ambrose's life come into sharper focus. The recollection recorded there, one of Augustine's earliest memories of Ambrose, is telling in the details recalled:

> Sed cum legebat, oculi ducebantur per paginas et cor intellectum rimabatur, vox autem et lingua quiescebant . . . sic eum legentem vidimus tacite et aliter numquam . . . ne auditore suspenso et intento, si qua obscurius posuisset ille quem legeret, etiam exponere esset necesse aut de aliquibus difficilioribus dissertare quaestionibus

32. See also *Conf.* 6.4. My text of the *Confessions* is L. Verheijen, ed., *Sancti Augustini Confessionum Libri XIII* (Turnhout, 1981).

. . . quamquam et causa servandae vocis. . . . Quolibet tamen animo id ageret, bono utique ille vir agebat. (6.3)

(When [Ambrose] read, his eyes scanned the page and his heart searched for under-standing, but his voice and tongue were quiet . . . and thus we saw him reading in silence, for he never read aloud. . . . Perhaps he was afraid that some obscure passage in the author he was reading might raise a question in the mind of an attentive listener if he read aloud, and he would have to explain the meaning or discuss the more difficult points. . . . Perhaps it was for the sake of his voice. . . . Whatever his reason, it was a good one.)

This portrait of Ambrose is important for several reasons. Because Augustine was raised in the classical rhetorical tradition, his reactions to Ambrose the reader reflect those of a classically trained intellectual viewing for the first time a Christian reader at work. When Augustine remembers Ambrose as a reader, therefore, he does so not as a fellow Christian offering praise to a beloved teacher, but rather as a yet-to-be converted Christian attempting to understand an important Christian figure and the new style of reading he practices. Augustine draws attention to Ambrose in the ways he does in this passage, there-fore, to accentuate the divisions between ancient and Christian modes of reading, stressing qualities that symbolize the transformation of rhetorical attitudes occurring in the fourth century.

The picture of St. Ambrose silently perusing a text seems inconsequential to modern eyes, but this picture of Ambrose's behavior has stuck firmly in Au-gustine's mind for reasons that bear importantly on assumptions about the best way to attain truth. It was not, after all, a normal practice in antiquity to read silently[33]—one normally read aloud or, better, had one's slave read to one. For his part, Augustine is not entirely clear at this point in his recollection as to the reasons for Ambrose's silence, but the emphasis he places on this quality of Ambrose's readerly habits reveals more than a sense of curiosity on his part. It speaks also to the revaluation of classical rhetoric itself, suggesting the transfor-mation of speech and oratory, to silent reading and writing.

This shift to silent reading implies a further development that corresponds to the positions suggested by Paulinus of Nola in his poetical epistles to Ausonius. Because Christian *caritas* is inherently part of each soul, because it is present to Christians by virtue of their status as Christians, the need to read in silence becomes an absolute necessity, for only through silent reading can one hear the pure and silent music of one's soul. The importance of this aspect of Christian

33. See B. M. W. Knox, "Silent Reading in Antiquity," *Greek, Roman, and Byzantine Studies* 9 (1968), pp. 421–35.

reading recalls the "silent song" of God's love described by Paulinus in his carmen 15. Because it is innate and most perfect, God's love, symbolized as a song in Paulinus's poem, cannot, like any mundane song, be "heard" in a normal sense. Rather, through God's *tacitus cantus*, a paradoxical image that best captures the sublimeness of God's music, Christians "hear" the love of God it represents.

At *Confessions* 12.26, Augustine articulates this new role accorded to reading more clearly:

> . . . vellem ergo, si tunc ego essem quod ille et mihi abs te Geneseos liber scribendus adiungeretur, talem mihi eloquendi facultatem dari et eum texendi sermonis modum, ut neque illi, qui nondum queunt intellegere quemadmodum creat deus, tamquam excedentia vires suas dicta recusarent et illi, qui hoc iam possunt, in quamlibet veram sententiam cogitando venissent, eam non praetermissam in paucis verbis tui famuli reperirent, et si alius aliam vidisset in luce veritatis, nec ipsa in eisdem verbis intellegenda deesset.

> . . . if I had been Moses and you had made it my task to write the book of Genesis, I should have wished you to give me such skill in writing and such power in framing words, that not even those who as yet cannot understand how God creates should reject my words as beyond their comprehension, and those who can should find expressed in the few words of your servant whatever true conclusion they had reached by their own reasoning; and if, in the light of truth, another man saw a different meaning in those words, it should not be impossible to understand this meaning too in those same words.[34]

Augustine longs for the most sublime truth in his engagement of obscure texts. Like Moses, he seeks the clarity of intellect that divine presence proffers, coupled with an ability comparable to Moses' to utter divine truths through human language so that dissonant passages of Scripture might ultimately reflect God's truth. The final statement of this passage is especially important. "If," Augustine writes, "in the light of truth, another man saw a different meaning in those words, it should not be impossible to understand this meaning too in those same words." This injunction to comprehensive meaning is both a manifesto of Christian rhetoric cast in the most personal of terms and also a recommendation of a special role accorded the Christian reader. Augustine's aim is personal, for he hopes to find a means to express the sublimeness of God in such

34. This and subsequent renderings come from R. S. Pine Coffin's translation in *Augustine: The Confessions* (Harmondsworth, 1961). P. Brown discusses this passage also in *Augustine of Hippo: A Biography* (Berkeley and London, 1967), p. 259, n. 7. See also J. J. O'Donnell, *Augustine: Confessions* 3 vols. (Oxford, 1992), vol 3., pp. 334–35.

a way as to make Him accessible to everyone. But it is also rhetorical, for he seeks to affirm the process of reading by which differing interpretations of language might abide simultaneously and in unity. In the same way that the cithara is innate to all Christian souls, then, so too, Augustine implies here, is Christian truth innately in language, in the signs that conspire through the aegis of syntax, diction, and vocabulary to give shape to Christian thought. Augustine's task was to postulate a way in which the discordant passages requiring interpretation might be mediated, a way in which the breach or cut of meaning could be healed.

Augustine's postulation is offered in two texts. At *Confessions* 12.18, he offers a theological consideration:

> Quid, inquam, mihi obest, si aliud ego sensero, quam sensit alius eum sensisse, qui scripsit? Omnes quidem, qui legimus, nitimur hoc indagare atque comprehendere, quod voluit ille quem legimus, et cum eum veridicum credimus, nihil, quod falsum esse vel novimus vel putamus, audemus eum existimare dixisse. Dum ergo quisque conatur id sentire in scripturis sanctis, quod in eis sensit ille qui scripsit, quid mali est, si hoc sentiat, quod tu, lux omnium veridicarum mentium, ostendis verum esse, etiamsi non hoc sensit ille, quem legit, cum et ille verum nec tamen hoc senserit?

> (How can it harm me that it should be possible to interpret . . . words in several ways, all of which may yet be true? How can it harm me if I understand the writer's meaning in a different sense from that in which another understands it? All of us who read [Moses'] words do our best to discover and understand what he had in mind, and since we believe that he wrote the truth, we are not so rash as to suppose that he wrote anything which we know or think to be false. Provided, therefore, that each of us tries as best he can to understand in the Holy Scriptures what the writer meant by them, what harm is there if a reader believes what you, the Light of all truthful minds, show him to be the true meaning? It may not even be the meaning which the writer had in mind, and yet he too saw in them a true meaning, different though it may have been from this.)

Because a Christian accepts the premise that the word of God is true, any interpretation of sacred Scripture in some way reflects that truth, provided that the reader engages the text actively and to the best of his abilities. Because reading is subjective, filtered through the prism of personal experience, it is manifold. This does not, however, lessen its truth value, but only heightens the sublimeness and congruence of God's divinity.

In the *De doctrina christiana,* Augustine confirms this notion of linguistic meaning by offering a rhetorical consideration of it, formulating in his handbook of Christian rhetoric the methods by which the readings of which he speaks in the *Confessions* obtain. Now the full-knowing reader comes to the fore as the central player in the construction of meaning. Augustine treats his version of the full-knowing reader from several angles. First, he analyzes language itself in the context of theological certainty. This discussion, which forms book 1 of the *De doctrina christiana,* concludes with a section on the kind of reader demanded by Scripture. Then, Augustine analyzes language as a norm of convention, concluding with a consideration of the relationship of rhetorical norms to Christian reading. Third, Augustine considers reading as a separate activity, and locates those activities a good Christian must learn and practice if full-knowledge of sacred Scripture or Christian truth is to follow. Finally, in book 4, Augustine considers each of the preceding facets of human communication—divine truth, language, and reading, in a comprehensive way.

As in the later books of the *Confessions,* Augustine sets for himself in the opening chapters of the *De doctrina christiana* the task of articulating the importance of sacred Scripture in Christian life and of determining the best ways in which this sublime, divine language can best be understood and disseminated. This involves "discovering" what must be understood and teaching what has been understood (1.1), goals achieved through the assistance of God, whose presence in each human soul effects the desired end. The process is solitary and spiritually rewarding. It necessitates a surrender of the individual to God's mercy and assistance (1.22). In this way, God "uses" his children, "applying His use of us to His own goodness." A hermeneutical circle arises, in which the Christian seeking understanding of God through language is led to an understanding of God through his revealed word by virtue of *caritas,* the intimate and tangible presence of God in each Christian's soul. This circular process demands, therefore, a search for wisdom that is centered and controlled by that which is being sought—God. And because each Christian will bring different temperaments, abilities, and intelligence to this search, the kinds of responses elicited of each Christian are bound to be various.

This variety forms a segue into a closer consideration of an active, meaning-making audience. This is, Augustine says, an audience that works alone, that seeks wisdom, that sustains its interpretation of language with God's love. As a result: "If anyone has derived from [reading] an idea that may be useful to him in building up his love, but has not expressed by [that idea] what the author whom he is reading demonstrably intended in that passage, he is not erring dangerously, nor lying. For inherent in lying is the will to speak falsehoods . . . [and] lying is always hurtful." (Quisquis vero talem inde sententiam duxerit, ut huic aedificandae caritati sit utilis, nec tamen hoc dixerit quod ille quem legit eo loco sensisse probabitur, non perniciose fallitur nec omnino mentitur. Inest quippe in mentiente voluntas falsa dicendi . . . [et] mendacium semper inutile est; 1.36ff.)[35] The important point for Augustine is not that truth is unilateral and fixed, but that it has varying qualities and resonances, that its manifold sublimeness cannot be comprehended entirely. Perhaps most important, no aspect of it can be gleaned without the participation of the reader of sacred Scripture, who must do the best he can to ferret wisdom from its disparate and imperfect language.

This tenet of Christian rhetoric does not translate into a radical relativism. Not all interpretations are equally valid, nor are all of equal value. But, like someone who leaves the road through error, but makes his way "through the field to the place where the road also leads," readers of lesser abilities can and must be shown that it is better not to leave the road (1.36). The process of demonstrating the appropriate paths to readers of lesser ability involves a comparison of passages as a means to control interpretation. A reader who arrives at a certain conclusion about Christian truth can control his own tendencies to wander off the beaten path by adducing other pertinent passages from Scripture. "If he agrees that [those passages] are true and definite, then the opinion which he had formed concerning the former passages cannot be true" (1.37). The reader must, therefore, attempt to control his own interpretations at every step in the process of reading. He must become his own classical orator, persuading himself of the certainty of his reading by measuring it against the dictates of *caritas* that inform the interpretive process. When the reader does this, he may approach the interpretation of Scripture "fearlessly" (1.40), for his readings will be supported by the strength of God's own love. The language he reads will be transformed, from its imperfect shape on a written page, to a natural form emanating from God.

Ideally, the community of Christian believers seeks as its goal a language that is silent and unspoken, a natural language that is felt in the soul. But Augustine knew that such a language, like such a goal, was difficult to attain. Most Christians were mired in the imperfect world and had to deal with conventional language, progressing slowly, if at all, to the ideal commended in book 1 of the *De doctrina christiana*. Conventional language is the locus of imperfection for Augustine, a vestige of original sin. Spoken language is mutable and

35. My text of the *De doctrina christiana* is G. M. Green, ed., *Sancti Aureli Augustini Opera: De doctrina christiana*, in *Corpus Scriptorum Ecclesiasticorum Latinorum*, vol. 80 (Vienna, 1963). Translations are from D. W. Robertson, *Augustine: On Christian Doctrine* (New York, 1958).

ephemeral, and written language open to "deception, obscurity, vagueness, manifold interpretation" (2.4–6). At every turn, an active, meaning-making reader is required to sort out the obscure from the plain, the obtuse from the clear. Yet the procedure of full-knowing reading harbors a divine order and plan. "It is with delight that we experience some trouble in searching for divine truth . . . for some passages from Scripture are easier, and they relieve our hunger; in the ones that are harder . . . practically nothing is dug out which is not discovered to be said very plainly in another place" (2.6).

Conventional language takes various forms—Latin, Greek, Hebrew—and the best readers will be able to use all three. In order to advance beyond the inherent limitations of Scripture's language, however, one must, regardless of the language, ingest the contents of sacred Scripture entirely, attaining a complete knowledge of them (2.8). This will enable the reader to weave his way through Latin translations of Scripture with some authority, even if his knowledge of Hebrew or Greek is less than complete. Throughout the process of reading, the dictates of logic, science, rhetoric, and dialectic—the best knowledge of antiquity—can be brought to bear. But the ultimate goal of these instruments of knowledge is not to attain an understanding of them, but rather to proceed somehow more closely to the truth of God whose wisdom they serve to reveal. Yet, the processes of acquisition of linguistic and analytical tools, facility in language, and a broad knowledge of scripture, grounded though they all are in conventional modes of instruction and communication, must be measured by the Christian reader in the larger context of Christian wisdom: "When unfamiliar things do not ensnare the reader provided with instruction—meek and humble of heart, easily brought under the yoke of Christ and weighed down by His light burden, grounded, rooted, and built up in love, beyond the power of knowledge to puff him up—let him advance to the study and thorough investigation of the ambiguous language of Scripture." (Hac igitur instructione praeditum cum signa incognita lectorem non impedierint, mitem et humilem corde, subiugatum leniter Christo et oneratum sarcina levi, fundatum et radicatum et aedificatum in caritate quem scientia inflare non possit, accedat ad ambigua signa in scripturis consideranda; 2.42.)

The process of "hearing" God with sure authority is more specifically located in the third book of the *De doctrina christiana*. There, Augustine gives attention to the ways in which the competencies required of a full-knowing reader must be brought to bear in the interpretation of God's word. The first competency is "attention and persistence" (3.5). One must always be on guard against interpreting figurative words literally, or vice versa. To exemplify this basic quality of reading, Augustine recalls the words of Paul: "the letter kills, but the spirit gives life" (2. *Cor.* 3.6). In other words, if a reader, in his subjective interpretation of language, comprehends only what the language "says" and ignores the "spirit" informing the words (one might say the context in which they are uttered), then that reader "reads carnally," without complete knowledge (3.5). A reader must not, in other words, be passive. The essence of language must be gleaned from an active consideration of the "strange and twisting lanes of speech."[36] If one simply takes words at face value, one "subjects intelligence to the flesh" (3.5).

Augustine goes on to qualify these principles by noting that "he who produces or worships any symbol (that is, language) unaware of what it means, is enslaved to a sign" (3.9); conversely, he who does not do this understands "reality," the level of meaning beyond the subjective to which "all symbols must be ascribed" (3.9). To ensure that the spirit, not the letter, of language is revealed, a reader must, therefore, be discerning: "Since things appear similar to each other in many ways [in language], we should not imagine there is any precept that we must believe that, because a thing has a certain analogical meaning in one place, it always has this meaning." (Sed quoniam multis modis res similes rebus apparent, non putemus esse praescriptum ut quod in aliquo loco res aliqua per similitudinem significaverit, hoc eam semper significare credamus; 3.25). Language, in other words, is semantically diverse, and only the perseverance of a full-knowing reader can clarify this diversity.

Perhaps the most striking consideration of a powerful reader in the *De doctrina christiana* comes in the first book, however, where Augustine links his description of the Christian reader to the crucified figure of Christ. Such a reader, Augustine begins, is a reader of "the word made flesh": in the same way that we "penetrate the mind of our listener through the ears of flesh, the word of God is carried in our heart and becomes a sound and is called speech" (1.13). The Word of God was made flesh in order that He might dwell among us—in our hearts, instructing us through love, that horrible pang, so Augustine recalls in the *Confessions,* that made him long for things he could not understand and did not yet know.[37] That love acts as a medicine upon our souls, healing us in our imperfection and instructing us in our ignorance.

The resonance of this passages does not end with its theological implications, as powerful and as congruous as they are, for the subsequent section (1.14) treats

---

36. *De Catech. Rud.* 10.15.
37. See *Conf.* 3.1 and 6.1., e.g.

the theme of the Word made flesh, and more specifically the crucifixion itself, as a hermeneutical prototype:

> Et quem ad modum medici cum alligant vulnera non incomposite sed apte id faciunt, ut vinculi utilitatem quaedam pulchritudo etiam consequatur, sic medicina sapientiae per hominis susceptionem nostris est accomodata vulneribus, de quibusdam contrariis curans et de quibusdam similibus. Sicut etiam ille qui medetur vulneri corporis, adhibet quaedam contraria, sicut frigidum calido vel humido siccum vel quid aliud eius modi, adhibet etiam quaedam similia, sicut linteolum vel rotundo vulneri rotundum vel oblongum oblongo ligaturamque ipsam non eandem membris omnibus, sed similem similibus coaptat: sic sapientia dei hominem curans se ipsam exhibuit ad sanandum, ipsa medicus, ipsa medicina. (1.14)[38]

> (And as physicians bind up wounds in an orderly and skillful manner, so that even a certain beauty may join the usefulness of the bandage, so the medicine of Wisdom, by assuming humanity, accommodated Himself to our wounds, healing some by opposite remedies and others by like remedies. A physician, in treating an injury to the body, applies certain opposites, as cold to hot, wet to dry; in other cases he applies like remedies, as a round bandage to a circular wound, or an oblong bandage to an oblong wound, not using the same bandage for every limb, but adapting like to like. Likewise, the Wisdom of God, in healing humanity, has employed Himself to cure it, since he is both the physician and the medicine.[39])

Sarah Spence has suggested[40] that one can read this passage not only as a discourse on Christ's *caritas* for humanity, but also as a *description* of Christian reading. This makes every sense in a treatise devoted to Christian rhetoric—the centerpiece of which was a powerful reader who required instruction in *how* to use her considerable powers. In Spence's view, the passage works on analogy: the *medicus* is God but also the Christian reader; the *vulnus* is the wound on Christ's body and also the dissonant language of Scripture; the *corpus* is Christ's body but also the text of Scripture itself. Helpfully, the word for "body" in Latin, *corpus,* can also mean "book."[41]

The implications of Spence's reading are not difficult to grasp: Augustine

38. Spence, *Rhetorics of Reason and Desire,* pp. 98–103 analyzes this passage and several subsequent ones to make her good points about Augustine's "hermeneutics of charity." I owe the discovery of this passage to this important study on rhetoric in the classical and medieval traditions.

39. On the *De doctrina christiana* in general, see D. W. H. Arnold and P. Bright, *De Doctrina Christiana: A Classic of Western Culture* (Notre Dame, 1995), and R. P. H. Green, *De Doctrina Christiana* (Cambridge, 1994), pp. ix–xxv.

40. See *Rhetorics of Reason and Desire,* esp. pp. 100–103.

41. LS, p. 472, s.v. *corpus,* B, b and II.

makes reading analogous to the crucifixion itself, framing it in the context of the defining event of Christianity and, therefore, enshrining it as the center-piece of Christian rhetoric. Moreover, as the next chapter will suggest, there may be more than theological considerations at work in this passage, for Augustine's use of the vocabulary of cutting and binding links to a tradition in place in antiquity in which allusion was described as a cut or a literary graft. Since he did not have allusion specifically on his mind in writing this passage in the *De doctrina christiana,* it is not possible to say that Augustine is keying into this allusion-specific tradition. But, given that antiquity consistently describes allusion in terms of cutting, the *association* of cutting and a powerful reader would have been easy to make to a fourth-century littérateur raised in the classical tradition. In the event, Augustine's *De doctrina christiana* ensured that a powerful reader was legitimated in the West for the first time. There would seem, given his legitimation, to be little coincidence in the fact that a term for allusion exists in the extant evidence for the first time in the West barely a century after Augustine wrote. Put another way, literary allusion and the requi-site competencies of full-knowing reading were normalized only *after* Augustine placed at the center of his interpretive paradigm an empowered reader possessing all of the competencies of our full-knowing reader. As the next chapter will suggest, antiquity had developed a consistent vocabulary for de-scribing allusion, but it became normalized in the Western tradition only on the influence of Augustine's own version of our full-knowing reader.

Chapter 4 Versions of Allusion

The lack of a term for allusion in antiquity is an oddity of Western literary history more often repeated than scrutinized. The evidence pulls allusion's students in contrary directions: on the one hand, ancient artists seem to allude frequently and with great sophistication; on the other, ancient literary culture, especially as represented by ancient rhetoric, seems to lack a clear-cut way to talk about the allusions which seem to form so important a part of their output. This makes for a curious situation, implying the absence of an antique notion of allusion and arguing for caution in applying our modern concept of allusion to ancient literary works.

But this lack is not in and of itself a profound piece of evidence. If an ancient term for allusion is lacking, yet if ancient literary works seem replete with allusions, it is counterintuitive to deny the existence of an ancient notion of allusion simply owing to that lack, for it is illogical to think that the concept and practice of allusion are coeval with the mere invention of a term for it. Concepts can exist absent terms to designate them. More to the point, it seems always to have been the case in ancient rhetoric that conceptualization and naming followed the invention and practice of rhetorical categories such as metaphor, simile, allegory, and the like.[1]

The more important question centers on function. The fact that there would seem to be moments of allusion in ancient literary works does not mean that those allusions function in a modern sense. Especially given the ways in which ancient literary forms negotiated the tensions between oral and written traditions,[2] function can only be determined by analyzing what seem to be ancient descriptions of allusion. Thus, the task for this chapter.

There are, as it turns out, a cohort of moments in Greek and Latin literature that would seem to describe allusion. These descriptions offer up a battery of key terms, images, words, consistently used.[3] Not coincidentally, this evidence accords both with the vocabulary used by Augustine to talk about a powerful reader, and with the vocabulary used by Macrobius to talk about Virgil's borrowings from Homer. These descriptions are most useful because they permit modern students of allusion to locate ways in which antiquity talked about allusion despite the lack of a good term to frame specific articulations. This cohort of terms, images, words is useful also in the ways it exposes allusion at the level of conceptualization, affording insight into the complexity and sophistication of the antique notion of allusion. Perhaps it is not surprising that ancient literary artists, not rhetoricians, offer the surest evidence by which to access an ancient notion of allusion, offering us not a single way of naming or conceptualizing allusion, but a variety of ways, consistently cast. And their consistency is the best witness to the validity of the claim of the following pages, namely, that antiquity conceived of (and described) allusion as (1) a species of textual movement and implantation; (2) a procedure in which the reader or audience is empowered at the expense of the author; and (3) as a kind of literary graft or cutting.

I begin by examining briefly some ancient rhetorical categories that would seem to (or have been made in modern criticism to) stand for or to mean

1. T. Cole, *The Origins of Rhetoric in Ancient Greece* (Baltimore and London, 1991); see also R. L. Enos, *Greek Rhetoric Before Aristotle* (Prospect Heights, Ill., 1993), esp. pp. 88–95; W. W. Fortenbaugh and D. C. Mirhady, eds., *Peripatetic Rhetoric after Aristotle* (New Brunswick, N.J., 1994); and G. A. Kennedy, *A New History of Classical Rhetoric* (Princeton, 1994).

2. On which see now F. Dupont, *L'Invention de la littérature: De l'Ivresse grecque au livre latin* (Paris, 1994).

3. I take for granted that *borrowing* is of the essence with allusion; thus I identify these descriptions on the basis of their interest in literary borrowing. On this essentialism, see above, chap. 2.

"allusion." Although several obvious categories—*imitatio, aemulatio,* for example—have affinities with allusion, the evidence suggests that they did not perform the rhetorical tasks that the term *allusio* eventually came to represent in Christian rhetoric. Indeed, ancient rhetoric, as we have seen, consistently ignores allusion formally, while taking cognizance of a powerful reader cautiously, a circumspection that makes every sense in a discipline devoted to the idea that an audience might be persuaded of any topic, provided the orator's rhetorical skills were in place. There could be on the part of rhetoric, in other words, little formal interest in allusion, with its demand for a powerful audience response of the kind represented by δεινότης, since to invite that sort of response would be to court rhetorical and oratorical failure (as the practitioners and theoreticians of δεινότης themselves knew). But what ancient rhetoricians feared to do, ancient literary artists pursued without hindrance. Several of them, in fact, as the bulk of this chapter will suggest, key into a tradition of naming allusion descriptively.

A BRIEF LOOK AT RHETORICAL CATEGORIES: *ALLUSIO*, μίμησις, ζήλωσις (AND SOME OTHER TERMS)

When modern students of allusion search for an antique term for allusion, the rhetorical categories most often mentioned are μίμησις, ζήλωσις, *imitatio, aemulatio,* or *paraphrase.* The most obvious term, *allusio,* does not exist in ancient rhetoric.[4] To be sure, it does come eventually to designate allusion, but as an ancient word, *allusio* does not perform the semantic tasks of its modern cognates until the late antique period, as we saw in the previous chapter. Several older categories of ancient rhetoric would seem to come close to performing these tasks in earlier centuries, but a closer examination of them reveals that they fall short of the mark. μίμησις and *imitatio,* for example, were common terms used by the ancients to account for one author's use of another's words. The Greek μίμησις, with a rich history spanning rhetoric and philosophy, became more proscribed in the Hellenistic period and was used to denote something as specific as the standardized human types (the braggart solider, the hot-headed man, for example) or something as general as character, thought, or natural phenomena, as long as generic distinctions were observed.[5]

In the Roman period, however, the comparable term *imitatio* came to be

---

4. LS, p. 94.
5. See A. Preminger and T. V. F. Brogan, eds., *The New Princeton Encyclopedia of Poetry and Poetics* (Princeton, 1993), p. 576, s.v. *imitation.*

closely associated with copying the "classics," the great models of achievement in each genre.[6] The key expressions of this view are given in the fragmentary *On Imitation* by Dionysius of Halicarnassus and in Quintilian's *Institutio oratoria* 10.2. This conception of *imitatio* involves on the part of a writer the use of an exemplary model, from whose works he selects, distills, employs the best features of language and presentation. In the hands of Quintilian, *imitatio* is rarely, if ever, a mechanism of slavish copying. As "Longinus's" *On the Sublime* suggests, the point rather is to imitate a spirit or a passion, a tradition bequeathed to medieval but especially to Renaissance notions of *imitatio*, as Vida's *Ars Poetica*, for example, makes clear.[7] But, of course, by the Renaissance, allusion already had existed for some time as a category expressing literary borrowing, quite apart from the concept of imitation bequeathed to it via the Roman notion of *imitatio*.[8]

In any case, a conception of imitation in which one selects a model for its exemplarism is hardly a credible substitute for a notion of allusion. Above all, it is too general. It accounts for the borrowing of words but not the creation of a space in which model and copy meet. The engagement is instead ornamental, a way of insinuating a particular work into a tradition, rather than engaging a particular work on specific and verifiable grounds. *Imitatio* is about shared language that can happen to be allusive, but it does not *mean* allusion to ancient littérateurs. [9]

Seemingly more specific is the notion of ζήλωσις or *aemulatio*, a concept employed in antiquity to talk about the appropriation of one author's words by another. The process is not a specific one in which prior words are brought forward into a newer literary work, however. More generally, ζήλωσις and *aemulatio* attend to the ways in which an author, contending with another, seeks to outdo the exemplarism of his model. Invariably the subsequent author would bruit his battle against his exemplary model by using the language of that model. But in this deployment of older words in a newer work of art, the

6. For a succinct discussion see D. A. Russell, "De Imitatione," in T. Woodman and D. A. West, eds., *Creative Imitation and Latin Literature* (Cambridge, 1979), pp. 165–88.

7. I am indebted in this discussion to Preminger and Brogan, *New Princeton Encylopedia*, pp. 576–77; cf. Vida, *Ars poetica* 2.422–44.

8. Cf. Blaise, p. 54, s.v. *adludere; MLWL*, p. 15, s.v. *allusio; Mitt. Wört.*, pp. 484–85, s.v. *alludere*; Niermeyer, p. 35, s.v. *allusio*; Sleumer, p. 98, s.v. *allusio; TLL*, vol. 1, fasc. 8, p. 1700, s.v. *allusio*.

9. See J. Farrell, *Vergil's Georgics and the Traditions of Ancient Epic: The Art of Allusion in Literary History* (Oxford, 1991), pp. 5–10 on the tradition in which classical scholars have generally held allusion to be a species of *imitatio*.

creative engagement of the two texts is never at issue. The dynamic at work is instead exclusively competitive, whereby an older work is evoked only to confirm the superiority of the newer work that takes shape from it. This paradigm might be useful to explain the psychology of the allusive author, or the dynamics of a literary culture that would seem to place heavy emphasis on tradition. But it does not explicate allusion, for allusion is not exclusively (if at all) an emulative or competitive form. It requires an engagement of the older work at issue, not a conjuring up of its best features in order to be outdone by a newer version.[10]

Aemulatio, like *imitatio,* gained a new lease on life in the Renaissance, when humanists of many stripes took pleasure in measuring classical Latin writers against their Greek models. But that measurement was never cast under the organizing principle of readerly desires. The obvious parallels were gathered together for the various authors, and the later work—say, Virgil's *Aeneid*—was judged according to the ways it did or did not succeed in emulating a Homeric parallel. The question was never one of Virgil's engagement of Homer or of Homer's enrichment of the meanings of the *Aeneid.* Instead, the focus was more narrowly on how a particular Virgilian passage would seem to fare verbally, rhetorically, and in terms of effect against its Homeric model. But, of course, the concept of allusion already existed by this time in Western criticism. Indeed, *aemulatio* is much akin to *paraphrase,* a Roman rhetorical invention that had in antiquity, and continued to have in later centuries, a specific identity apart from allusion.[11]

Even when we turn from the general to the specific, searching in the history of προσπαίζω, the transliterated Greek form of *alludere,* for qualities of allusion, we come up short. προσπαίζω has no literary connotations.[12] But to search in ancient rhetoric is to look in perhaps the most obvious but least likely place for ancient versions of allusion. Rhetoric, by nature a conservative discipline, would have been wary of allusion anyway. As a mode of discourse requiring an

10. This is essentially the point of Harold Bloom relative to allusion. See *Anxiety of Influence,* pp. 45–56. On imitation and literary borrowing in general in the Renaissance, see T. M. Greene, *The Light in Troy: Imitation and Discovery in Renaissance Poetry* (New Haven, 1982) esp. pp. 19–80.

11. Paraphrase was developed and fully articulated by the Romans. On its history see M. Roberts, *Biblical Epic and Rhetorical Paraphrase in Late Antiquity* (Liverpool, 1985), pp. 5–36. Though one might argue that paraphrase is akin to allusion, Roberts demonstrates that the goal in using paraphrase was not to evoke an older model but to outdo it, or better it, whence the idea of *aemulatio* comes into play. See esp. pp. 219–25.

12. LSJ, p. 1522.

empowered audience or powerful reader, allusion could only be considered a potential obstruction to the desired persuasive goal of the orator. The power assigned to rhetoric, in any case, as the arbiter of ancient literary categories is probably overplayed.[13] Rhetoric is reactive to literature. And literary artists, in their works, have recorded complex and sophisticated descriptions of allusion. Rather than see allusion in the rhetorical categories of paraphrase, *imitatio,* *aemulatio,* μίμησις, or ζήλωσις, then, we should see it in the following descriptions and others like them dispersed throughout the remains of Greek and Roman literature.[14]

ARISTOPHANES' EURIPIDES

Although the first committed description of literary allusion in the Western tradition would seem to occur in his *Acharnians,* Aristophanes evidences in many of his extant dramas an interest in the tension between authorial intent and audience interpretation, a tension he seems to consider of fundamental importance in his overall notion of literary and dramatic production. That tension is resident in the *Knights,* for example, where Aristophanes assails Cleon for his scurrility by pairing him with one more scurrilous still, who can match his linguistic prowess point for point. It is resident also in the *Clouds,* which lampoons Socrates for, among other things, his ability to ponder unimportant minutiae and to make them sound important through the clever use of language.

In much the same vein, the *Wasps* condemns the popular law courts and their tendency to judge fact through the filter of subjective perception. Here, the orator's ability to sway and move an audience is held up for special derision. Aristophanes' point is both to condemn a rhetorical notion of language that posits the correlation of intent and interpretation, and at the same time to ridicule the audience which, knowing better, nonetheless bases legal conclusions on the best-argued or best-ornamented speech, disregarding in the process the truth-value of what is said.

His larger sensitivity to the negotiation between authorial intent and audience interpretation is perhaps one reason why Aristophanes would seem more than any other extant Greek artist to consider the form and function of allusion in his dramas. The *Frogs* establishes a vocabulary for allusion that centers

13. See Cole, pp. 3–5.
14. In what follows, my discussion is meant to be suggestive rather than exhaustive.

especially on the power of the audience to make meaning.[15] That power is initially qualified in the *Frogs,* not coincidentally, by the adjective δεινός, a word, as we have seen, which allows us entry into a rich vein of evidence in Greek literature that considers the implications of a powerful reader. Aristophanes takes the discussion one step further, however, by tying δεινός language directly to depictions of allusion. He does this at the end of the *Frogs,* when Euripides and Aeschylus, set to do battle in the hopes of fulfilling Dionysus's search for a tragic poet, banter to and fro, each condemning the ways the other practiced the art of drama. The chorus sets up the scene by framing this bantering in the context of δεινός language, declaring that both Euripides and Aeschylus are poised with their most forceful mouths to provide phrases and little bits of verses (δεινοτάτοιν στομάτοιν πορίσασθαι / ῥήματα καὶ παραπρίσματ᾽ ἐπῶν; vv. 880–81). Here Aristophanes uses δεινός to underscore the ways in which the approaching contest will rely on the ability of the audience to connect the language they are about to hear to earlier dramas, affirming not the intention of the authors involved but the powers of the audience as readers and viewers of drama.

Much the same point is made later in the drama, too, as Aeschylus and Euripides characterize the ways in which they intended their words to affect their audiences. Needless to say, each poet insists that the other's intentions were not realized. Euripides condemns Aeschylus, for example, because, in his opinion, he always keeps his audience guessing, duping them into paying attention to one aspect of a drama while simultaneously furthering the plot. Aeschylus is also held out for scorn because he uses hard-to-understand expressions (vv. 819–930).

In this bantering, the role and function of the audience command special attention. For some time before this scene opens, Dionysus has been listening to Euripides condemn Aeschylus when, at verse 918, he asks Euripides why Aeschylus wrote in such a way, suggesting that he himself might prefer the silences of Aeschylus to the chatterings of Euripides (whose characters are portrayed throughout as hopelessly wordy). The word Dionysus uses to describe Aeschylus, ὁ δεῖνα, meaning something like "Mr. So-and-so," puns on δεινός, but in so doing suggests the stakes involved in Euripides' deprecation of Aeschylus. In calling Aeschylus ὁ δεῖνα in a discussion of the demands made of

15. The general discussion of literary culture attending to the *Clouds* in the more specific context of Aristophanes' views of language is well analyzed by D. E. O'Regan, *Rhetoric, Comedy, and the Violence of Language in Aristophanes' "Clouds"* (Oxford, 1992); on the *Frogs,* see K. Dover, ed., *Aristophanes, Frogs* (Oxford, 1993), pp. 298, 307–08, 325.

an Aeschylean audience, Aristophanes symbolizes those demands in a humorous play on words that links to a term in the Greek literary tradition used to describe a powerful audience.

When Aeschylus's turn comes to criticize Euripides, one of his more humorous lines of reasoning is also one of the more important for students of allusion. Having established the discussion of Aeschylian and Euripidean drama in the context of readerly or audience power, Aristophanes now turns, beginning at line 1063, to insinuate that discussion into the more specific context of allusion. At this point in the *Frogs,* Aeschylus has been discussing for some time the stately vestments worn by his own characters, symbolic of the noble, if tragic, lives they lead. When he turns to consider the garb of Euripides' characters, however, he can only note with more than a hint of disdain that Euripides' heroes all wear rags and appear beggarly (πρῶτον μὲν τοὺς βασιλεύοντας ῥάκι᾽ ἀμπισχών, ἵν᾽ / ἐλεινοὶ / τοῖς ἀνθρώποις φαίνοιντ᾽ εἶναι; vv. 1063–64). The use of ῥάκιον, "little rags," functions here to confirm in a humorous way the fact that Euripides in no less than nine of his dramas makes his heroes parade around in inappropriate garb.

Aeschylus's condemnation of Euripides works at another level in this scene, however. Euripides' beggars can be understood to function symbolically, implying a textual point being made that is more systematically treated in his earlier comedy, the *Acharnians,* a drama that directly considers the powers of the audience in a concrete description of allusion. The *Acharnians* is not centrally about dramatic composition, but when Dikaiopolis makes a visit to Euripides' house to find some "shreds" of a drama that he can use to compose a speech, Aristophanes plays on the fact that Euripides frequently repeats parts of earlier dramas in his later works, creating a web of associations between his works.

In highlighting the role of the author who would use older language and the author whose language is to be used, the dilemmas and delights of borrowing older language, described as "rag-picking," and the attitudes toward such borrowings from the perspective of an empowered audience, Aristophanes allows his lampoon to be viewed as a careful description of allusion. Perhaps most important, his vocabulary in the lampoon seems to be deployed strategically: his words apply not only to the comical lampoon he creates but also to the level of allusive description which would seem to inform it.

This level of meaning is revealed in several ways. The scene in question (vv. 393 ff.) begins with a dialogue in which Dikaiopolis and Kephisophon argue over whether Euripides will make an appearance to talk with Dikaiopolis. Euripides is at first not particularly agreeable and Dikaiopolis, fearing that he will not have his way, obstinately refuses to leave, declaring: "I won't go away; I'll knock at the door" (οὐ γὰρ ἂν ἀπέλθοιμ᾽, ἀλλὰ κόψω τὴν θύραν; v. 403).[16] The verb used in this declaration is important in a way not obvious at first. On the surface, ἀπέρχομαι is an ordinary verb whose presence can be explained by the general activity described here. It customarily implies movement away from something, or, more generally, departure, and it works to evoke such meanings here, at least initially.[17]

But ἀπέρχομαι applies to the act of allusion also, since the verb carries with it the idea of arrival and departure,[18] a denotation that carefully anticipates the discussion of allusion about to be broached in the scene itself: Euripides' plays themselves frequently depart and arrive in each other, after all, making them appear to be a quilt of phrases stitched together from previous works, any one of which could be taken from one context and moved to another. Dikaiopolis himself is also poised at this point in the drama to depart from his own language and arrive on the surer ground of Euripides' words, for he is in search of a kind of language that will impress the audience he will soon be addressing. Importantly, too, throughout this initial scene, it is the audience or "reader" of Euripides' dramas, namely Dikaiopolis, who holds the power to compose and to interpret, as subsequent phrases and images that center on begging and rag-picking make clear.

Dikaiopolis declares, for example, once Euripides finally agrees to see and to talk to him, that his main business is to get a "rag of one of his old plays" (ῥάκιόν τι τοῦ παλαιοῦ δράματος; v. 415). The use of ῥάκιον (the diminutive substantive of τό ῥάκος[19]) is suggestive of the physical rags being bandied about in the comedy, but it is also symbolic of the "textual" rags solicited at this point. The repetitions and quotations found throughout Euripides' plays, the parts torn or cut away from one text and implanted into another, are, after all, textual moments that have been literally torn from their author's works. In this regard, they are analogous to allusions, those places in writing where "little rags," rent from earlier texts, are sewn back into the fabric of a later work.[20]

Euripides eventually consents to Dikaiopolis's requests and offers some

16. My text is F. W. Hall and W. M. Geldart, eds., *Aristophanis Comoediae,* 2 vols. (Oxford, 1906).
17. LSJ, p. 187, s.v. ἀπέρχομαι, I.
18. LSJ, p. 187, s.v. ἀπέρχομαι, 2.
19. Usually occurring in the plural, meaning "little rags." See LSJ, p. 1564.
20. They also help more specifically to situate the full meaning of ῥάκιον when it is used later in the *Frogs;* see vv. 1063, 1066.

"rags" (τρύχη, v. 418), that is, the use of some of his best characters, to Dikaiopolis. But Dikaiopolis does not passively allow Euripides to make the choice for him. Once his initial offer of such figures as Oeneus and the blind Phoenix (vv. 420–22) is refused, Euripides mutters to himself "whose rendings does he want" (ποίας ποθ᾽ἁνὴρ λακίδας αἰτεῖται πέπλων; v. 423), before going on to ask whether Dikaiopolis might have use for Philoctetes, Bellerophon, or even Telephus (vv. 424–30). The figure Dikaiopolis finally finds agreeable is indeed Telephus, and having found the figure in whom Dikaiopolis takes pleasure, Euripides has his slave throw down Telephus's rags.

Because these rags represent words that Dikaioplois can use in the construction of his speech, they cannot simply be understood to represent the clothes worn by Euripides' heroes. Dikaiopolis is not, after all, searching merely for clothes, and Aristophanes plays on the rag-tag quality of Euripides' heroes to make a point about allusion. The rags that Euripides throws down to Dikaiopolis are in this sense as much bits and pieces torn from prior dramas as they are rags to be worn. They are, in fact, special kinds of rags, full of holes since everyone (including Euripides) has been rending them, but also worn out from compositional wear and tear. This special kind of wear, implying the ability of language to be rent from a prior text and to arrive in a subsequent text, is in fact confirmed in the word used by Euripides to describe the rags he offers to Dikaioplois—τρῦχος. Importantly, it is never used in the dramas of Euripides merely to describe garments worn out from being overused and, as is the case here, there is always a metaphorical value to the term when Euripides uses it.[21] Like the rags bandied about at this point in the *Acharnians*, then, τρῦχος accounts in its meaning for the special kind of wear denoted in this scene.

When Dikaiopolis goes on to describe the figure he seeks from Euripides as a clever speaker (δεινὸς λέγειν, v. 429), the characterization has a special resonance, given the associations of δεινός to a powerful reader or audience in the Greek tradition. In making this declaration, Dikaiopolis does more than assert his preference for a "good talker." Because the word symbolizes also the dangers of a meaning-making audience, Dikaiopolis can be understood to demand a speaker from one of Euripides' dramas whose words will evoke an appropriate response on the part of his intended audience, a speaker whose words will remind them of, and make them consider the implications of, Euripides' words in his own speech. Dikaiopolis desires, therefore, an audience willing to ponder the sources of his language and willing to take on the important task of

21. See, e.g., Euripides, *El.* 185, *Ph.* 325; LSJ, p. 1831, s.v. τρῦχος, 1.

accounting for his words' meanings by pondering the context in which they originally were cast. In short, Dikaiopolis is an allusive writer who understands the power granted to the allusion's audience or reader whenever an allusion is encountered. Specifically, Dikaiopolis seeks to exploit the allusion's ability to remind the reader of its source and to urge on certain associations in the reader's mind based on its origins.

Dikaiopolis is not simply a symbol of the allusive author, however. He also assists Aristophanes in dramatizing more closely the competencies of a powerful reader or audience, for he is a reader or listener of Euripides also. Those competencies are highlighted especially in the dialogue form that drama always takes, for the dialogue dramatized here between Euripides and Dikaiopolis about pieces of older texts mirrors the act of allusive writing itself, which also occasions a dialogue set in text that mediates the tension between the written form in which it exists and the dialogical form that it assumes when it is read. In this regard, Aristophanes dramatizes the unique competencies demanded of the figure I have called the full-knowing reader, especially to the extent Dikaiopolis is shown to be an active searcher after words, whose intended meanings in their original Euripidean context have little, if any, importance in the subsequent contexts in which Dikaiopolis uses them. Ultimately, it is his interpretive powers that matter here, not Euripides'.

If anything, the tension between authorial intent and readerly or audience power increases as the corresponding tension between Euripides and the allusive rag-picker, Dikaiopolis, is heightened. After additional banter, in which Euripides is induced into assisting Dikaiopolis in other ways, the exasperated master finally says: "The man will take away from me my tragedy" (ὤνθρωπ' ἀφαιρήσει με τὴν τραγῳδίαν; v. 464). The verb ἀφαιρέω[22] is germane to allusion in several ways. It can mean "taking away" in the broadest sense, denoting, say, the act of robbery, but it also can imply a separation of something from something else, an exclusion of something from another thing, or a subtracting or dividing out, a usage that takes pride of place in dramatic texts.[23] This connotation implies a subtler act than robbery, for although robbery implies a loss over which an owner presumably has no control and which, in any case, can be redressed, Euripides descries here the fact that his drama, which once was whole, has been made to suffer a subtraction or loss. In this sense, it can be said that Euripides fears something more sinister than a simple "robbery." He fears

22. Generally meaning "to take away;" see LSJ, p. 285, s.v. ἀφαιρέμα, II, 2.
23. LSJ, pp. 285–86, s.v. ἀφαιρέμα, II, 2 ff.; and see the examples drawn from Aeschylus especially.

an extraction or division of extreme proportions that will leave him (so he exaggerates) "lacking any plays" (φροῦδά μοι τὰ δράματα; v. 470).

Allusive function is also implied in Dikaiopolis's response once Euripides has granted him the shards and scraps for which he has begged. He is emboldened by his encounter with the dramatist (vv. 484–89) and is, so he says, "full of Euripides" (καταπιὼν Εὐριπίδην; v. 484). He can now face his intended audience with courage. This courage is not merely a function of an in-person encounter with Euripides, however, but is also resident in the fact that Dikaiopolis's language is drawn from Euripides' works. Dikaiopolis has not only encountered Euripides personally; he has also become the owner of words that were once Euripides'. In an allusive sense, then, Dikaiopolis's language is a shared medium, and Dikaiopolis has use for this language only as long as it remains the common property of himself and Eurpides. It is, after all, Euripides' reputation and skill that Dikaiopolis means to evoke by using the dramatist's language, but the meanings of Euripides' words will all be changed in the evoking.

Dikaiopolis is perhaps most consistently a figure in the *Acharnians* who highlights the rift between authorial intention and readerly power. He characterizes himself as a "beggar" (πτωχὸς, v. 498) when the worried chorus asks of him what he will "say" with his newfound rags (vv. 490 ff.). Like other allusive authors, Dikaiopolis has confronted the words that make up his literary tradition, and the process of incorporating those words suggests the instability of written language to remain the property of its author. In this regard, however, the allusive author is revealed in a rather negative light, as someone always prone to the powers of the reader or audience. Dikaiopolis himself is, after all, reduced to little more than a rag-picker who, from the point of view of the author of the text being mined for phrases and words, emaciates the earlier text so that it, too, becomes rag-tag. Those rags only become beautiful through the process of reconstruction that is symbolized here in the choral anticipation of what Dikaiopolis will say. In that process, the new text composed of bits and pieces torn from an older work becomes comely, a work of art unto itself containing elements drawn from the imaginative limits of its creator's mind but finally made to function only in the minds of full-knowing readers.

The powerlessness of Euripides comes in for special attention as the lampoon draws to a close. Aristophanes is careful to portray the great dramatist as perturbed and resigned to the pilfering leveled against his dramas by Dikaiopolis. Initially ornery and less than cooperative, he nonetheless comes to hawk his wares beginning at verse 420, as if a salesman plying his best merchandise. Eventually he consents to Dikaiopolis's theft with something that reaches beyond simple resignation, participating willingly in the process of the dismemberment of his texts, realizing the peculiarly fluid status of his own dramas once they are committed to writing, once they can be read. The control over his own language slips away from Euripides as the lampoon proceeds. At its conclusion, he is bereft of all power and Dikaiopolis, the allusive artist, is poised to throw to his audience, to what he hopes is good effect, the allusive rags of Euripides that are now part of his discourse. The locus of authority at the scene's end rests entirely, and definitively, with Dikaiopolis's audience—of full-knowing readers.

TERENCE AND *CONTAMINATIO*

Aristophanes would seem to conceive of allusion in terms of cutting, rending, and begging, and always with a powerful audience or reader in mind. A similar perspective on allusion is offered by Terence in his frequent discussions of poetic "contamination." *Contaminatio* is normally defined as the adulteration of something integral by the addition of alien material. In a literary sense, an older work of art is used as a model and as a source of language by a new artist, and stands, by virtue of its incorporation into the newer work, "contaminated." The term does not seem to have been used in antiquity specifically to designate allusion,[24] but Terence's discussions of it in the prologues to his comedies reveal affinities to allusion that have gone unnoticed. In particular, Terence is interested in exposing the artistic assumptions of those who practice and condemn *contaminatio* and the demands placed on the audience confronting a contaminated work. His discussions conform in terms of detail and vocabulary to the narrative description of allusion found in Aristophanes' lampoon of Euripides.

As a practitioner of *contaminatio,* Terence is a defender of the assumptions implicit in its practice. Terence's rival, Luscius Lanuvinus, so Terence himself tells us, has criticized Terence's artistic habit of using bits and pieces of older Greek dramas in his newer productions, that is to say, of alluding to older Greek literary works. Lanuvinus, Terence goes on to say, cannot see his way past the necessity of preserving Greek models, an urge on his part that would seem to include a prohibition against their language being used in later works by admiring artists. Terence, on the other hand, as an artist, cannot hope to

24. Although Farrell, *Vergil's Georgics,* uses it, correctly I think, to frame a particular species of allusion; see pp. 94 ff.

articulate for his audience a coherent comedic tradition without using those models as he sees fit, even if that use involves the wholesale implantation of parts of those models into his newer production.

A conflict between contrary conceptions of language animates this dispute. Lanuvinus, who is held up for special scorn by Terence as a rhetorical pedant, defends a practice in which language is fixed and immutable. Once a drama has been written, it is sacrosanct. It cannot be adulterated by the piecemeal appropriation of its parts for use in later works. Terence, on the other hand, aside from musing over the narrowmindedness of one who would attempt the kind of rigid control recommended by Lanuvinus, asserts that even those works that Lanuvinus considers sacrosanct are themselves contaminated. Every artist who is truly an artist practices *contaminatio,* he says. Only untalented pedants attempt to control this basic aspect of creativity by denying the undeniable.

In drafting his side of the issue more fully, Terence analyzes several qualities of *contaminatio* that pertain directly to allusion. He locates his discussion of *contaminatio* in the credible aims of verbal art when it relies on the use of older material, the controls, if any, that need to be placed on the use of older material in a newer work of art, and the role assumed by the audience when it confronts borrowed material. The context in which *contaminatio* ought to be considered is sketched generally in the prologue to Terence's first play, the *Andria.* Terence's vocabulary in this prologue is crisp: he uses words that link to Aristophanes' lampoon of Euripides, but that also anticipate (as we will see) Virgil's discussion of allusion as grafting in the second *Georgic:*

> quae convenere in Andriam ex Perinthia
> fatetur transtulisse atque usum pro suis.
> id isti vituperant factum atque in eo disputant
> contaminari non decere fabulas.
> faciuntne intellegendo ut nil intellegant?
> qui quom hunc accusant, Naevium Plautum Ennium
> accusant quos hic noster auctores habet,
> quorum aemulari exoptat neglegentiam
> potius quam istorum obscuram diligentiam. (13–21)

(The author admits that he has transferred anything suitable from the latter play to his adaptation of the former and made free use of it. This is the practice attacked by his critics, who argue that by so doing he is "spoiling" the original plays. Surely they miss the point here, for all their cleverness. In attacking the present author they are really attacking Naevius, Plautus, and Ennius, whom he takes for his models and whose "carelessness" he would far rather imitate than his critics' dreary accuracy.[25])

Terence uses *convenere* initially to describe what he has done to his Greek models. He has, he said, literally made them "come together" by transferring (*transtulisse*) material from Menander's *Perinthia* to his own work. This sense of *convenere* accords neatly with the meanings of ἀπέρχομαι, used by Aristophanes in the *Acharnians*. Both verbs suggest arrival, departure and movement from one form to another. Beyond the affinities of *convenere* and ἀπέρχομαι, Terence confirms in his use of *transferre* the distinctive quality of what he has done, for this verb connotes the physical "copying" of one part of a book into another.[26]

Later prologues offer other angles on Terence's notion of *contaminatio*. In the Prologue to the *Heauton Timorumenos*, for example, Terence discusses the role of the audience confronted by a contaminated play. To articulate its role more clearly, Terence has his leading actor, Turpio, say that it might be Terence's intention to inform his audience of the author of the model on which he has drawn in composing the play, or even to tell them some details of its plot, "if I hadn't judged that the better number of you knew it already" (ni partem maxumam / existumarem scire vostrum; vv. 8–9). This statement presupposes an audience whose conversance with the traditions in which he wrote enables Terence to take for granted a certain informed participation in and engagement of his drama. For this reason, Turpio goes on to mention Terence directly in the Prologue, creating a dramatic representation of allusion in which the words of an author, spoken by another, are overtly linked to that author in the acting of the scene. This scene becomes, in short order, a symbol for the larger compositional habits practiced by Terence, which devolve onto the audience's ability to make certain connections between and among various dramas, to become, in short, full-knowing readers. For this reason, Turpio informs the audience that Terence desires for them to be his judge (*iudicium*, v. 12). It has now become their responsibility to recognize and to make sense of the contaminated material in the comedy.

Turpio goes on to stress two further points which bear importantly on allusion. First, after widening his appeal to the audience to be the final arbiters

25. My text is R. Kauer and W. M. Lindsay, eds., *P. Terenti Afri Comoediae* (Oxford, 1958). Translations are from B. Radice, *Terence: The Comedies* (Harmondsworth, 1976).

26. It refers also to the act of arboricultural cutting and grafting, and anticipates in this regard the meditation on allusion in the second *Georgic*. See LS, p. 1889, s.v. *transfero*, I, B and 2.

of Terence's talents, Turpio then makes a plea for himself, asking the audience to "assist me with your fair-minded spirit and through your silence to allow me to perform" (adeste aequo animo, date potestatem mihi / statariam agere ut liceat per silentium; (vv. 35–36). This silence is, on the one hand, a plea for the audience to be well mannered, for audiences, as Terence himself points out, were prone to leave the theater to view more popular performances, such as boxing or tightrope walking.[27] But this comment gains greater significance in light of the remark Turpio makes near the end of the Prologue, when he declares that the play the audience is about to see is the embodiment of "pure speech" (in hac est pura oratio; v. 46). Although the phrase *pura oratio* might easily be brushed aside as the bravado of an actor and his playwright, one is tempted to posit a connection between *silentium* and *pura oratio*. The language of the drama is "pure" in this light because of the interpretive responses it elicits. Because the drama's language demands both an appreciation of the drama's presentation and an engagement of its borrowed language, the audience is enjoined to be silent in order to be in the best position to consider the full meaning of those borrowings. Too, in evoking the notion of *pura oratio,* Terence bruits his war with Lanuvinus yet again. *Pura* (as the substantive *purum*) is the opposite of *contaminatio.*[28] The artistic practices of Terence are made to be in this passage, therefore, exactly what Lanuvinus says they are not.

In the Prologue to the *Eunuchus,* Terence turns his attention to the author who practices *contaminatio,* and finds himself in the position of defending his latest play against Lanuvinus's newest charge: that Terence is a thief (*fur,* v. 23). First, Terence responds in general terms to Lanuvinus's charge that he has pilfered his new play wholesale. He admits he has "transferred" (*transferre,* v. 32) certain characters from Greek models but he goes on in greater detail to answer the charge that he has "stolen" something. He declares that he has not pilfered anything, because, after all, there is "nothing that is spoken now that has not been said before already" (nullumst iam dictum quod non dictum sit prius; v. 41). In effect, Terence declares that it is impossible in literary terms to be a thief.

27. See *Hekura,* Prol., vv. 20 ff; it is important to note that this Prologue, where the poet defends his own plays against other forms of amusement, does not discuss *contaminatio.* Logic dictates, of course, that a drama must be watched and I do not want to downplay that silence does also refer here to the fact that Terence's audiences were notorious in their restlessness, as he himself tells us. On the other hand, his audience was not composed of bumpkins, only entertained by glitter and extravaganza. Rather, meanings that pertain both to allusion and to the exigencies of production exist here.

28. LS, p. 1494, s.v. *purus* (*purum*), esp. II A.

Because artists work in a closed system of tradition and innovation, to recall prior moments in works or to recall, on a larger scale, themes or issues, is not to plagiarize or to steal, any more than beggary is thievery. To steal, after all, is to take something which is not one's own under cover and with the intent of not being caught. In a literary context, beggary, as Aristophanes demonstrated, must involve two willing people.

Terence sees the issue in exactly these terms. He cannot be accused of thievery because he has not attempted to hide what he is doing. If he were a plagiarist, Terence suggests implicitly, he would desire coversion, concealment. He has already proven, through his stated reliance on the audience both to judge him and to recognize the traditions in which he works, that coversion is not part of his artistic agenda. The thief or plagiarist may not want to advertise the fact that he is using older material, but the artist who borrows older literary material desires just such an advertisement.[29]

Terence's famous statement that there is nothing new to say can be viewed in two ways. On the one hand, it is probably true that everything worth saying in art had, by his time, already been said in one way or another. The basic plots of all dramas are, after all, reducible presumably to a dozen or so scenarios in which characters' names and modes of behavior change, but in which the basic story-lines remain constant. Yet, viewed from the standpoint of allusion, a view invited by Terence's introduction of thievery into his ongoing discussion of *contaminatio*, it is also true that literary language by nature, because it exists in a closed system of texts, repeats from work to work words, phrases, and images that have been used before. This would be especially true, moreover, in the Roman literary tradition, which had to appropriate Greek models to Latin forms, itself an act of *transferre* that always involved the use (or reuse) of older language. In this sense, Terence's best defense is found not only in an argument from tradition but also in the ways his logic points to the inevitable results of allusion, which no artist can ignore if that artist is truly to engage and challenge the traditions in which he writes.

VIRGIL, VARRO, AND THE METAPHORS OF NATURE

Aristophanes and Terence dramatize allusion as a form of textual movement and implantation; as a kind of literary cut; or as a literary form that empowers

---

29. Terence makes much the same point later in the Prologue to the *Adelphoe,* where he asks the audience to judge whether or not his inclusion of a scene found in the Greek original but omitted in Plautus's subsequent version constitutes "thievery" on his part (vv. 10 ff.).

the reader or audience. In the second *Georgic,* Virgil would seem to mediate these notions, framing them in an allegory of arboricultural grafting that pertains also to literary allusion. Although any interpretation of a Virgilian poem cannot be above dispute, many of the difficulties that surround this particular poem's tone and detail abate when it is read as an allegory of allusion. The ways in which Virgil would seem to sanction violation to trees, for example, has always proved troublesome to commentators, for in this poem, as in the *Aeneid,* Virgil depicts tree violation without having the perpetrators of such violence offer the normal oaths or, lacking them, suffer divine retribution for defiling so sacred a symbol.[30] Since most of the grafts Virgil describes in the poem are impossible to achieve in nature, their function as symbols of the bounty and perfection of nature is also problematic, leading one recent scholar to assert that Virgil tells lies.[31] Moreover, if the grafts stand as symbols of something, what precisely are they meant to evoke, given their unnatural qualities and the violence that leads to their strange bounty?

If one approaches Virgil's poem from the angle of literary allusion, problems such as these lose the logic they otherwise hold. There is, for example, a tradition of conceiving of language metaphorically in natural and, more specifically, arboricultural terms. Virgil himself had already suggested the connection in the fourth *Eclogue* and Statius would mediate this tradition down to the first century C.E. in his *Silvae,* on the model of several of Horace's *Odes* (esp. 1.16, 1.22) that conceive of literary production in terms of natural bounty and landscape. But Varro is perhaps most exemplary of this trend, both for the committedness of his treatment and for the fact that the treatise in which it comes, the *De lingua latina,* is specifically a consideration of language.

Varro makes wide use of the metaphor of the tree in attempting to explain language's wily function. In describing the difficulty of attaining a complete knowledge of the meanings of words, for example, Varro notes that he will do his best to follow the course of his proposed "four levels" of etymology in each of the words he considers, "even if [the word] has directed its roots beyond its own domain[;] for often, the roots of a tree . . . spread out under a neighbor's cornfield" (Sed qua cognatio eius erit verbi quae radices egerit extra fines suas,

30. I owe these insights to R. F. Thomas, "Tree Violation and Ambivalence in Virgil," *TAPA* 118 (1988), pp. 261–73. See *Aen.* 3.22 ff., 6.179 ff., and 12.766 ff.

31. D. O. Ross, Jr., *Virgil's Elements: Physics and Poetry in the Georgics* (Princeton, 1987), p. 110. See also Ross's article "Non Sua Poma: Varro, Virgil, and Grafting," *Illinois Classical Studies* 5 (1980), pp. 63–71, esp. pp. 65–68 and n. 6; and A. S. Pease, "Notes on Ancient Grafting," *TAPA* 64 (1933), pp. 66–76.

persequemur. Saepe enim ad limitem arboris radices sub vicini prodierunt segetem; 5.13.3–6). Words, like trees, harbor much that cannot be seen. An accounting of meaning, by implication, leaves much unstated and fails to consider much that is harbored in the history of words. Even the best investigators, Varro concedes, will not be able to uncover everything about the etymology of certain words: "though one uses tools to uncover the desire of the one who imposed the word, much remains hidden" (cum haec amminicula addas ad eruendum voluntatem impositoris, tamen latent multa; 7.2.1–2), yet the "fruit" (*fructus*) of the linguistic tree is often obscured by the fact that poetic employment of words does not include the history of those words (7.2.2–5). These and other moments like them can be understood to inform Virgil's poem of the earth. At the least, they allow one to realize that in writing a poem about arboriculture, Virgil was not exclusively keying into Greek didactic poems on husbandry and farming.

Virgil's second *Georgic* ties into the tradition of talking about language in several other ways also. The poem's initial invocation to Bacchus, for example, strikes a resonant cord. Bacchus, in his Greek form of Dionysus, is the god of drama and of drink. The mention of this divinity allows Virgil to situate the opening of his poem in the context of dramatic composition, represented by the god's powers over drama, and of skewed perception, represented by the god's mastery over drink. Moreover, given the role accorded to Dionysus in classical drama (especially the *Bacchae*), linkages to the topic of human perception are strengthened. So, too, are linkages to the tradition mediated in Greek drama in which linguistic function in general is considered under the rubric of δεινός language. When Virgil declares in verse 2, therefore, that "now, I will sing you, Bacchus" (nunc te, Bacche, canam),[32] he links his poem to a divinity whose abilities to manipulate language are notorious, and to one whose special venue, drama, includes a rich tradition of talking about δεινός language.

Other aspects of the poem's opening relate to an allegory on language also. Virgil goes on to enjoin Bacchus, for example, to "plunge your naked legs with me in the new vintage and remove your buskins" (veni nudataque musto / tinge novo mecum dereptis crura coturnis; vv. 7–8). Such an invitation is hardly credible. Bacchus's participation in Virgil's poem can only obtain in a subjective suspension of belief on the part of the reader, in the reader's willingness to make Virgil's words work in an artificial, literary world where gods and poets can languish together in a perfect scene. The mechanism that fosters this perfect

32. My text is R. A. B. Mynors, ed., *P. Vergili Maronis Opera* (Oxford, 1969).

scene is language itself: language becomes the vehicle by which the impossible is rendered real. That reality remains, however, a construction of the reader's interpretive powers. Such a power is an appropriate offering to Bacchus in any case, who mediates, in his role as an arbiter of human perception, the ability to make things appear to be, as here, what they are not.

This special power of language to create and sustain unnatural worlds is ratified in Virgil's subsequent treatment of grafting. His discussion is controlled in part by Theophrastus and in part by Varro (vv. 9–31),[33] but the bulk of it is pure invention, a list of arboricultural *adynata*. "Experience," (*usus*, v. 22), Virgil tells us, "has discovered other ways to propagate trees," and in going on to relate some of the ways in which *usus* has refined the art of grafting, Virgil describes several kinds of grafts between species and even families that are impossible to achieve in nature (vv. 32 and 72). Because *usus* does not sanction the kinds of grafts Virgil goes on to describe, his intentions in these lines are not apparent. As in the opening invocation to Bacchus, the reader must suspend belief and follow Virgil into the poem despite its contradictions.

In following him, one is confronted with what looks to be a *recusatio*, which, upon further inspection, becomes a statement of literary aims that center on allusion. Speaking to Maecenas, Virgil claims that he will hold fast to his intended topic, eschewing digressions that he would not pursue even if he had one hundred tongues: "I do not wish to embrace everything in my verses, even if I had one hundred tongues, one hundred mouths, and an iron voice" (non ego cuncta meis amplecti versibus opto, / non, mihi si linguae centum sint oraque centum, /ferrea vox; vv. 42–44). Already in establishing his Dionysian scene and its marvelous, unnatural bounty, however, Virgil has spoken with many tongues. Moreover, this kind of speech is implied in the very language used to discount it, for the highlighted words in these lines comprise an allusion to Homer (*Il.* 2.489–90), which centers attention on the ways in which audience response and literary language conspire to create unreal and marvelous worlds—beyond the scope of artistic articulation, yet present allusively at the same time. Such a conspiracy places a burden for making meaning on the audience: a writer can use language to create unreal worlds, as Virgil has done with his grafted forest, but such a writer cannot hope to control the responses of an audience which willingly follows him into such a world, even if he possessed one hundred tongues and mouths or an iron-strong voice. And proclaim

33. See Thomas, "Tree Violation and Ambivalence," p. 271 and his *Virgil, Georgics,* 2 vols. (Cambridge, 1988), vol. 1, pp. 157–61; see also R. A. B. Mynors, ed., *Virgil, Georgics* (Oxford, 1990), pp. 101–13.

though he might that he does not intend to follow digressions as he makes his way in the poem, the truth is that those digressions are implicit in the Homeric allusion in these lines. The poet does not have to follow them. That will be the job of the full-knowing reader.

Virgil would seem to set for comparison in these lines both the image of his grafted trees (unnatural and impossible in nature) and the image of his own grafted language (equally unnatural and, within the context of a fixed notion of linguistic meaning, impossible to control). When, therefore, he declares that he will not detain Maecenas with fictive songs, sung through wandering paths and long preludes (non hic te carmine ficto / atque per ambages et longa exorsa tenebo; vv. 45–46), he does so not merely as a means to move on with his topic. He also seems to suggest that such details as would be found on wandering paths or in long preludes are allusively present already. He cannot entertain a closer look at them because he cannot control their reception, any more than he can effect in nature the unnatural grafts which dominate this section of his poem. Those grafts, like the Homeric allusion, are a matter of audience con-struction, over which the poet has no control. As if to highlight the dialogical quality of allusion being described here, Virgil uses words that apply to speak-ing, not writing, a tactic all the more telling in that the *Georgics* were not written as poems to be performed. The presence of *lingua, ora,* and *vox* in these lines can be ascribed credibly to writing, to be sure, but these words suggest also the oral quality of communication being described, the ways in which the "voice" of Homer is present dialogically to readers.

The topic of reading is more specifically addressed when Virgil considers the "nature" of soils" (solo natura subest; v. 49) and the "wild spirit" of trees (silvestrem animum; v. 51). The instructions he offers in these lines for the cultivation of soils that will assist in the bounty of the impossible grafts can be understood to apply to the act of reading itself, and the effort described can be seen to flesh out the details involved in the careful (and unnatural) process involved in full-knowing reading. The point would seem to be that when a reader entertains the presence of an allusion, he must be willing to participate in what is, from the standpoint of "normal" reading, an unnatural act, dividing his attention between two texts and attempting to make sense of the textual "graft" before him. When that graft is given the attention it deserves, it, like the grafts of these verses, bears fruit.

The fecundity of these allegorical, literary grafts is championed in the next few lines, where Virgil goes on to describe grafting between families or species, precisely the kind of grafting impossible to achieve in nature:

Nec modus inserere atque oculos imponere simplex.
nam qua se medio trudunt de cortice gemmae
et tenuis rumpunt tunicas, angustus in ipso
fit nodo sinus; huc aliena ex arbore germen
includunt udoque docent inolescere libro.
aut rursum enodes trunci resecantur, et alte
finditur in solidum cuneis via, deinde feraces
plantae immittuntur: nec longum tempus, et ingens
exiit ad caelum ramis felicibus arbos,
miratastque novas frondes et non sua poma. (vv. 73–82)

Nor are grafting and budding simple. For the buds push out from the bark, and burst their soft sheaths, in the place where a narrow slit is made in the knot; from an alien tree a bud is inserted in this and they teach it to grow into the sappy bark. Or, again, plain trunks are cut open and a path is cut, deep into the core with wedges; then fruitful slips are introduced, and before long a great tree shoots up to the sky with happy boughs and wonders at its new leaves and fruits not its own.

The careful attention paid here to the process of arboricultural grafting functions as a way for Virgil to specify certain features of literary grafting. Attention to the verbs Virgil uses is instructive along these lines, allowing a firmer association to notions of movement, implantation, and cutting featured prominently in Terence and Aristophanes. The verbs demonstrate Virgil's ability to pull the full resources of Latin to his needs, for he offers here an array of verbal forms, as if to suggest through voice, morphology, and mood the manifold nature of literary grafting.[34] The first two verbs, *inserere* and *imponere,* are both easily associated with grafting, the former having as its first meaning to "ingraft,"[35] and the latter taking as its primary meaning "to put, place, or set into or upon,"[36] but with collateral meanings that generally fall outside the context of arboriculture. These would seem to be the basic verbs that Virgil would associate with grafting, and their similarity to the verbs used by Aristophanes and Terence—ἀπέρχομαι, *convenere, transferre*—is noteworthy.

Other words are consistent with the evidence analyzed above in Aristophanes and Terence. *Trudunt* (v. 74), for example, though it is used to magnify the natural process of budding and growth in the host tree, anticipates the process of grafting in the ways it connotes a pushing or sending forth within

34. Four of the verbs are passive; five are compounded; two are infinitive; one is frequentative. The verbs all correspond in their tense (present).

35. LS, p. 964, s.v. *insero,* I, II.

36. LS, p. 906, s.v. *impono,* I, A.

the broader context of pressure or thrusting, both of which suggest the insertion (thrust) of the graft and the subsequent pressure applied in binding the graft to the host tree.[37] *Rumpunt* (v. 75), used to describe the site where the graft ought to occur, suggests the underlying violence of grafting with its connotations of ripping, rending, cutting, or tearing.[38] *Includunt* and *inolescere* (v. 77) alter the focus of the scene from the implicit violence involved in grafting to the more productive results of arboricultural cutting. The graft is "inserted" (*includunt*) and then permitted to grow (*inolescere*). *Inolescere* highlights both the fecundity and the implicit perversion of grafting, for it is an inclusive verb of growth predicated on the idea of an implantation or introduction of something in, to, or on something else.[39] It does not connote organic growth or the innate potential of living things to increase their size.

The sense of manipulated growth implied in *inolescere* is ratified in the verb *resecantur* (v. 78), which Virgil uses to describe the process of cutting the host tree. The verb is powerful in the ways it connotes abbreviation and suppression of growth, exactly what the host tree suffers when it is pruned and surgically altered, for this verb has the sense of "cutting loose," or "cutting off," "curtailing," "checking," or "restraining."[40] That aspect of grafting is ratified in the verb *finditur*, which suggests the "cleaving" and "splitting" required of the host tree to support the proposed graft, a sense also gained in the connotation of *immittuntur* and *exiit* (vv. 80–81).

Virgil goes on to conclude his description of grafting with the observation that the transformed tree "wonders at its new leaves and fruits not its own" (miratastque novas frondes et non sua poma; v. 82). Wonder is an important aspect of Virgil's description of grafting, affirming the poet's own knowledge of the unreal quality of the literary graft. At the same time, it highlights the power of language to lead its willing readers down paths into worlds of unreal dimensions, as it affirms the necessity of allusion's readers to be strong, committed meaning-makers of the texts they read.

Yet in articulating these positions, Virgil works within a tradition that is confirmed by the witness of Varro. Virgil, remember, refused to take Maecenas down "rambling paths" (vv. 45–46) and yet he led him (and his poem's readers) into a forest of grafted trees. In book 5, Varro characterizes the search for etymological meaning as a walk through a forest (5.5.6–11). Words, like trees,

37. LS, p. 1905.
38. LS, p. 1605, s.v. *rumpo*, I.
39. LS, p. 959, s.v. *inolesco*, II.
40. LS, p. 1577.

direct their roots beyond their own domains; words harbor, like trees, much that cannot be seen, yet can be inferred. Any accounting of meaning must leave much unstated. The fruit of meaning, he concludes, is often obscure. For Virgil, this obscurity is a source of marvel. Fostered by language's ability to reconfigure and reconstruct nature into new and wondrous shapes, controlled by the ability of readers to explore differing parts of the grafted tree and its bounty—but never the entire tree—literary grafting in the second *Georgic* is manifold and diverse, the bounty of language's paradoxical nature.

In the second *Georgic*, then, Virgil would seem to mediate the evidence of Aristophanes and Terence by concentrating on the notions of cutting and implantation operative in these earlier authors. More specifically, he focuses on the kinds of cutting involved in literary borrowing and the results of this literary surgery. The cuts are not rag-tag rips or tears, as they are in the *Acharnians*. Qualified carefully by the verbs Virgil employs in his descriptions of grafting, they are surgically precise. Grafting itself is a precise and carefully wrought image, implying the transformation of the host tree and the new bud (the older and newer texts).

This Virgilian allegory has an analogue in more direct (and contemporaneous) descriptions of literary borrowing. One is offered at *Controversiae* 7.1.27, where the elder Seneca describes Cestius in the act of appropriating words Virgil had used at *Aeneid* 8.26–27. Virgil, Seneca reports, had himself owed the words used by Cestius to Varro. Varro, in turn, was translating Apollonius's *Argonautica* 3.749–50. Seneca goes on to report that Ovid preferred a certain emended form of the words in question, and concludes that "Varro developed the idea he wanted excellently, while Ovid found in Varro's verse an idea of his own. The abbreviated line will mean something different from the complete one" (Varro quem voluit sensum optime explicuit, Ovidius in illius versu suum sensum invenit; aliud enim intercisus versus significaturus est, aliud totus significat). In the *Suasoriae* (3.7), Seneca takes up Ovidian reading again, this time reporting on Ovid's use of Virgil's phrase *plena deo*.[41] He says that Ovid "did something with Virgil's Latin that he had done with many other lines of Virgil," making use of Virgilian language "not for the sake of plagiarism, but intending that his open borrowing would be noticed" (non subripiendi causa, sed palam mutuandi, hoc animo ut vellet agnosci).

These passages from Seneca are historically consistent with what we know about ancient, especially Roman, attitudes concerning the use of another

---

41. The phrase is not found in our texts of Virgil.

writer's words, the occurrence of which became more prominent in imperial writing, especially in the development of the so-called pointed style, of which Seneca's son is an exemplary model. As Henry Nettleship pointed out more than a century ago, to use the words of another author was to do that author an honor.[42] It was part of the process of *imitatio* and *aemulatio,* as we have seen. Seneca the Younger himself articulates this idea when he says, writing to Lucilius (*Ep.* 79.6), that "he who writes last comes off best, for he finds the words ready to hand and, if he arranges them differently, they have the appearance of being new: nor is he laying hands on what belongs to another, since words are common property" (Praeterea condicio optima est ultimi; parata verba invenit, quae aliter instructa novam faciem habent. Nec illis manus inicit tamquam alienis; sunt enim publica). In *Epistle* 84 Seneca goes on to discuss the ideal compositional habits of a writer. Reading, he says, ought to be alternated with writing, wherein a lapse of time is allowed for assimilating into writing what has been read. The man of real talent will impose his own stamp on all he has absorbed so that the separate components will form a unity in which the identity of any author "imitated" is not perceptible.[43] In saying this, Seneca would seem to follow Horace's dictum in the *Ars Poetica:* "in public space will be private rights, if you do not delay upon the common and open way" (publica materies privati iuris erit, si / non circa vilem patulumque moraberis orbem 131–32).[44]

But it is one thing to sanction the use of older material in a newer work of art with the aim of making the older material an imperceptible part of the newer work, as Seneca the Younger does. It is quite another to make use of older material with the express aim of desiring the older material to be noticed. Seneca the Elder describes the latter process in the *Suasoriae.* His interest in the audience's response to Ovid's use of Virgil's phrase allows one to see in his remarks something akin to our modern notion of allusion. That similarity can be found also in his concluding remarks in the passage cited above from the *Controversiae.* In it, the elder Seneca describes not an imitative process in which a borrowing is concealed, but an act of reading, in which the desires of the reader lead to a specific shaping of the older material in a newer work of art, the aim of which is to draw attention to the older material in the newer work.

42. H. Nettleship, *Ancient Lives of Vergil with an Essay on the Poems of Vergil in Connection with his Life and Times* (Oxford, 1879), p. 62.

43. I follow here E. Fantham, *Seneca's Troades: A Literary Introduction with Text, Translation, and Commentary* (Princeton, 1982), pp. 24–25.

44. Ibid., p. 24, n. 28.

The elder Seneca's remarks in the *Suasoriae* are one of the few extant moments in Latin literature which would seem to consider directly the implications of allusion. Seneca's reasons for offering up such a consideration are difficult to know. They may inhere in Stoic notions of linguistic meaning, which came to privilege, in the face of long-lived cultural norms, reading and writing as authentic venues for knowledge, and which were often predicated on difficult-to-understand language that demanded an active interpretation by the reader or listener. Or they may inhere more generally in changing attitudes toward styles of language represented by the pointed style, then ascendant, and warned against in no uncertain terms by Quintilian in the coming decades. His rationales aside, Seneca can be understood to anticipate a growing tendency on the part of littérateurs under the early empire to consider the implications of allusion more fully, even as rhetoricians turned a blind eye to it.

Seneca's attitude with respect to a powerful reader anticipates Augustine. There is something more than coincidental, in any case, in the fact that Augustine and Macrobius both use a cohort of words in their considerations of an empowered reader that conform to descriptions of allusion analyzed in this chapter. The verbs used by Macrobius to describe Virgil's "borrowings" from Homer—*trahere, inserere, mutuari, proferre, transferre, subtrahere*—all easily qualify under the rubrics of textual movement, implantation, and cutting. Augustine, needless to say, uses words that attend more directly to notions of cutting—*corpus, alligare, vulnus.* It is perhaps easier to call this coincidence, but these affinities of theme and vocabulary must also portend the ways in which a fuller place for allusion was made in Western literary culture—as we know it was, from the time of Augustine down to our own day.

Part Three **Reading Allusion:**

Catullus to Pound

Chapter 5 Swinburne's Battle: Catullus, Callimachus, Anacreon, Sappho

[Although] a more beautiful translation there never was and never will be
. . . compared with the Greek it is colourless and bloodless, puffed out by
addition and enfeebled by alterations. Let anyone set against each other
the first two stanzas, Latin and Greek, and pronounce.
—Algernon Charles Swinburne

The small body of poetry written by Catullus has engendered a vast
scholarly output. Much of that work has focused on the ways in which
Catullus made use of the Greek literary tradition. Yet few of his readers
have framed Catullus's Hellenism in terms of allusion, choosing instead to analyze his engagement of Greek materials as instances of
translation—a tradition that is now long established.[1] Assessments of
these "translations" are often cast in terms similar to Swinburne's

1. The tradition of Catullus as translator is much taken for granted, much less
   scrutinized. The broadest treatment remains G. Lafaye, *Catulle et ses modèles*
   (Paris, 1893). More specific is D. E. W. Wormell, "Catullus as Translator," in
   *The Classical Tradition: Literary and Historical Studies in Honor of Harry Cap-
   lan*, ed. L. Wallach (Ithaca, 1966), pp. 187–201. Most recently, W. Fitzgerald,
   Catullan Provocations: Lyric Poetry and the Drama of Position (Berkeley and
   London, 1995), discusses translation briefly at pp. 194–95.

consideration of carmen 51, Catullus's famous adaptation of Sappho's φαίνεταί μοι κῆνος ἴσος θέοσιν, and tend either to dragoon Catullus into the ranks of Greek imitators or, conversely, to emphasize his originality as against his dependency on tradition. Such assessments, however, fail to consider the possibility that both conformity and novelty inform Catullus's aesthetic choices, and that some other literary form, such as allusion, controls those choices.[2]

It is easy enough to question Swinburne's premises, for if carmen 51 is a translation, it is hard to know what sort of translation it is supposed to be. Since there are important alterations of the Greek throughout, especially at the poem's conclusion, it is not literal enough to function as a crib of its original, nor is it free enough to induce the reader to forget Sappho's poem entirely. In fact, many of Catullus's so-called translations from the Greek are hybrids, simultaneously inviting scrutiny in the light of prior Greek models and boldly asserting their independence from those models. My claims in this chapter are that these "hybrid" translations are in fact instances of allusion and, more specifically, that Catullan allusion conforms to the practices laid out by Terence under the rubric of *contaminatio*. Indeed, I would suggest that Catullus's poems often *appear* to be translations precisely because Catullus inherited from Terence a conception of allusion that was founded on the wholesale importation of large parts of older material into a newer work of art on the model of *contaminatio*.

His conformity to the practices of Terence is not surprising, given that Catullus was a close reader of Terence who (like Terence) was engaging the Greek tradition with few, if any, prior Latin models to follow. As few other Latin writers could, therefore, Terence demonstrated to Catullus the ways he might negotiate the movement from Greek model to Latin poem, a process that involved, as we have seen, the cutting and implanting of older models, and a reliance on the reader's abilities to identify those models and to make them mean in coherent ways. Because he was literally implanting Greek materials into his own literary productions, therefore, Catullus's poetry seems inlaid, like a montage of Greek and Latin materials framed by the sturdy wood of Catullus's own confection.

In pressing my claims in this chapter, I am aware of arguing against a long tradition in Catullus studies that downplays the cogency of seeing in ancient texts anything approximating allusion; as I am working against an equally

2. T. P. Wiseman, *Catullus and His World: A Reappraisal* (Cambridge, 1985), p. 152, gets around this problem by calling the poem a translation, an adaptation, and an independent poem. His discussion would seem to suggest that Catullus alludes throughout.

vibrant tradition which holds that Catullus was an eager translator who practiced his craft over most of his poetic career. That Catullus was a translator there
can be no doubt. That he is as frequent, or as varied, a translator as has been
claimed is the question at hand. It is not a question we need to examine in the
dark. After all, we know something of the habits of Catullus as a translator, for
we possess in carmen 66 an example of Catullan translation rendered incon-
trovertible by the fact that Catullus tells us in no uncertain terms that this poem
is, in fact, a translation from the Greek (sed tamen in tantis maeroribus, Ortale,
mitto / haec expressa[3] tibi carmina Battiadae; 65.15–16). Carmen 66 is a
control, therefore, by which to measure other poems which are thought to be
translations from Greek models. We are fortunate also to have recovered earlier
in this century substantive parts of the Greek poem that Catullus set for
translation in 66—from Callimachus's fourth book of *Aetia*. It is possible,
therefore, not only to determine what poems Catullus considered translations,
but also, by comparing the Latin of 66 with its Greek exemplar, to assess the
standards he applied when translating from the Greek.

One finds that the standards set are very high indeed. Carmen 66 is a close
rendition of the Greek, replicating much of the word order, sound, and rhetorical polish that characterize Callimachus's poem. Every resource available in
Latin is brought to bear in this effort. No other Catullan poem even comes close
to matching the skill and precision with which Callimachus's Greek is brought
over to Latin.[4] The care evinced in carmen 66 makes Catullus's other so-called
translations from the Greek pale by comparison. This substantial difference
cannot simply be ignored. I would locate the source of this difference in an
artistic choice on the part of Catullus to engage much of Greek poetry through
allusion rather than translation, given the high standards he sets for himself
in 66.

Nor can one ignore the general role assigned to translation in the age when
Catullus wrote.[5] It is easy to forget that Latin literature, especially in the
Republican period, was formed in the glare of Greek models. This required on

3. Terence first uses the word *exprimere* to designate literal translation and Cicero, *De fin.* 3.15
   takes up the use later (*De opt. gen. Or.* 5.14 and *De or.* 1.44.155); from Plautus's time onward
   vertere always means free translation.
4. See Wormell, "Catullus as Translator," pp. 194–95, for a line-by-line comparison of Greek
   to Latin, and p. 198, esp. n. 20, for a summary of Catullus's translative habits relative to
   Callimachus's fourth book of *Aetia*.
5. On the tradition in general, see D. P. Kubiak, "Cicero, Catullus, and the Art of Neoteric
   Translation," Ph.D. diss., Harvard University, 1979.

the part of all Latin writers a verbal engagement of exemplary Greek writers as part of the indispensable process by which literary tradition was kept alive and transformed to Roman tastes and temperaments. A writer of Latin letters could not forgo engaging Greek material because that engagement constituted his very entry into literary culture. The foray into that culture by definition involved translating from the Greek words and phrases for appropriate placement in the newer, Latin creation.[6] How else could a writer working in the elegiac traditions of Callimachus, for example, hope to engage Callimachus but by making use of Callimachus verbally? By the same token, how could such an engagement proceed without the translation of Greek words, images, phrases, so as to make them functional in the newer, Latin creation?

Our attention, then, needs to be focused on the specific function of allusion: that is, on *how* Catullus brings Greek material forward into his own work of art.[7] As this chapter will suggest, the general dictates of *contaminatio* laid out in the previous chapter loom large in Catullus's practices. Like Terence, Catullus often writes his own poems with a specific Greek model in mind—an epigram of Callimachus, an elegy from Anacreon, a Sapphic fragment. And, like Terence, he often clusters (translated) Greek material (words, short phrases, a key name) in his newer Latin version, which serves to flag the reader to the Greek model he has in mind. Like Terence, too, it is rarely the case that Catullus engages in a single poem more than one prior Greek work. Indeed, it is the norm for Catullus to have a single Greek model in mind and, as in *contaminatio,* to use it throughout his newer Latin work to the exclusion of other prior works.[8]

Unlike Terence, however, Catullus's purpose in engaging prior Greek works is often enough to call into question the literary, artistic, or aesthetic assumptions of his models. Allusion becomes in this way a mechanism of literary tradition as well as mode of literary innovation, that is, a way to affirm but also

6. See N. I. Herescu, "Catulle traducteur du Grec et les Parfumés de Berenice: Catulle 66, 77–88," *Eranos* 55 (1957–1958), pp. 153–70, esp. 168–69, for a brief outline of the history of translation in Latin literature; and Wormell, "Catullus as Translator," for comments on that history also.

7. Especially since the habits attending to his practice of it rule out translation as an explanation of the function in many of Catullus's poems.

8. I do not mean this to be a blanket statement, any more than one can argue unproblematically that Virgil alludes exclusively to Homer in the *Aeneid,* or exclusively to Theocritus in the *Eclogues,* or exclusively to Hesiod in the *Georgics.*; Rather, this is one kind of allusive practice in antiquity that all ancient writers at some time in their work follow.

to expand upon prior literary assumptions. In this regard, allusion especially bears witness to the dual roles assumed by Catullus in his poetry. He is Catullus the lover—amorous Catullus—a character in his own verse. But he is also Catullus the poet—artistic Catullus—giving shape to emotional and intellectual experiences through language. These identities bruit themselves at various points, and in various ways, in the poetry of Catullus, but, as the following discussions suggest, they are most vigorously had in the play of allusive space.

CALLIMACHUS 25 AND CATULLUS 70

Ὤμοσε Καλλίγνωτος Ἰωνίδι μήποτ' ἐκείνης
    ἕξειν μήτε φίλον κρέσσονα μήτε φίλην.
ὤμοσεν· ἀλλὰ λέγουσιν ἀληθέα τοὺς ἐν ἔρωτι
    ὅρκους μὴ δύνειν οὔατ' ἐς ἀθανάτων.
νῦν δ' ὁ μὲν ἀρσενικῷ θέρεται πυρί, τῆσ δὲ ταλαίνης
    νύμφης ὡς Μεγαρέων οὐ λόγος οὐδ' ἀριθμός.

(Callignotus swore to Ionis that he would hold neither man nor woman dearer than her. He swore it: but what they say is true, that lovers' oaths are not heard by the gods. And now his flame is a man, while of poor Ionis, as with the Megarians, there is, neither count nor reckoning.)

Nulli se dicit mulier mea nubere malle
    quam mihi, non si se Iuppiter ipse petat.
dicit: sed mulier cupido quod dicit amanti,
    in vento et rapida scribere oportet aqua.

(My woman says that she would not want to marry anyone other than me, even if Jupiter himself were seeking her. She says it, but what a woman says to her desirous lover should be written in wind and running water.)

The affinities of Catullus's carmen 70 and Callimachus's epigram 25 have long been noted by commentators, who have made much of Catullus's reliance on Callimachus.[9] Several terms have been used to qualify this reliance over the

9. My texts are R. Pfeiffer, ed., *Callimachus*, vol 2., *Hymni et Epigrammata* (Oxford, 1953); and R. A. B. Mynors, ed., *C. Valerii Catulli Carmina* (Oxford, 1958). C. J. Fordyce, *Catullus: A Commentary* (Oxford, 1961), p. 361, says that Catullus 70 is "reminiscent of Callimachus Epig. 25." K. Quinn, *Catullus: The Poems* (London, 1970), p. 399, says that "an epigram of Callimachus provides the starting point." R. Ellis, *A Commentary on Catullus* (Oxford, 1889), p. 435, says that 70 is "obviously modelled on Callimachus." W. Kroll, *C. Valerius Catullus* (Leipzig, 1923; rpt. as *Catull* [Stuttgart, 1959]), p. 221, is inclined

years ("adaptation," "imitation," "translation"). Given their disparities, however, notions of adaptation or imitation, not to mention translation, are curiously at odds with the verbal evidence either poem commends. In fact, the poems are distinct situationally, in terms of both content and characters; they are of unequal length (Catullus's poem is shorter by one couplet); and either poem takes a different interpretive tack with respect to maxim that lovers' vows are unstable. That vow itself would seem chiefly to provide the evidence for commentators who argue for the poems' affiliation.

That vow clearly links the poems; the question centers on what sort of linkage exists between the two works. Although the Catullus poem cannot umproblematically be called a formal translation, or even adaptation, of Callimachus's Greek exemplar, the evidence at hand clearly supports an allusive reading of 70, for key words in Catullus's Latin link to comparable words in Callimachus's Greek. Three such linkages are of the moment: the anaphora of ὤμοσε . . . ὤμοσεν, which is nearly replicated in *nulli se dicit . . . dicit;* the mention of ἀθανάτων, which links to Jupiter; and the identical placement of ἀλλὰ and *sed* in their respective lines. These affinities are too sketchy to be used as evidence of translation, but by the standards of allusion they allow one to locate in Catullus 70 vestiges of Callimachus 25 traceable to this particular epigram and to no other.

An allusive reading of 70 reveals a web of interpretive tensions established by Catullus and evidenced initially in syntactical diversion, implying divorcement from, not, as many have suggested, confirmation of, Callimachean aesthetic practices.[10] The Latin phrase *nulli se dicit . . . dicit,* which alludes to the phrase ὤμοσε . . . ὤμοσεν, is exemplary in this regard. These phrases constitute the opening words of their respective poems, are fairly close in meaning, and suggest a connection of the Latin to the Greek. In the play of allusive space,

---

to see the poem as independent. Other possible allusive sources include Sophocles (as noted by Quinn), elucidated by P. Laurens, "A propos d'une image Catullienne (c. 70.4)," *Latomus* 24 (1965), pp. 545–50.

10. D. O. Ross, Jr., *Style and Tradition in Catullus* (Cambridge, Mass., 1969) has suggested the novelty of the elegies as against the conformity of the polymetricals to the Greek tradition. Like K. Quinn, *Catullus: An Interpretation* (New York, 1973), esp. p. 277 and n. 60, I find this unconvincing, but would note that allusion supports Ross in the reading of carmen 70, to the extent that Catullus turns away from Callimachus in it. Allusion teaches us, however, that the novelty of the polymetricals in their Greek context is just as stark.

however, the way that the Greek words, ὤμοσε . . . ὤμοσεν, are almost—but not quite—replicated by the Latin words *nulli se dicit* . . . *dicit* suggests that the opening of Callimachus's poem is not quite right.

It turns out that the final couplet of Callimachus 25 is not quite right, either, for Catullus rejects those lines entirely, concluding his poem two lines earlier than his Greek exemplar. Because Catullus does not say as much as Callimachus, he renders the emotional situation imagined in his poem more fluid. Callimachus's final words, after all, report the devastation resulting from Callignotus's vow: Callignotus, having sworn to Ionis his true love, has run off with another man. In the Latin poem, by distinction, Catullus simply records that Lesbia has stated a preference to marry him, even if Jupiter himself were to woo her. None of the finality of the Callignotus-Ionis episode obtains in carmen 70. All we know is that Catullus would seem to doubt Lesbia's word, since he notes that the sentiments of a lover cannot be trusted any more than they can be written on the wind or water. The finality of Callimachus's poem, the narrative certainty it offers, is rejected in carmen 70. Catullus the lover is not, at least yet, akin emotionally to Ionis, because Catullus the poet explicitly refuses a connection between Lesbia and Callignotus.

That refusal also reverberates at an aesthetic level, implying generic challenges to Greek epigram. The semantic distinctions preserved in the verbs ὤμοσε and *dicit* are a case in point. Callimachus talks of oaths sworn in the past and reported to his readers from the purview of an omniscient narrator, while Catullus records the discourse of his two lovers in indirect statement. These differences translate into practical correctives for elegy. Catullus specifies the topic of epigram more centrally than does Callimachus in personality and in dialogue, choosing to concentrate on a discrete situation of discourse, faithfully recorded. Callimachus, by distinction, offers only generalities, and places the burden of his poem's knowledge on pronouncements reported from on high, not in the actions and words of specific characters. Elegy, Catullus would seem to say, must focus on human emotion and the force of personality, not on divine oaths and the certitude they do or do not imply.

This sentiment, too, harbors the potential for gauging the mood of carmen 70 more specifically. The final couplet of the poem cannot be read as a cynical dig at pie-in-the-sky hopes once held. Because Catullus the poet refuses the aorist tense of Callimachus,[11] opting to make his poem function exclusively in

11. Which I presume he would have rendered in the perfect or pluperfect.

the present tense, the expectations of Catullus the lover must be read as ambiguous and, to a certain extent, controllable. Amorous Catullus does not know anything beyond what the present can tell him, and that is not very much at all. He tempers his own uncertainty by choosing to reflect on the instability of Lesbia's words, but that sentiment can be chalked up to simple caution. Lesbia and Catullus, after all, do have a history, and not a very tame one. In the event, the mood of the poem can be rescued from the forlorn resignation of its Callimachean predecessor. Catullus the lover might not marry Lesbia, but Catullus the poet refuses to let the possibility of that outcome function in the context of Ionis's history. And because the poem exists exclusively in the present, there is still a chance that amorous Catullus will pull this one off. Lesbia is many things, but she is not another Callignotus—because Catullus the poet refuses to make Catullus the lover another Ionis.

The temporal divergences in either poem are preserved in the Latin phrase *dicit: sed,* which alludes to ὤμοσεν· ἀλλὰ (verse 3 in both poems). These phrases help to situate more specifically the preferred qualities of elegy and the ways in which those qualities can best be presented artistically. In Callimachus, ὤμοσεν is used of an oath-taking: "he swore it: but what they say is true" (ὤμοσεν· ἀλλὰ λέγουσιν ἀληθέα). The mendacity of the oath leads to the poem's crux, proving that the gods do not hear lovers' oaths. The emotional life of Callignotus and Ionis concerns Callimachus much less than the declaration that lovers' oaths are never heard by the gods. In this regard, Callignotus and Ionis are simply used by Callimachus to exemplify a more general point of limited emotional appeal that has no present relevance to Callignotus and Ionis, or, therefore, to readers of their history.

Catullus's poem, by contrast, places a premium on the lives of its characters. Catullus's speaking is personal, divorced from the strictures of religion implied in an oath taking. Furthermore, Lesbia swears no oath in carmen 70. Catullus's Jupiter is not akin to Callimachus's gods, therefore, since he highlights not Lesbia's spirituality but rather her resolve to marry Catullus. Callimachus's gods, by contrast, are the focal point of his poem. The wisdom of an old maxim proffered from on high in Callimachus's epigram is replaced in carmen 70 by a living voice, speaking in the present, who reveals the poem's wisdom through personal reflection. Moreover, it is the lover himself, not an omniscient narrator, who speaks in carmen 70.

Artistically, the divergences of *dicit* and ὤμοσεν point to choices of elegiac presentation recommended by Catullus. Elegy ought to avoid the mere reportage of past action and instead proffer the faithful recording of speech. The status accorded to speech in turn highlights the desired effects that tense and presentation help to achieve. Intimacy and presence are the chief qualities that result. Moreover, because readers of the poem join its action through characterization, not narration, the emotion and sentiment of the poem appear to the reader front-face, as a present event in which they play a part.

The intimate presence of Catullus's characters works also to effect interpretative possibilities. Because this poem exists in an eternal present, future and past harbor no threat. The remoteness of future and past confers a sense of control to the situation of discourse that does not exist in Callimachus's poem. Catullus the lover may not be able to orchestrate to his full liking the marriage he would seem to desire, but insofar as he can talk, he can also work to bring about its occurrence, and, through strategic choices of tense and presentation, Catullus the poet ensures that his readers will be in on the talking.[12]

In the broadest sense, then, Catullus 70 is about the necessity and the difficulty of the elegist's task as he attempts to inscribe speech—dialogue—in writing. Such a task is by definition impossible, since inscription freezes dialogue and in turn alters the quality that makes it a speech: its ability to be spoken. But elegiac epigram must proceed despite this powerful obstacle. Its generic purpose is to supersede the writing that constitutes it. Catullus's prescription for supersession includes those qualities of elegy he has already recommended: the use of present tense, an emphasis on recorded speech, attention to characterization as against narrative intrusion—those things that Callimachus avoids in his own elegy.

When Catullus centers attention onto speech and writing in his final couplet, therefore, he would seem to affirm the spoken and written forms that elegy must ideally merge. Like Lesbia's vow, elegy itself must be written on air and swift-flowing water, harboring in its writing the qualities that can release it from writing's limitations. To the extent that allusion reveals this important goal of elegy, it, too, can be considered part of Catullus's reckoning of elegiac practice. The bulk of those practices, after all, have themselves been revealed outside of the language of carmen 70, in the mind of the full-knowing reader. As we shall see, poetry itself will often move in Catullus's hands in this privi-

---

12. See R. F. Thomas, "Catullus and the Polemics of Poetic Reference," *AJP* 103 (1982), pp. 144–64.

leged space, where writing attempts dialogue, and divorced from Callimachus's reality, where writing exists but means little anymore.

CATULLUS 7 AND CALLIMACHUS'S "HYMN TO APOLLO"

Carmen 7 functions in ways similar to carmen 70.

Quaeris, quot mihi basiationes
tuae, Lesbia, sint satis superque.
quam magnus numerus Libyssae harenae
lasarpiciferis iacet Cyrenis
oraclum Iovis inter aestuosi   5
et Batti veteris sacrum sepulcrum;
aut quam sidera multa, cum tacet nox,
furtivos hominum vident amores:
tam te basia multa basiare
vesano satis et super Catullo est,   10
quae nec pernumerare curiosi
possint nec mala fascinare lingua.

(You ask how many of your kisses, Lesbia, are enough and more than enough for me. As great as the number of Libyan sand that lies on silphium-bearing Cyrene, between the oracle of hot Jove and the sacred tomb of old Battus; or as many as are the stars, when night is silent, that see the stolen loves of men; to kiss you with so many kisses, Lesbia, is enough and more than enough for mad Catullus; kisses, which neither curious shall count up nor an evil tongue bewitch.)

Φοῖβος καὶ βαθύγειον ἐμὴν πόλιν ἔφρασε Βάττῳ
καὶ Λιβύην ἐσιόντι κόραξ ἡγήσατο λαῷ,
δεξιὸς οἰκιστῆρι καὶ ὤμοσε τείχεα δώσειν
ἡμετέροις βασιλεῦσιν· ἀεὶ δ' εὔορκος Ἀπόλλων.
ὤπολλον, τολλοί σε Βοηδρόμιον καλέουσι,
πολλοὶ δὲ Κλάριον. πάντη δέ τοι οὔνομα πουλύ·   70
αὐτὰρ ἐγὼ Καρνεῖον· ἐμοὶ πατρώιον οὕτω.
Σπάρτη τοι, Καρνεῖε, τόδε πρώτιστον ἔδεθλον,
δεύτερον αὖ Θήρη, τρίτατόν γε μὲν ἄστυ Κυρήνης.
ἐκ μέν σε Σπάρτης ἕκτον γένος Οἰδιπόδαο
ἤγαγε Θηραίην ἐς ἀπόκτισιν· ἐκ δέ σε Θήρης   75
οὖλος Ἀριστοτέλης Ἀσβυστίδι πάρθετο γαίῃ,
δεῖμε δέ τοι μάλα καλὸν ἀνάκτορον, ἐν δὲ πόληι
θῆκε τελεσφορίην ἐπετήσιον, ᾗ ἔνι πολλοὶ

ὑστάτιον πίπτουσιν ἐπ᾽ ἰσχίον, ὦ ἄνα, ταῦροι.

ἲν ἲν Καρνεῖε πολύλλιτε, σεῖο δὲ βωμοί   80

ἄνθεα μὲν φορέουσιν ἐν εἴαρι τόσσα περ Ὧραι

ποικίλ᾽ ἀγινεῦσι ζεφύρου πνείοντος ἐέρσην,

χείματι δὲ κρόκον ἡδύν· ἀεὶ δέ τοι ἀέναον πῦρ,

οὐδέ ποτε χθιζὸν περιβόσκεται ἄνθρακα τέφρη.

ἦ ῥ᾽ ἐχάρη μέγα φοῖβος, ὅτε ζωστῆρες Ἐνυοῦς   85

ἀνέρες ὠρχήσαντο μετὰ ξανθῆσι Λιβύσσης,

τέθμιαι εὗτέ σφιν Καρνειάδες ἤλυθον ὧραι.

(Phoebus, too, told Battus of my own fertile city and in the form of a raven, auspicious to our founder, led his people as they entered Libya and swore to dedicate a walled city to our kings. And the oath of Apollo is ever sure. O, Apollo, many call you Boedrominus, and many call you Clarius: everywhere your name is on the lips of many. But I call you Carneius; in the way of my fathers. O Carneius, Sparta was your first foundation; then Thera; but third was Cyrene. From Sparta the sixth generation of the sons of Oedipus brought you to Thera; and from Thera lusty Aristoteles established you in the Asbystian land, and built you a most beautiful shrine, and in the city established a yearly festival in which many bulls, O Apollo, fall on their haunches for the last time. Hie, Hie, Carneius, god of many prayers, your altars are adorned in spring, even all the pied flowers which the hours lead forth when Zephyrus breathes dew, and in winter the sweet crocus. Undying evermore is your fire, and the ash never feeds about the coals of last evening. Greatly, indeed, did Phoebus rejoice as the belted warriors of Enyo danced with the yellow-haried Libyan women, when the appointed season of the Carnean feast came around.

Catullus alludes to Callimachus's hymn at three points in his carmen 7:[13] verse 3, "quam magnus numerus Libyssae harenae," takes shape from verse 86 of Callimachus's hymn: μετὰ ξανθῆσι Λιβύσσης; verse 4, "lasarpiciferis iacet Cyrenis," alludes to verse 73 in Callimachus's hymn: δεύτερον αὖ Θήρη, τρίτατόν γε μὲν ἄστυ Κυρήνης; and verse 6, "et Batti veteris sacrum sepulcrum," alludes to verse 65 in Callimachus's hymn: Φοῖβος καὶ βαθύγειον ἐμὴν πόλιν ἔφρασε Βάττῳ.[14]

13. There are surely more allusions than this; I have chosen these because they are commented on in the scholarship and because a lengthy article explicates them; see V. Bongi, "Spunti Callimachei e Alessandrini in Due Carmi di Catullo (70 e 7)," *Atene e Roma* 20 (1942), pp. 173–83, esp. 174–76. Pp. 180–82 offer other possible allusions in carmen 7. Fitzgerald, *Catullan Provocations*, pp. 53–54, discusses the Callimachean element of 7 most recently.

14. I extrapolate in part from the discussion of Bongi, "Spunti Callimachei e Alessandrini," pp. 174–76.

The allusive play sanctioned by these linkages reveals a broader structural connection between both poems, inhering in the ways that the beginning and ending of carmen 7 are akin to the concluding section of Callimachus's hymn. Catullus's poem begins with a question that centers on quantity: how many of Lesbia's kisses are enough for him (Quaeris, quot mihi basiationes / tuae, Lesbia, sint satis superque? vv. 1–2). Catullus ends his poem, by distinction, with the declaration that he wants to kiss Lesbia enough to jumble the count that the curious (*curiosi*, v. 11) might be secretly keeping. If their count is thwarted, Catullus says, the *curiosi* will not be able to envy them their passion through wicked gossip or vexation.

The issue of quantity and an exhortation to envy also inform the conclusion to Callimachus's hymn, which is set off from the rest of the poem contextually and situationally. In these lines, Callimachus turns from venerating Apollo to take up an old aesthetic quarrel with Apollonius Rhodius. Envy (φθόνος) figures into this narrative as an allegorization of Apollonius himself and their quarrel centers on the rectitude of writing lengthy poetry. Beginning at verse 106, the personified figure of Envy denigrates Callimachus (τὸν ἀοιδὸν) on just this score, for not being able to write a long poem,[15] before going on to whisper to Apollo that he—Envy—does not cotton to the poet who does not sing as much as the sea ('οὐκ ἄγαμαι τὸν ἀοιδὸν ὅς οὐδ' ὅσα πόντος ἀείδει; v. 106).[16] The implication is that Callimachus is incapable of writing a lengthy poem. Callimachus's hymn also features prominently at its conclusion the poet's exhortation to Apollo to let Blame go where Envy dwells (χαῖρε, ἄναξ· ὁ δὲ Μῶμος, ἵν' ὁ φθόνος, ἔνθα νέοιτο; v. 113).

Callimachus reacts sharply to the blame leveled against him. He has not written a large poem, so he knows, but he bears the criticism and casts Envy, along with Blame, out. He makes up with quality, so he says, what he lacks in quantity. The Euphrates is great, he notes, but it is also teeming with filth. The priestesses of Demeter do not carry quantitatively every drop of water to their

15. The scholiast reports, apropos of v. 106, that "in these words he [Callimachus] rebukes those who jeered at him for not being able to write a big poem." This line itself comprises an allusion, in any case, to *Arg*. 3.932. See A. W. Mair, *Callimachus, Lycophron, Aratus* (Cambridge, Mass., and London, 1921), pp. 21–22; F. J. Williams, *Callimachus: Hymn to Apollo: A Commentary* (Oxford, 1978), pp. 85–90 brings the discussion of these lines up to date. On Callimachus in general, see A. Cameron, *Callimachus and His Critics* (Princeton, 1995).

16. ὅσα easily applies to expressions of quantity and sound; see LSJ, p. 1261, s.v. ὅσας, I, III, and IV.

goddess as an offering, only the pure water that trickles down from the holy fountain (vv. 108 ff.). The point is that the quality of their water, like the quality of his poetry—particularly this hymn—is what counts for most. Like the bloated Euphrates, lengthy poetry harbors much that is unnecessary and unsavory.

The controversy recalled in Callimachus's conclusion has the effect of forming, as it were, a containing structure which controls Catullus's poem, whose beginning and end are framed by it. Carmen 7 is thereby brought into an aesthetic controversy centering on the rectitude of writing a certain kind of poetry. The detractor in Callimachus's poem, Apollonius, has an analogue in the *curiosi* of Catallus's poem, who (like Apollonius) feel envy and threaten the equilibrium of the scene. And, much like Callimachus's response to Apollonius, Catullus determines to push on and ignore his detractors. He writes what he deems appropriate to write and in the way he deems appropriate to write it.

Though he uses Callimachus's poem to level a corrective at the *curiosi* of his own poem, Catullus also uses allusion to frame a debate about the necessity of poetry written to venerate divinity, thus posing an aesthetic challenge to Callimachus in the play of allusion's space. This challenge takes shape in the context of those attributes of Apollo that are, in Callimachus's view, most praiseworthy. These would include his abilities to build cities, to foster order, and to procure the goods of the earth for people in the remotest places of the earth. In the end, concord results from these activities, whose benefits are symbolized in the celebratory dance of the warriors of Enyo and the Libyan woman (vv. 85 ff.). In his role as builder and civilizing force, therefore, more than in any other role, Apollo gives humanity reason for veneration.

The allusions to Callimachus's hymn in carmen 7 center precisely on those lines in the Greek poem that stress, via the Libyan woman (v. 3), Cyrene (v. 4), and Battus (v. 6), these most important Apollonian qualities. The language that forms amorous Catullus's answer to Lesbia's question (quot mihi basiationes . . .), therefore—a question centered on the passions of two lovers—links allusively to a different sort of passion for a divinity. When Catullus tells Lesbia that he will be satisfied only when he has kissed her as many times as there are sands in Libya, lying across Cyrene, amid Jove's temple and Battus's tomb, his sentiment is rendered in the context of Callimachus's veneration of Apollo.

The play sanctioned in allusive space transcribes and then alters the Latin versions of these exemplary Greek figures. The vibrant Libyan woman, dancing with the warriors of Enyo in celebration of the concord proffered by Apollo, are, in their Latin version, mere pieces of dust and sand. Cyrene, the vital city founded with Apollo's assistance, is now *lasarpiciferis* (v. 4)—reduced to offering rare plants in the desert sun. Battus, whom Apollo assisted in the founding of Cyrene, is now quietly ensconced in his tomb. Only Jove appears in these lines as a vital presence, the correlative in the Latin poem to Callimachus's Apollo, yet even the role assigned to this god is transformed in the play of allusion's space. Jove is made to symbolize sexuality in these lines, for he is *Iovis aestuosi*, "sexy," "hot" Jove (v. 5), and his passion, in any case, devolves quickly onto the kissing that Lesbia and Catullus pursue. But with that devolution, divinity, as always in Catullus's poetry, disappears.

This disappearance corresponds to a poetic corrective formulated in the play of allusive space. There, the propriety of the topic chosen by Callimachus for his hymn is challenged, and the corrective to Callimachus's misplaced veneration inhabits the shifting vision set to work in the latter half of carmen 7. There, the dry sands of Callimachus's Apollonian scene are forsaken for the cool darkness of a starry night. Catullus says that he desires limitless kisses, but by focusing in his declaration on the stars of heaven, of whom Apollo is the chief luminary, and by personifying those stars as public spectators peering into private places (vv. 7–8), Catullus expresses his own poetic and emotional reconfiguration of Callimachus's veneration of Apollo.

When he personifies the limitless stars in verse 7, therefore, and translates himself and his lover to a world of heady carnal pleasure, Catullus does more than simply count kisses and frame an answer for his lover. In allusive space amorous Catullus makes Lesbia his Apollo. At the same time, Catullus the poet challenges Callimachus's veneration of Apollo. The public world of this brilliant god, with his attendant political and social bounties, is replaced by the private world of *basia*, with their heady pleasures and unlimited delights. Apollo's veneration has no place in this private world, but neither would there seem to be much place for the kind of poetry represented by Apollo's hymn. In the hands of Catullus the poet, Callimachus's veneration becomes little more than a *furtivus amor*, exemplary of a moribund tradition, now unveiled by a poet emboldened by the power of Lesbia's kiss.

CATULLUS 27 AND ANACREON 51/11

In carmina 7 and 70, we have witnessed the collusion of artistic and amorous identities, variously assumed by Catullus. In carmen 27, which has long been read as a translation of Anacreon fragments 51 and 11, Catullus the lover is absent, and allusion allows a full-knowing reader to view Catullus the poet as he wends his way through Anacreon's vision:

Minister vetuli puer Falerni
inger mi calices amariores,
ut lex Postumiae iubet magistrae
ebrioso acino ebriosioris.
at vos quo lubet hinc abite, lymphae,
vini pernicies, et ad severos
migrate. hic merus est Thyonianus.

Φέρ' ὕδωρ, φέρ' οἶνον, ὦ παῖ.
φέρε ⟨δ'⟩ ἀνθεμόεντας ἡμὶν
στεφάνους ἔνεικον, ὡς δὴ
πρὸς Ἔρωτα πυκταλίζω.

ἄγε δὲ φέρ' ἡμὶν ὦ παῖ
κελέβην ὅκως ἄμυστιν
προπίω, τὰ μὲν δέκ' ἐγχέας
ὕδατος, τὰ πέντε δ' οἴνου
κυάθους, ὡς ἀν ὑβριστιῶς
ἀνὰ δηὖτε βασσαρήσω.
ἄγε δηὖτε μηκέτ' οὕτω
πατάγωι τε κἀλαλητῶι
Σκυθικὴν πόσιν παρ' οἴνωι
μελετῶμεν, ἀλλὰ καλοῖς
ὑποπίνοντες ἐν ὕμνοις.[17]

(Boy, minister of the old
Falernian, bring me stronger cups, as
the law of Postumia, mistress of the
revels, orders, Postumia drunker
than the drunk grape. And water,
destroyer of wine, go away and take
up with the severe ones: here the
wine is Bacchus.)

(Bear water, boy, bear wine,
bear me garlands of flowers: fetch
them so that I may fight with love.)

(Come, boy, bear me a bowl so that I
may drink without breathing; pour
in ten ladles of water and five of
wine, so that I may once again be
wanton with decorum. Come
again, let us no longer practice
Scythian drinking with noise and
shouting over wine, but let us drink
moderately amid beautiful songs of
praise.)

Verses 1–2, "Minister vetuli puer Falerni / inger mi calices amariores," allude to
v. 1 of Anacreon's fragment 51, Φέρ' ὕδωρ, φέρ' οἶνον . . . ; and *migrate* (v. 7) links
to the Greek ἄγε (frag. 11.1, 7). Other correspondences—the mention in both
poems of Bacchus, wine, water—confirm the affiliation of the poems.

These affiliations, which connect the poems in allusive space, reveal important divergences of the Latin from the Greek, which point, as in carmina 7 and

17. My text is D. L. Page, ed., *Poetae Melici Graeci* (Oxford, 1962).

70, to correctives of vision and topic within the larger fabric of the Greek literary tradition. παῖς and *minister puer* are akin, for example, but *minister puer* is an expansion of the Greek that discloses information about tone and mood. The expansion of παῖς might be viewed as a way for Catullus to poke fun at his own poem, lending to it a staged, bombastic quality, an ironic twist on the Greek. But the mocking is bilateral, because the tone of the Latin poem reveals itself in the context of its Greek predecessor. The result is tonal ambiguity: Catullus may be mocking his own witty bombast, but he may also be correcting Anacreon, improving on his vision through addition. Moreover, because this is a poem that celebrates Bacchus, the perceptions of the poem's speaker cannot necessarily be trusted. Catullus the poet may be putting into the mouth of his speaker puffery because his speaker is drunk—or about to become so.

Other linkages, based also in divergence, expand this interpretive line of reasoning and help to control the sentiment of the poem as its situation unfolds. There is a likeness in grammar (mood), sound (rhyming "er"), and, initially, in meaning, between φέρ' and *inger* (both qualify a carrying of some sort). But the Latin *inger* is an expansion of the Greek, a stronger word both in terms of sound (disyllabic) and sense, symbolizing the penetration (*in*) of drink into a privileged space where Bacchus and Postumia rule. The Greek φέρ', by comparison, is blunt. The differences between a "bringing in" (*inger*) and a "carrying" or "bearing" (φέρ') make the Greek setting much less special, neither separated from the wider world nor divulging a privileged space. What is brought forth is also distinct in either poem. Catullus's *puer* is told to bring in stronger cups of old Falernian (vetuli . . . Falerni / . . . calices amariores). Anacreon's παῖς offers wine, water, and garlands (ὕδωρ . . . οἶνον / στεφάνους), in anticipation of an erotic evening. By distinction, Catullus goes on to refuse water in his poem completely, exhorting *lymphae* (v. 5), the destroyer of wine (*vini pernicies,* v. 6), to go away (*migrate,* v. 7).

The denigration of water points to broader correctives that function both in the poem itself and in the tradition of sympotic verse. Anacreon's fragments center not only on drink but also on love. The first fragment, 51, is personal. The second fragment, 11, is communal and public. The speaker moves about the scene as if an arbiter of drink, much like Catullus's Postumia, who is, in fact, a *magistra bibendi.* Unlike Postumia, however, Anacreon's speaker recommends the dilution of the wine set for consumption and enjoins his concelebrants to moderation.

Catullus, by contrast, has taken over the personal voice of fragment 51, but never relinquishes it, even as he makes his way allusively into fragment II, refusing, as he joins the two poems, the communal voice of Anacreon's fragment II. This refusal of the communal voice of sympotic verse harbors, on an artistic level, a correction of narrative strategy. The traditions of sympotic verse, with its detached narration of events and its broad, social vision, are replaced now by a personal voice controlled increasingly by Bacchus's power. For this reason, Catullus's speaker casts out any severe ones (*severos*) who would worry, as Anacreon does, about moderation and control.

The issue of control is central to the playing out of the poem's situation of discourse and brings readers to a point allusively where both poems diverge completely. Catullus has already established the special flavor of his night of revelry about to begin for his speaker, or already, as in the case of Postumia, begun. His speaker rejects moderation out of hand, and declares: "hic merus est Thyonianus." This is a powerful declaration that can be read in a number of ways. *Merus* is an adjective here, meaning "pure" or "undiluted," but it is so closely associated with wine that it can stand as a substantive for "wine."[18] In the same way, *Thyonianus,* literally, "born of Thyone," designates Bacchus, the god of wine, or it can simply mean "wine" itself. *Hic* grammatically can go with *Thyonianus* or *merus,* or stand adverbially, with no alteration of meter. The phrase is governed by a simple copula. One can construe the line in several ways, each harboring increased clarity: the most common way to render the line is "this wine is undiluted," but one can also say, "here, wine is Bacchus," "here, wine is undiluted," or more simply, and preserving the Latin word order, "here, wine is wine."

Because the point of Catullus's poem is to refuse the dilution of wine recommended in Anacreon's poem, the various readings of the final line of carmen 27 need to be viewed in the pure, undiluted context from which they proceed. Allusion allows one to witness the rejection on the part of Catullus's speaker of all manner of dilution, and this rejection is both aesthetic as well as internal to the poem's situation of discourse. Aesthetically, the poem refuses generalities of address or of subject, revealed, as we have seen, in the ways the Greek words παῖς, ὕδωρ, and οἶνον are expanded in the Latin, in the rejection of the moderation and control implicit in the figure of Postumia, and in the ways Catullus's speaker casts out water from his poem. At the poem's conclusion, therefore, the

18. Apart from the neuter form, *merum,* which also means "wine." See LS, p. 1137, s.v. *merus* I, *merum.*

vision Catullus crafts for his readers retains its integrity, on every level. The wine is pure in the same way the poetry is pure, undiluted by any taint of the old tradition of sympotic verse.

Often read as a poem written in that tradition, where a narrator or spectator enjoins his compatriots to moderation and control, carmen 27 transforms the social setting of sympotic verse into a private and privileged moment. And because that moment is personal, intimate, pure—like its wine—it eventually celebrates precisely what sympotic verse traditionally scorned. In resonating at the level of tradition, moreover, Catullus allows a full-knowing reader to view an articulation of lyric correctives that take shape from the integrity, gusto, and wholeheartedness of the wine of his poem, the special place it is to be drunk, the purity of the celebration of which it is the centerpiece.[19] Integrity, purity, wholeness are also attributes of sympotic verse, reformulated now into a new, purer form that centers upon private emotion, not social practices redeemed in moderation. In this sense, Catullus pulls the rug out from under a tradition (the *severos* of v. 6) that would dilute both its wine and its poetry. In so doing, he shapes sympotic verse in a way his predecessors never did, locating in it the pure, undiluted mood of life's joy that is the hallmark of Dionysian celebration, and compelling his readers to join him in this night of wholeness, if only to share in the purity of spirit that he has shaped allusively to fuller form.

SAPPHO AND CATULLUS

> And if some lover, such as we
>   Have heard this dialogue of one,
> Let him still mark us, he shall see
>   Small change when we are to bodies gone.
> —Swinburne, "The Ecstasy"

When Swinburne read Catullus's version of Sappho's φαίνεταί μοι κῆνος ἴσος θέοσιν, he filtered his assessment of the poem through the prism of Sappho's Greek, begging the question of Catullus's artistic aims in engaging Sappho as he does and ignoring, in any case, the interpretive potentials occasioned in the Latin poem when it is read outside of the context of translation. Allusion reveals

19. The ancient topos holding that inspired poets were drinkers seems less than apt here, since Catullus is not incontrovertibly the speaker of his poem, as he is elsewhere. On Anacreon in general in the context of allusion, see P. Rosenmeyer, *The Poetics of Imitation: Anacreon and the Anacreontic Tradition* (Cambridge, 1992).

that Catullus's handling of the Greek tradition is rarely a straightforward affair; infrequently, if ever, does he merely better an older model, after the fashion of Swinburne's battle. Interpretive divergence is as much a part of Catullus's method as conformity to prior models. Much of the preceding discussion has focused on assessing these interpretive divergences in the context of allusion. Sappho is perhaps Catullus's most important allusive source.

An analysis of Sapphic allusions in Catullus is difficult because so much of Sappho is lost, but the possible interpretive benefits make the risks salable. The fragmentary nature of Sappho's poetry cannot be underestimated, and it renders the foray into allusive space more difficult,[20] but the connections between Catullus's verse and Sappho's inhabit a special world that ought not be denied simply because it cannot be viewed with complete authority. There can be no doubt, in any case, of a cause-effect relationship at work. Of all of antiquity's poets, Sappho comes closest to Catullus in terms of evoking personality and emotional detail, and of deploying lyrical rhetoric—the deft manipulation of pronouns and, sometimes, tense—to infiltrate the emotions of readers.[21]

More concrete evidence cannot be overlooked: there is the fact that the name of Catullus's *puella* easily evokes the figure of Sappho and all of the associations of refinement and sophistication attending the women of Lesbos. The resonance of the name Lesbia has been noted, of course, but it can be understood, given the previous discussion of Catullus's engagement of the Greek tradition, to function as more than a simple honorific for his lover. We have seen above that Catullus the poet often enables his readers to see allusively corrections, modifications, confirmations of prior artistic habits—while Catullus the lover goes about his amorous pursuits, which are also modulated in the play of allusive space. In the Lesbia cycle, this convergence of identities is no less a part of the interpretive landscape. And by invoking the name of his closest Greek model every time he talks about his hardest and longest love, Catullus the poet

20. The broadest treatment of this relationship, Lafaye, *Catulle et ses modèles,* esp. pp. 95–119, is unfortunately very old. Cf. A. L. Wheeler, *Catullus and the Traditions of Ancient Poetry* (Berkeley, 1934), esp. pp. 153–83; G. B. Donzelli, "Di Catullo e Saffo," *Studi italiani di filologia classica* 36 (1964), pp. 117–28; G. Jachmann, "Sappho und Catull," *Rheinisches Museum* 107 (1964), pp. 1–33; Wormell, "Catullus as Translator," p. 190; and Wiseman, *Catullus and His World.* pp. 116–37.

21. On lyrical rhetoric in antiquity, see W. R. Johnson, *The Idea of Lyric: Lyric Modes in Ancient and Modern Poetry* (Berkeley and London, 1982), esp. pp. 1–24, 38–49, 108–23.

can be seen paying obeisance to Sappho through the emotional history of Catullus the lover.

Passer and στρουθός

It is only recently that the connection between the *passer,* Lesbia's pet sparrow, and Sappho's στροῦθοι, the sacred birds of Aphrodite, has been made to function in a substantive way. It has been normal in the commentaries to note the similarity, but not to make that similitude the basis for interpretive connection. If one reads the *passer* as an allusion to Sappho 1, however—a poem, it should be said, that we have substantially in completion—the *passer* poems take on a different look.

The grounds for proposing this linkage have always been considered tenuous. In fact, the evidence is hardly convoluted. As F. E. Brenk has shown, the use of στρουθός as an amatory symbol is extremely rare in extant Greek literature: the bird is so used only in the *Lysistrata* at verse 723 and in Xenophon's *Ephesiaca* 1.8.[22] References to *passer* in Latin in a comparable context are also sparse: the word appears once in Plautus's *Casina* (v. 138) and twice in the *Asinaria* (vv. 664–65, 691–95).[23] On the other hand, Cicero presumes a knowledge of the *passer* as an erotic symbol at *De finibus* 2.75, although it is hard to know the source of his knowledge.[24] Clearly, however, Catullus is not drawing on an Alexandrian tradition, since Alexandrian poets seem not to have been interested in the στρουθός. The word does not appear in any of the Alexandrian poets Catullus seems to have known best, nor in any of the pet or insect poems of the *Greek Anthology.*[25]

Granted the connection of Catullus and Sappho artistically and temperamentally, and the dearth of extant passages that point the full-knowing reader elsewhere in the Greek or Latin traditions, it is not a leap of faith to assert an allusive connection between Catullus's *passer* and Sappho's στρουθός—indeed, quite the contrary. At the least, the tendency represented by Wilhelm Kroll, who thought that the *passer* ought to be considered a spontaneous outpouring of emotion, unconnected to Greek epigram,[26] can be rejected. If anything, a

22. F. E. Brenk, "Non Primus Pipiabat: Echoes of Sappho in Catullus' *Passer* Poems," *Latomus* 39 (1980), p. 712.
23. Ibid., p. 704.
24. Ibid., p. 706.
25. Ibid. See also K. J. Dover's discussion of bird symbology on Greek vases in his *Greek Homosexuality* (Cambridge, 1978), esp. pp. 77–81.
26. Brenk, "Non Primus Pipiabat," p. 707, reports Kroll's comment: "Das Gedicht scheint

full-knowing reading of Catullus based on a *passer*-στρουθός linkage suffers only for an inability to be placed in its complete Sapphic context. Let us begin to examine this allusion, therefore, by seeing what Catullus and Sappho make of their respective birds:

Passer deliciae meae puellae,
quicum ludere, quem in sinu tenere,
cui primum digitum dare appetenti
et acris solet incitare morsus,
cum desiderio meo nitenti   5
carum nescio quid lubet iocari,
et solaciolum sui doloris,
credo, ut tum gravis acquiescat ardor:
tecum ludere sicut ipsa possem
et tristis animi levare curas!

(Sparrow, delight of my girl, with whom she is accustomed to play, whom she holds in her lap, to whom she gives her fingertip to peck and to provoke sharp bites, it's fun for her, hot after me, to tease the bird with sweet whatnots, little games to soothe the pain. If I'm right when she does it, she does it to cool down. I wish I could play around like this, cool down, not feel so bad.)

Ποικιλόθρον᾽ ἀθανάτ᾽ Ἀφρόδιτα,
παῖ Δίος δολόπλοκε, λίσσομαί σε,
μή μ᾽ ἄσαισι μηδ᾽ ὀνίαισι δάμνα,
πότνια, θῦμον,
ἀλλὰ τυίδ᾽ ἔλθ᾽, αἴ ποτα κἀτέρωτα   5
τὰς ἔμας αὔδας ἀίοισα πήλοι
ἔκλυες πάτρος δὲ δόμον λίποισα
χρύσιον ἦλθες
ἄρμ᾽ ὑπασδεύξαισα· κάλοι δέ σ᾽ ἆγον
ὤκεες στροῦθοι περὶ γᾶς μελαίνας   10
πύκνα δίννεντες πτέρ᾽ ἀπ᾽ ὠράνωῖθε-
ρος διὰ μέσσω·
αἶψα δ᾽ ἐξίκοντο· σὺ δ᾽, ὦ μάκαιρα,
μειδιαίσαις᾽ ἀθανάτωι προσώπωι
ἤρε᾽ ὄττι δηῦτε πέπονθα κὤττι   15
δηῦτε κάλημμι,
κὤττι μοι μάλιστα θέλω γένεσθαι
μαινόλαι θύμωι· τίνα δηῦτε πείθω

---

ganz spontan enstanden und hat mit den griechischen Epigrammen auf Lieblingstiere (vgl. auch Mart. 1,7) nichts zu tun." Cf. W. Kroll, *Catull* (Stuttgart, 1959), p. 3.

σάγην ἐς σὰν φιλότατα; τίς ς', ὦ
ψάπθ' ἀδικήει;   20
καὶ γὰρ αἰ θεύγει, ταχέως διώξει,
αἰ δὲ δῶρα μὴ δέκετ', ἀλλὰ δώσει,
αἰ δὲ μὴ φίλει, ταχέως φιλήσει
κωὐκ ἐθέλοισα.
ἔλθε μοι καὶ νῦν, χαλέπαν δὲ λῦσον   25
ἐκ μερίμναν, ὄσσα δὲ μοι τέλεσσαι
θῦμος ἰμέρρει, τέλεσον, σὺ δ' αὖτα
σύμμαχος ἔσσο.[27]

(Ornate-throned deathless Aphrodite, wile-weaving daughter of Zeus, please don't overpower my heart, mistress, with ache and anguish, but come, if in the past you ever heard my voice from afar and relented and came, leaving your father's golden house, with chariot yoked: beautiful swift sparrows whirring fast-beating wings brought you above the dark earth down from heaven through the mid-air, and soon they were here; and you, blessed one, with a smile on your immortal face, asked what was the matter with me this time and why I was calling and what did I have in mind for my grand passion: "Whom am I to persuade this time to lead you back to her love? Who hurts you, Sappho? If she runs, she will soon pursue; if she does not take gifts, she will offer them instead; if she does not love, soon she will even love against her will." Come to me now once more and relieve me from inescapable care; fulfill all that my heart longs to fulfill and you yourself be my comrade in arms.)

The *passer* has been understood to symbolize a charm, the penis, even a rival lover. Each of these interpretations relies on evidence that Catullus the lover supplies in this and other poems. With linkages to Sappho, however, evidence supplied by Catullus the poet appears. In its Sapphic affiliation, the *passer* functions much less in a sexual, physical context and symbolizes instead a conception of ideal love that Catullus (both poet and lover) finds insufferable.[28]

In that Sappho assists readers in getting to this interpretive point,[29] it is important to analyze the function of her sparrows in poem 1. The poem is justly famous, and the story well known: Aphrodite has been summoned from her father's house to rescue Sappho, who stands praying at far remove. An old problem has returned: Sappho is again in love and in need of some of Aphro-

27. My text is E. Lobel and D. Page, eds., *Poetarum Lesbiorum Fragmenta* (Oxford, 1955).
28. See E. N. Genovese, "Symbolism in the *Passer* Poems," *Maia* 26 (1974), pp. 121–24, for the variety of interpretations of the *passer*.
29. I pass over the tendency of earlier scholars to think of the στροῦθοι as swans. See Ellis, p. 7 for a condemnation of the swan-*passer* connection.

dite's potion to induce her intended to come around. Aphrodite has helped before, Sappho says; will she please help again? The στρούθοι appear in the poem as a prized mechanism by which such help can be proffered by the goddess. When the goddess came before, Sappho remembers, she harnessed her sparrows to her golden chariot and came hurrying down from the ideal space of heaven to the dark earth below. This recollection places a premium on the power of the sparrows as the means by which Aphrodite is translated from ideal to real space. They are the means, therefore, by which the prayers of lovers are answered in this world of imperfection and yearning, mediating between the ideal world of Aphrodite, filled with light (cf. vv. 1–12) and the imperfect world of Sappho, symbolized by darkness (vv. 13 ff.).

For her part, Sappho summons the goddess from her ideal world with a specific request, articulated in a way whose temporal dimensions are important for Catullus's poem. Although memories of prior loves are invoked in order to remind Aphrodite of prayers formerly answered,[30] the prayer of poem 1 is not about the past. Sappho now seeks from the goddess assistance with a new love, not for a return to past loves who have already offered their favors. The implication is that the intended of Sappho perhaps does not know of her intentions, or is not in the mood to reciprocate. Sappho's prayer is directed, therefore, to a future whose outcome cannot in any way be predicated on past activity. The poem's concluding optatives and imperatives help to confirm this temporal situation more securely. In Sappho's poem, therefore, the sparrows not only mediate between ideal and real space, but also symbolize competing versions of love based in temporally separate realities—present and future. In their role as the privileged birds of Aphrodite, the sparrows represent an ideal love harbored in the future, therefore, yet insofar as they convey Aphrodite to earth they also symbolize an earthly, more physical love resident in a present time.

In grabbing one of Sappho's sparrows and making it the centerpiece of his poem, Catullus also brings into his poem's situation of discourse these competing notions of love embodied by Sappho's birds. Catullus concentrates his visual focus in carmen 2 on the lone sparrow, but it is the contrasting effects of the sparrow on Catullus and Lesbia that form the poem's crux. First, the bird plays with and about Lesbia. While the verb used to describe the playing (*ludere*, v. 2) evokes sexual nuance, the *passer* also excites in Catullus a burning

---

30. Sappho's poem is technically a cletic hymn. See A. P. Burnett, *Three Archaic Poets: Archilochus, Alcaeus, Sappho* (Cambridge, Mass., 1983), p. 247 and n. 38.

desire by virtue of what he does while at play. He flits about her lap (*sinus*), which preserves in its meanings the folds of clothing covering Lesbia's body, or better, her breasts. Fingertips then appear (v. 3), as the bird gently nibbles at Lesbia's hand. Then comes the explanation that must be offered in order to make sense of the scene. The understood question that arises after verse 4 is: "Why does she play with the bird in these ways?" The putative answer, framed in verses 5–7, is fraught with sexual tension: "It's fun for her, hot after me, to tease the bird with sweet what-nots, little games to sooth the pain" (cum desiderio meo nitenti / carum nescio quid lubet iocari, / et solaciolum sui doloris).[31] But Catullus the lover is hardly sure of this self-serving explanation. He goes on to say that "if I'm right, when she does it, she does it to cool down" (credo, ut tum gravis acquiescat ardor; v. 8).[32] There follows this optative: "I wish I could play around like this, cool down, not feel so bad" (tecum ludere sicut ipsa possem / et tristis animi levare curas; vv. 9–10).

Catullus the lover has attempted, in self-serving terms, an explanation of the sparrow's function in Lesbia's life. Full-knowing readers can spy an additional function for her bird, revealed in the play of allusive space. There, much as in Sappho's poem, the *passer* points to emotional attitudes and possible outcomes, symbolizing an ideal love represented by Aphrodite, and a real love represented by Sappho's own longings. Since Catullus seeks more than he can get in carmen 2, jealously and curiously eyeing the plaything that soothes his intended's passions, full-knowing readers can register his conception of love in real, physical, terms, akin to Sappho's own longings in her poem. Lesbia, by distinction, is affiliated in allusion's space with an ideal love represented by Aphrodite. This love, since it is ideal, must be viewed as the construct of Lesbia's mind, reflective of an ideal emotional and physical passion that has no place in the real world that Catullus the lover inhabits. In the play of allusion's space, therefore, the sparrow mediates these competing notions of love. It is enough for Lesbia to contemplate hoped-for affairs in the privacy of daydreams and intimate reflection—hence the sort of solace the sparrow would seem to give to her. It is not at all enough, by distinction, for Catullus the lover to contemplate the sparrow in a similar way. Like Sappho's plea in her prayer to Aphrodite, Catullus has no use

31. Vv. 5–7 are variously translated. I take *cum* as a preposition, governing *desiderio meo, nitenti* as the dative of person with *lubet*, and *carum nescio quid* and *solaciolum sui doloris* as objects of *iocari*, the complementary infintive required of *lubet*.

32. I am indebted to the discussions of Wiseman, *Catullus and his World*, pp. 137–39, in articulating this translation.

for idealism. Like Sappho, he simply needs a strong dose of divine intervention to make his intended come around.

Other linkages to Sappho's poem confirm this reading. *Gravis ardor,* for example, alludes to μαινόλαι θύμωι (v. 18). The Greek context is interrogative, but the question asked there is analogous to the implied question, suggested above, that Catullus answers in verses 5–8. The lines in which μαινόλαι θύμωι function take shape around a recollection. Sappho had summoned Aphrodite before, and she came to the lover's assistance, asking, "what did I have in mind for my [Sappho's] grand passion?" (κὤττι μοι μάλιστα θέλω γένεσθαι / μαινόλαι θύμωι; vv. 17–18). The hoped-for outcome is obvious in Sappho's poem, and Aphrodite eventually uses her powers to help achieve it. In carmen 2, the question helps to clarify the situation of discourse in the light of the *passer—* στρουθός allusion, allowing one to view Lesbia and Catullus as potential, not real, lovers. The poem does not catch this pair *in mediis rebus.* Catullus is smitten, but Lesbia prefers to dawdle with the *passer.* The hoped-for outcome of Sappho's poem is implicit in the function of the bird, to be sure, but the poem only takes its readers so far. Catullus wants what Lesbia will not give, and she cannot give it because she is unable to fathom it—yet.

Much the same logic underpins the linkage between Sappho's θῦμον (v. 4) and Catullus' *animus* (v. 10). Sappho's word falls in the adonic of strophe one; Catullus's word comes in the final line of carmen 2. In allusive space, Sappho's first strophe resonates in the forlorn wish of Catullus's conclusion. Both passages are optative in tone. Sappho prays for Aphrodite not to forsake her; Catullus wishes privately that he could take pleasure in Lesbia's *passer.* The plea of Sappho's first strophe is mediated by the sparrows, the agents of Aphrodite's intervention in Sappho's poem. In the same way, the *passer* is the object that connects Lesbia and Catullus, and though it also symbolizes allusively here Lesbia's disinterest in Catullus, it functions at the same time to bring the couple together, a linkage which enables Catullus's optatives to be realized, though not until later. Correspondingly, Catullus's optative in verse 10 can be read as parallel with verses 25–26 in Sappho, where the poet implores Aphrodite to release her from an "inescapable care." *Curas* alludes to μερίμναν and allows a full-knowing reader to see in the linkage further vestiges of Catullus's hoped-for-outcome.

Although readings such as these are hardly contentious, they do harbor broader implications for the interpretation of Catullus's poetry. They allow one to see in carmen 2, for example, a logical chronology of presentation. Many commentators have wondered over the role of this poem and its function in the "collection" as we possess it.[33] Allusion allows a full-knowing reader to posit the logic of placing this poem at the very beginning of the collection. The play in allusive space suggests that the affair has not yet even begun; that Catullus pursued Lesbia, not the other way around; that Lesbia was interested in the idea of loving before she was willing (at least with Catullus) to act on those interests. In short, allusive space introduces the psychology of the Lesbia cycle, however one wishes to construct that cycle. That an introduction of this sort should occur in the second poem of the collection makes good sense. Its sets the terms by which amorous Catullus will pursue Lesbia, and those terms are articulated in a pursuit of another sort, the literary pursuit of Sappho, bruited allusively in the language of Catullus the poet.

In the event, allusion allows one to see in Catullus's deployment of the *passer* the sine qua non of the poem. As long as this bird is around, Lesbia will never be his: all he will be able to do is watch her pet flitter about her body, touching places that are emotionally his property, nibbling fingers that he ought to be biting, soothing her until she can act on the notions of love that themselves flitter about her mind in idealized caricature. In this sense, then, the whole future of the affair hinges on the presence or absence of the *passer*. And because Sappho's poem is technically a prayer, the sense of spiritual and emotional vulnerability, the handing over of oneself to a higher power, also obtains in Catullus's poem. Below its surface lightheartedness, therefore, allusion preserves a deeper, more solemn tone. But Catullus's private prayer goes, as it must, unanswered, for Catullus the poet could not make Catullus the lover his god.

Atalanta, Milanion, and Carmen 2b

God or not, Catullus's prayers are answered in carmina 2b and 3. In carmen 2b, mythology serves the purpose of framing specifically the kind of Lesbia that Catullus desires. Carmen 3, by distinction, announces with mock solemnity the death of the *passer*, making explicit, and commencing, the sexual dimension of the affair. The allusive linkages found in carmen 2 conspire to make carmen 2b a perfect ending to the poem it follows. The relationship of 2b to 2 has vexed commentators since Guarino, who was the first to posit a lacuna after 2.10 (the

---

33. Arguments about the "collection" concern questions of chronology and position that probably can never be answered. On the ordering of the polymetricals, see M. Skinner, *Catullus' Passer: The Arrangement of the Book of Polymetric Poems* (Salem, N.H., 1981). See also Quinn, *Catullus: An Interpretation*, pp. 1–53, for a succinct statement of the arguments for and against seeing a conscious ordering in the collection.

manuscripts all give 2 and 2b as one poem).[34] Allusion can assist full-knowing readers in dealing with this well-worn issue in a new way, allowing them to read verses 11–13 as an exemplary conclusion to carmen 2.[35]

There is no difficulty in making these lines fit the grammatical structure of verses 9–10, the concluding lines of carmen 2. *Possem* can stand as an optative expressing an unrealizable wish, and verses 9–10 segue clearly enough into carmen 2b. The five lines in question come out meaning something like this: "If only I could play around like this, cool down, not feel so bad, I'd be as thankful as nonstop Atalanta was for the golden apple that dissolved her girdle—she'd been celibate too long" (tecum ludere sicut ipsa possem / et tristis animi levare curas! / tam gratum est mihi quam ferunt puellae / pernici aureolum fuisse malum, / quod zonam soluit diu ligatam).

Grammatical consonance is paralleled by the ways in which carmen 2b forms a logical conclusion to the narrative of carmen 2. Carmen 2b reports the history of Atalanta, who was beaten by Milanion in a footrace only because Aphrodite assisted him in attaining a victory that no one else had been able to achieve. In due course, Atalanta became Milanion's lover. In evoking Aphrodite, whose presence is implicit in the mythology of Atalanta's race and in the mention of the golden apple (*aureolum malum,* 2b.2), Aphrodite's fruit and a symbol of "last favor,"[36] Catullus brings these lines into the constellation of allusions sanctioned by the *passer*-στρουθός connection, where Aphrodite and love's psychology play, as we have seen, so central a role in the poem's situation of discourse.

Carmen 2b helps to specify the situation of discourse in carmen 2 in various ways. Its lines are spoken by Catullus the lover and yet they report the history of Atalanta, whose past is analogous to Lesbia's. Atalanta's story is, after all, about a long-sought-after woman who is finally ensnared in love's clutches by a determined suitor armed with Aphrodite's assistance. The interpretive twist is perfect, especially when considered in the context of the linkage of *passer* and

34. Most editions and commentaries have followed Guarino.

35. Relative to the relationship of 2 to 2b, see Quinn, *Catullus: The Poems,* pp. 94–96, who discusses the problem succinctly. He prints 2 and 2b as one poem, as the mss. attest, but thinks that vv. 11–13 (our 2b) are fragmentary, as has virtually every commentator since the Renaissance. G. P. Goold, *Catullus* (London, 1983), p. 32, considers the poems as one, and translates them as such, making some alterations in words and, in one case, transposing a line (v. 8 for 7). See also the views of J. Loomis, "Dissecting Catullus: Carmen 2," *Epistemonike Epeterida* (Thessalonica, 1976), pp. 161–69, who argues that poem 2 is insipid "beyond belief" unless fragment 2b is read as the final 3 lines of the poem.

36. Burnett, *Three Archaic Poets,* p. 267 and n. 102.

στρουθός. The story of Sappho's poem is virtually identical to the story of Atalanta: Aphrodite helps a lover with an intended. In Catullus, the story is a specification of the wish Catullus articulates in verses 9–10; were the *passer* to please him as much as it does Lesbia, he would be as happy as Atalanta.

But in specifying Catullus's wish as it does, Atalanta's story also transforms the poem whose conclusion it supplies. Because her story is about love's conquest, the resonance of that conquest cannot go unheeded in the poem's situation. The implication is that what happened to Atalanta will happen to Lesbia, and will make Catullus more than thankful. The symbology of Atalanta portends, therefore, the future of the affair. Catullus will be like Atalanta when Lesbia is like Atalanta. All that stands in the way is the *passer*. In the poem's symbolic scheme, enhanced throughout by the play of allusion, two erotic symbols—the *passer* and Atalanta—are poised like competitors. One symbol will have to go. Carmen 3 tells us which symbol went.

Catullus 3 and Sappho, frag. 140

Lugete, o Veneres Cupidinesque,
et quantum est hominum venustiorum:
Passer mortuus est meae puellae,
passer, deliciae meae puellae,
quem plus illa oculis suis amabat.   5
nam mellitus erat suamque norat
ipsam tam bene quam puella matrem,
nec sese a gremio illius movebat,
sed circumsiliens modo huc modo illuc
ad solam dominam usque pipiabat;   10
qui nunc it per iter tenebricosum
illud, unde negant redire quemquam.
at vobis male sit, malae tenebrae
Orci, quae omnia bella devoratis:
tam bellum mihi passerem abstulistis.   15
o factum male! o miselle passer!
tua nunc opera meae puellae
flendo turgiduli rubent ocelli.

(Mourn, Venuses and Cupids, and all you whom the Venuses love. The sparrow of my girl is dead, the sparrow, delight of my girl, whom she loved more than her own eyes; for he was sweet he was and knew his mistress as well as the girl knew her mother. Nor would he move from her lap but, hopping now here, now there, would only chirp to his mistress. Now he goes along the dark road, whence they say no one returns. But curse upon you, cursed shades of Orcus, which devour all beautiful things! Such a beautiful sparrow you have taken away. O, cruel deed! O poor little bird; all because of you my girl's eyes are heavy and red with crying.)

Catullus begins carmen 3 by ordering "Venuses and Cupids" to mourn the death of the *passer*. Sapphic resonances abound in this imperative, for Aphrodite, who is evoked in this reference, has been, as we have seen, a consistent character in the play of allusive space in 2 and 2b. In carmen 3, Aphrodite is invited centrally into the poem's situation, but unlike the prior Sapphic contexts, the invitation is cosmetic. Aphrodite's power holds no dominion over this poem or its poet. Nor does she have a part to play in the poem's situation of discourse. She is invoked to be dismissed, and allusions to Sappho help to situate this tone and its implications in the opening verses of the poem.

Verse 3 announces the passer's death and alludes to Sappho, fragment 140:

κατθναίσκει, Κυθέρη᾽ ἄβρος ᾿Αδωνις· τί κε θεῖμεν;
καττύπτεσθε, κόραι, καὶ κατερείκεσθε Κίθωνας.

(Delicate Adonis is dying, Cytherea; what to do? Girls, beat your breasts and tear your clothes.)

This allusion has been noted by several critics.[37] Normally it is considered ironic. Catullus the lover invokes Aphrodite, as love's goddess, in order to construct mock solemnities for the dead *passer*. In the third verse of carmen 3, therefore, when Catullus declares that the *passer* is dead, the imperative to Venus is whimsical. Venus needs no prompting to mourn the death of her own bird.

If the allusion to Sappho is considered, however, irony and whimsy are not nearly the sentiments involved here. The line seems calculated to offend the goddess—and, by implication, to devalue the function of divinity in the love affairs of men and women—for the allusion to Sappho 140 recounts the death of Adonis, the one figure whom Aphrodite herself loved beyond all else, and lost. If one imagines the opening lines of the poem as pronouncements of Catullus to the goddess—or to what she represents via the function of the *passer*-στρουθός allusion—a full-knowing reader can spy vestiges of a competition with Aphrodite, who is herself, along with her bird, confined to the reaches of Orcus.

The competition harbors intimations of a perceived and imminent victory.

37. By Brenk, "Non Primus Pipiabat," p. 709 and originally by Genovese, "Symbolism in the *Passer* Poems," p. 124.

At the conclusion of carmen 2b, Atalanta and the *passer* stood as symbolic competitors. Here, by invoking the mythology of Aphrodite's own lost love, Catullus implies that he has won his battle with love, a battle which pitted the *passer* and an ideal notion of love that pleased Lesbia against Catullus himself, who takes the role of the victimized Atalanta. As we have seen, the Atalanta mythology functions in another way also, suggesting the submission of Lesbia, another lover long sought through the power of Aphrodite's intervention. The point now, however, is that Catullus has not relied on divine intervention to get Lesbia, and yet here, in carmen 3, he is well on his way to getting her, as carmina 5 and 7 confirm. We are not privy to his method, but it has worked. He has bested Aphrodite and her bird, symbolic of Lesbia's intransigence; he has brought about the hoped-for outcome. And because the *passer* is dead, the affair can proceed apace, as it does in carmina 5 and 7 with a vengeance.

Carmina 8 and 51 and Sappho 31

Carmina 5 and 7 appear now in the light of allusive play as celebrations of hard-fought physical and emotional battles. Idealized notions of physical and emotional connectedness, symbolized by the *passer*, are replaced by the reality of physical contact:

> Vivamus, mea Lesbia, atque amemus,
> rumoresque senum severiorum
> omnes unius aestimemus assis!
> soles occidere et redire possunt:
> nobis cum semel occidit brevis lux,   5
> nox est perpetua una dormienda.
> da mi basia mille, deinde centum,
> dein mille altera, dein secunda centum,
> deinde usque altera mille, deinde centum.
> dein, cum milia multa fecerimus,   10
> conturbabimus illa, ne sciamus,
> aut ne quis malus invidere possit,
> cum tantum sciat esse basiorum.

(Let us live, my Lesbia, and love, and place no value on all the talk of severe old men. Suns can set and rise again. For us, when the brief light has once set, there is one unbroken sleep. Give me a thousand kisses, then a hundred, then another thousand, then a second hundred, then yet another thousand, then a hundred. Then, when we have made up many thousands, we will confuse the counting, that we may not know it, nor any evil person blight them with evil eye, when he knows that our kisses are so many.)

Carmen 5, with its emphasis on kissing, marks the first step in the progress of the affair on Catullus's terms. The poem is preemptive, offering reasons why the affair should move to a physical stage. Because the topic has been broached, one knows that Lesbia is not the same as she was in carmen 2, and for reasons carmen 3 makes clear. The memory of the *passer* infiltrates carmen 5 throughout, however. The images that dominated Catullus's suppressed desires there— the bird flitting about his intended's breast and lap, nibbling fingers that he should be biting, eliciting playful strokes from Lesbia's hand—are relocated. Catullus has taken the place of the *passer* and the next step is to move from requests for kisses to kissing itself. Carmen 7 articulates this next step.

Here, as we saw above, allusions to Callimachus correct prior lyric assumptions. Catullus the poet has a new set of aesthetic priorities to pursue. Allusion allows a full-knowing reader to view those priorities with some clarity and to watch, at the same time, Catullus the lover finally get his hard catch.

Things go sour as easily as the hope of carmina 2 and 2b was fulfilled, however. Carmen 8 marks a clear turning point in the affair, and the image of the sun that dominates carmen 5 now reappears in sad irony:

Miser Catulle, desinas ineptire,
et quod uides perisse perditum ducas.
fulsere quondam candidi tibi soles,
cum uentitabas quo puella ducebat
amata nobis quantum amabitur nulla.   5
ibi illa multa cum iocosa fiebant,
quae tu uolebas nec puella nolebat,
fulsere uere candidi tibi soles.
nunc iam illa non volt: tu quoque impote⟨ns noli⟩,
nec quae fugit sectare, nec miser vive,   10
sed obstinata mente perfer, obdura.
vale, puella. iam Catullus obdurat,
nec te requiret nec rogabit invitam.
at tu dolebis, cum rogaberis nulla.
scelesta, uae te, quae tibi manet vita?   15
quis nunc te adibit? cui uideberis bella?
quem nunc amabis? cuius esse diceris?
quem basiabis? cui labella mordebis?
at tu, Catulle, destinatus obdura.

(Wretched Catullus, it is time to stop and account as lost what you see is lost. Once the days shone bright on you when you used to go so often where the girl led, she who was loved as none will ever be loved. There and then were given us those joys, which you wanted and which she did not deny. Bright days truly shone for you. Now she desires no more, no more should you desire, wretch, nor follow her who flees, nor live in misery, but with firm mind endure, persist. Farewell, my girl; now Catullus is firm; he will not seek you nor ask you against your will. But you will be sorry when you aren't asked for favors anymore. Poor wretch, what life is left for you? Who now will visit you? To whom will you seem pretty? Whom now will love you? Whose will you be called? Whom will you kiss? Whose lips will you bite? But you, Catullus, be resolved and persist.)

Irony abounds in the solemn reversals that the poem creates, and in the painful tangents that only remind the poet more acutely of his pain. Eventually the poet is forced to stop for his own good. The more he affirms his resolve, the more it disintegrates before his eyes with horrifying ease. All that remains is the memory of lip biting lip. That image returns readers to carmen 2, where the *passer*, not Catullus, nibbled Lesbia's fingertips. Presumably Catullus the lover is back to where he started in that complex, allusive poem.

An allusion to Sappho 31 helps to situate the tone and emotional nuance of carmen 8 more specifically. Sappho 31, perhaps her most famous poem, is fragmentary. The last line as we have it, however, forms the basis for an allusion in the last line of carmen 8: ἀλλὰ πᾶν τόλματον ἐπεὶ † καὶ πένητα †[38] (but now I must endure all things, since I am poor). Catullus says "destinatus obdura" (v. 19): "be resolved, persist." The situation of discourse in Sappho 31 is well-known and need not be analyzed at length here. The lover of her poem, overcome physically by the glories of her lover, presses on with love's affliction. Love's sickness is not remedied in Sappho's poem; indeed, the poem is more a celebration of the sublime power of love's emotions than an antidote to the suffering it occasions. Reality becomes an affliction, a painful, almost overwhelming rush of feeling, eventually leading to an inability to act. Only sure, steady repose can save the emotional equilibrium of the lover.

Allusively, these sentiments reverberate at the end of carmen 8, rendering the poem's situation of discourse in crisper terms. Pronouns are manipulated and shifted, preserving important emotional and tonal changes. Catullus talks to himself as a speaker to an audience (I-you) in the opening verses (*tibi*, v. 3), but that posture quickly becomes an interior monologue (I-I; *nobis*, v. 5). At verse 12, another shift occurs, and Catullus addresses Lesbia (I-you; *vale, puella*). The poet concludes the poem by talking to himself again as a speaker to an audience

---

38. The daggers around καὶ πένητα are unimportant to my argument, since I focus here on τόλματον, which links to *obdura*.

(I-you; *at tu, Catulle,* v. 19), suggesting the attempt to objectify his situation in order to control it.

But the previous verse, "whose lips will you bite," (*cui labella mordebis?* v. 18), had found the lover reflecting on the most intimate details of the affair and suggesting, in the motions of biting, the nibbles of the *passer* in carmen 2 that so excited him and led in turn to the course of events recounted in prior poems. The allusion to Sappho confirms the return to intimate detail and denies the procedure recommended by the poet throughout the poem. He will be firm, strong, and endure, but not because he has achieved mental hygiene. Like Sappho's lover in fragment 31, endurance is a hard but necessary medicine because the affair is still fresh in Catullus's mind, as the allusion to Sappho confirms. Through allusion, therefore, Catullus the poet ensures that what Catullus the lover says does not deflect what he truly feels.

Perseverance is a central theme of many of the short poems subsequent to carmen 8. Catullus takes up this issue perhaps most directly, however, at the end of carmen 51, his famous version of Sappho 31. The reasons that make this poem seem less a translation than a series of allusions to Sappho's equally famous poem are perhaps now clearer. Leaving aside the linkages of the first three stanzas will allow a more detailed consideration of the poem's final stanza, which has always troubled commentators. L. P. Wilkinson believed that this poem was the first sent to Lesbia. "It was," he says, "intended as a test, a 'feeler.' If she were in love with him, she would understand what he meant; if not—after all it was only a translation."[39] In the constellation of allusive space revealed in the preceding sections, such a claim is rendered less than certain.

Catullus the poet rarely, if ever, corrects Sappho artistically through allusion, after the fashion of his corrections of Callimachus or Anacreon. When his poetry alludes to hers, the engagement almost always harbors the consonance of their poetic aims and visions. In 51, this is clearly not the case, especially in the final lines of Catullus's poem. In carmen 8, as we have seen, the final line of Sappho 31 as we have it is used by Catullus the poet to suggest the emotional dilemma faced by Catullus the lover. In carmen 51, by contrast, Catullus begins to veer from Sappho long before Sappho's fragment breaks off. The final point of collusion would seem to be at verse 12, where Sappho describes the ringing in her ears and the clouding of her vision, portending a faint. Verses 11–12 of Catullus replicate these images. There are a full four lines of Sappho, dealing

39. Quoted by Quinn, *Catullus: The Poems,* p. 241, from Wilkinson's paper in Fondation Hardt, *Entretiens sur l'antiquité classique* 2 (1956), p. 47.

with sweat, trembling, and "skin the color of grass," before the fragment breaks off with verse 17. The final four lines of Catullus, by distinction, shift the focus entirely, from Lesbia and the *ille* of verse 1 to Catullus alone. These lines form the crux of the poem. *Otium* is Catullus's chief problem, he says; it is *molestum.*

If this poem, and especially these lines, are meant to entice Lesbia in the ways Wilkinson and others have suggested, it is hard to know where the enticement is to be found. If the point is that *otium* offers a setting for seduction, then it is curious that Catullus should call it *molestum,* especially since it has offered him the chance to compose such a beautiful poem. In the play of allusive space, moreover, the correction of Sappho's fragment cannot be ignored. That correction implies a shift of vision and tone. Indubitably, Sappho evokes the horrors of love's power. Sappho does something in her fragment that is denied by Catullus in his final stanza, however. She sings of two people who are together—and who remain together. Catullus denies this implicit unity in his final stanza by removing himself from the poem's situation of discourse, which, in effect, shifts that situation onto the lover exclusively.

The denial of the final lines of Sappho's vision helps one to locate in Catullus's poem the sentiments of a spurned, not a prospective, lover. The poem, in this regard, is aptly placed, if one believes in the theory of a three-book collection, near the end of the "first book" of that collection. A full-knowing reader stands physically in the collection, then, and emotionally in its language, with a solitary and brooding lover. Now the nuances of *otium* become clearer. *Otium* is and will remain a double-edged sword. It enabled Catullus the lover to spend time with Lesbia, plotting his strategies of seduction. It made the affair possible, offering the leisure for the lovers to pursue their thousands of kisses. And it now offers the time for tortured reflection, of the kind that has brought down kings and wealthy cities.

The play of allusion also allows a full-knowing reader to understand in *otium* the agency of forbearance, survival, and, eventually, healing. Through linkages to Sappho's fragment 31, carmen 51 mimics the difficult curative process that eventually leads Catullus, in carmen 76, to prayer and pleading. The affiliation of the poems establishes the concord of the lovers' plights, but in refusing Sappho's conclusion, such as we have it, Catullus the poet recommends the psychological medicine Catullus the lover must take. He must draw back from the situation, take stock, refuse to indulge in the emotions or the memories recounted in the opening stanzas of carmen 51. It is a bothersome and difficult task, as Catullus makes clear in carmen 76 (difficile est longum subito deponere amorem; v. 13)—*otium molestum est*—yet vestiges of recovery are in place already in the comparison fronted in the poem's final verses. After all, to contrast oneself to kings and wealthy cities is no mean approximation. That comparison, which posits a translation from internal, emotional lassitude to the broader concerns of politics and society, represents a final, resolute turning away from Lesbia and, as allusion reveals, from the poetry of Sappho.[40]

Carmen 11 and Sappho 105a and 105c

The process of recovery for Catullus seems never to occur. The elegies reveal the see-saw of Catullus's emotional strengths and weaknesses. Carmen 85 represents a melding of submission and defiance in the face of emotion's oppression, where Catullus declares that he loves and hates Lesbia (*odi et amo*), but this elision of contrary feelings is the exception. The collection as a whole would seem to give more expressive shape either to love or to hate, but not to both at the same time. More often, the rigors of emotional shifts harbor the potential for mental exhaustion. In carmen 52, the dangers of this possibility are given firm expression by Catullus the poet, who links the amorous Catullus of carmen 51 to the despondency and resignation of carmen 52:

> Quid est, Catulle? quid moraris emori?
> sella in curuli struma Nonius sedet,
> per consulatum peierat Vatinius:
> quid est, Catulle? quid moraris emori?

> (What's the point, Catullus; why don't you hurry and die? The tumor Nonius sits in a curule chair; Vatinus swears falsely through the consulship. What is it, Catullus? Why don't you hurry and die?

Kings and cities, symbolic of social and political space and suggestive, as we have seen, in the conclusion of carmen 51 of emotional recovery, are represented here by Nonius the aedile and Vatinius the consul. Yet laced in these public and political identifications is Catullus's question, stylized through anaphora: "What's the point, Catullus? Why don't you hurry and die" (Quid est, Catulle? Quid moraris emori? vv. 1, 4). Much earlier in the collection as we have it, in

40. E. Fraenkel, *Horace,* (Oxford, 1970), pp. 211–13, argues that the idea of *otium* causing the fall of kings and cities is a Hellenistic paradeigma. In this sense, what Catullus goes on to say in the final stanza "evolves naturally from the statement otium . . . tibi molestum est, . . . as a general rule established in history" (p. 213). Although Fraenkel adduces historical evidence to support this contention (see esp. p. 212, n. 3), which would no doubt explain how Catullus came to include this verse in his poem in the context of literary history, the questions of why he put it here and how it should be read are not necessarily answered.

carmen 11, foreign cities and public lives attracted Catullus's comment. There, public and private images were merged. No matter where his friends Furius and Aurelius go, Catullus will wish them to bear a message to Lesbia. That message contains the declaration of the lover's resolve: "Don't expect to find in me yesterday's lover; it's her fault love has died, like a flower cut down on the meadow's edge, when it has been touched by the plow passing by" (nec meum respectet, ut ante, amorem, / qui illius culpa cecidit velut prati / ultimi flos, pratereunte postquam / tactus aratro est; vv. 21–24). The emotion of these lines is taut. The flower, symbolizing the love of Catullus for Lesbia, is perched on the meadow's edge: so far from the blades of the plow, so close to safety, yet this time, the plow grazes it and kills it.

The resilience of this scene is enhanced by an allusion in verses 22–24 to several of Sappho's fragments.[41] Fragment 105a seems to address the issue of virginity, but it also articulates conceptions of equilibrium and proper behavior. It assists full-knowing readers in situating Catullus's condemnation of Lesbia in a more focused psychological paradigm:

> οἶον τὸ γλυκύμαλον ἐρεύθεται ἄκρωι ἐπ᾽ ὕσδωι
> ἄκρον ἐπ᾽ ἀκροτάτωι, λελάθοντο δὲ μαλοδρόπηες,
> οὐ μὰν ἐκλελάθοντ᾽, ἀλλ᾽ οὐκ ἐδύναντ᾽ ἐπίκεσθαι

(As the sweet apple reddens on the tree top, on the top of the topmost bough; the apple-gatherers have forgotten it, though not entirely; but they could not reach it.)

These lines suggest that the equilibrium effected of chastity and sexual activity is hard to maintain. The apple must be perfectly ripe for the full pleasures of union to be achieved, and for the full measure of social assent to be granted. The virgin remains unplucked until the right time: she is never out of mind even if she is out of touch.[42] But equilibrium is a delicate thing, and sometimes, as in 105c, it is destroyed.

> οἶαν τὰν ὑάκινθον ἐν ὤρεσι ποίμενες ἄνδρες
> πόσσι καταστείβοισι, χάμαι δέ τε πόρφυρον ἄνθος. . . .

(Like the hyacinth which shepherds stomp in the mountains, and on the ground the purple flower. . . .

41. On this allusion see H. A. Khan, "On the Art of Catullus *Carm.* 62–39–58, Its Relationship to 11.21–24, and the Probability of a Sapphic Model," *Athenaeum* 60 (1967), pp. 160–76. On *carmen* 11 itself, see M. C. J. Putnam, "Catullus 11: The Ironies of Integrity," *Ramus* 3 (1974), pp. 70–86.
42. I follow here Burnett, *Three Archaic Poets*, pp. 216–17.

The tender blossom of full and fertile fruit is crushed, like the hyacinth under the indifferent foot of the shepherd. The hyacinth, not coincidentally, is Aphrodite's flower, commonly ascribed to her meadows,[43] and here her flower is violated and eventually destroyed, along with the delicate social and physical equilibrium that Sappho would seem to proffer in these lines.

Catullus reverses what would be considered normal sexual imagery in his final stanza, making himself the delicate flower, and Lesbia the masculine plow,[44] and such a reversal affirms a characterization that is typically Sapphic, and fundamental to the image Sappho draws of herself in poem 1. There, recall, Sappho marches out and claims Aphrodite as a comrade in arms. Throughout, stark militaristic images prevail. A Homeric allusion linking to images of war in the description of the flittering wings of the sparrows accentuates a prevailing sense of the power of love and of love's goddess.[45] Now Catullus has been run down by this power. He refused Aphrodite's assistance in carmen 2 and perhaps even mocked the goddess in carmen 3, holding his powers as Lesbia's conqueror up for comparison to Aphrodite's *passer*. He has come out, in the end, on the wrong side of the battle and Lesbia, like the plow of Sappho's fragment, is oblivious to it all. She whisks across him and their love, easily, even indifferently. Like another death recorded earlier, this death relies on Sapphic allusion for a fuller sense of the poem's situation, but the death of the flower, unlike the death of the *passer*, is no cause for celebration.

Catullus the poet does not often merge his voice with that of his amorous namesake. When he does, as in carmina 85 and 52, the effect is emotionally laden and highly charged. Carmen 85 preserves in its two simple lines the private worlds of emotion manifested publicly. The sentiment of *odi et amo* is crisp. The phrase expresses conflict and competition, yet elision smooths over the narrative dissonances, reflecting the gentle balances and momentary equilibriums that, together with the sweeps of despair and gloom, form the crux of Catullus's collection as a whole.

Even here, then, in this short and emblematic poem, Catullus the poet would seem to work against allowing Catullus the lover the last word. The poet's abilities to manipulate language into the smooth cadences of elided vowels put to the lie the volatile emotionality that informs amorous Catullus's narrative. In the play of allusion's space, however, there is a clearer articulation

43. Ibid., p. 269, n. 110.
44. See Khan, "On the Art of Catullus *Carm.* 62–39–58," p. 161.
45. See Burnett, *Three Archaic Poets*, esp. p. 257.

both of the manifold quality of Catullus's identities and of the ways in which those identities are mutually inclusive. One finds, too, a deeper sense of the significance of Catullan self-dialogues and a firmer notion of how tradition was received and deployed. One is reminded of Swinburne's assessment of Catullus and Sappho, two poets who manifested, in his view, a battle of sound and form. In the play of allusive space, a full-knowing reader is empowered beyond this superficial competition. Such a reader sees different battles bruited, sees, at the very least, that Catullus the poet often engaged in battles of which Catullus the lover was unaware.

Chapter 6 The Wounded Body:

Augustine and Horace

Peccabam ergo puer, cum illa inania istis utilioribus amore praeponebam
vel potius ista oderam, illa amabam. Iam vero unum et unum duo, duo
et duo quattuor odiosa cantio mihi erat et dulcissimum spectaculum
vanitatis equus ligneus plenus armatis et Troiae incendium atque ipsius
umbra Creusae.

(So I sinned as a boy when I preferred empty romances to more valuable
studies, even though I loved the one and hated the other. But then "one
and one are two, two and two are four" was a loathsome song, while the
wooden horse and its crew of soldiers, the burning of Troy, and even the
ghost of Creusa made the sweetest dream, futile though it was.)
—Augustine, *Confessions* 1.13

. . . infelix simulacrum atque ipsius umbra Creusae
visa mihi ante oculos et nota maior imago.

(. . . there before my eyes was seen the sad phantom and ghost of Creusa
herself, a form larger than in life.)
—Virgil, *Aeneid* 2.772–73

Augustine's attitudes toward classical literature have normally been
articulated in the context of *Confessions* 1.13, his famous deprecation of

Virgil's *Aeneid*.[1] There, Augustine rejects the emotional hold of Virgil's epic and laments time wasted weeping for Dido that might better have been spent attending to spiritual improvement. The fact that Augustine inserts a Virgilian half-line at the conclusion of this justly famous chapter, gently allowing the poet of the *Aeneid* the last word, tells us something apart from what he ostensibly says in 1.13.

On one level, this moment is radically dissonant. The Virgilian material seemingly affirms, perhaps even celebrates, the poet of the *Aeneid*, even as Augustine has just completed a thorough debasing of the poet's worth to Christian education. And if one is meant simply to come away from this moment with a sense of Virgilian cadence—that is, to understand Virgilian hexametrical rhythm to embody something like the rudiments of education that every literate Christian must know—then it is hard to see how Augustine meant for any further associations to be suppressed.

The claim of this chapter is that no such suppression was contemplated by Augustine because the kind of reading demanded at 1.13 represents a specifically Christian mode of allusion, deriving from a conception of the literary work as a secular form of Scripture and requiring the same sort of readerly response in order for meaning to occur. As we saw in Chapter 3, the crucifixion is the normative symbol in Augustine's hermeneutical model. The wounded body of Christ required the healing of the Father's love, just as the Christian reader applies the salve of charity in order to heal the wounds on the body of Scripture, that is, the dissonant passages requiring understanding. Augustine's pun on the word for body, *corpus*, which also means "text," neatly ties the analogous levels together. In the *Confessions*, therefore, allusive moments, like dissonant passages from Scripture, are wounds on the *corpus* that is the secular literary work.

---

1. On these attitudes, see H.-I. Marrou, *Saint Augustin et la fin de la culture antique* (Paris, 1958); P. Courcelle, *Les Confessions de Saint Augustin dans la tradition littéraire: Antécédents et Postérité* (Paris, 1963); for the artistic and literary contexts of the *Confessions* I have found useful R. J. O'Connell, *St. Augustine's Confessions: The Odyssey of the Soul* (Cambridge, Mass., 1969); J. J. O'Meara, "Augustine the Artist and the Aeneid," in *Mélanges Christine Mohrmann* (Utrecht, 1963), pp. 252–60; H. Hagendahl, *Augustine and the Latin Classics* (Göteborg, 1967); J. J. O'Donnell, "Augustine's Classical Readings," *Recherches augustiniennes* 22 (1980), pp. 144–75; R. McMahon, *Augustine's Prayerful Ascent: An Essay on the Literary Form of the Confessions* (Athens, Ga., 1989); E. De Mijolla, *Autobiographical Quests: Augustine, Montaigne, Rousseau and Wordsworth* (Charlottesville, 1994); M. R. Miles, *Desire and Delight: A New Reading of Augustine's Confessions* (New York, 1992).

More to the point, such allusions require a powerful reader to make them mean, or, in analogous terms, to heal them, just as the dissonant moments in sacred writing require a powerful reader to heal them, to make them mean.[2]

That healing reveals a literary landscape in which the qualities of book 2 of Virgil's *Aeneid,* so filled with death, defeat, lost hope, and firm determination, resonate in the *Confessions.*[3] The theology of the moment, which is predicated on a rejection of Virgil, does not suffer, because, at the least, one can make strategic connections between Aeneas, the bewildered, hopeless, exile, and Augustine, who is spiritually akin to him at this point in his life. These qualities of spirit lend dimension to the theological point being made and portend also the glories of the later books of the *Confessions,* where Augustine, like Aeneas, finds what he has for so long been seeking. Yet the very fact that Augustine has used Virgilian material to make this point undermines the ostensible narrative of 1.13. Virgil's *Aeneid* is not futile, empty, an enchanting dream, if, in fact, his poem can help readers make sense of the spiritual longings and emotional ennui of Augustine.

This moment in the *Confessions,* then, is of the essence, betokening an important development of allusive practice in the Western literary tradition. This development marks an advance on antique notions of allusion in Latin writing, based, in the Latin tradition at least, on the model of *contaminatio.* Now the inclusion of prior materials in the newer literary work is more eclectic. Instead of the dominance of a single, prior model informing the allusive program of Augustine, as one commonly finds in the individual poems of Catullus, one encounters in Augustine's *Confessions* multiple prior works informing an individual passage—a harbinger of the more complex kind of allusive practice that became the norm in Western writing in the wake of Christianity's rise.

More specifically in the context of Augustine's autobiography, too, allusion signifies an awareness on Augustine's part of the tension he constantly negotiated between his faith and his love of classical literature—a negotiation that

2. I owe my understanding of the basic paradigm to S. Spence, *Rhetorics of Reason and Desire: Vergil, Augustine, and the Troubadours* (Ithaca, 1988), esp. pp. 95–101.

3. On the literary qualities of the confessional genre see M. Skutella, A. Solignac, E. Trehorel, and G. Bouissou, eds., *Les Confessions* in *Oeuvres de Saint Augustin,* Bibliothèque Augustinienne 13–14 (Paris, 1962), pp. 9–11; O'Connell, *St. Augustine's Confessions,* pp. 7–8, and esp. p. 7, n. 11; and R. A. Markus, "St. Augustine and Signs," in R. A. Markus, ed., *Augustine: A Collection of Critical Essays* (New York, 1972), pp. 61–85.

often found Augustine wondering over the efficacy of writing in general. His aim in allusive moments such as the one at 1.13 seems to have been to set out for readers not some perfected version of his life but a more substantive, because more real, version of his past, in which the dissonances were as much a part of the fabric of experience as the unities and symmetries that reflection always proffers.

In the play of allusive space, therefore, Augustine's life becomes itself a text, a *corpus,* that demands to be read, healed, in order to be made fully consonant. The task for this chapter is to articulate this sort of reading/healing. The function of allusion in *Confessions* 4 is exemplary in this regard.[4] There, Horatian linkages preserve a consideration of the form and function of Christian writing, the dilemmas it proposes, the attractions it offers, the spiritual efficacy it harbors, an issue that is expanded and resolved at 4.7, where an allusion to Horace's *Odes* 2.16 helps a full-knowing reader to see in Augustine's dark night of the soul a firm commitment to spiritual equilibrium forged in the act of writing. I turn first to 4.6, then, which establishes the problem of writing in general, thence to 4.7 and an analysis of the solution.

CONFESSIONS 4.6 AND ODES 1.3

vide, quia memini spes mea, qui me mundas a talium affectionum immunditia, dirigens oculos meos ad te et evellens de laqueo pedes meos. Mirabar enim ceteros mortales vivere, quia ille, quem quasi non moriturum dilexeram, mortuus erat, et me magis, quia ille alter eram, vivere illo mortuo mirabar. Bene quidam dixit de amico suo: dimidium animae meae.—(Augustine, *Confessions* 4.6.27–28)

(Look deep within. See these memories of mine, for you are my hope. You cleanse me when unclean humors such as these possess me, by drawing my eyes to yourself and saving my feet from the snare. I wondered that other men should live when he was dead, for I had loved him as though he would never die. Still more I wondered that he should die and I remain alive, for I was his second self. He said it well of his own friend; he was the other half of my soul.[5]

4. One might also analyze *Confessions,* 9.1.9 ff., where *Odes* 1.18.4 is normative, or 6.10.38, where *Epodes* 2.3 is normative. Horace exists in other places in the *Confessions* to be sure. For a partial list of Horatian allusions, see P. Keseling, "Horaz bei Augustin," *Philologische Wochenschrift* 51 (1931), pp. 1278–80, or, the *Index Scriptores Profani* in M. Skutella, ed., *S. Aureli Augustini Confessionum Libri XIII* (Stuttgart, 1969), pp. 378–79.

5. My text is L. Verheijen, ed., *Sancti Augustini Confessionum Libri XIII, Corpus Christianorum, Series Latina* (Turnholt, 1981). Translations are from R. S. Pine Coffin, *Au-*

> Sic te diva potens Cypri,
> sic fratres Helenae, lucida sidera,
>   ventorumque regat pater
> obstrictis aliis praeter Iapyga,
>   navis, quae tibi creditum   5
> debes Vergilium, finibus Atticis
>   reddas incolumem, precor,
> et serves animae dimidium meae.—(Horace, *Odes* 1.3.1–8)

(Let the powerful goddess of Cyprus, let Helen's brothers, bright stars, and the father of the winds, confining all but Iapyx, rule you so, ship, who owe to us Virgil entrusted to you, may you bring him safe to Attic shores, I pray, and preserve the half of my soul.)

One often finds Augustine in the *Confessions* reflecting on the intractable qualities of his life before conversion: the necessity and the meaning of death, his blindness to the love and the glory of Christ, the pervasive constancy of God as Christ, who always, so Augustine knows, guided him, even through the darkest mazes of spiritual languor. These qualities of spiritual life are perhaps nowhere more compactly presented than in *Confessions* 4.6, the famous chapter in which Augustine recounts the death of his youthful best friend in terms that balance the doubts about death against the countervailing sustenance of God's mercy.

Confessions 4.6 is laced with spiritual self-recrimination and doubt. The old bogey of death is raised by Augustine to new heights ("I was sick and tired of living but afraid to die" [taedium vivendi erat in me gravissimum et moriendi metus]; 4.6.12) and the sure presence of God's sustenance is nearly lost in the haze of psychological disintegration, almost to the point of making the reader forget that a Christian is the author of this passage, and that the events described in it are decades in the past. Easily unnoticed in the closing lines of 4.6 are two allusions—one classical and one Christian—that help to situate the larger context of this bitter memory more securely. In most translations, the words of Horace, taken from *Odes* 1.3, are lost in the grief of Augustine's prose: "he said it well of his own friend: he was the other half of my soul." Equally unobtrusive are the words of the psalmist, recalling the guidance of God's love to "save my feet from the snare."

In the narrative structure of 4.6, these allusions are hardly quiescent. They

---

gustine: The Confessions (Harmondsworth, 1961), sometimes modified. The newest edition is J. J. O'Donnell, *Augustine: Confessions: Introduction, Text, Commentary* (Oxford, 1992).

attract the attention of a full-knowing reader because Augustine specifically mentions the speaking of Horace (*dixit*), though not the poet's name. The reportage of these words, coming as they do directly on the heels of the psalmist's words, are intrusive, forcing the narration of a past event into the harsh reality of its present reconstruction. Both allusions signal, if only momentarily, a narrative shift, from historical recollection to present rumination. In the play of allusive space, more than simple emotion informs that rumination.

The allusions function in a complementary way. Scriptural language helps to cement the theological issue at stake, highlighting the detail of the passage. Horatian language, by contrast, affords glimpses into the larger concerns of the moment, whose focus is removed from theological concerns. First, theology: Augustine uses the words of Psalm 24:15 and links his recollection to the middle portion of this psalm, which recommends the guidance and assistance of God. Boldness is the key quality scorned in this psalm. Its singer tells us that sinners are led by God (8), but those sinners are specifically called "humble," for humility affords men the justice of God (9), relieving great guilt (11) and loosening the snare of pride (15). It is not simply a matter of spiritual cleansing that haunts Augustine here. A question of pride, arrogance, boldness has caught his fancy. His recollection, for reasons that will become clearer later, harbors intimations of what the Romans called *audacia*.

With the details of theology in place, Augustine turns to the words of Horace, spoken of Virgil in *Odes* 1.3. How was it that I lived, Augustine asks, when my friend was dead, for he was, "as [Horace] says, the other half of my soul." In the play of allusive space, this seemingly simple phrase harbors a wider discussion of *audacia* because these words in their Horatian context link to Horace's own questioning of Virgilian *audacia*. One moves, therefore, in Augustine's reckoning, from death, to spiritual *audacia,* to mimetic *audacia*. The consideration of his friend's death, in other words, leads Augustine to worry over the boldness of his spiritual naiveté in the context of the boldness of his own mimetic recollection of it. In this way, the theological dissonance of 4.6 is framed in a mimetic context that places in doubt the morality of writing about topics such as those considered in 4.6, topics whose articulation poses risks to those who would write about them.

A detailed examination of *Odes* 1.3, the so-called propempticon for Virgil, allows a full-knowing reader to locate those risks more securely.[6] Horace

6. My text is E. Wickham, ed., *Q. Horati Flacci Opera* (Oxford, 1901). I review the reception of this ode in my "Horace and Virgilian Mimesis: A Re-Reading of Odes 1.3,"

broaches the issue of mimetic *audacia* carefully in *Odes* 1.3. The issue hinges on the function and meaning of the phrase *animae dimidium meae,* which controls the various levels of this poem's situation of discourse. That phrase, which has generally been translated as if *dimidium* were a synonym for *pars,* and as if its sentiment confirmed Horace's devotion for Virgil, would seem actually to place into doubt Horace's esteem for the poet of the *Aeneid.* One can spy suggestions of this less positive tone in the ways Horace works his way toward the introduction of the phrase, spoken as if to Virgil, in verse 8. Preceding verse 8 are a series of periphrases that mingle epic and lyric diction. Venus, for example, is *diva potens Cypri* (v. 1); Castor and Pollux are *fratres Helenae* (v. 2); Aeolus is *ventorumque pater* (v. 3). These roundabout ways of naming suggest collectively the idea that what Horace seems to be saying in this ode may not actually be what he means to say. This interpretive dissonance is ratified in the ways epic language is adduced in the poem. Venus is called after her epic title, *diva potens,* while the phrase *fratres Helenae* suggests not only Helen herself, so imposing an

---

Classical World 87 (1992), pp. 156–72, with full bibliography. The standard treatment is J. P. Elder, "Horace C. 1.3," *AJP* 73 (1952), pp. 140–59. For the variety of interpretations, see S. Commager, *The Odes of Horace* (New Haven, 1962), p. 118; R. G. M. Nisbet and M. Hubbard, eds., *A Commentary on Horace: Odes Book 1* (Oxford, 1970), pp. 44–45, who argue that 1.3 "is an accomplished piece of versification, but little more. The poet . . . shows none of his usual tact and charm; there is not a hint of Virgil's poetry and it is wrong to argue . . . that the ode's sombre and religious tone is directed specifically towards the recipient. The second part of the poem is equally unsatisfactory; . . . here the trite and unseasonable moralizing seems out of place in a poem of friendship. . . . Nor is the flatness of the thought redeemed by any special excellence in the writing. . . . We miss the Horatian virtues of brevity and incisiveness." G. Williams, *Tradition and Originality in Roman Poetry* (Oxford, 1968), p. 159, makes much the same comment, calling the ode "undistinguished," and concluding that there is not "the slightest sense of a personal relationship in the greater part of the poem." K. Prodinger, "Zu Horazens Ode I.3," *Wiener Studien* 29 (1907), p. 165, and A. W. Verrall, *Studies Literary and Historical in the Odes of Horace* (London, 1884), p. 120, both assert that 1.3 is actually two poems. Verrall argues that the first eight verses of the ode are a true *propempticon* simply added to vv. 9 ff., which were written earlier and not as a *propempticon.* G. L. Hendrickson, "Horace's Propempticon to Virgil," *Classical Journal* (1907–1908), pp. 100–104, argues that the first eight lines were all that Horace intended Virgil to hear (thus establishing Horace in his view as following Menander in the form of the *propempticon*) and that the rest of the poem was out of Virgil's ear-shot. An antidote to these views is R. Carrubba, "The Structure of Horace, Odes 1.3: A Propempticon for Vergil," *AJP* 105 (1984), pp. 166–73, who has argued for the coherency and structural integrity of this ode. A. Hahn, "Horace's Ode to Vergil," *TAPA* 76 (1945), xxxii–iii, spies comedy at work in 1.3.

epic figure, but also the image of the Dioscuri in their single epic, aspect.[7]
Lucida sidera would seem also to have an epic provenance, implying not only St.
Elmo's fire but also the serene images of epic night.[8] Here, again, the implication is that the putative topic of the ode is going to hinge more on epic than on
lyrical sentiments, that what this poem would seem to be may not actually be
what the poem is—or will become.

The symbolic value of the Dioscuri, mentioned at verse 2, helps to control
the various identities, ostensible and implied, that the poem assumes and the
naming of Castor and Pollux situates 1.3 in a personal context. Castor and
Pollux are twins, representatives (presumably) of the closest relationship possible in human terms. Since 1.3 is also about a personal relationship, one can see
preserved in the naming of the Dioscuri an analogue for the relationship of
Horace and Virgil, a relationship, as we have seen, that takes shape in periphrases and the introduction of epic diction to lyric form. The mythology of the
Dioscuri tells us something else about this relationship, however, establishing a
context in which the phrase *animae dimidium meae* will function later. Though
Pollux was inconsolable at Castor's death, one version of their story has it that
they were allowed to be together for half of the time, while another version
holds that Castor was allowed to live again, but only at the expense of the life of
Pollux, so that they lived on alternate days. In both myths, the twins live, but
always separated and divided from each other. The details of their mythology
highlight, therefore, not the closeness of their birth but rather their division or
separation played out in the history of their lives.

Commentators often cite Horace's effusive praise of Virgil in the *Satires* as
conclusive proof that *animae dimidium meae* implies devotion and friendship.
His first published work, it is true, leaves no doubt that Horace shared a
friendship with Virgil equally as intimate as the one he shared with Maecenas.
Beginning at *Satires* 1.5.39, for example, Horace mentions his friends Plotius
and Varius in the same breath as Virgil, and describes them all as "whitest souls
earth ever bore, to whom none can be more deeply attached than I" (animae
qualis neque candidiores / terra tulit neque quis me sit devinctior alter; vv. 41–
42). Yet the evidence in the *Satires* cannot be adduced in a discussion of 1.3
because of chronology. *Satires* 1 was written sometime before 35 B.C. It represents a collection written by a Horace who refuses to call himself a poet yet
("First I will remove my name from the number of those as I would allow to be

7. R. Basto, "Horace's Propempticon to Vergil: A Re-Examination," *Vergilius* 28 (1982),
    pp. 33–35.
8. Ibid.

poets" [primum ego me illorum dederim quibus esse poetas, / excerpam numero]; *Sat.* 1.4.39–40; cf. vv. 41 ff.), and who praises a Virgil who represents the pastoral traditions of Theocritus ("To Virgil the Muses rejoicing in rural life have granted simplicity and charm" [molle atque facetum / Vergilio adnuerunt gaudentes rure Camenae]; *Sat.* 1.10.44–45 ff.; cf. 1.10.81 f.). This specification of the role and function of the Virgil that Horace finds praiseworthy in the *Satires* demonstrates that Horace's view of (and praise of) Virgil in the *Satires* is a praise of Virgil the pastoral poet. And Horace himself is a different sort of writer at this point. At this early date, the lyrical project of the *Odes,* which certainly is the task of a *poeta,* lies somewhere in the distance. Horace is not yet, by his own admission, a poet.

He is clearly a poet, on the other hand, in 23 B.C.E., when *Odes* 1–3 were published.[9] Virgil, too, is a poet, but now he is the poet of the *Aeneid,* not a pastoralist. It is hard to imagine two more different genres of poetry than epic and lyric. It is equally hard to imagine that the friendship praised by Horace in the *Satires,* some ten years earlier, suffered no strain in the intervening years, when Horace discovered his poetic voice and Virgil began to practice a poetry constructed on vastly different terms from Horace's chosen form. That a separation of some sort should have occurred seems inevitable and that separation, as we have seen, is mirrored in the history of the Dioscuri, who in times past had been close but who eventually came to inhabit, though not by choice or predilection, separate worlds.

The meaning of *dimidium* corroborates these changes and the separation implied by them, as a brief look at its etymology attests. *Dimidium* is related to *dimidiare,* a verb rarely found in finite form in classical Latin, meaning "to divide into two equal parts," "to halve."[10] Its perfect passive participle, *dimidiatus,* means "half" or "halved," and refers to a whole that has been divided. The substantive *dimidium* takes from its verbal kin this sense of divided whole, connoting a part of something that has been cut off from something else that was divided (and so is truly half of what was formerly whole).[11] It is not

9. *Odes* 1.3 is generally considered late; no ode was written before 32 B.C.; the first book of the *Satires* was written before 35 B.C.E., the date of its publication. See Basto, ibid., pp. 36–37, on the issues of dating. Virgil died four years after Horace published *Odes* 1–3. By 23 B.C.E. the first two-thirds of the *Aeneid* would have been in presentable form (all of the allusions to Virgil in Horace come from books 1–7), so that Horace would have a very good idea of what the *Aeneid* was—in his view—about.

10. Thus LS, p. 581, s.v. *dimidio.*

11. LS, p. 581, s.v. *dimidius,* III A (*dimidium*).

equivalent to *pars,* the word most commentators consider synonymous with it, citing *Odes* 2.17.5 *meae . . . partem animae* as exemplary of the friendship Horace shared with Maecenas. Lewis and Short offer no verbal root in Latin for *pars* but the noun *portio,* a word which means "a share, a part, a portion,"[12] is listed as kindred to *pars,* and the Greek πόρω "to furnish, to offer, to give,"[13] is listed as kindred to both these nouns. These etymological data corroborate what we already can sense in a reading of this ode. *Pars* is inclusive. Horace and Maecenas share their worlds through friendship. *Dimidium,* on the other hand, is exclusive, implying permanent separation, the cutting asunder of something that was once—but is no longer—whole. This, too, corroborates the evidence found in 1.3, where separation, not devotion, subsists. The function of *dimidium* in 1.3 centers on halving, then, and reveals the relationship of Horace and Virgil to be grounded in a former unity that is now changed, a wholeness cut asunder. The "souls" of Horace and Virgil, as it were, once joined, are now— for reasons that will become clearer as the ode progresses—halved into separate but equal parts. Much like the Dioscuri, these two figures were once inseparable but are now entirely apart.

Now the epic elements preserved in the diction of the ode's opening lines come into clearer focus. Horace and Virgil have been separated on aesthetic grounds. Verses 9–24 specify those grounds in no uncertain terms: "to him was oak and triple bronze encircling his chest who first committed his fragile boat to the savage sea" (illi robur et aes triplex / circa pectus erat, qui fragilem truci / commisit pelago ratem / primus; vv. 9–11). *Ratis* is especially noteworthy, for although it is described here in terms of fragility, it also represents, as often in Augustan writing, poetry itself. So, too, is the mention of the "first traveler" important, preserving in its meanings the literary analogue of Virgil's pathbreaking travels through Latin letters. Those travels are articulated beginning at verse 13, where Horace's vision considers in turn various images, themes, and locales traceable to the *Aeneid.* In locating those travels in the *Aeneid,* Horace confirms that it is Virgil the epicist whom he is describing here, not the pastoral Virgil recalled in the *Satires:*

> . . . nec timuit praecipitem Africum
>   decertantem Aquilonibus
> nec tristis Hyadas nec rabiem Noti,
>   quo non arbiter Hadriae   15

12. LS, p. 1401, s.v. *portio,* I.
13. Technically, πόρω is presumed to be the present form of the aorist active ἔπορον, on which see LSJ, p. 1452, s.v. πόρω.

maior, tollere seu ponere vult freta.
>   quem mortis timuit gradum,
> qui siccis oculis monstra natantia,
>   qui vidit mare turbidum et
> infamis scopulos Acroceraunia?   20
>   nequiquam deus abscidit
> prudens Oceano dissociabili
>   terras, si tamen impiae
> non tangenda rates transiliunt vada.

(. . . he feared not the rushing southwest wind fighting with the North, nor the gloomy Hyades, nor the rage of Notus, than whom there is no mightier master of the Adriatic, whether he desires to excite or quiet the seas. What form of Death's approach feared he who with thirsty eyes gazed on the swimming monsters, on the stormy sea, and the infamous cliffs of Acroceraunia? Pointlessly God chopped off the lands from the incompatible ocean, if impious boats still cross the seas he meant should not be touched.)

At this point it becomes clear that Horace has not written what so many commentators have claimed he wrote: a *propempticon*—a poem praying for the safe return of a love one. Like so much else in this ode, what seems to be the case is often not supported by the evidence the poem itself supplies. The catalogue comprising verses 9–23, after all, is hardly written to make the prospective traveler feel more comfortable for its having been written, filled as it is with storms, winds, monsters, promontories, and evil tidings. Moreover, at verse 23 the *ratis,* the vessel that symbolizes poetry itself, having made its way through the uncharted waters of the *Aeneid,* becomes of a sudden *impia.* As the putative traveler on the *ratis,* therefore, Virgil becomes the singular example of the *audax gens humana,* rushing to ruin through crimes prohibited them. The ode rests now firmly in the context of epic mimesis as practiced by Virgil:

>   audax omnia perpeti   25
> gens humana ruit per vetitum nefas.
>   audax Iapeti genus
> ignem fraude mala gentibus intulit.
>   post ignem aetheria domo
> subductum macies et nova febrium   30
>   terris incubuit cohors,
> semotique prius tarda necessitas
>   leti corripuit gradum.
> expertus vacuum Daedalus aera
>   pennis non homini datis: 35

perrupit Acheronta Herculeus labor.
　　nil mortalibus ardui est:
caelum ipsum petimus stultitia, neque
　　per nostrum patimur scelus
iracunda Iovem ponere fulmina.   40

(Bold to allow all things, humanity runs, despite prohibition, to crime. Iapetus's daring son by impious craft brought fire to the tribes of men. After fire was stolen from its home in heaven, poverty and a new company of ills fell upon the earth, and the necessity of death, rermote once, quickened its pace. Daedalus tried the empty air on wings not given to man; the toiling Hercules burst through Acheron. Nothing is too steep for mortals. Heaven itself we seek foolishly, and through our sin we let not Jove lay down his bolts of thunder.)

The transformation of *ratis* from *fragilis* (vv. 10–11) to *impia* (vv. 23–24) is fundamental to the lecture on mimesis that comprises the remaining lines of the ode. That lecture centers on the figures of Prometheus, Daedalus, and Hercules. Beyond their appropriateness as epic heroes, figures who "did it all"—or tried to—are their priority and their arrogance. Each pursued practices no one had ever dared before. Each was, in his own way, supremely bold in doing what he did, and his *audacia* was in due course punished. But, since "nothing is too steep for mortals" (nil mortalibus ardui est; v. 37), Jupiter can scarcely afford to rest the *fulmen,* the mechanism of punishment.

If Horace is less convinced that Jupiter's thunderbolt will come crashing down on Virgil's head, nevertheless he clearly believes that there are problems reserved for littérateurs who are bold, prideful, arrogant, and special problems for literary *audacia* of the kind represented by Virgil the epicist. To be sure, Horace does not excuse himself from the company of those who try to do bold things with language. He makes the last verbs of the poem first person plural (*petimus, patimur,* vv. 38, 39) for just this reason. But poetry ranges the creative spectrum, from the purely personal singing of lyric to the comprehensive song of epic. Epic, in any case, is not lyric. The song of self embodied in lyric is not the same as the song of epic, which always seeks, as Horace himself says, "heaven itself" (caelum ipsum). The boldness, the *audacia,* involved in epic journeying of a Virgilian kind is fundamentally to challenge the gods at their own game, to try to recreate "everything" in the epic genre as if the poet were a god of creation himself. The desire to achieve this kind of mimesis is akin to the desire to move about the world over the water or to give fire to men or to try to fly. To attempt such acts invites, if not divine punishment, then surely mimetic failure, a failure portended in the fates suffered by Hercules, Daedalus, and

Prometheus. Readers move over the poetic waters of *Odes* 1.3 with Horace, then, from the figure of Virgil as a bold epicist to the condemnation of epic mimesis as a supreme example of verbal *audacia*.

Audax is key word in this ode. It is a special word in Horace's vocabulary, most often used in his poetry to describe figures who foolishly seek great accomplishments (with the idea that these accomplishments should not be sought). In *Epistles* 2.1.182, for example, it is used to describe a kind of poet who is showy, who writes only to gain the attention and approbation of the audience. Although Horace claims the highest respect for such a poet, there is a sense of irony in this epistle, addressed, after all, to Augustus and prominently mentioning as it does another *audax poeta*, Virgil himself. In *Odes* 4.2 (v. 10), *audax* is also used of the would-be Pindaric poet, the poet whom Horace says he cannot be. In *Odes* 1.12, *audax* is used of Athena in a poem that emphasizes— while it seems to close—the gap that remains between what humanity can do and what it wants or seeks to do.[14] So it is here also, in 1.3, used in the same way. Literary *audacia*, no less than other forms of human boldness, requires divine punishment. If, therefore, Horace and Virgil have or will become *lucida sidera*, immortal through their writing, the achievements that render them immortal are nevertheless cast in different terms and harbor different moral implications. Both seek heaven as the practical effect of their poetry's worth. But both are separated by the aims their poetry seeks and achieves. And while both may suffer punishment—aesthetic or otherwise—Horace would seem to repose at his poem's end in the sure knowledge that there are some things verbal mimesis cannot achieve, that some things are better left unsaid.

Horace's study of human *audacia* is central to the aims of Augustine's reminiscence in 4.6, a recollection framed initially in the words of the psalmist. In the play of allusive space, the words of Horace and the verses of the psalmist represent complementary meditations on human *audacia*. The psalmist is satisfied to resign himself to the mercy of divine guidance. Theologically, this satisfaction infiltrates Augustine's recollection, offering a corrective to Augustine's extreme reaction to his friend's death. The *audacia* that has led to Augustine's resignation, conceived as the snare of wordly immersion, is balanced by the soothing hand of God's judgment, whose saving grace reflects his redemptive powers in the lives of Christians.

On a broader level, Augustine also raises the issue of mimetic *audacia* by

14. See also *Odes* 3.4.56, 3.18.13, 3.27.28; *Epistles* 2.2.51; *Satires* 1.1.30, 2.3.165, 2.5.29, 1.10.76; *Ars Poetica*, v. 237.

linking his recollection to Horace. The stakes in this linkage lie outside the sure mercy of God's love, for the sin of *audacia*—symbolized by the act of recollecting in writing the emotional desolation occasioned by his friend's death—has already been accomplished. The implication of the Horatian linkage is moral and literary, therefore, before it is theological: like Virgil, Augustine has sought heaven itself in committing this story to writing, has performed a literary act akin to the doomed adventures of Hercules, Daedalus, and Prometheus. The consequences of this act, harbored in the play of allusive space, allow one to take the full measure of Augustine's moral attitudes toward writing, attitudes which eventually occasion a theological paradox that is resolved, as it was broached, through the mediation of Horace's wisdom.

Augustine intimates the moral issue at stake in the opening line of 4.6: "Why do I talk of these things?" (quid autem ista loquor; 4.6.1) In fact, this talking is a writing and it is the moral implications of writing to which Horace's ode speaks most clearly. It is, after all, the inability of humans to achieve all they would seek to do that gives Horace pause. In a literary sense, epic is doomed to failure, offering little more than problematical considerations without coherent answers. For Horace, this insufficiency is both unsatisfactory and potentially dangerous, highlighting problems that reveal the weakness of human solutions. To practice epic is to accentuate human weakness under the veneer of human accomplishment.

The moral issues preserved in *Odes* 1.3 are present also in Augustine, and he meditates on them in different ways in 4.6. In a more specific sense, because Augustine would seem to be writing after a fashion a Christian epic, recounting in the *Confessions* the total emotional and spiritual milieu of his life, confessional writing itself is called into question. We have seen above in Chapter 3 that Christians placed a premium on writing and reading, but the issue here is shifted from the reading of sacred Scripture and the exegetical consideration of its truths to a reading of the self and the constitution of an evolving Christian consciousness on the most personal of levels. The issue for Augustine, as for Horace, is one of degree. It is one thing to devote oneself to scriptural reading and exegetical writing, quite another to devote oneself to the exegetical consideration of one's self. Because personal musings, self-reflexive analyses, are not sacred Scripture, only the accumulated history of imperfect human action, a writing that centers, as the *Confessions* does, on a comprehensive accounting of personal activity is problematic.

Unlike Scripture, which is imbued with the quality of divine sanction, such a writing would seem to be false. It lends to the experiences recounted a fixed and therefore potentially dangerous permanence. In the event, the ultimate aim of Christian communication, to attain to the truth of God, is put off, not enhanced, both for the reader of the *Confessions* and, more important, for Augustine himself as the writer of the work. By definition, writing cannot adequately give shape to the longings of personality and self-awareness in such a way as to make them intelligible. Augustine's musings in 4.6, like Virgil's wanderings in the *Aeneid*, raise more questions than they can possibly answer. The vision becomes skewed—and solipsistic. The focus is eventually shifted, from Christian truth to personal indulgence.

Solipsism raises a corollary issue in the play of allusive space that focuses on the rectitude of presenting such a vision in the guise of a monologue addressed to God. Different sorts of audiences seem to be anticipated in the *Confessions*, but Augustine is clear from the first lines of the *Confessions*, other audiences aside, that God is the most important intended of his work. In 1.3, Horace holds that nothing is too steep for mortals, for which reason Jove can scarcely afford to rest his thunderbolts. His words in verse 38, "foolishly, we seek heaven itself," have a special resonance when they are read allusively in Augustine's passage. The writing of the *Confessions*, no less an instance of seeking heaven, is rendered in the play of allusive space analogous to the foolish exploits of Hercules, Prometheus, Daedalus, all of whom sought heaven itself. Writing *of* God is not the same as writing *to* God. The former was, and remains, the mainstay of Christian exegesis. The latter, by contrast, would seem to occasion the unhappy circumstance of making God into an intimate confessor. The theology of such a position is sound but the balance is skewed in Augustine's presentation because his writing to God is so personal, so centered in the emotion and detail of a single life. The effect is to center as much attention onto the imperfect Christian as onto God.

Now the stakes are raised. Horace's moral question is transformed to a theological position: it is immoral and improper to write to God. Not even the corrective wisdom of Psalm 24 can mitigate this dilemma, since its wisdom argues for the avoidance of sin, for a belief in, and a reliance on, divine assistance to preclude sin. The sin of writing, by distinction, has already been committed, and on a grand scale. In this regard, Augustine is no different for his knowledge of God's potential assistance than Hercules, Prometheus, and Daedalus. All of them are bold sinners, conscious sinners, and all are sinners who sin despite, and perhaps as a result of, the knowledge of their own turpitude.

The pious acknowledgment of God's assistance that lingers allusively in the words of Psalm 24, no matter how surely felt or sincerely expressed, cannot be sustained in the mimetic inscription of the *Confessions*, with its discourse reaching ever further to heaven itself. The only course of action for Augustine is to forbear, and the contours of that forbearance help a full-knowing reader to situate the dilemmas and the delights of writing to God that linger in 4.6. The question with which Augustine frames 4.6 returns in this regard with special significance: "Why do I talk of these things?" This question, which summarizes a series of queries that conclude 4.5, is also proleptic, anticipating in a general sense the kind of "talking" that comprises 4.6.

The questioning of language's morality in a Horatian context devolves ultimately onto the figure of God, with implications about the very ways in which we conceive of and talk about Him. In this sense, the Horatian allusion highlights the absolute sublimeness of God, and so the absolute absurdity involved in the detailed writing to God about one's (God-given) life as if He were a confessor-priest. This act, which might on one level seem submissive, is, in a larger sense, the boldest act a human can attempt, bolder even than the *audacia* of Hercules, Prometheus, or Daedalus. The problem, much as in *Odes* 1.3, is one of degree. How does a Christian get around the thorny problem of human *audacia* when, whenever he writes in the ways Augustine does here, he is himself being supremely bold?

The play of allusion in 4.6 offers no solutions. Psalm 24, as we have seen, is limited by the proscriptions it demands. Augustine clearly did not stop writing, although the theology that informs 4.6 would seem to require that he do just this. Horace offers no solution either, since he includes himself in the company of bold Virgil, and intimates that he, like Virgil, delights in the prospect of being translated to the heavens through the immortality his poetry will grant. In the analysis of 4.7 that follows, one firm answer will be offered to this dilemma, through allusion to *Odes* 2.16. Here, however, in 4.6, Augustine seems satisfied to ruminate on the paradox in which he is caught. He implies all the same several reasons why seeking heaven in the ways he does is important to a theologically astute Christian.

Because allusion allows a full-knowing reader to gauge Horace's ambivalent attitude toward verbal mimesis (he worries over it, but practices it nonetheless), one is able to see this ambivalence in place in the *Confessions* also. Augustine is not extolling the virtues of pride and arrogance. The fact that 4.6 is so surely grounded in the morality of Psalm 24 precludes this interpretation. Instead, Augustine would seem to test the limits of faith from the perspective of human imperfection, opting to proceed for putative benefits in spite of obvious perils.

One can conceive of those benefits at once in the play of allusive space. Horace, after all, though he condemns Virgilian mimesis and opts for the more limited purview of lyric, is nonetheless a sinner after the fashion of Virgil. He may seek heaven in a more proscribed way, but his search is still *audax*. The putative benefit is beauty, the beauty of language shaped to mature forms, the beauty of wisdom finely wrought, or the beauty of immortality attained through the staying power of written language, a staying power Horace extols in no uncertain terms in *Odes* 3.30. For Augustine, these benefits, and their attractiveness, are no less real. One thinks of *Confessions* 1.13, and the subtle inscription of Virgilian language into a passage that rejects Virgilian myth. The alluring quality of language itself, and of its carefully wrought wisdom, is difficult to deny. A Christian may be sidetracked by this beauty, but a Christian who keeps the words of the Psalms in mind may find something else again in language's beauty that brings him closer, if only momentarily, to God.

What that Christian will find is a richer understanding of what it means to be a Christian in a postlapsarian world. Such a world harbors a multitude of temptations and the best of Christians will feel the pulls and tensions of their allure. The *Confessions* is a witness to those pulls, to the continual emotional dialectic that finds a Christian now certain in his love for God, now tempted by his love of earthly life and its attractive charms. The rhythm of this dialectic is preserved in the texture of allusion itself, in the ways the language of 1.13 points at the same time toward a Christian truth and a Virgilian moment, or in the ways 4.6 points to a spiritual corrective that is challenged in its Horatian context. Christian life is not easy. The sure solitude of the Psalms is never permanent. The Christian who is true to his own faith, to the love of God that he feels within him, will recognize the dialectical quality of Christian life. And if they are careful perceivers of their own limitations and imperfections, Christians will glimpse more securely their own frailties, and witness more intimately the majesty of God's perfection. If a Christian is to make his way in the world, fallen and imperfect as it—and he—may be, he is going to have to succumb, even knowingly, to the snares of temptation and of arrogance. The acknowledgment of imperfection, the ability to recognize error, places a Christian in a much firmer position relative to God, even if one consciously sins, knowingly errs. To act solely on the basis of proscription, after all, is to doubt the efficacy of faith itself, for if faith is efficacious, its truths, however imperfectly realized, will take the erring Christian farther than simple conformity will.

There is an air of paradox in such a view and, as always in the *Confessions*, the sentiment is personal and self-reflexive, conceived for Augustine more than for the community of believers. The function of allusion in the language of 4.6 also mirrors this paradox, for it offers a way of meditating on this problem at a distance, allusively, without being subsumed by it, recreating the dialectic of spirit and emotion that envelops Augustine in 4.6 both in a theological and a literary way. Augustine is able to suggest both the dilemma and the delight of the issue, to participate in the temptation of it, and to worry over the spiritual implications of it, to acknowledge the imperfection and the brazenness of his sin, and to learn from it in the process. Yet the paradox remains. The attractiveness of talking to God always subsists in the theological dilemmas it poses. But the glories of that attractiveness sometimes outweigh the spiritual perils, as Christian writers for a millennium would bear witness in their own portrayals of human personality and selfhood.

CONFESSIONS 4.7 AND ODES 2.16

> Quo enim cor meum fugeret a corde meo? Quo a me ipso fugerem? Quo non me sequerer? Et tamen fugi de patria. Minus enim eum quaerebant oculi mei, ubi videre non solebant, atque a Thagastensi oppido veni Carthaginem.
> —(Augustine, *Confessions* 4.7.19–22)

> (Where could my heart find refuge from itself? Where could I go, yet leave myself behind? Was there any place where I should not be a prey to myself? None. But I left my native town. For my eyes were less tempted to look for my friend in a place where they had not grown used to seeing him. So from Thagaste I went to Carthage.)

> quid brevi fortes iaculamur aevo
> multa? quid terras alio calentis
> sole mutamus? patriae quis exsul
>   se quoque fugit?
> —(Horace, *Odes* 2.16.17–20)

> (Why do we strive so hard in our brief lives for so much? Why do we change our own land for lands warmed by an alien sun? What exile from his country ever escaped himself as well?)

Confessions 4.6 considers the moral implications of confessional writing. The issue is broached but remains fundamentally unsolved. At *Confessions* 4.7, this issue is considered from another angle, and a solution is ventured. Its articulation centers on the function of writing as a source of spiritual sustenance. The theological dilemmas of confessional writing may be counterbalanced by the putative benefits confessional writing commends. Those benefits are postulated in the context of spiritual ennui, psychological flight, and the ability of writing to achieve for its practitioners a mental space divorced from the dictates and the tensions of the wider world. The Christian who writes in the confessional mode does more than offer autotelic and hubristic ruminations on human imperfection. This writer is also a seeker of the soul. The search fronted in writing can harbor undesirable spiritual consequences, but it also empowers a writer to create an inner space, a verbal reckoning of the soul's quiescence, where solitary contemplation can proceed.

Confessions 4.7 focuses on Augustine's attempts to construct this inner world. In the wake of the death of his best friend, so Augustine tells us, his soul was a burden, bruised, bleeding. Neither the charms of the countryside nor the sweet scents of nature could please it. Mental and spiritual peace were elusive: "[My soul] found no peace in song or laughter, none in the company of friends at table or in the pleasures of love, none even in books or poetry" (Non in amoenis nemoribus, non in ludis atque cantibus nec in suave olentibus locis nec in conviviis apparatis neque in voluptate cubilis et lecti, non denique in libris atque carminibus adquiescebat; *Conf.* 4.7.6–9).

As he moves on to consider his wretched state, Augustine remembers that he came to a point of no return, a proverbial dark night of the soul, where he could no longer flee from fleeing. Burdened by inner turmoil and repelled by outer distractions, Augustine decides to leave Thagaste for Carthage, replacing one city for another and returning thematically to *Confessions* 3.1, where he recalls his arrival in Carthage "in the midst of a hissing cauldron of lust" (Veni Carthaginem, et circumstrepebat me undique sartago flagitiosorum amorum; 3.1.1–2). Needless to say, Augustine did not find what he was seeking. Carthage represents the nadir of Augustine's spiritual life.

The plaints that form the concluding lines of 4.7, with their spiritual gloom and mental dissonances, are owed to Horace, *Odes* 2.16. This ode, too, centers on the issues of mental hygiene, spiritual peace, emotional consonance. The ode begins boldly with the triple anaphora of *otium,* which alludes to the final stanza of Catullus 51. The linkage preserves in the language of Horace's ode vestiges of loves won and lost that linger in Catullus's poem, but Horace follows Catullus in his shifting perspectives, since the allusion to 51 centers on the closing lines of Catullus's poem, which are divorced from the emotionally laden verses that precede it, and which focus on public and political settings. For his part, this shift of focus helps Catullus to specify the function of *otium* in his own life. It is, as we saw in the previous chapter, a double-edged sword. *Otium* has led to the affair with Lesbia, enabling Catullus to spend time with his lover and to plot strategies of seduction, offering the leisure for petting, kissing, and, eventually, consummation. But *otium* also offers the time for pained reflection of the kind that brings down kings and cities. *Otium* also is the sine qua non of poetry itself, affording to Catullus the opportunity to spend long hours swapping verses with friends or practicing his craft alone. *Otium* represents, in these ways, a comprehensive social, personal, and poetic space, and an analogous emotional and spiritual posture, at once symbolic of spiritual and physical repose and of emotional victimization.

These themes resonate in the *Confessions* by virtue of Augustine's allusion to *Odes* 2.16. In that poem, *otium* is a complex word, difficult to translate. The word is more comprehensive, as we shall see, than those meanings normally given it in English (something like "leisure," "peace," "freedom from care and trouble").[15] Fraenkel comes closest to describing the nuance of the word by suggesting that it embodies a private sort of wisdom.[16] The importance of Catullus 51 in 2.16 further complicates the meaning of the word, for Catullan *otium,* as we have seen, harbors connotations of both "leisure" and "peace of mind."[17] In 2.16, too, the word represents both a physical setting in which spiritual balance obtains and the mental equilibrium made possible by that physical setting. For Horace, however, writing is specifically located as the mechanism that helps to achieve *otium,* "peace of mind"; moreover, it is the most important action any human can pursue who finds himself with *otium,* "leisure," on his hands.

Horace plays upon the notion of outer and inner equilibrium by constructing in 2.16 key situations controlled, in addition to *otium,* by the phrases *tumultus mentis* (vv. 10–11) and *laetus animus* (v. 25). These, in turn, are controlled at the poem's conclusion by Horace's evocation of his small farm and delicate breath of the Greek Muses. Each of these images—*otium, tumultus*

15. See C. E. Bennett, *Horace: Odes and Epodes* (Boston, 1901), p. 292. See also A. Kiessling and R. Heinze, eds., *Q. Horatius Flaccus Oden und Epoden* (Berlin, 1930), p. 224, who see embodied in the opening of the ode "Das Lebensideal der hesuchia . . . der Zustand, wo luketai pas ho tes psuches cheimon," grounding the ode in Epicurean sentiment. But even they go on to admit that though "die curae spielen im römischen Denken eine viel grossere Rolle als im griechischen frontides or merimnai, bei H[oraz] sehr häufig alle Empfindugen umfassend, die, durch Gegenwärtiges oder Zukünftiges veranlasst, den Seelenfrieden stören"; cf. R. G. M. Nisbet and M. Hubbard, *A Commentary on Horace: Odes Book II* (Oxford, 1978), pp. 254–55; 258–59; and V. Pöschl, *Horazische Lyrik: Interpretationen* (Heidelberg, 1970), pp. 131–33.

16. E. Fraenkel, *Horace,* (Oxford, 1970), p. 214.

17. On which see J. A. Richmond, "Horace's 'Mottoes' and Catullus 51," *Rheinisches Museum* 113 (1970), pp. 197–204.

mentis, laetus animus, spiritum Graiae tenuem Camenae—is mutually inclusive: the *otium* of the opening stanzas leads Horace to consider at verses 10–11 the setting that best occasions the diminution of *tumultus mentis. Tumultus* is specified in another way at verse 25, where Horace considers the pleasures that make one's soul happy (*laetus animus*). Then these considerations are placed in a personal context at the ode's end, where the poet situates himself in relation to the preceding discussion. This collusion of public and private worlds will have, as we shall see, a special resonance in Augustine's search for spiritual peace in 4.7.

But Horace's ode begins with *otium,* a word whose function has long perplexed commentators.[18] Because *otium* functions in the larger context of the poem in close association with the images of *tumultus mentis* and *laetus animus,* it is easiest to garner the sense and function of this crucial word by allowing the later verses of the poem to control the ways in which this word functions. When so read, *otium* becomes a catch-all word, symbolizing human longing. We can approach this understanding of *otium* by considering in turn the figures who are said to pray for it at the onset. Horace gives three incongruous examples of figures who seek *otium.* Each figure is described in its own unique element. The man on the sea prays for *otium,* for example, when the clouds appear and the stars cannot be fixed in the sky. The Thracians, though maddened by war, seek *otium* also, as do the Medi, though they are armed with their quivers. We are also told, at the conclusion of this catalogue, that *otium,* whatever it is meant to symbolize, is something that cannot be bought.

Two qualities control the presentation of these figures. First, Horace moves

---

18. The scholarship on this ode has centered less on interpreting its lines and more on determining the authenticity of the so-called Cura-strophe, vv. 21–24. On this see Pöschl, *Horazische Lyrik,* pp. 122–42, who offers a history of the controversy, pp. 122–23, and nn. 1–5. This amounts to a reworking and expansion of his earlier paper, "Die Curastrophe der Otiumode des Horaz," *Hermes* 84 (1956), pp. 74–90. W. L. Liebermann, "Die Otium-Ode des Horaz (c. II.16)," *Latomus* 30 (1971), pp. 294–316, reconsiders the issue more recently. See also K. Latte, "Eine Ode des Horaz (II, 16)," *Philologus* 90 (1935), pp. 294–304; K. Barwick, "Drei Oden des Horaz," *Rheinisches Museum* 93 (1950), pp. 249–67. Latte and Barwick offer interesting structural rationales for preserving the ode as the ms. tradition gives it to us. Liebermann concurs. K. Büchner, "Horaz über die Gelassenheit," *Humanitas Romana* (Heidelberg, 1957), pp. 176–202, argues for the excising of the Cura-strophe altogether; on Büchner specifically see also the comments of Pöschl, p. 122, and the full bibliography there, n. 1. The translation of *Odes* 2.16 is by C. E. Bennett, *Horace: The Odes and Epodes* (Cambridge, Mass., and London, 1927), with some modifications.

from the personal consideration of a single figure, a sailor overtaken at sea (*prensus,* v. 2), to the general consideration of large groups of people who share a bond of temperament or birth, or both (*Thrace,* v. 5; *Medi,* v. 6). In this way, he highlights the comprehensive quality of the point he is about to make: it will touch everyone, either as individual or as part of the crowd. Second, these figures seek *otium* in incongruous contexts, for although it is not to be doubted that *otium* is a desirable thing for which to pray, the settings in which the sailor, the Thracians, and the Medi seek *otium* are hardly of a kind that ought to elicit prayers. Why, for example should a sailor at sea, the Thracians contemplating war, or the Medi armed with their characteristic quivers pray for *otium.* They are, after all, in their element, doing what they presumably want to do and do well. They are not in any sort of situation that ought to discomfit them; indeed, quite the opposite.

Because the external situation of these figures is in order, one must posit an internal disorder, a mental dissonance, in the figures named in the opening verses of 2.16. In this regard, one encounters in the sailor on the sea, the Medi, and the Thracians figures who are victimized by inner conflicts. This victimization is self-inflicted, a psychological dilemma, and it would seem, given the information offered in these lines, to center on the disparity between desires, which propel humans to action, and the insufficiency of achievements attained as a result of that action, which occasions a spiritual deficit, a longing for something after all that has been desired has been attained. This deficit ensures that happiness is elusive. Expectations outweigh actualities.[19]

Given this opening gambit, Horace's consideration of *tumultus mentis* in verses 10–11 is sensible. Having established a situation of discourse in which human longing is always incommensurate with human action, Horace begins to consider the dynamics of human psychology, the mental and spiritual space where longing gives way to action, where the inequality of desire to action is harbored: "For it is not treasure nor even the consul's lictor that can banish the wretched tumults of the soul and the cares that flit about the paneled ceilings" (non enim gazae neque consularis / summovet lictor miseros tumultus / mentis et curas laqueata circum / tecta volantis; vv. 9–12). Now the focus of the poem is internal, describing a mental setting where tumults and cares are immune to the glories of political power or the luxury that riches offer. All of the figures of the ode mentioned up to this point, therefore, are located in verses 10–11 in a psychological dynamic. Their prayers for peace are prayers for inner fortitude,

19. See H. Womble, "Horace's *Carmina* II.16," *AJP* 88 (1967), pp. 385–409, esp. 388.

mental consonance. And the attainment of this preferred mentality is not easy
to come by.

Some things assist in its attainment, however:

> vivitur parvo bene, cui paternum
> splendet in mensa tenui salinum
> nec levis somnos timor aut cupido
>   sordidus aufert.
> quid brevi fortes iaculamur aevo
> multa? Quid terras alio calentis
> sole mutamus? patriae quis exsul
>   se quoque fugit. (vv. 13–20)

(He lives happily upon a little on whose frugal board gleams the ancestral salt-dish,
and whose soft slumbers are not banished by fear or sordid greed. Why do we strive so
hard in our brief lives for so much? Why do we change our own land for lands
warmed by an alien sun? What exile from his country ever escaped himself as well?)

Living simply, for example, can assist one's search for *otium*. If one lives modestly, with a sparse table, unmolested by fear or base greed, then *otium* will
follow. The sleep extolled here is especially important, for it symbolizes the sort
of inner strength, the mental consonance, to which the prayers for *otium* speak.
The sleep of one who lives modestly is the healthy sleep of one whose desires are
commensurate with actions, whose aims in life and their achievement are
enough.

When Horace broaches the rhetorical questions of verses 17–20, therefore,
the symbology of the opening verses is focused onto a single situation with
universal application. The question asked in these lines is begged. Flight, of a
kind imagined in verses 1–8, is pointless. The sailor flitting over the sea wishes
he were somewhere else; the Medi and the Thracians, perched to march into
new territories for conquest or for skirmish, wish for something else. Unless one
reposes in peace in one's own mind, unless the *tumultus mentis et curas* are
controlled by a life whose desires and pursuits are in balance, no change of
physical surrounding is apt:

> scandit aeratas vitiosa navis
> Cura nec turmas equitum relinquit,
> ocior cervis et agente nimbos
>   ocior Euro.
> laetus in praesens animus quod ultra est   25
> oderit curare et amara lento

temperet risu; nihil est ab omni
    parte beatum.
abstulit clarum cita mors Achillem,
longa Tithonum minuit senectus,   30
et mihi forsan, tibi quod negarit,
    porriget hora. (vv. 21–32)

(Morbid care boards even the brass-bound galley, nor fails to overtake the troops of
horse, swifter than stags, swifter than Eurus when he drives the storm before him. Let
the soul be joyful in the present, let it disdain to be anxious for what the future has in
store, and temper bitterness with smile serene. Nothing is happy altogether. Achilles
for all his glory was snatched away by an early death; Tithonus, though granted a
long old age, wasted to a shadow; and to me maybe the passing hour will grant what it
denies to you.)

External flight is tautological. The cavalry on their swiftest horses will not
win the race with care, which is "swifter than stags" (vv. 22–23), and those who
cannot gain pleasure in attaining their desires, whose longings lead them
ceaselessly on to new pursuits that will be equally dissatisfying, run the risk of
repeating the histories of Achilles—whose longings were extinguished not by
internal consonance but an early death—and Tithonus—who achieved his
desire of eternal life without attaining eternal youth. This is why, Horace
suggests in verses 25–29, one must attend to the happiness of one's *animus,*
putting to the side worries over the future and bearing with a peaceful smile
whatever comes one's way.

This is a simple piece of wisdom, and, as often in Horace's poetry, the
simplicity harbors broad and profound implications. Those implications are
found in the final stanzas of the ode, where Horace locates his ode's wisdom in
the context of his own life:

te greges centum Siculaeque circum
mugiunt vaccae, tibi tollit hinnitum
apta quadrigis equa, te bis Afro
    murice tinctae
vestiunt lanae: mihi parva rura et
spiritum Graiae tenuem Camenae
Parca non mendax dedit et malignum
    spernere vulgus. (vv. 33–40)

(Around you low a hundred herds of Sicilian kine; in your stables whinnies the
racing-mare; you are clothed in wool twice dipped in African purple. To me Fate that
does not belie her name has given a small domain, but she has vouchsafed the fine
breath of Grecian song and a scorn for the envious crowd.)

Grosphus, the recipient of the ode, and Horace, its author, are contrasted in these lines. Although the connection between the disatisfied figures of prior lines and Grosphus is not explicitly made, the distinction between Grosphus's luxuriant prosperity, his herds, sleek horses, and expensive clothes, and Horace's simple farm makes such a connection obvious. The ode functions, in this sense, as a missive, proffering wisdom, extolling a spiritual position, offering order to a difficult human problem.

That order centers, as it must, on the difference between internal and external palliatives. Grosphus, with his estate, like the sailor flittering on the sea, or the Medi or the Thracians about to march to war, or any *exsul* who has fled himself, only worsens the problem he seeks to alleviate by flight, especially if that flight is external, involving the movement from one place to another. The sure wisdom of verses 19–20 affirms the futility of this sort of flight in no uncertain terms: "What exile from his own country ever fled himself as well?" Verse 20, *se quoque fugit*, which is the midpoint of the poem, its crux both thematically and structurally, is a crisp rejoinder to all those who would seek *otium* externally. The antidote to this sort of flight is offered by Horace in the example of his own life. He is ensconced on the Sabine farm. And though he, as he himself makes clear, flees to this farm to spurn the crowd, his wandering, unlike the crowd's, is to himself and to the delicate breath of the Greek Muse. His flight, in other words, is to writing.

The final adonic line of the ode, *spernere vulgus,* is a loaded phrase that suggests much about Horace's own spiritual dynamic that remains unstated in the poem's discourse. The crowd is an all-purpose symbol in this line. On the one hand, it represents the setting from which Horace seeks respite. In another way, however, it represents something more sinister. Crowd psychology is a perilous force. People will do in crowds what they would never do as individuals. One thing that the crowd does that Horace rejects is partake of the wearisome pursuit for more than what they already possess. They seek, as the earlier verses of the poem suggest, to be happy, they seek *otium,* but what they seek is never consonant with what they attain. The dissonance is a function of spiritual ignorance. Happiness cannot exist lacking the balance of desire and action, and that balance is attained only through self-examination and inner reflection. And this is why writing is important. For Horace, self-examination and inner reflection are mediated by writing, by the delicate breath of Greek poetry. Writing functions as a mechanism of spiritual equilibrium, made possible by a life of *otium,* but offering as its most cherished effect a mental *otium* that neither the crowd, nor Grosphus, can fathom.

The *otium* Horace extols in 2.16 is translated in the play of allusive space to *Confessions* 4.7. The situation of discourse of 4.7 centers on a theological point, but allusion reveals a larger issue at stake, centering on the function and effects of writing in the attainment of spiritual peace. Writing, as we have seen, is enough for Horace. Writing is restorative, curative. It allows for the creation of an inner world, where the benefits of *otium* are realized. One of the chief benefits of writing is psychological consonance, what contemporary readers might call a stable conception of self. For Horace, selfhood is constituted in writing, enabling the objectifying forces of the crowd, which harbor more peril than benefit, to be replaced by language's ability to assist in the development of self-conception. In this way, the differing kinds of flight imagined by Horace in 2.16, which reflect analogous flights from self-knowledge, are checked. Writing makes any and all forms of flight unnecessary.

Augustine, as we have seen in 4.7, pines in a way identical to the figures imagined by Horace in his poem, seeking externally the *otium* that seems so elusive. Augustine flees to Carthage in the same way that the *exsul patriae* exchanges for his country lands "burning with an alien sun" (2.16.18–19). The result, as Augustine reports subsequently in 4.8 is error: "My greatest comfort and relief was in the solace of other friends who shared my love of the huge fable which I loved instead of you, my God, the long-drawn lie which our minds were always itching to hear, only to be defiled by its adulterous caress" (Maxime quippe me reparabant atque recreabant aliorum amicorum solacia, cum quibus amabam quod pro te amabam, et hoc erat ingens fabula et longum mendacium, cuius adulterina confricatione corrumpebatur mens nostra pruriens in auribus; 4.8.9–13). This powerful statement of spiritual ennui and misalliance alludes to 2 Timothy 4:3, which cautions against the lies of teachers who spread "deceitful spirits and doctrines of devils." The teachers implicitly meant here are the various false prophets of astrology and Manicheanism. The antidote to false teaching and spiritual error, so Timothy continues, is piety and appropriate shepherding by a pastor. This antidote leads, in turn, in Augustine's narrative, to spiritual deliverance, reckoned in no uncertain terms at *Confessions* 4.10 in the words of Psalm 79:8: "O God of hosts, restore us to our own; smile upon us, and we shall find deliverance, for wherever the soul of man may turn, unless it turns to you, its clasps sorrow to itself. Even though it clings to things of beauty, if their beauty is outside God and outside the soul, it only clings to sorrow" (Deus virtutum, converte nos et ostende faciem tuam, et salvi erimus. Nam quoquoversum se verterit anima hominis ad dolores figitur alibi praeterquam in te, tametsi figitur in pulchris extra te et extra se).

One could not ask for a more succinct resume of the spiritual assumptions of *Odes* 2.16: the false allure of external luxury and beauty contrasted to inner peace and consonance, the dichotomy between outer and inner worlds, the sorrow occasioned by the glories of the larger world, even the mention of the smile of God, recalling Horace's *lentus risus* (vv. 26–27). Horace and Augustine are in virtual agreement on the dynamics that underpin human happiness. They diverge only in assigning a cause for that happiness. For Augustine the cause is divine. This does not lessen the importance of spiritual examination and self-reflection, but it makes the arduous journey of self less harrowing. For Horace, no cause is recommended other than the need of humans to attain spiritual solitude.

Causes aside, both Horace and Augustine are witnesses to the efficacy of writing in the search for spiritual consonance, and this would seem to be the main point revealed in the play of allusive space. Because Horace recommends the Greek Muses as the antidote to spiritual lassitude, one can see in Augustine's allusion to 2.16 a similar appeal. Questions about writing's moral and theological currency, raised allusively in a Horatian context in 4.6, are now reconsidered. The bogeys of absurdity, hubris, *audacia* are replaced by firmer notions of writing's function and benefits. Not only is writing aesthetically compelling; it is also theologically necessary. Writing serves in turn as a mechanism of self-expression and, in the face of an all-powerful and ultimately intangible god, as the only available means by which an imperfect Christian may approach the sublimeness of God's truth.

In this way, writing implies for a Christian an economy of divine ascent: one harbors, in theological terms, the love of God in one's soul. That love is, in the excellent phrase given us by Paulinus of Nola, "a silent music played upon the soul's cithara." One feels this love constantly in the pangs of desire, emotion, longing. But feeling is not enough, as the history of Augustine's own journey to God in the *Confessions* makes clear. The love that he feels for his dead friend, in fact, is but one of many examples in the *Confessions* of the stirrings of divine love in the soul. To get from the point of feeling to the point of knowledge is a difficult, arduous procedure. Yet, until one is conscious of the source of love and can act on the dictates established by that love, spiritual consonance and happiness are impossible. Contemplation occasions this consciousness, the process of restoration and slow deliverance that Augustine recommends, in the words of the psalmist, at the beginning of 4.10. Augustine suggests in the play of allusive space that written contemplation is a vital component of human understanding in Christian terms, that writing, far from trivializing spiritual problems and skewing one's focus away from God, is the only means for a Christian to proceed from feeling God's love to understanding it, and, having understood it, to act upon it.

Writing is vital for other reasons made clear in allusion's space also. As Horace suggests, writing centers one's attention onto the self, because writing is a self-reflective process. It is also a personal process, engaging both emotion and reason through the filter of personal experience. As writing centers one's attention on the internal dynamics of feeling and perception, a slow awareness of the sources of those feelings and the constructions of those perceptions emerges. We see this process at work both in Horace's ode, which moves from exotic locales to the delicate breath of writing itself, and in *Confessions* 4.7, where Augustine slowly shifts his attention from outer turmoil and the insufficiencies of the world to an inner space where flight becomes unnecessary.

Augustine, like Horace, flees to writing. Horace flees the crowd and reposes with Greek poetry. Augustine flees to the *Confessions*—and also, at least in 4.6 and 4.7, to the lyrics of Horace. Pronouns offer a sure gauge to the efficacy of either author's flights to writing. Horace includes himself in the rhetorical question asked in verses 17–18: "Why do we strive so hard in our brief lives for so much?" (quid brevi fortes iaculamur aevo / multa?). Then he shifts, at verse 37, to a personal pronoun: "Fate has given to me a small farm and Greek Muses." The wisdom of the ode, the spiritual benefits of writing that it recommends, is achieved on a personal level in the poem's situation of discourse. One leaves Horace alone, on his farm, with his poetry, apart from the crowd and all its ill-begotten cares and misplaced seekings.

Augustine also moves from a public and external space to an inner space in 4.7. We find him at the beginning of this chapter pining over the inability of anything in the world to please his bruised soul. The countryside, the sweet smells of the garden, song, laughter, even friendship, leave him cold. As he proceeds to the point near the end of 4.7 where he alludes to Horace, however, the focus is altered and the vision becomes internalized. External forms are replaced by a concern for internal consonance. The vocabulary he uses highlights this flight to an inner space, symbolizing Augustine's concentration on his own situation and its implications in the most personal of terms. There is literally an expression of self for every line of this chapter, confirming for readers that confessional writing leads to a confrontation of self and, by implication, a confrontation with God, however imperfectly rendered.[20] There can be in a

---

20. The words in question are: *ego, eram, aestuabam, suspirabam, flebam, turbabar, portabam,*

passage of spiritual loss and deprivation no clearer measure of writing's benefits, for while the narrative of the passage tells a story of spiritual exile and emotional wandering, the language of the passage reveals the extent to which writing has shifted its author's focus, offering a cure for exile and wandering. The "I," the self, that Augustine seeks in this passage is, if not found, then at least created in the act of writing, and that is at least half of the hard work that must be done in the difficult search for *otium*.

By implication, therefore, writing empowers selfhood, gives to it a form and creates in the process a medium by which meditation, contemplation, and even ascent can be realized. This, too, is a flight, but it is, in Horace's terms, the appropriate kind of flight. And even though the Augustine of 4.7 did go on to flee in an inappropriate way, hustling to Carthage to escape his desolation, Augustine the converted Christian recalls this moment in his life from the wiser purview offered by *otium*, confirming its presence in his own life in the comprehensive and satisfying context revealed in the play of allusion's space.

Through the process of full-knowing reading, then, dissonant moments in Augustine's life are, like the contradictions of Scripture, mediated by a powerful reader, in the same way that the wounded body of Christ is healed by the soothing balm of *caritas*. This process by which consonance is reached is intimately bound up with the textualizing of Augustine's own life, with the empowerment of Augustine himself as the reader, the healer, of his own wounded body. But consonance is a sweet and fragile thing, carefully, painfully achieved in the *Confessions*. It is dissonance that abides. The story of the straight and narrow path traveled, gloriously, perfectly, to God, is not possible here, for Augustine has wandered long and hard, though, in the words of the psalmist, these have been the wanderings of a Christian true to himself: "My steps have been steadfast in your paths, my feet have not faltered . . . that I might behold your face and be content in your presence."[21]

---

me, ponerem, inveniebam, sciebam, volebam, valebam, cogitabam, meus, conabar, me, ego, mihi, remanseram, possem, meo, me, fugerem, me, sequerer, fugi, veni.

21. Ps. 16:5, 15, with minor alterations.

Chapter 7 The Unhealable Wound:
Abelard, Ovid, and Lucan

Unde vehementer indignati et adversum me coniurati, nocte quadam, quiescentem me atque dormientem in secreta hospitii mei camera, quodam mihi serviente per pecuniam corrupto, crudelissima et pudentissima ultione punierunt, et quam summa admiratione mundus excepit, eis videlicet corporis mei partibus amputatis quibus id quod plangebant commiseram. Quibus mox in fugam conversis, duo, qui comprehendi potuerunt, oculis et genitalibus privati sunt;

(Wild with indignation they plotted against me and one night as I slept peacefully in an inner room in my lodgings, they bribed one of my servants to admit them and there took cruel vengeance on me of such appalling barbarity as to shock the whole world; they cut off the parts of my body whereby I had committed the wrong of which they complained. Then they fled, but the two who could be caught were blinded and castrated.)—Peter Abelard, *Historia Calamitatum*

Readers of Peter Abelard's epistolary autobiography, the *Historia Calamitatum,* are familiar with these lines, the famous scene of castration, in which the arrogant Abelard is given his comeuppance at the hands of the henchmen of Fulbert of Chartres, the aggrieved uncle of

Abelard's lover, Heloise.[1] It would be more accurate, however, to call this a scene of *castrations*, for Abelard also remembers in these lines that two of Fulbert's henchmen were mutilated in the same way for their crime. It is easy enough to overlook these secondary mutilations in the glare of Abelard's own wounding, which so readily dominates the interpretive fabric woven here. More difficult to overlook are the rhetorical differences attending to these castrations.

The description of the henchmen's injury is vivid and direct: there can be no doubting the meaning of the declaration that the "two who could be caught were blinded and castrated" (duo, qui comprehendi potuerunt, oculis et genitalibus privati sunt). By distinction, Abelard's description of his own castration is a tissue of subterfuge. *Genitalis* is not used, nor is the strong verb *privare*. Instead, Abelard renders his wounding in a periphrasis dependent upon a relative clause that explains his disfigurement in the context of its perpetrators' displeasure: "they cut off the parts of my body whereby I had committed the wrong of which they complained" (corporis mei partibus amputatis quibus id quod plangebant commiseram). The descriptive bluntness attaching to the

1. My text is J. T. Muckle, C.S.B., "Abelard's Letter of Consolation to a Friend (Historia Calamitatum)," *Medieval Studies* 12 (1950), pp. 163–213, cited using page numbers (Muckle has no line numbers in his edition). Translations are from B. Radice, trans., *The Letters of Abelard and Heloise* (Harmondsworth, 1974). The *Historia* is properly the first of eight letters that presumably passed between Abelard and Heloise. The first letter was not called the *Historia Calamitatum* by Abelard (although by Petrarch's time the title *Historia Suarum Calamitatum* was in wide use); more probably, a working title for the *Historia* in the century after Abelard's death was *Ad Amicum suum Consolatoria* (though this would not seem to be owed to Abelard, either; see Muckle, p. 163). There are nine mss. of the letters, none of which is earlier than the late thirteenth century. There is no independent ms., so far as is known, of the *Historia Calamitatum*, although Heloise speaks of possessing one in *Ep.* 2. The letters were brought out in the thirteenth century, presumably based on a collection of documents pertaining to the Paraclete that came directly from Heloise (this is the argument offered by R. W. Southern, "The Letters of Heloise and Abelard," in *Medieval Humanism and Other Studies* [Oxford, 1970], p. 103). Editions of the letters appeared in 1616 (by d'Amboise and by Duchesne), 1718 (Rawlinson), 1841 (Orelli, includes only the *Historia* and the personal letters), and 1849 (Cousin). There is also an edition (really d'Amboise's text with Duchesne's notes) by J.-P. Migne in *PL*, vol. 178 (Paris, 1853). In addition to his version of the *Historia*, J. T. Muckle has edited six of the letters in *Medieval Studies* 15 (1953), pp. 47–94 (letters 1–4); 17 (1955), pp. 240–281 (letters 5–6). Letter 7, edited by T. P. McLaughlin, is in *Medieval Studies* 18 (1956), pp. 241–92. J. Monfrin, ed., *Historia Calamitatum: Texte critique avec introduction* (Paris, 1962) is a more recent edition. Many translations of the letters exist. For a complete accounting see Radice, *Letters of Abelard and Heloise*, pp. 50–55, itself a translation of the first order.

castration of Fulbert's thugs evanesces in Abelard's rendition of his own castration into a simple "cutting of body parts." It is no exaggeration to say that without the relative clause, "that which they complained" (*id quod plangebant*), the sort of cutting performed on Abelard would be difficult to determine.[2]

The way in which Abelard describes his castration might be credited to modesty or to the painful nature of the recollection, were it not for the presence in virtually the same sentence of an identical image rendered so much more concretely, and for the obvious rhetorical polish attaching to this passage, which lessens considerably the chance that the reminiscence is somehow too much to endure. Nor would Abelard's choice of words seem to be owed to some desire to use a vocabulary beholden to the standards of sacred Scripture. As Abelard himself makes plain not too many lines later in quoting from the Old Testament teachings on castration, scriptural language is precise and frank in its descriptions of castration. Importantly, the key word used by Abelard in his rendering of his own castration, *corpus,* is nowhere to be found in the scriptural passages Abelard cites. Readers take from this passage, therefore, a vivid image of Abelard's own wounded *corpus,* rather than a specific vision of castration.

My claim in this chapter is that Abelard focuses on the word *corpus* in rendering his castration in order to evoke the Augustinian program of Christian reading, which, as we have seen, makes the wounded *corpus* and a powerful reader the centerpieces of its design. His aim is doing so is to press a fundamental analogy: that his body, like Christ's, has been wounded and is in need of healing.[3] This analogy works historically, as a means to affirm Abelard's own view of the severity of his wounds, for they appear now as analogous to Christ's wounds, as Abelard becomes a Christ figure, harshly and unfairly criticized and scourged. But it also functions in the rhetorical and literary senses established by Augustine, in which the wounded body of Christ becomes the wounded text of Scripture, whose wounds, the contradictions and logical gaps inherent in Scripture itself, require healing through interpretation. Now, however, it is not Scripture that requires healing, but Abelard's own life story, the *Historia* itself.

In Scripture, of course, the wounds of the text are inherent in the narrative

2. Indeed, the margin of ms. T contains a gloss in the second hand that reads, "De plaga illa corporis quomodo scilicet castratus est." See Muckle, p. 190 and nn. 16a and 17.

3. My views on corporeality, especially with respect to Abelard and Heloise, are much indebted to the important work of S. Spence, *Texts and the Self in the Twelfth Century* (Cambridge, 1996). On recent approaches to the body more generally, see L. Lomperis and S. Stanbury, eds., *Feminist Approaches to the Body in Medieval Literature* (Philadelphia, 1993).

fabric. One expects a multiauthored work written over the course of centuries to present problems of interpretation, to be, at the very least, internally inconsistent. By distinction, Abelard's *Historia,* written by him in mature retrospect, could offer no such ready-made inconsistencies. The wounds of this newer text, therefore, needed to be introduced carefully by its author—and allusion supplies these wounds.

But it is allusion of a special sort, for Abelard confects the *Historia'*s allusions from quoted material, often announcing the source of the language directly or otherwise drawing attention to the fact that the words he is about to use are not his own. Abelard's use of quoted material makes good sense, to be sure. Quotations, after all, are *literal* wounds to the text in which they are placed, that is, they are obvious and self-announced "cuts" to the body of the text. In the *Historia,* therefore, they remain a visually striking reminder of the physical cuts Abelard suffered to his real body at the same time that they function rhetorically as wounds to his textual body that require healing—interpretation. Moreover, the interpretations sanctioned by these allusions are consistent with the larger themes of the *Historia.* As the sections below will suggest, a cohort of passages from Lucan's *De bello civili* and Ovid's *Metamorphoses, Amores,* and *Remedia amoris* link to moments in ancient Latin poetry in which cutting, wounding, passion, and emotion figure prominently—precisely the themes of Abelard's own life. I begin with a cluster of allusions to the work of Ovid, which situate the emotional state of Abelard more securely in the opening lines of the *Historia,* before turning to consider Abelard's allusions to Lucan's *De bello civili,* where the psychological and spiritual stakes of Abelard's own life are vetted more fully in the play of allusive space.

OVID IN THE OPENING LINES OF THE *HISTORIA CALAMITATUM*

The first hundred or so lines of the *Historia* take the reader through the early controversies Abelard experienced with his teachers, recount his own successes as a teacher himself, and conclude with Abelard's recollection of his initial plans to insinuate himself into the household of Heloise. These lines form a coherent narrative, cohesive as to topic and form, the details of which center on a cluster of stock images—most important, military imagery associated with intellectual activity. The first thing we learn about Abelard's father, for example, was that he "had acquired some knowledge of letters before he was a soldier" (Patrem autem habebam litteris aliquantulum imbutum antequam militari cingulo insigniretur). We are then told that later on his passion for learning was such "that he intended all his sons to have instruction in letters before they were trained to arms" (Unde postmodum tanto litteras amore complexus est ut quoscumque filios haberet litteris antequam armis instrui disponeret).

The first thing we learn about Abelard, too, is that he fell so in love with learning that he renounced the glory of a soldier's life, gave up his rights of inheritance as his father's eldest son, and "withdrew from the court of Mars in order to kneel at the feet of Minerva" (Martis curiae pentius abdicarem ut Minervae gremio educarer). More important than the renouncing of wordly arms is the transference of those arms in symbolic terms to the world of scholarship. Philosophical and theological pursuits become the venues for intellectual battle. The weapons of dialectic, Abelard says, "I preferred over all the other teachings of philosophy, and armed with these, I chose the conflicts of disputation instead of the trophies of war" (Et quoniam dialecticarum rationum armaturam omnibus philosophiae documentis praetuli, his armis alia commutavi et trophaeis bellorum conflictus praetuli disputationum).

These lines are carefully constructed so as to articulate an intellectual arming of sorts. The young knight is now equipped, prepared to go on the attack or to defend himself, as need be. Like a true peripatetic, he travels from place to place, seeking the arms of other philosophers, battling for ideas, gaining strength, testing new strategies and maneuvers. Importance attaches in these lines to details: only enemies are named, and they are figured as players on opposing fields. William of Champeaux, who inhabits the heights that Abelard seeks to reach, is identified carefully several times by name because he is such a fierce enemy. William has soldiers, too, the other students, who gain their identity through their attachment to him and his growing irritation with Abelard.

Arms, of course, lead to war, and the battle lines are eventually drawn over a proposed school that Abelard seeks to found at Melun. William uses all the means at his disposal to thwart Abelard's plans, but Abelard wins this battle and eventually, so he says, the fame of William contracted and died away, whereupon Abelard transferred his school to Corbeil, nearer to Paris, then was forced from the battle scene by ill health. William, meanwhile, carefully manipulates his next moves like a tactician planning an offensive. He is wounded, but not mortally so. A showdown comes not much later.

The two combatants circle each other soon enough over a philosophical dispute that Abelard easily wins. His victory is well received, so Abelard reports, and William's successor as the head of the Paris school, a man carefully left unnamed because he is not an enemy, offers Abelard his own chair. William is, of course, enraged, and his aggression and violence do justice to any epic hero. He is eaten up with envy (*invidia*), burning with angry pain (*dolor*). Furylike, he hounds the unnamed successor who put Abelard in his old chair, eventually forcing Abelard to leave Paris and to return to Melun.

At the apogee of William's *invidia* and *dolor*, Abelard turns to Ovid for verbal assistance, noting that the more William's envy pursued him, the more famous Abelard became: "the more his jealousy pursued me, the more widely my reputation spread, for, as Ovid says: 'envy seeks the heights, the winds sweep the summits'" (quanto manifestius eius me persequebatur invidia, tanto mihi auctoritatis amplius conferebat iuxta illud poeticum: Summa petit livor, perflant altissima venti; *Hist. Cal.*, p. 179). Here, the *invidia* of William becomes the measure of Abelard's success in climbing to the summit, and Ovid's words (from *Remedia amoris* 1.369) assist readers in reaching that summit directly. The major themes of Ovid's *Remedia* now infiltrate the *Historia*—in particular, the appropriate topics one might treat in writing, charges made by enemies, the delight of fame, and love (*amor*). The first three of these themes are easily applicable to Abelard in the context of the *Historia* already established, for Abelard's autobiography treats each of these subjects in its opening lines. It is perhaps surprising, however, to encounter the fourth theme, love, at this stage of the *Historia*, for this is a topic not taken up directly in the *Historia* until dozens of lines later. The prominence of this theme in Ovid's poem, however, makes it difficult to suppress its resonance at this point in the *Historia*.

Ovid's larger purpose in the *Remedia*, of course, is to disentangle lovers from love's snares. His injunction at verse 358 that "love needs to be fled" sums up his work's grand theme. But the resonance of this allusion in the *Historia* is somewhat broader than this injunction allows. The theme of amorous avoidance is present allusively in the *Historia* through this quotation, to be sure, but so too is the more palatable notion that love is a prominent quality of life, even at the summit of philosophical success. In making love a central topic in a place we do not necessarily expect to find it, at or near the summit of philosophical prominence, then, this allusion establishes an important connection between what are commonly held to be competing identities in Abelard. Here, at least, Abelard the philosopher and Abelard the lover are configured as discrete aspects of one identity.

Emotion, if not love, figures prominently in subsequent lines of the *Historia*, as the battles between William and Abelard continue. Each ratchets up the intensity of their disputes, while vying for the allegiance of students and the intellectual high ground from which to launch further assaults. Abelard describes this latest (and final) series of run-ins with William as sieges launched against an enemy. Eventually, William abandons his school and is converted to the monastic life. Further skirmishes carried out between William's supporters and Abelard's followers lead only to the ultimate victory of Abelard. His final success is qualified through an allusion to another passage from Ovid, this time drawn from the *Metamorphoses* (13.89–90), where the words Abelard assumes are Ajax's: "And I shall not go too far if I boldly say with Ajax that . . . 'if you demand the issue of this fight, I was not vanquished by my enemy'"(Illud vero Aiacis, ut temperantius loquar, audacter proferam: . . . si quaeritis huius / Fortunam pugnae, non sum superatus ab illo; *Hist. Cal.,* p. 180).

With this allusion, several of the interpretive threads suggested thus far in the *Historia* begin to form a tighter fabric. The imagery of battle is confirmed in the recollection of one of Western's literature's great soldiers. The theme of self-assessment is also broached, however, for Ajax pursues in these lines the arms of Achilles, the prize he seeks most of all, in the same way that Abelard has described himself as hankering after the trophies of professional success. Yet in transferring his own narrative into the mouth of Ajax, Abelard does more here than simply offer up old words for fresh interpretation. Indeed, the larger Ovidian story evoked by these words changes the context of the *Historia Calamitatum* violently, conjuring up images of suicide, mental dissonance, and cutting, images that will have important places not too much later in the *Historia*.

The lines quoted by Abelard are, in their Ovidian context, spoken by Ajax to the Greek chieftains as Ajax begins to articulate his claim to the arms of Achilles. The specific context is Ajax's own estimation of his duel with Hector, in which Ajax came out the better. Much more than bravado informs the lengthy speech Ajax delivers here, however, of which Abelard has snatched but a few lines. Ajax's words flow freely and Odysseus comes in for considerable criticism as the issue shifts from past glories to present insults. Ajax appears, in Ovid's rendering, a boisterous, bitter, envious figure, a great fighter, a good talker, passionate, flawed. He is, in short, all of the things Abelard has shown himself to be in the *Historia* thus far. The connections of temperament seem even starker in the light of Abelard's careful construction of himself as a soldier, since the Ovidian context hinges on the exploits and details of lives spent in contention.

As much as Ajax is a glorious soldier of impressive power and talent, however, it cannot be forgotten that Ovid's narrative is not a victory yarn but the story of a suicide. Ovid's comment is apt: "pain conquered the unconquered hero" (invictumque virum vicit dolor; v. 386). Of a sudden, in the play of allusive space, a cluster of images and themes intrudes on the *Historia*. Where formerly Abelard could consider the function of emotion at the summit of philosophical prominence, now he is evinced as a figure saying bold and fearless words, but lunging simultaneously toward an end fraught with pain and grief. That end is rendered, moreover, entirely in internal terms. *Dolor* conquers Ajax just it wracked the mind of William of Champeaux. William went, so Abelard tells us, to a monastery. Abelard will continue on, superficially bold, until, like Ajax, he too is cut by a sword. Abelard's wound, unlike Ajax's, is not self-inflicted, nor does he die from it. But this allusion brings into high relief images of cutting and wounding, and makes starker the symbol of the wounded *corpus* in the *Historia*.

SUBLIMIS QUERCUS: LUCAN AND ABELARD

A few lines after comparing himself to Ajax, Abelard offers another analogy, likening his old master of theology, Anselm of Laon, to a rotting tree by alluding to Lucan's[4] *De bello civili:*

> Ad hanc itaque cum accessissem ut fructum inde colligerem, deprehendi illam esse ficulneam cui maledixit Dominus, seu illam veterem quercum cui Pompeium Lucanus comparat, dicens:
>
> Stat magni nominis umbra,
> Qualis frugifero quercus sublimis in agro . . . .[5] (*Hist. Cal.,* p. 180)

> ("I had come to this tree [Anselm] to gather fruit, but I found it was the fig tree which the Lord cursed, or the ancient oak to which Lucan compares Pompey: There stands the shadow of a noble name, like a tall oak in a field of corn . . . .")

Abelard fronts this comparison initially, however, not by referring to the oak that represents Anselm, but by recalling the fig tree of the Lord. The introduction of this tree into the narrative of the *Historia* is important in the context of

4. P. von Moos, "Lucan und Abaelard," in G. Cambier, ed., *Hommages à André Boutemy,* Collection Latomus 145 (Brussels, 1976), p. 415, proves the close reliance of Abelard on Lucan's text, not on florilegia or some second-hand collection. Lucan always appears in the medieval handlists of the school curriculum; more important, all of the books of the *De bello civili* are used in quotation in both the prose and poetry of the twelfth century. See more generally J. Crosland, "Lucan in the Middle Ages," *Modern Language Review* 25 (1930), pp. 32–51, and also B. Marti, "Literary Criticism in Medieval Commentaries on Lucan," *TAPA* 72 (1941).

5. Muckle, p. 180

the previous Ovidian allusions, for the fig tree personifies the commission of original sin—Adam and Eve hid their nakedness from the Lord under fig leaves. It thereby accentuates the theme of hidden intentions and the conflicts that arise from human passions, themes the Ovidian allusions take up directly. In a context that already harbors allusively the idea that one cannot flee from oneself, the symbolism of the fig tree is apt. God knows all; nothing can be hidden from him. So, too, as the history of Ajax attests, is it impossible to hide from oneself. This is why we are, or often become, like Ajax, our own mortal enemies. The fig tree intimates the power of human self-reflection, then, and the importance of self-knowledge. At the same time, the image of one tree that symbolizes the failure of deception leads naturally to another, similar tree, the rotten oak found in the first book of Lucan's *De bello civili.*

This tree is equally deceptive, but for less obvious reasons. The ostensible role of the allusion is affirmative for Abelard's life. Anselm is established in the *Historia* as a famous, if elderly, figure. Abelard is almost immediately disappointed with him, however, for his reputation seems greater than his talents. Sustained exposure confirms Abelard's belief that Anselm is the purveyor of blue smoke and mirrors. There is little to recommend him anymore except, perhaps, his past successes. Like a great but dying tree, he stands, as if by habit, stately and ominous, but entirely benign. Given these qualities, it seems apt to symbolize Anselm as a rotten tree in order to conclude the metaphor of fruit gathering that represents Abelard's search for theological answers. The answers he seeks cannot be found, because the "tree of knowledge" from which he seeks nourishment is but a husk. By distinction, Abelard would appear in these lines to be the vigorous upstart, ready to reject the past and forge defiantly and confidently into the future.

The play of allusion's space muddles this seemingly easy foray into the future, however, for the connection of Anselm and Pompey, as against the presence of a young and vigorous Abelard, requires the introduction of Caesar into the interpretive fabric of the *Historia,* since Caesar is a dominant presence in Lucan's poem, where his actions counterbalance the waffling and incertitude of Pompey. In the process of making these necessary connections, the ostensible affirmation of Abelard's ascendancy is undercut.

The allusion to the first book of the *De bello civili* renders the roles played by Abelard and by Anselm in the larger fabric of human volition and the psychology of human discord that dominates Lucan's poem.[6] It takes Lucan but a few

6. My text is D. R. Shackleton Bailey, ed., *M. Annaei Lucani De Bello Civili* (Stuttgart, 1988).

verses to move from "wars more than civil" (Bella . . . plus quam civilia; v. 1); to the haunting images of suicide, recalling now the allusion to Ajax; then to Nero (the latest and best representative of such images); then to the issue of peace, which is scarcely sustained; then, finally, to discord, which is the norm in human activity. Into this matrix of philosophical and historical musings Pompey is introduced at verse 135, the first of Lucan's "heroes," and the antidote to Caesar, who is introduced a few lines later (v. 143).

With the introduction of Pompey and Caesar, Lucan shifts his focus from the inherent discords of human history to the psychology that would seem to make discord possible and ensure its dominance in human history.[7] The focus is now narrowed from universal to particular concerns, centering on these two

7. Such imaginings fill much of the *De bello civili.* Lucan's description of human life, which is cast in terms of the *concordia discors,* is a prominent example. The prevalent quality of human life is discernible only in terms of *discordia.* It is not simply happenstance that whenever concord is mentioned in book 1 it is always "bad" (e.g., "O male concordes," v. 87) nor is it mere coincidence that *concordia* in general is unattainable in the *De bello civili.* The ending of book 9 addresses the failures of concord in the lament of Caesar that "concordia mundo / nostra perit" (9.1097–98), and elsewhere Lucan suggests the inability to achieve *concordia* in even the best of circumstances. Even a casual examination of the words *discors* or *discordia* in the *De bello civili* demonstrates the permeation of this condition in the worlds Lucan creates. For *discordia* see esp. 2.272, 6.780, and 9.217 (and, less importantly, 5.299 and 646); on *discors* see, apart from 1.79,98,266, and 589, 3.313, 6.687, 7.198. *Discordia* is present even in the underworld in book 6 (vv. 780 ff.). It is present also at the beginning of book 10—the very point in the poem where discord would seem to be at an end—where Lucan makes Caesar sense discord in the breasts of those he is about to address in Egypt. Lucan shapes this scene not only because the particular concords of the triumvirs were based on fictions and deceptions, but also because concord, on account of human nature, cannot abide. Lucan's apt comment is that "Magnumque perisse / non sibi" (vv. 12–13). Caesar—nobody—can escape *discordia* so well represented by Pompey, not even his survivors, who by virtue of their survival contain *discordia* within their breasts. Such a view is corroborated in book 4, when Lucan depicts friend running out to greet friend from behind opposing ramparts (4.196 ff.). The intent of these lines would seem to be less to extol the possibility of such a concord than to highlight the impossibility of concord under the best of circumstances. Lucan's own reading of history leads him immediately to crash this vision of *concordia* to the ground. In the following verses (4.205 ff.) the brutal images of Petreius dominate, who, though he is a partisan of Pompey, comes to represent something other than lines of battle formerly drawn. At this juncture, Lucan transcends the political or historical aims of his poem to condemn, with equal weight, though by different means, the human participants in this scene who have failed. My readings of Lucan are much indebted to W. R. Johnson, *Momentary Monsters: Lucan and His Heroes* (Ithaca and London, 1987).

figures. Neither figure comes in for happy qualification. Pompey, Lucan tells his readers, has decided to rest on his laurels in the bright glare of momentary peace. He is neither overcome by Homeric divinities nor even captured by Virgilian self-doubt and tragedy. In Lucan's evocation of him, he has simply taken the easy way out. He is "more tranquil in declining years" (vergentibus annis / . . . tranquillior; vv. 129–30), he has become a "a seeker of fame" (famae que . . . petitor; v. 131), he "believes in his former greatness" (priori / credere fortunae; vv. 134–35). Trusting in his own press, as it were, Pompey chooses to continue to live his own history, making the past serve his future. In a larger sense, such a decision, and the exercise of freedom it implies, allow Lucan to imagine the nature of life after the fall away from the Gods, from Stoic *sympatheia,* when freedom leads not to greater and better things but to a point where higher standards are forsaken for volition.

Caesar, on the other hand, is nothing more than an earlier version of Pompey, avaricious for fame and, in Lucan's estimation, almost unearthly in his powers of persuasion and in his abilities to lead. He is depicted in the first book of the *De bello civili* in terms that make him akin to a supernatural force. He makes his entry into the poem as a bolt of lightening (vv. 151 ff.) that cannot be controlled, spreading destruction across a wide path. And not for nothing: soon the debilitating force of Caesar's power comes to dominate Lucan's vision. Beginning at verse 185, for example, Caesar spies the personified Roma, garbed in rags, sobbing, admonishing him to give up his treasonous plans and allow peace to prevail. He is initially troubled by this image, but the logic of his mind is skewed by the perversions of his deep longing for power, so that his original feelings are countered by subsequent justifications of what he is about to do.

Lucan gives shape to Caesar's justifications—and their illogicality—by offering the normal reaction first, noting that "the horror of the deeds physically affected Caesar, by making him tremble" (tum perculit horror / membra ducis; vv. 192–93). But quickly on the heels of this vivid image comes a second reaction perverted by the lust for power. Soon, then, Caesar speaks at length and defends what he is about to do (vv. 195–203). The breaker of the peace, the one who thirsts for power and brings discord, so Caesar says, is not Caesar but his enemy, "who has made me the enemy of Rome" (ille erit . . . qui me tibi fecerit hostem; v. 203). The old bromide that would make one's enemies the authors of one's own excesses informs Caesar's response to those who would charge him with treason.

In subsequent verses, Caesar is depicted as a wild lion. There are putative strengths to be associated with a lion, but Lucan's lion is made to live on the unplowed Libyan fields, where he becomes a ravenous hunter. This lion's prowess in hunting, moreover, is directly the result of his own prompting, for this lion fills himself with rage by lashing his body with his tail. His anger is so great, Lucan reports, that a blow to the chest head-on by a spear would sail right through his body, so quickly and fiercely does the beast pursue its prey (vv. 205–12).

When we next meet Caesar, he has taken on the swiftness and the rage of the Libyan lion directly. Lucan reports that, after deciding to "follow Fortune" (te, Fortuna, sequor; v. 226), Caesar became "faster than the bullet whirled from the Balearic sling or the arrow which the Parthian shoots over his shoulder" (in-piger, et torto Balearis verbere fundae / ocior et missa Parthi post terga sagitta; vv. 229–30). In the next verse, Lucan reports that Caesar, much like a raging lion, brought destruction to many towns on his march back into Italy (vv. 231 ff.).[8]

In allusive space, the mistakes of the two protagonists in this conflict become analogous to those acted out by Anselm and Abelard. Caesar and Pompey, each in his own way, represent the acme of human volition. The growing crisis of Republican Rome becomes the field upon which the terrors of human volition gone awry are played out. The "suicide" of Rome, depicted by Lucan as the thrust of Rome's own spears and javelins against her body, is made also to function on the level of individual experience. And to the extent that Caesar has become a perversion of moral discernment, so too is Pompey a symbol of the same lack of discernment, for he is unable to muster the courage to do anything about the doom he knows is imminent and which he has to a great extent made possible. In allusion's space, the analogy is vivid: Anselm is too old and too set in his ways to care anymore about theological truth. Like Pompey, he will do exactly as he pleases. Abelard appears in no more positive a light, however. Allusion reveals him to be, like Caesar, much more interested in himself than in truth. He acts according to his own whims and desires, unable—or unwilling—to distinguish moral differences any longer, or perhaps now disinterested in moral choices altogether.

In a larger sense, the notion of unity that is lacking in Lucan's vision of human experience is also lacking in Abelard's recollection of his early training under various theologians. It is a stark moment when full-knowing readers

---

8. Other examples: by the opening of *De bello civili* 3, Caesar makes so bold as to compare himself to the forces of nature and when he arrives at a sacred grove at 3.399 ff., the linkage to Pompey seems natural and somehow completed. Daring to desecrate a grove that even nature-gods dare not harm, Caesar for a moment becomes the embodiment of nature and convention, seems to have fused his freedom into an overwhelming force of human volition that cannot be stopped.

begin to sense that Lucan's pessimistic rejection of order as a constant in human affairs also impinges upon the *Historia*. One can hardly fail to make the connection. Absent the sure ordering principle offered by moral discernment, one is left with the wreckage sanctioned by the free reign of desire of a kind represented by Caesar or Pompey. Lucan's concern in the first book of the *De bello civili* is to teach that humanity rarely seeks the ideal, to assert that human greatness cannot be sustained either socially or psychologically. The human desire to act under a higher law that demands self-sacrifice, intensity of desire, constant vigilance is always checked by human weaknesses, and this is most vividly seen in the contest between concord and discord.

The lack of moral discernment and the inability to curb human volition are the key interpretive constructs revealed in the play of allusive space. These fundamentally negative insights into human nature, commended as givens by Lucan and filtered allusively into the fabric of the *Historia Calamitatum*, offer little interpretive room for the soothing salve of Christian reading. One is left with the image of a disreputable Anselm of Laon, but the analogous figure of Abelard as Caesar is no less ignoble. The competing worlds of this allusion, centering ultimately on the symbol of the fig tree that was cursed by Christ, do not lead to any sort of interpretive clarity. Instead, they offer only clusters of interpretive options, none of them positive assessments of Abelard's life, all of them portending the personal, social, and theological dilemmas faced by Abelard not too much later.

CORNELIA AND POMPEY / HELOISE AND ABELARD

Quae quidem, memini, cum eius adolescentiam a iugo monasticae regulae, tam-quam intolerabili poena, plurimi frustra deterrerent ei compatientes, in illam Cor-neliae querimoniam inter lacrymas et singultus, prout poterat, prorumpens ait:

O maxime coniux!
O thalamis indigne meis! hoc iuris habebat
In tantum fortuna caput? cur impia nupsi,
Si miserum factura fui? Nunc accipe poenas,
Sed quas sponte luam. (*Hist. Cal.*, p. 190–91)

(There were many people, I remember, who in pity for her youth tried to dissuade her from submitting to the yoke of monastic rule as a penance too hard to bear, but all in vain; she broke out as best she could through her tears and sobs into Cornelia's famous lament:

O noble husband,
too great for me to wed, was it my fate
to bend that lofty head? What prompted me
to marry you and bring about your fall?
Now claim your due, and see me gladly pay.)

When Lucan is next invited into the interpretive fabric of the *Historia Calamitatum*, much has transpired in the story Abelard tells in its lines. The carefully wrought plot to seduce Heloise has succeeded, their son, Astralabe, has been born, they have been married in secret, and, finally, Abelard has suffered his humiliating wound at the hands of Fulbert's henchmen. Almost immediately after the description of his castration, Abelard turns to consider the next phase of his life. Both he and Heloise decide, at his urging, to take monastic vows—Abelard at the Benedictine abbey of St. Denis, Heloise at the convent of Argenteuil. Implying that most people seemed to understand his decision to enter the monastic life, Abelard reports in no uncertain terms that many did not understand Heloise's decision to become a nun, especially given her youth and the severity of the "yoke of the monastic rule" (iugu[um] monasticae regulae; *Hist. Cal.*, p. 190). In the face of the complaints leveled against her, however, Heloise determines to go ahead with her vows and is able even to repeat the lament of Cornelia, spoken in the eighth book of Lucan's *De bello civili* (vv. 94–98). With that lamentation, a full-knowing reader is invited into allusive space.

This quotation has been interpreted by a variety of readers on different levels, eliciting responses that range across the spectrum of possibility. Abelard's use of this quotation has been considered, on the one hand, expressive of important spiritual longings in Heloise,[9] a way in which Abelard might somehow medi-

9. Thus P. von Moos, "Cornelia und Heloise," *Latomus* 34 (1975), p. 1050: ". . . und Heloises zitathaftes Lebenszeugnis zeigt eindeutig, dass hier der Klostereintritt mit dem Freitod gleichgesetzt wird, nicht etwa einem ethisch verwerflichen Selbstmord, sondern einem heldenhaften Opfertod aus selbstloser Liebe." See also his "Le Silence d'Héloïse et les Idéologies Modernes," in *Pierre Abélard, Pierre le Vénérable: Les Courants philosophiques, littéraires et artistiques en occident au milieu du XII siècle; abbaye de Cluny 2 au 9 Juillet 1972* (Paris, 1975), esp. pp. 442–44, where he takes Peter Dronke to task for writing "contre l'idée saugrenue d'une fonction spirituelle atribuée aux lettres d'Héloïse, . . . en renversant l'argument "puritain," . . . prouver leur historicité exactement par cette incohérence qui, selon lui, ne peut être inventée, parce qu'elle exprime la contradiction existentielle des partenaries." Von Moos refers here to Dronke's "Heloise and Marianne: Some Reconsiderations," *Romanische Forschungen* 72 (1960), pp. 223–56. See also von Moos's n. 35, pp. 442–43.

tate on, and draw attention to, the "conversion" of Heloise to a different way of life and mode of perception. On the other hand, comedy and melodrama have also been seen to inform this quotation, wherein Abelard would seem to accentuate his own foibles and flaws as if they were now an almost forgotten part of the "conquered" past. The quotation has also been viewed as expressing if not historical fact, then the historical context in which emotion and passion were felt and played out, a gauge wherein true feeling might be seen at work in the lives of two medieval people.[10] Although some have stressed the improbability that these words as constituted in the *Historia* reflect actual circumstance,[11] nothing has been made of the quotation in the context of allusion.

Analogy is important in the play of this allusion's space. If Abelard and Heloise are married (and they are) and if Heloise is made to play Cornelia (as she is), then a strategic shift in the dramatis personae has occurred. To this point in Abelard's narrative, allusion suggested that Abelard was playing Caesar to Anselm's Pompey. Now, as the husband of Cornelia, Abelard has become Pompey, that is to say, he has become like the rotten tree depicted by Lucan in the first book of the *De bello civili*. In effect, therefore, Abelard has become both a moribund thinker, like Anselm, and morally dead to the world and to his own wretched situation. He is but a shadow of his former self, weakened, waiting for a bolt of lightning to end the charade of his existence.

But this moment is finely honed in the play of allusion's space. The larger shift of identities—from Abelard-as-Caesar, avaricious for fame and drunk with the power of his own desires, to Abelard-as-Pompey, tired, defeated, waiting for the end—parallels a thematic shift in the *Historia* from personality to emotion, for the emotion of the moment recalled allusively is highly charged. The opening of *De bello civili* 8, in addition to serving the needs of this moment, reads almost as a resume of Abelard's career up to the point of Heloise's lament. For example, both authors stress the fame their characters achieved early in life, a characterization made stark by the ways in which both turn to images of a fall. So too is the idea of destiny, mentioned in verse 10 (memor fati) by Lucan, important in Abelard's rendition of his own career. Lucan's description of the *multi* (v. 14) awaiting Pompey at the Pharsalian camp also recalls Abelard's descriptions of the crowds who met him after hearing of his castration, and of the support that they gave him, which made him (so he says) forget the pain of his wound.

10. See P. Dronke, *Abelard and Heloise in Medieval Testimonies* (Glasgow, 1976), pp. 10–14, for a summary of these and other views.

11. Thus von Moos, "Cornelia und Heloise," pp. 1049–50.

Thus, though the words are Lucan's, many points apply equally to Abelard, who has become Pompey now:

Iam super Herculeas fauces nemorosaque Tempe
Haemoniae deserta petens dispendia silvae
cornipedem exhaustum cursu stimulisque negantem
Magnus agens incerta fugae vestigia turbat
implicitasque errore vias. pavet ille fragorem
motorum ventis nemorum, comitumque suorum
qui post terga redit trepidum laterique timentem
exanimat. quamvis summo de culmine lapsus
nondum vile sui pretium scit sanguinis esse,
seque, memor fati, tantae mercedis habere
credit adhuc iugulum, quantam pro Caesaris ipse
avulsa cervice daret. deserta sequentem
non patitur tutis fatum celare latebris
clara viri facies. (*Bel. civ.* 8.1–14)

And now beyond wooded Tempe, the Gorde of Hercules, Magnus headed for the lonely forests of Thessaly in a roundabout way; as he urged on his horse, worn out from swift flight and deaf to the spur, he confused the path of his retreat and made a labyrinth of his tracks. He dreads the sound of the trees in the wind; and any of his comrades who falls back to join him frightens him in his agitation and fear. Though fallen from the heights, he knows that the price of his blood is still high; and, mindful of his career, he believes that his death can still earn as great a reward as he would give for the severed head of Caesar. Though he seeks solitude, his known features don't allow him to hide his disaster in safe concealment.

Here, Pompey is made to look the fool, botching his retreat, exhausting his horse, fearing his own men and the sound of the trees, that all-important symbol of impotence. He has fallen from his former eminence but is still mindful of his former career. His comrades and others are reported to be astounded by his change of fortune, and he would choose, so Lucan says, to be unknown to all (cunctis ignotis gentibus esse / mallet; 8.19–20), now feeling that he achieved too much too soon, now cursing his youthful exploits and successes. Most of all, Pompey seeks places forsaken by the rest (deserta petens, v. 2; deserta sequentem, v. 12), though, ultimately, his fame is too great to allow that. Much like Abelard, Pompey has lost the accouterments of past glories and seeks the desert places: "I admit that it was shame and confusion in my remorse and misery rather than any devout wish for conversion which brought me to seek shelter in a monastery cloister" (In tam misera me contritione positum confusio, fateor, pudoris potius quam devotio conversionis ad monasticorum latibula claustrorum compulit; *Hist. Cal.,* p. 190). And much like Abelard, fortune will not allow Pompey to forget his past, especially the exploits of his youth:

> Nunc festinatos nimium sibi sentit honores
> actaque lauriferae damnat Sullana iuventae,
> nunc et Corycias classes et Pontica signa
> deiectum meminisse piget. sic longius aevum
> destruit ingentis animos et vita superstes
> imperio. nisi summa dies cum fine bonorum
> affuit et celeri praevertit tristia leto,
> dedecori est fortuna prior. quisquamne secundis
> tradere se fatis audet nisi morte parata? (*Bel. civ.* 8.24–32)

(Now he feels that his honors came too quickly; now he curses the exploits of his triumphant youth in Sulla's day; now he hates to remember the fleets of Cilicia and the armies of Pontus. Thus old age and life surviving power destroy the proudest heart. Unless the end of life comes together with the end of happiness, and anticipates sorrow with a quick death, past greatness is a mockery. Who dares to trust prosperity, except he has the means of death at hand?)

Full-knowing readers will recall the implications of Ajax's boast bruited earlier in the *Historia*. With that boast, Abelard recounted giving up Mars for Minerva and accomplishing what were, given his age, a series of exemplary intellectual achievements. But those achievements resonate also in the conclusion of that boast, Ajax's suicide. The reality of that suicide hovers, like a portent, uneasily close to the surface of the *Historia*. Particularly chilling in this regard are Lucan's subsequent words about the consonance of life and happiness. If the end of life does not come at the same time as the end of happiness, Lucan says, then past greatness is mockery. One ought to commit suicide, Lucan concludes, rather than muddle on after the fall (8.29–32).

Pompey and Abelard find themselves in the midst of their descents from the summit. For his part, Pompey is still made of puffery and bravado. His entry onto Lesbos, where Cornelia awaits him, is recounted in the context of her swooning vision of him, against the backdrop of her nightmares and her longed-for death. Yet, in reviving her, Pompey blusters on about his glory and his destiny: "Love that I have been conquered. For I bring you greater distinction now, when the magistrates and devoted ranks of the Senate and all my retinue of kings have gone: from this time be the sole follower of Magnus" (quod sum victus ama. nunc sum tibi gloria maior, / a me quod fasces et quod pia turba senatus / tantaque discessit regum manus. incipe Magnum / sola sequi; *Bel. civ.* 8.78–81). Unexpectedly, however, Pompey concludes his verbal thrashing with a sudden and profound shift of tone. Having just instructed Cornelia that her signal fidelity ought to be grounded in her mourning for him as a dead man, as against her premature mourning for him while he is still alive, Pompey goes on to add, uncharacteristically: "My defeat has brought no loss to you; for Magnus survives the battle, though his greatness has gone; what you weep for is what you really loved" (tu nulla tulisti / bello damna meo: vivit post proelia Magnus, / sed fortuna perit. quod defles, illud amasti; *Bel. civ.* 8.83–85).

Now the stakes are considerably altered. Pompey had seemed to ground his reproaches in the context of social and even political norms. But of a sudden he shifts the terms of his appeal. There is no reproach in the simple phrase "quod defles, illud amasti" (what you weep for is what you really loved). The *quod* and *illud* of this phrase are normally interpreted to refer to the trifles for which Cornelia would seem to cry, for which reason they make a fitting rebuke to her grief when Pompey uses them to conclude his condemnation of her mourning. They can also, and more fittingly, refer to Pompey himself, or, better still, to the essence, the "thing" that bound them. Understood in this sense, the final line of Pompey's reproach transforms his bombast and her pathos into a rendition of something essential and powerful.

Though Lucan's "heroic" Pompey is little more than a caricature of prior epic heroes, here Pompey has his moment of lucidity and, one might even say, his moment of tragic heroism. All is not lost, he would seem to suggest, if he and Cornelia can cling, in their own imperfect and difficult ways, to their love. That point looms largest. And because it is a point couched in the darkest of scenes, it represents a countervailing force against the rush of oblivion, the potency of something essential, something that abides in the face of historical and personal abandonment. This scene, then, though it describes the vortex of personal disintegration, also offers the means to reclaim lost potential, to undo the desolation of striving without success, and the ability to make good the absence of consolation in the sterile world of emotional lassitude.

Cornelia's lament represents a rush of emotional and spiritual integrity into the disintegrating worlds of Lucan's *De bello civili.* For one moment, order abides, centering upon the strength and consonance of emotion. This consonance, constructed amid faltering personalities and the gloom of profound defeat, becomes the centerpiece of Abelard's emotional state, and Heloise's. The consonance, however, is fragile, as consonance always is in Lucan's poem and in Abelard's *Historia.* Full-knowing readers can spy its fragility in subsequent quotations in the *Historia* to Jerome's *Contra Jovinianum*—Jovinian questioning the spiritual superiority of celibacy to marriage; they can view it in Abelard's more mundane considerations of new enemies, whose voices, so Abelard says, flitter about like the "poetic creation Echo" (illius poetici figmenti quod Echo dicitur; *Hist. Cal.* p. 202)—Echo, whose history is so replete with the longings of love and the dilemmas of emotion. They can also see it in the scriptural tags Abelard adduces as his story concludes. It is resonant in the quotation from Psalm 61.2, the prayer of the King in exile, that "from the ends of the earth I have called to you, when my heart was in anguish" (A finibus terrae ad te clamavi dum anxiaretur cor meum). It resounds in Paul's defense of his own epistle in 2 Corinthians 7, 5: "There are troubles from without and fears within" (Foris pugnae, intus timores). And it is resident in the quotation from Proverbs 12.21, with which Abelard concludes the *Historia:* "Whatever shall fall to his lot, the just man will not be saddened" (Non contristabit iustum quidquid ei acciderit).

One gains a sense of this fragility perhaps most vividly, however, in the carefully offered ironies of Abelard's self-presentation that exist quite apart from the narrative he tells, the architecture it offers, or the social and cultural norms used to articulate it. Indeed, while he demands that *his* readers key into the Augustinian program of reading, while he compels them to use their own power to heal his text and, in essence, make sense of the wounds to his body (the sort of work this chapter has ventured), Abelard dramatizes his own inability to be such a reader.

This inability is perhaps the most important feature of Abelard's life after the fall, after he has become, as it were, Pompey. Prior to his castration, Abelard depicts himself as a powerful reader of a kind commended by Augustine. Indeed, the very foundation of his intellectual activity is based on a novel approach to reading Scripture that depends on readerly power for its best function. Immediately after his castration, however, Abelard depicts himself as a failed reader, devoid of bold powers, lost in the "killing letter of the law":

> Nec me etiam parum confundebat quod secundum occidentem legis litteram tanta sit apud Deum eunuchorum abominatio ut homines amputatis vel attritis testiculis eunuchizati intrare ecclesiam tamquam olentes et immundi prohibeantur, et in sacrificio quoque talia penitus animalia respuantur [liber Levitici capitulum XXII]: Omne animal, quod est contritis vel tunsis vel sectis ablatisque testiculis, non offeretis Domino. [Deuteronomii capitulum XXIII]: Non intrabit eunuchus attritis vel amputatis testiculis et absciso veretro ecclesiam Domini. (*Hist. Cal.*, p. 190)

> (I was also not too little confounded that according to the killing letter of the law, a eunuch is such an abomination to the Lord that men made eunuchs by amputation

or mutilation of their members are forbidden to enter a church as if they were stinking and unclean, and even animals in that state are rejected for sacrifice. "Ye shall not present to the Lord any animal if its testicles have been bruised or crushed, torn or cut"; "no man whose testicles have been crushed or whose organ has been severed shall become a member of the assembly of the Lord").

This rumination on scriptural evidence relating to eunuchs is couched in a specific vocabulary that ties into the Augustinian program of reading, the very program so obviously in place to readers of the *Historia*. The scene focuses on Abelard's mental capacity in the hours and days after his castration, when the future could not have seemed bleaker. Contemplating his course of action, Abelard recalls the Old Testament teachings about eunuchs. Scripture is not vague about the topic, as Abelard remembers, for eunuchs are, in his recollection, foul and unclean, unworthy to hold sacred office or to enter sacred places. By virtue of their wound, they are an abomination to God. This causes Abelard, as he says, to be "not too little confounded" (Nec me etiam parum confundebat . . .).

What is more striking than his confoundment, however, is the way in which Abelard recalls Paul's phrase the "killing letter of the law"[12] to frame his own interpretation of the Scripture, precisely the phrase used by Augustine to frame his own discussion of Christian reading. At *Confessions* 6.4, as we saw above,[13] Augustine remembers that Ambrose often said in his sermons that "the literal level kills, but the spiritual level proffers life" (littera occidit, spiritus autem vivificat), a recollection immediately subsequent to the important scene in which Ambrose is praised as a silent reader of Scripture, as someone able to render intelligible through the application of Christian charity any text set before him. He was able to do this, Augustine recalls, because Ambrose understood, after St. Paul, that the literal level when taken by itself kills, but that the spiritual level, when coupled with the literal, proffers sense.

Importantly, Abelard makes no mention of the spiritual level of meaning in his rumination on the scriptural evidence relating to eunuchs. Instead, he plays on the fact that he is somehow caught at the literal level of interpretation, the level that makes such a stark case against eunuchs. Yet clearly Abelard knew that the passages in question from the Old Testament had been interpreted for centuries under the Augustinian model in such a way as to make them applicable only to *self-mutilated* eunuchs. The direct language of the Old Testament,

12. From 2 Cor. 3.6.
13. For a contrary view see M. McLaughlin, "Abelard as Autobiographer: The Motives and Meaning of His 'Story of Calamities,'" *Speculum* 42 (1967), pp. 463–88.

the killing letter of the law, did indeed announce a harsh reality for all eunuchs. But the traditions of readerly interpretation adduced through the application of charity, the spiritual level of understanding, had mollified this harsher view, so that Abelard had nothing to fear from the Church or from Christian culture in general now that he had become a eunuch.[14] The fact that Abelard surely knew this seems precisely the point. The teachings constructed from charity, from the spiritual law, were no longer available to Abelard after his castration. The wounds to his physical body made healing the wounds of his textual body impossible—for him.

The *Historia Calamitatum* recreates in the play of allusive space multiple scenes in which the Augustinian program of Christian reading functions for its reader, yet for Abelard the wounds to his textual body do not, or cannot be made to, heal any longer. Analogously, this outcome results from the fact that Abelard conceives of the wounds to his physical body as incomprehensible in the terms given to him by his culture. Abelard's failure to read his body is not merely an intellectual defect specific to him, therefore. Rather, it points to a cultural deficiency centering on the ways Christians had been taught to conceive of and view the world. His failure calls into question the very efficacy of the Christian rhetorical model as an authentic tool in the comprehension of human experience. Christian charity was not uniformly applicable, its soothing salve did not, as Augustine claimed it always did, heal the wound. After his castration, therefore, reading, the fundamental act of Christian intellection, was at an end for Abelard. Now, for him, only the "killing letter of the law" abided.

By erasing himself from the readerly program of the *Historia*, therefore, Abelard suggests his own cultural divorcement but also the importance of passion in human experience. There is just as much sense, and just as much spiritual rectitude, he seems to say, in calling to one's lover from the desert places, in constructing the mental habitat to fend off troubles from without, and in affirming the social and spiritual importance of one's experience. By inviting his readers to affirm the Augustinian program of reading and by forcing them to view his own competencies outside of that program, Abelard makes the claim for a strong reader in general, not only in the reading of Scripture, a claim that allusion would continue to foster in subsequent centuries in the West.

14. See Muckle, p. 190, n. 33.

Chapter 8   *Scala a Dio:* Dante and Ovid

Dicevano gli antichi che la poesia
è scala a Dio. Forse non è cosi
se mi leggi. Ma il giorno io lo seppi
che retrovai per te la voce . . . .

(The ancients said that poetry is the ladder to God. Maybe this is not the
case if you read my poetry. But on the day that I found my voice once
more through you I knew it . . . .)
—Eugenio Montale, *Siria*

Dante's relationship with Ovid is at once obvious and enigmatic—
obvious because allusions to the *Metamorphoses* are so numerous in the
Divina Commedia, yet enigmatic because its dynamics remain in large
part to be articulated.[1] The more prominent connection of Virgil and
Dante has always commanded priority of place in Dante studies, while
most assessments of Ovid and Dante make Ovid play the role of a

---

1. A good start on articulating the details is R. Jacoff and J. T. Schnapp, eds., *The
Poetry of Allusion: Virgil and Ovid in Dante's "Commedia"* (Stanford, Calif.,
1991); see also M. U. Sowell, ed., *Dante and Ovid: Essays in Intertextuality*
(Binghamton, NY, 1991); and M. Picone and B. Zimmermann, eds., *Ovidius
Redivivus: von Ovid zu Dante* (Stuttgart, 1994).

a poet who symbolized for Dante myth, grotesque metamorphosis, and divine power. But allusion allows readers to see in Dante's version of Ovid a poet of *humanitas* and to assess many of the key moments of Dante's *Commedia* as meditations on the powers and limits of human action in face of divine retribution.

My claim in this chapter is that Dante alludes to Ovid's *Metamorphoses* in order to subscribe in the *Commedia* to Ovid's particular brand of *humanitas,* that is, to Ovid's own celebrations of those qualities of heart and mind that confirm a common human identity. Further, I claim that this identity is framed in Ovid's poem, and thus in Dante's, in the context of victimization, wherein volatile and idle gods pursue humans relentlessly and with much pleasure in order to corner them, taunt them, and then change them into new forms. Vestiges of human identity always abide in these transformations, however, for these traces of identity are foundational to who and what humans would truly seem to be. These traces are, in other words, those aspects of identity that are not socially or culturally constructed, that abide in and out of time, the essences in which Ovid seems to have believed and about which his epic poem of change would seem to take best shape. This essentialism, the foundation of Ovidian (and Dantean) *humanitas,* is especially revealed in a variety of ways in the *Commedia,* but perhaps most fully through allusion.

Dante's Ovidian essentialism is perhaps not surprising, but how he chooses to express Ovidian *humanitas* through allusion is noteworthy. To be sure, Dante's engagement of Ovid conforms to the practice of allusion made prominent in the Christian tradition by Augustine, that is, through a careful deployment of key words that inform fundamental moments in the *Commedia.* But now the reader must be even more diligent, more devoted to the allusive text, for Dante's allusive practice is more subtle than his predecessors'. There is not a rejection here of the terms of Christian interpretation, as there was in Abelard's *Historia,* much less a modeling process, as we witnessed in the allusive practices of Catullus, in which whole poems were brought allusively to bear in later works. Indeed, just the opposite tack is taken here: Dante works throughout the *Commedia* to enmesh his poem to Ovid's so vigorously as to blur the lines between the language of his own poem and the words of his exemplar. In this way, Dante helps to articulate a more complex allusive practice, one based in the normative assumptions in place since the time of Augustine, but requiring now even more readerly power.

This power, in the end, has both an external, historical cogency as well as an internal, interpretive point. While announcing a ratcheting up of the competencies required of the reader, Dante's allusive responses to the *Metamorphoses* of Ovid also mete out the kind of human power that best exemplifies the essentialism of his poem. The experience of readerly fortitude in the recognition and interpretation of Ovidian material becomes in this way an important means by which human power itself is affirmed, the very power that Ovid and Dante celebrate in their respective poems—indeed, the very power that smooths our ascent up the ladder of God, as Montale taught, the power that allows us, as Dante himself taught, to reach the plenitude of paradise.[2]

THE SCENE OF ALLUSIVE READING: *INFERNO* 3 AND 4

That power is called upon at once, in the opening cantos of the *Inferno*, where Ovid is held up for special consideration. In the fourth canto, Dante faints and is aroused from his slumber by a clap of thunder. Attempting to determine his surroundings, he looks hard but can see precious little except darkness itself. Then Virgil, who bids for his attention by suddenly speaking, appears to Dante to have lost all color (tutto smorto; v. 14) and tells Dante to follow him into the blind world below (or discendiam qua giù nel cieco mondo; v. 13). This exchange follows:

"Io sarò primo, e tu sarai secondo."
E io, che del color mi fui accorto,
   dissi: "Come verrò, se tu paventi
   che suoli al mio dubbiare esser conforto?"
Ed elli a me: "L'angoscia de le genti
   che son qua giù, nel viso mi dipigne
   quella pietà che tu per tema senti.
Andiam, ché la via lunga ne sospigne." (*Inf.* 4.15–22)[3]

("I will be first and you will be second." And I, who saw his color, said, "How can I come if you are afraid who, when I am in doubt, are my comfort?" And he said to me: "The anguish of the people who are down here marks my face with the piety that you think indicates fear. Let us go, for the long way compels us.")

It is necessary to read this exchange in poetical as well as spiritual terms and

2. See T. Barolini, *The Undivine Comedy: Detheologizing Dante* (Princeton, 1992), pp. 194–96, on this theme in Dante's poem.

3. My edition is C. S. Singleton, ed. and trans., *Dante Alighieri: The Divine Comedy: Inferno, Purgatorio, Paradiso*, 3 vols. (Princeton, 1970–75). My renderings are made with help from Singleton, J. D. Sinclair, *Dante: The Divine Comedy*, 3 vols. (London, 1939–46), and J. A. Carlyle, T. Okey, P. H. Wicksteed, trans., *The Divine Comedy of Dante Alighieri* (New York, 1959), and I follow Sinclair verbatim for *Purg.* 4.

to view it both as the conclusion of the third canto and the beginning of the fourth. In the third canto, recall, Dante and Virgil had entered through the gate of Hell and, after expressing his fear of the place, Dante had been instructed by Virgil to put all cowardice aside. Virgil, speaking at length for the first time after his introduction to the poem in the second canto, easily assumes the role of guide and takes pains to apply a hard logic to his comments about the "neutrals." The gist of Virgil's wisdom in this canto, however, centers as much on emotional as on rational insights, for although Dante grants Virgil the benefit of his experience assumed under the guise of reason, he also characterizes Virgil in no uncertain terms as an interpreter of secret things (mi mise dentro a la segrete cose; *Inf.* 3. 21).

The broader connotation of these secret things is, of course, far afield from Christian Hell, for the journey to the underworld in the sixth book of the *Aeneid* forms the context in which Dante's journey into Hell takes place. Hell might exist theologically in Christian terms without Virgil, but a poetical trip to the underworld without Virgil cannot proceed. More important, by virtue of Virgil's poetical presence in this canto, neither can a reader of Dante ignore the details of Aeneas's journey to the underworld. The linkage of Dante and Virgil on the lip of Christian Hell, therefore, sanctions the clearing of allusive space, whereby the *Inferno* and the sixth *Aeneid* are also linked. In the play of allusion's space, Dante begins to consider the spiritual ramifications of his own journey into Hell, a consideration that will owe much to Virgil and that will point to larger habits of thought relative to the classical poets and the wisdom harbored in their poetry.

The wisdom of Virgil's sixth *Aeneid* appears at once. The ostensible reason for Aeneas's journey, to glean information about the future from his father, is overshadowed by the emotional appeal Virgil makes in constructing the scene in which Aeneas and his father meet. Aeneas spies the shade of his father and tries three times to embrace it without success. He attempts to shield his pain by casting his glance elsewhere and spies the fields of Elysium, which are described in terms of their verdant richness. This act of pain averted, symbolized in the movements of Aeneas's vision to these fertile and green fields, comes eventually to symbolize the enduring qualities of growth and fecundity that nature herself represents in the course of the seasons, a topic Virgil had taken up with less resolve earlier in the *Georgics*.[4] But the greenery that meets Aeneas's gaze is also

4. On which see G. Miles, *Virgil's Georgics: A New Interpretation* (Berkeley and London,

symbolic of those things which do abide in life as in death. The green promise of spring, for example, perseveres through the cruel course of winter, whose cruelty is as much a harbinger of spring as a destroyer of it. So, too, do human essences abide, though through the crueler course of death that leads to eternal life, either in Christian heaven or in Virgilian Elysium.

By virtue of this linkage, then, Dante would seem to center his own vision of Christian Hell squarely within the fold of Virgilian *humanitas,* sharing with Virgil a broad conception of the facets of human existence that abide in and out of time. Virgil's position is fundamentally a spiritual one and Dante incorporates it into his own poem without losing any of the spiritual vigor it proffers. This is the grandest secret told by Virgil in *Aeneid 6.* That secret allows canto 3 to be read less severely in the context of Christian teleology, and more emotionally as a commentary on humankind's spiritual state. It is, Virgil asserts in his portrayal of Aeneas and Anchises, on emotional grounds, in the guise of love and hate, that we forge our most permanent and enduring existence, so that how we live our emotional lives has a normative bearing on what we become in death. As much as Virgil sounds the severe tones of Christian eschatology in his instructions to Dante to "go down into the blind world" below (*Inf.* 4.13), those words also shimmer with humane connotations revealed in the play of allusive space. That world is blind because it is the acme of sin and necessary punishment, but it is blind in a more humane sense also in that it offers to Dante exposure to the suffering of humans cast in the context of life's very imperfections, whose details are affirmed by Virgil's physical and textual presence in this and the prior canto.

Moreover, when Dante goes on in the next verse to misconstrue the color of Virgil's countenance, he exposes himself not only as a frightened sinner but also as an incompetent reader, as one unable to interpret experience correctly. Virgil, of course, corrects Dante and then goes on immediately to assert that "I will be first and you will be second" (Io sarò primo, e tu sarai secondo; v. 15), his words suggesting both poetical as well as physical priority, and forming a complete picture of Dante's relationship to Virgil established in the third canto. Virgil will lead Dante, correcting misreadings, and offer to him a more secure view of human experience, which will take shape in both theological and poetical

---

1980), pp. 141 ff. and M. C. J. Putnam, *Virgil's Poem of the Earth: Studies in the Georgics* (Princeton, 1979), pp. 56–59.

terms, a view that will be owed, therefore, as much to classical *humanitas* as to the dictates of Christian theology.

The progress they will make will be slow and long, Virgil says (Andiam, ché la via lunga ne sospigne; v. 22), portending the dual activities of theological instruction and poetical engagement that will ensue presently, but Dante gets down to the hard work of engaging the poetical tradition almost at once when he has Virgil take him into the company of the other classical poets. No more vivid a scene in Western writing can be found by which to symbolize the ongoing process of reading, engaging, and challenging tradition. And given the way in which allusion functions in the third and fourth cantos, full-knowing readers can spy in this grand meeting of the great poets of the West an equally grand clearing of allusive space, where the masterworks of classical poetry are merged, mixed, matched, abandoned, or embraced. In constructing this scene, therefore, Dante advertises not only those poets other than Virgil that are important to him, but also the fact that much of the business of the *Commedia* will involve locating and making use of earlier poetry, will involve, in other words, the function of allusion.

When Dante describes his descent to the first circle of Hell in *Inferno* 4, he uses terms that apply as much to textuality and reading as to theology.[5] He offers first a discussion of the virtuous heathens, whose membership includes Virgil himself, and broaches this discussion in the context of things that are heard. Dante "hears," for example, the sighs of the sufferers of the first circle (vv. 25–27) and "listens" also to Virgil's various explanations of the places they behold together. He closes this scene in much the same way: "We did not stop because of his speaking, but continued passing through the forest (for this is what it looked to be) of gathered spirits" (Non lasciavam l'andar perch' ei dicessi, / ma passavam la selva tuttavia, / la selva, dico, di spiriti spessi; *Inf.* 4.64–66).

At the point where he first encounters the spirits of the approaching *poetae,* however, Dante adds to his vocabulary key verbs that embody vision, symbolizing a shift in his own perceptual framework, from a passive listener to an active reader of the experience he is about to recount. Dante sees, so he says, a blaze of light, not far from the place where he had been sleeping at the opening of the canto: "We had not gone far from where I slept when I saw a blaze of light which was encircled in a hemisphere of darkness. We were still a short distance

5. This manner of poetical construction has been analyzed elsewhere in the *Commedia* by J. Freccero, "Manfred's Wounds and the Poetics of the Purgatorio," in R. Jacoff, ed., *Dante: The Poetics of Conversion* (Cambridge, Mass., 1986), pp. 195–208.

from it yet not so far that I couldn't in part make out that an honorable company occupied that place" (Non era lunga ancor la nostra via / di qua dal sonno, quand' io vidi un foco / ch' emisperio di tenebre vincia. / Di lungi n'eravamo ancora un poco, / ma non sì, ch'io non discernessi in parte / ch'orrevol gente possedea quel loco; *Inf.* 4.67–72).

Vision is central to the functioning of these verses and the importance of seeing, as against hearing, is accentuated by the fact that the light that Dante sees is surrounded by darkness. The tactic of carefully manipulating the visual contours of a scene recalls for full-knowing readers the similar strategy used by Virgil in *Aeneid* 6 in describing Aeneas's gaze averted from the shade of his father. Although Dante cannot at this point quite make out what it is he sees in the light, he half-way discerns (discernessi in parte; v. 71) the presence of an honorable group in the glare of light that is intently the object of his vision. Yet, not trusting his own reading of the scene, he asks Virgil to interpret it for him and is careful to describe Virgil as one honorable in science and in art (O tu ch'onori scienzia e arte; v. 73), as if to ensure the well-roundedness of the interpretation Virgil is set to offer. After Virgil renders praises for the figures in general terms, both Dante and Virgil hear an unidentified voice from on high enjoin them vaguely to honor the highest poet (Onorate l'altissimo poeta; v. 80). This injunction to obeisance neatly links to the characterization of Virgil himself at verse 73, where the poet was described as one who does honor to science and art. But the voice falls immediately into silence, which allows readers to make various associations and appraisals of the meaning of the lines. Thereupon, four figures approach Dante and Virgil, and Virgil proceeds to identify the figures for Dante: "Mark him there with the sword in his hand who comes before the three as their master; he is Homer, the sovereign poet. Horace is next the moralist, Ovid is third, and Lucan is last" (Mira colui con quella spada in mano, / che vien dinanzi ai tre sì come sire: / quelli è Omero poeta sovrano; / l'altro è Orazio satiro che vene; / Ovidio è 'l terzo, e l'ultimo Lucano; *Inf.* 4.86–90).

The introduction of the classical *poetae* to the lines of Dante's new epic are curiously skewed, inviting attention by virtue of the inconsistencies they highlight. The unnamed voice who introduces the arrival of the poets, for example, speaks only of one poet (l'altissimo poeta; v.80), though six poets are present if Dante is included. More important, perhaps, are the problems raised by the ways in which Dante qualifies the classical poets present to him. Homer offers no difficulty, for the first poet named is easily characterized by Virgil specifically as a poet of war. The accounting of the three remaining poets is much less straightforward, however. Though he clearly possessed a firm sense of the motives and visions of Horace, Ovid, and Lucan, Dante gives no clear indication of how to gauge that sense. Of Horace Dante says only that he is a moralist (l'altro è Orazio satiro che vene) and there is truth to this qualification, for the medieval reception of Horace did emphasize the moral positions of the *Satires* and *Epistles*. But there was already in place by Dante's time a clear conception of the illustrious and singular power of the *Odes,* though there is no mention of them here. In the same way, the almost dismissive tone assigned to Ovid and Lucan strikes the wrong chord, for the medieval reception of both Ovid and Lucan was enthusiastic and comprehensive. Lucan is one of the most popular of the classical poets in the Middle Ages. Ovid, moreover, always popular in the guise of a poet of love and of mythology, seems oddly underqualified here, for he was perhaps the most popular of the classical poets in the Middle Ages, owing, among other reasons, to the wealth of stories and lore retrievable from the *Metamorphoses* and applicable in countless way to the allegorical and moralizing bents of medieval littérateurs.

The tone of this passage, already curiously off, is skewed even more when Virgil concludes his remarks by noting that "therefore, because the name accorded each of them is suitable to each and to me, they welcomed me" (Però che ciascun meco si convene / nel nome che sonò la voce sola, / fannomi onore; vv. 91–92).[6] Now the prior qualifications seem unnecessary, since Virgil suggests that the unnamed voice meant to include all of the poets with the phrase "l'altissimo poeta" (v. 80). But this cannot be true historically, for the poets named here are divided by language, epoch, and temperament. It can only be true, therefore, in a textual sense, if each poet is understood to stand in relation to the others allusively, wherein the poem of one is present in the other, obscuring that point where originality takes over and influence evanesces.

If this is so, then the qualifying attributes stand out all the more, for beyond confusing the issue by their inadequacy, they become anachronistic, impossible in the context of allusive space where their glories and visions are played out. When Dante goes on, then, at verse 103 to join their ranks and discuss with them things that are, so he says, "apt for that place, of which it is good to be silent" (parlando cose che'l tacere è bello, / sì com' era 'l parlar colà dov' era; vv.

6. Singleton has: "Since each shares with me the name the single voice has uttered, they do me honor, and in that they do well" (p. 41); Sinclair has: "Since each shares with me in the name the one voice uttered they give me honourable welcome" (p. 63); Carlyle-Okey-Wicksteed print this rendition: "Because each agrees with me in the name, which the one voice sounded, they do me honour" (p. 28).

104–5), there is a sense in which that silence betokens future allusive moments in the *Commedia* where full-knowing readers will be empowered to speak for the company of these poets. In allusive space these silences will be transformed into utterance.

Dante would seem to confirm this interpretive line of reasoning as he concludes canto 4. After conferring with his poets in silence, he and they arrive at a meadow of fresh verdure (prato di fresca verdura; v. 111), whose details recall Virgil's description of Elysium in the sixth *Aeneid.* Thereupon, Dante describes the figures he spies in this meadow, all of whom turn out to be characters resident in classical literature. Once again, vision becomes an important quality as Dante focuses on the eyes of these figures, which are, so he says, "grave and slow to move" (con occhi tardi e gravi; v. 112). The gazes of Aeneas averted from his father in *Aeneid* 6 and the gaze of Dante himself earlier in the canto cannot help but be recalled now. Thereupon, green, that color so prominent in the sixth *Aeneid,* takes priority of place when Dante goes on to catalogue the classical figures who, so he says, are arrayed on the green enamel ('l verde smalto). The textual quality of this scene is ratified now in the ways that Dante's classical ekphrasis, etched upon the green meadow with its enamel figures, demands interpretation by those who see it. It will be interpreted, of course, as a textual piece, in the contexts and settings that link the characters it depicts to particular classical moments.

The connection to *humanitas* returns also, for after the presentation of these figures, Dante has the *poetae* regard with reverence a host of philosophers, the embodiment of reason. A clear distinction is made, in the process, between the function of poetry, which exalts *humanitas,* and the function of philosophy, which is grounded in reason. The *poetae* come to represent in these closing scenes the power and resiliency of the human spirit, for which reason Dante places all of the figures in a setting reminiscent of the meadow in the sixth *Aeneid,* where that same point was initially made, and where the *Commedia* as a whole commences allusively.

There is one final circumstance in Dante's presentation that gives pause. Though he is extraordinarily efficient at tying together the various levels of his narrative, attention to the pedigree of figures set to be read on the green enamel of his ekphrastic meadow offers a curious silence all its own. Those figures named there—Electra, Hector, Aeneas, Caesar, Camilla, Penthesilea, Latinus, Lavinia, Brutus, Lucretia, Julia, Marcia, Cornelia—are epic figures who play prominent roles in the poems of Homer, Virgil, and Lucan. But Ovid, the other epic poet of the group, does not figure at all here. With the exception of Caesar, the main character of Lucan's *De bello civili*, and Aeneas, the hero of Virgil's *Aeneid*, not one figure who plays a role in the *Metamorphoses* is mentioned here. This is especially noteworthy given the glut of figures that fill the pages of that poem. There exists, then, in Dante's catalogue no overt mention of Ovid. In the context of silence implicit in the earlier moment in the canto, when Dante refused to report what he and the *poetae* said to each other, this omission seems strategic, all the more so when Dante goes on to take his leave of the *poetae* by noting that his words sometimes fail him (che molte volte al fatto il dir vien meno; v. 147). All of the connotations associated with silence and its application to reading now come into play. Unable to say what he wants, he cuts himself short, leaves the presence of the *poetae* for good, and continues on his way to a place where no light shines (E vegno in parte ove non è che luca; v. 151), on to the harsher dictates of theological necessity.

Though Dante makes much of the silence he observes when he is introduced into the company of the classical *poetae*, his own silences concerning Ovid stand out for their starkness. Not only does Dante underrepresent figures from the *Metamorphoses* in his "green enamel" of classical *figurae*, but he also refuses to qualify Ovid, except to call him "third." These approaches to Ovid are not unimportant, for Ovid, as one of his best critics has noted, is everywhere and nowhere in the *Commedia*,[7] that is to say, is everywhere in the verbal texture of the *Commedia* allusively, but nowhere accorded a rank or status akin to that granted to Virgil. In spite of the fact that Ovid is present in the *Divina Commedia* verbally in a way comparable to Virgil, it is usually granted— because he openly advertises it as fact—that Virgil is the poet of choice for Dante, the poet from whom he gained his greatest insights about experience and with whom he shared a firm belief in the power of poetry to exalt. Virgil, so the argument goes, is the central poet of the *Commedia* and of Dante's poetic development and what can be profitably said about the other *poetae* must be said in the light of this hard fact.[8]

---

7. W. Wetherbee, "Poeta che mi guidi: Dante, Lucan and Virgil," in R. von Hallberg, ed., *Canons* (Chicago, 1983), p. 20.

8. The role and status of Ovid in the intellectual life of Dante has only recently been confirmed in a positive way. Students of Dante have generally held that Dante knew Ovid mostly through glosses, accessus, and the details of the commentary tradition. This position has been most recently argued by A. Robson, "Dante's Use in the Divina Commedia of the Medieval Allegories on Ovid," in *Centenary Essays on Dante by Members of the Oxford Dante Society* (Oxford, 1965), pp. 1–38; or his "Dante's Reading of the Latin Poets and the Structure of the Commedia," in C. Grayson, ed., *The World of Dante: Essays*

But Dante's public homage to Virgil ought not to be the only grounds upon which, nor the only context in which, his poem is studied, especially since Dante himself seems so impatient to lead us to Virgil, to tell us in no uncertain terms that Virgil is his *buon maestro*. This impatience is itself an important fact to ponder. It is the result of the importance he attaches to the idea of tradition, to the influence of the past, and to the necessity of acknowledging both in his own work. In paying his debts before his readers' eyes, in announcing that Virgil is his master and teacher, Dante begins to set the account aright. In making good this debt he also gives readers insight into an intimacy that might otherwise go undisclosed. But other debts remain to be paid and many moments in the *Commedia*, like canto 4, render a clear accounting of the payment through allusion. Because he draws attention by negation to the role and status of Ovid, full-knowing readers would seem to be accorded a special invitation to scrutinize the ways in which the *Metamorphoses* and the *Commedia* play at each other in allusive space. One finds, as we shall see, that the ladder to God for Dante often enough included ruminations on the most fundamental of human concerns, cast within the context of Ovid's own renditions of human longing and suffering at the hands of divinity.

INFERNO 25.97: "TACCIA DI CADMO E D'ARETUSA OVIDIO"

Inferno 4 problematizes the figure of Ovid and affords Dante the venue by which to broach his own complex relationship with him and the other classical *poetae*.[9] In *Inferno* 25, Dante returns to the figure of Ovid for a more specific consideration of this poet and his craft. Superficially, the invocation proclaimed at verse 97, in the midst of a chilling recollection of transformation, is both negative and stereotyped. Ovid is summoned forth to be silenced because Dante, presumably, is now able to offer a new and better brand of transformation poetry. But allusion allows readers to construe the invocation in a much different light. Far from constituting a rejection of Ovid's peculiar brand of transformation poetry, or, worse yet, offering his own newer brand to replace it, Dante challenges in these lines the very notion that Ovid is a poet of transfor-

---

on *Dante and His Times* (Oxford, 1980), pp. 81–121. Cf. R. Hollander, *Allegory in Dante's "Commedia"* (Princeton, 1969), pp. 201–5.

9. J. T. Schnapp, "Dante's Ovidian Self-Correction in *Paradiso* 17," in Jacoff and Schnapp, *Poetry of Allusion*. pp. 214 ff., discusses *Inferno* 4 and other moments in the *Commedia* in which Dante evokes Ovid, doing so as a means to discuss the presence of Ovid later in the *Paradiso*.

mation. In this light, full-knowing readers can understand the invocation to Ovid in canto 25 explicitly to be a rejection of the traditional views of Ovidian poetry as a simple repository of myth and grotesque metamorphosis. Ovid's poetry, Dante would seem to say, is about something else again.

This position is gleaned in the careful ways Ovid is evoked verbally in Dante's lines. The canto takes shape in an initial sighting of Cacus and the Centaur. In turn, these grotesque figures demand of Dante a description that is so grotesque that even he has reason to doubt it. Thereupon he beholds several Florentine figures, who quickly become part of a bizarre scene of transformation involving serpents, which occupies the remaining verses of the canto. In the midst of his description, Dante mentions Ovid directly:

> "Taccia Lucano omai là dov' e' tocca
>   del misero Sabello e di Nasidio,
>   e attenda a udir quel ch'or si scocca.
> Taccia di Cadmo e d'Aretusa Ovidio,
>   ché se quello in serpente e quella in fonte
>   converte poetando, io non lo 'nvidio;
> ché due nature mai a fronte a fronte
>   non trasmutò sì ch'amendue le forme
>   a cambiar lor matera fosser pronte. (*Inf.* 25.94–102)

("Let Lucan be silent with his stories of wretched Sabellus and Nasidius and let him wait to hear what now comes forth; Let Ovid be silent about Cadmus and Arethusa; for if in his lines he turns him into a serpent and her into a fountain, I do not grudge it to him, for he never so transmuted natures face to face that both kinds were ready to exchange their substance.")

The superficial connection between Lucan's tales of Sabellus and Nasidius and Ovid's renditions of Cadmus and Arethusa is clear enough. Like the figures involved in Dante's recollection, these earlier figures suffered transformation of a horrific kind. But this scene also draws attention to Dante as a stiff and hard-headed challenger of Ovid as a poet of grotesque detail. The inherent competition involved in Dante's silencing of Ovid compels a full-knowing reader to ponder with more consideration the details of the transformations of Cadmus and Arethusa in the context of Dante's newer scene.

That attention skews the presentation of transformation in the canto and helps to situate more securely Dante's estimation of Ovid. Ovid's *Metamorphoses* are fraught with scenes of transformation of the most bizarre and arcane natures. The histories of Cadmus and Arethusa, on the other hand, do not come to mind as obvious candidates in a competition predicated on the details of grotesque metamorphosis. Indeed, in returning to Ovid's versions of the histories of Cadmus and Arethusa, one is struck by the tameness of Ovid's presentations. These figures have little to do with the horrible images Dante would seem to set for comparison with them. Cadmus and Arethusa are memorable in fact not so much for their grotesque transformations as for their fundamental humanity. It is their flaws, their unmistakable passions, the fears they endure, that readers take most vividly away from their stories. In this regard, their transformations become little more than foils to their emotions, a way for Ovid gently to caricature the vicissitudes of human vicitimization.

There is a solemn sadness in Cadmus's plea to his wife, who has borne all of his trials with him, especially as this plea comes on the heels of Ovid's description of his transformation, which is almost tender by comparison to Dante's description in *Inferno* 25:

> Dixit et, ut serpens, in longam tenditur alvum
> durataeque cuti squamas increscere sentit
> nigraque caeruleis variari corpora guttis
> in pectusque cadit pronus, commissaque in unum
> paulatim tereti tenuantur acumine crura.
> bracchia iam restant; quae restant, bracchia tendit,
> et lacrimis per adhuc humana fluentibus ora
> "accede, o coniunx, accede, miserrima" dixit
> "dumque aliquid superest de me, me tange manumque
> accipe, dum manus est, dum non totum occupat anguis." (*Met.* 4.576–85)[10]

(He spoke stretched out in long form like a snake; he felt his skin hardening and scales growing on it, while iridescent spots dotted his darkening body. He fell prone upon his belly, and his legs were gradually bound together into one and fashioned into a slender pointed tail. His arms remained; while they remained, he stretched them out, and with tears flowing down his human face he said: "Come close, oh, come, most wretched wife, and while there still is something left of me, touch me, take my hand, while there is a hand, while still the serpent does not totally take me over.")

This moment of Ovidian pathos relies on the deft manipulation of emotion and victimization for its bittersweet effect. The manipulation hinges, on the one hand, on Cadmus's lucidity, for he is aware of his fate as it befalls him. It

10. My text is W. S. Anderson, ed., *P. Ovidii Nasonis Metamorphoses* (Leipzig, 1977).

also hinges on his seemingly instinctive desire to spend the last moments of his human life with his wife, an instinct grounded, it would seem, in the consonance of their emotional life together before the transformation. It relies also on the utter loss of power evident in Cadmus's plea. If Cadmus's appeal were the result of a natural process, all would be different; the story would not be sad, only real. But as a victim who understands his victimization and hankers after the object of his love, Cadmus finds his fate sealed in a lingering sadness that is symbolic of the encroachments and brutal forces of divine power.

The final scene of Cadmus's transformation is also quietly horrible in the ways it qualifies his subdued submission to fate. As often in the *Metamorphoses,* Ovid's narrative verges precariously near the edge of melodrama. The balance here is achieved by Ovid's careful attention to the nuances of human personality. Cadmus and his wife are believable because of their devotion to each other in the face of their predicament. And the consonance of their love allows them, once they have both been transformed into serpents, seemingly to enjoy their new forms by virtue of their companionship. While their comrades are filled, understandably, with horror, the two serpents slither off into the woods, *placidi dracones,* mindful of who they were and yet knowing what they have become. What is striking, then, is not the metamorphosis recalled in this narrative but the humanity affirmed in the face of it, couched in the details of victimization and emotional fortitude that qualify this story most directly.

Arethusa's tale is no less compelling in the same way:

quid mihi tunc animi miserae fuit? anne quod agnae est,
siqua lupos audit circum stabula alta frementes,
aut lepori, qui vepre latens hostilia cernit
ora canum nullosque audet dare corpore motus?
non tamen abscedit; neque enim vestigia cernit
longius ulla pedum: servat nubemque locumque.
occupat obsessos sudor mihi frigidus artus,
caeruleaeque cadunt toto de corpore guttae,
quaque pedem movi, manat lacus, eque capillis
ros cadit, et citius, quam nunc tibi facta renarro,
in latices mutor. (*Met.* 5.626–36)

(How did I feel then, wretch that I was? Was I not the lamb, when it hears wolves howling around the stables? Or the hare hiding in the brambles that sees the dogs' deadly muzzles and dares not make the slightest move? But he wasn't gone, for he saw no traces of my feet further on; he watched the cloud and the place. Cold sweat poured down my choked limbs and the dark drops fell from my whole body. Wherever I put my foot a pool ran out, and from my hair the drops fell; and sooner than I can now tell it, I was changed to a stream of water.)

Ovid's description is especially harrowing here because he allows his readers the opportunity to witness the events of her transformation from Arethusa's privileged position. By virtue of following his words, readers are privy to Arethusa's chilling vision, try on with her the various identities of other victims, breathe her breaths and hope her hopes for freedom. Then, the sweat of fear, which also represents the toil of her struggle to be free, becomes the sweat of a curse. No sooner is the line that describes the sweat comprehended than readers discover—to their horror, for they have been won over to her side by her own telling of this story—that she has lost. She becomes a river and plunges to her fate. The episode recalling Arethusa's fate, then, much like the narrative of Cadmus and his wife, hinges on the carefully wrought emotional appeal of its protagonist, this time rendered in the manner of a first-person narration. The horror of the metamorphosis is vivid, but the pathos of the figure transformed is served by that horror, so that the emotion of the victim impresses more than the terror of her fate.

Allusive play allows a full-knowing reader the option of reading Dante's boast in *Inferno* 25 as a corrective to tradition. Dante qualifies Ovid in the normal way, as a poet concerned with myth and bizarre transformation, and he succeeds in writing transformation poetry that would seem to outdo even Ovid in terms of horror and grotesque detail. But when readers return to the Ovidian moments specifically held up for comparison, they can hardly concur that the histories of Cadmus and Arethusa offer instances of grotesque transformation. Transformation is part of these stories, to be sure, but Ovid's narratives are much more stories about the terrors of human victimization, about quiet bravery, about fortitude of spirit in the face of insuperable odds.

In calling forth Ovid in the ways he does in *Inferno* 25, Dante would seem to create a new identity for his classical *auctor*. He creates a false Ovid, with whom he associates the poetry of myth and transformation and whom he silences. At the same time, he sends his readers back to the text of Ovid's *Metamorphoses*, the source of myth and transformation, where the real Ovid subsists in the stories he tells. In doing this, Dante would seem to offer a qualifying attribute for Ovid that is lacking, as we have seen, in *Inferno* 4, a qualification that centers not on mythography or transformation, but on the features that set humans apart from the gods and from nature's brutal forces. Dante's qualification in *Inferno* 25 points, then, to a whole other side of Ovidian poetry in the *Metamorphoses,* a side of Ovid revealed and ratified in other allusive moments in the *Commedia.*

PURGATORIO 2.7–9: THE DAWN IN *PURGATORIO* AND ARACHNE'S CHEEKS

One such moment occurs in *Purgatorio* 2. There, making his way into that middle realm between Hell and Paradise, Dante pauses, as he often does in these cantos, to set the scene in epic and physical terms. Using the details of astrology to situate the sky in the context of the evanescent night and the burgeoning sun, Dante reaches for a metaphor to frame the picture of dawn in *Purgatorio:*

> Giá era 'l sole a l'orizzonte giunto
>   lo cui meridian cerchio coverchia
>   Ierusalèm col suo più alto punto;
> e la notte, che opposita a lui cerchia,
>   uscia di Gange fuor con le Bilance,
>   che le caggion di man quando soverchia;
> sì che le bianche e le vermiglie guance,
>   là dov' i' era, de la bella Aurora
>   per troppa etate divenivan rance. (*Purg.* 2.1–9)

(Already the sun had reached the horizon whose meridian circle covers Jerusalem with its highest point, and night, circling opposite it, was issuing from the Ganges with the Scales, which fall from her hand when she exceeds the day, so that, there where I was, the white and rosy cheeks of fair Aurora, with her increasing age, were turning orange.)

This picture of dawn is cast in terms that recall Ovid's description of Arachne:[11]

> sed tamen erubuit, subitusque invita notavit
> ora rubor rursusque evanuit, ut solet aer
> purpureus fieri, cum primum Aurora movetur,
> et breve post tempus candescere solis ab ortu. (*Met.* 6.46–49)

(though Arachne did turn red, for a sudden flush marked her unwilling cheeks and

---

11. Much recent work treats the function of Arachne in the *Commedia* via Ovid's version of her story in the *Metamorphoses.* No work, to my knowledge, treats the allusion in *Purg.* 2. For a review of the literature and Dante's treatment of the Arachne myth, see P. R. Macfie, "Ovid, Arachne, and the Poetics of Paradise," in Jacoff and Schnapp, *Poetry of Allusion,* pp. 159–72.

again faded: as when the sky grows crimson when the dawn first appears, and after a little while when the sun is up it grows white.)

The specific points of allusion are *rubor, Aurora,* and *candescere* in Ovid, corresponding to *vermiglie, Aurora,* and *bianche* in Dante. Because these linkages point specifically to Ovid, they sanction allusion and reveal a connection between Dante's dawn and Ovid's Arachne, allowing the natural scene evoked in *Purgatorio* 2 to be personalized in terms of human emotion cast in an Ovidian guise.

Ovid's version of Arachne's story is a study in contrasts between human longing and divine retribution. Ovid's handling of it, moreover, places a premium on Arachne's vulnerability by contrasting it to her pride (not arrogance) and confidence in her own abilities. The details of her sad life, her mother's death, her father's menial job, and Arachne's own low birth and station in life, conspire to render her a defenseless figure in the world. Arachne's one claim to fame is her extraordinary ability at weaving. Arachne's lowly position is not detailed by Ovid simply for the sake of pathetic indulgence, however. Ovid is careful as he proceeds in his story to contrast the earthly impotency of Arachne with her seemingly god-granted powers of weaving. He never directly says that Arachne was taught to weave by Athena, but he does admit that Arachne's talents would lead one to think that she had been so taught (*scires a Pallade doctam; Met.* 6.22). Arachne's defense of her innate abilities, when taken in the context of her lowly existence, makes her a sympathetic, because human, figure.

When Athena appears before Arachne in disguise and almost bursting with jealousy, therefore, the stage has been set for a classic confrontation between good and evil. And, once again, as at other points in the *Metamorphoses,* Ovid removes any chance of his story becoming melodrama by his deft handling of characterization. The emotions ascribed to Arachne are believable because their context has been carefully presented. The deceptions of Athena, therefore, only add to the power of Arachne's position. Athena becomes the bully who is afraid to show her face, the symbol of a kind of wickedness that finds contentment in making victims of the less powerful. There is no bravado or burgeoning ego implicit in Arachne's question of the disguised Athena—"why does the goddess avoid fighting the good fight?" (*cur haec certamina vitat? Met.* 6.42)—just the dictates of fairness and propriety of action. Morally, the frail human girl is, at this moment, far superior to her divine persecutor.

In answering Arachne's question—*venit,* "she has come," Athena says—the goddess reveals herself to her victim. Ovid's portrayal of Arachne's response to the ruse that she now understands all too well is perfect in the balances it achieves between narrative, as against emotional, descriptiveness. Arachne is unafraid, according to Ovid, who declares that she alone remained so (sola est non territa virgo; *Met.* 6.45), yet that declaration of feeling, coming as it does from an omniscient narrator, is deftly balanced by a physical description of Arachne that belies her fearlessness. Arachne does, after all, blush slightly upon realizing her predicament. That blush fades as quickly as it appears, to be sure, but this detail of emotional vulnerability confirms the humanity of Arachne and the righteousness of her position. Arachne's blush, like the dawn of which it reminds Ovid, is metaphorical, underscoring in symbolical terms the per-durability of the righteous position in the face of insuperable odds. The blush of Arachne's cheeks represents also, and perhaps most important, the point of no return for Arachne, the moment in which she determines, in a flush of anger and determination, to contend with Athena.

The linkage of Arachne's blush to *Purgatorio* 2 underscores several themes. It sets into high relief the human dimension of the canto, while simultaneously accentuating the durability and righteousness of the good soul. In confirming the *humanitas* of this moment in the poem, allusion also allows full-knowing readers to spy in its play the affirmation of those traits—singular talent, devotion to duty, self-praise and confidence—that are uniquely and powerfully Arachne's. That affirmation is corroborated in several ways subsequently, most notably by the presence of Casella, Dante's dear friend.

Immediately following the Ovidian allusion in the opening of the canto, the angel of God arrives with his boatload of sinners eager to climb to the top of the mountain for absolution. As Dante soon recognizes, among the company of these sinners is Casella,[12] who, like Arachne, is an accomplished artist. Remembering Casella's penchant for song, Dante asks him to sing and soon the friend begins an old piece of Dante's, "Amor che ne la mente mi ragiona." Even Virgil is charmed and listens intently, enthralled by the perfection of Casella's voice. The virtuosity of Casella's performance, so perfect that the stern Cato must banish Virgil, Dante, and the souls of the dead from their momentary repose, ratifies more than the talents of Dante's friend, however. Casella's song is emblematic also of a higher and more profound power that reverberates allusively in this scene, gaining resonance in the light of Arachne's virtuoso performance. The connection between the two artists in this canto devolves onto the

12. For a reading somewhat at odds with my own, see J. Freccero, "Casella's Song (*Purg.* 11,112)," *Dante Studies* 91 (1973), pp. 73–80.

issue of those qualities that abide beyond the limits of temporal life and the finite world. The power of any art to survive the great transference of human souls from the world of the living to the world of spirit affirms the emotional consonances that give rise to all art, and ratifies the righteousness of celebration that art confers onto those moments of human experience worthy of art's veneration. Allusion allows full-knowing readers to understand that, in this conferral and celebration, the highest aims of the living achieve a glorious repose within the furthest reaches of the world of spirit.

A broader aesthetic issue is also broached in the play of allusion's space, centering on the morality of mimesis. It is difficult, after all, not to read Ovid's rendition of Arachne's story as an allegory of mimesis whose conclusion (that art disfigures and presumably can kill) renders dubious Ovid's approbation of Arachne's actions. This diminution of Arachne's position does not in the least diminish those qualities of her character that Ovid has already set for praise and acknowledgment: her lowly status, her glorious talent, her swift and sure determination in the face of harsh odds. But once those qualities have been certified in the narrative, that is, once Arachne has blushed, Ovid's tone changes. She makes a mistake, Ovid says, in "rush[ing] to her fate" (*in sua fata ruit; Met.* 6.51). There can be no putting off this contest, nor its inevitable outcome. One way or the other, Athena will win.

The figure of Arachne, therefore, is both a positive and a negative symbol. On the one hand, she represents a fortitude and pride that are hallmarks of achievement and artistic accomplishment. She perseveres and does so well knowing the difficulties involved. On the other hand, she represents the dangers of extremism, of placing too much emphasis on art at the expense of experience itself. Ovid's worry here has to do with balance. It is important in the practice of art to keep clearly in mind the distinctions between the reality that inspires mimesis (the archetype) and the copy of the reality that becomes the finished work of art. Mimesis is moral only if the balance between archetype and copy is sustained. Art's value inheres chiefly in the ways it compels us, challenges us, to partake of better, of richer, of more profound experiences. Experience, in the end, is what counts for most. This is why the lesson of Arachne's fate is so stunningly cruel. Arachne is allowed to continue to experience life as an artist—Athena's penalty is to condemn Arachne to live, after all, not to die ("vivit," she says)—but at what price?

In the play of allusive space, however, Dante would seem to refuse the stern moral lessons that Arachne symbolizes. The allusion to Ovid's rendition of Arachne's story, after all, links to the moment of revelation in its lines, the point when Arachne fully realizes the implications of her position. That scene, with its harrowing realities and burgeoning emotions, depends for its effect on the careful introduction of Arachne, the deft qualification of Athena as wily and bitter, and the confirmations of Arachne's superb artistry. Full-knowing readers, then, have every reason to see in this allusion a strategic refusal of the latter part of Arachne's story as rendered by Ovid. Arachne is not a symbol of human volition gone awry, of improper moral choices, only of human fortitude and righteousness.

The issue of mimetic rectitude is held at bay in allusive space. In *Purgatorio* 2, allusive play would seem to affirm not lectures about the morality of mimesis, but the abiding quality of verbal or visual artistry that proffers the bounty of eternity to human experience. Arachne's fate might be seen to infiltrate *Purgatorio* 2, but only as a means to confirm a discourse on permanence. If Arachne's struggle against Athena is emblematic of the good soul's struggle against mortality and the terrors of the *Inferno,* if Casella's song, replaced eventually by the healing words of the Psalms, illuminates what abides in and out of time, then the human qualities of fortitude and right action, cast within the context of the mimetic arts, are worth the price they might exact. Transcendence and permanence are things worth fighting for, if Arachne is any witness, and the music of *Purgatorio* 2 is itself a verbal reckoning of some magnitude that confirms the efficacy, the morality, of mimesis as it seeks a transcendence from the world which gave rise to it. The redemptive power of art, Dante would seem to say, is worth the moral price we pay to be redeemed, even if, in celebrating its *humanitas,* we only advance to the base of the mountain in Purgatory.

PURGATORIO 4.137–39: BELACQUA, PHAETON, AND THE PROBLEMS OF IDENTITY

Allusion reveals the celebration of *humanitas* in *Purgatorio* 4 also, where Ovid's words are put to good use to confirm the power and the problems of self-identity. At the end of this canto, Dante has occasion to make use of Ovidian vocabulary as a way to embellish the details of the midday sky:

> . . . Vienne omai; vedi ch'è tocco
> meridian dal sole e a la riva
> cuopre la notte già col piè Morrocco. (*Purg.* 4.137–139)

(Come now, see, the meridian is touched by the sun and already on the shore night sets its foot on Morocco.)
dum loquor, Hesperio positas in litore metas
umida nox tetigit; non est mora libera nobis; (*Met.* 2.142–143)

(While I speak dewy night has reached her goal on the far western shore. Delay is no longer an option for us.)

Like the linkage to Ovid's Arachne, this allusion relies on language used by Ovid of humans in order to qualify aspects of geography. The points of collusion here—*nox, notte, litore, riva*—sanction full-knowing reading and link the ending of *Purgatorio* 4 to a dramatic point in Ovid's rendering of the story of Phaeton and Apollo, that point at which the sun has first risen on the new day and Apollo comes to terms with the notion that he is about to allow his son to commit suicide.[13]

The crazy-quilt series of events that has led to this moment in the second book of the *Metamorphoses* has its origin in the story that concludes Ovid's first book of that poem.[14] There, Phaeton demands of his mother information about his paternity and ends with her injunction that he seek for himself the glorious father he feels compelled to meet. Book 2 opens with Phaeton standing before the palace of the sun, dazzled by its splendors and warmly admitted by Apollo to it and to the paternity that only the sun god can proffer. The actions of father, mother, and son collude at this juncture to ratify a fundamental point about human (and divine) nature, namely, that humans (and gods) are inclined to seek confirmation of their identities even at some risk to themselves or to others. Clymene, for example, is carefully qualified by Ovid as only too willing to tell Phaeton of his own identity lest she suffer an insult to her own.[15] Phaeton, on the other hand, is only too willing to deliver that insult in the attempt to claim his own identity,[16] an identity that is confirmed by Apollo, who himself willingly assumes the role of *pater* in the process of performing this confirmation.[17]

Those risks only grow starker as Phaeton and Apollo meet in book 2. Phaeton is embraced by Apollo, who has taken off his crown of light, so as not to blind and burn his son. But Apollo, caricatured in perfect form by Ovid here

13. See also on Phaeton, K. Brownlee, "Phaeton's Fall and Dante's Ascent," *Dante Studies* 102 (1984), pp. 135–44. Cf. the discussion of Phaeton in the larger context of the *Paradiso* in Schnapp, "Dante's Ovidian Self-Correction in *Paradiso* 17," in Jacoff and Schnapp, *Poetry of Allusion,* pp. 214–23 and esp. p. 217 and n. 15.

14. See *Met.* 1.747–79 for the details of this portion of the story.

15. See esp. Ovid's qualification of Clymene at *Met.* 1.765–79.

16. See esp. *Met.* 1.755–61, where Phaeton grows "red with rage" (erubuit . . . iramque) at the doubts raised by Epaphus about his paternity, which leads presently to his confrontation with Clymene.

17. *Met.* 2.34–48 are dominated by words stressing fatherhood or paternity: *progenies, parenti* (v. 34), *pater* (vv. 36, 49), *genitor* (vv. 38, 40), *propago* (v. 38), *paternos* (v. 47), e.g.

as the somewhat befuddled father trying to please his long-lost son, no sooner has confirmed Phaeton's paternity than he says something he almost immediately regrets: "'And so that you don't doubt me, seek from me what you will, so that you might receive it from me as a gift. And let the pool where the gods swear—which I have not seen—witness my promise to you.' Scarcely had he stopped talking when Phaeton asked Apollo for his chariot, and the right to drive his winged horses for one day." ("quoque minus dubites, quodvis pete munus, ut illud / me tribuente feras. promissis testis adesto / dis iuranda palus, oculis incognita nostris." / vix bene desierat, currus rogat ille paternos / inque diem alipedum ius et moderamen equorum; *Met.* 2.44–48).

Ovid renders this scene with a deft emotional balance, contrasting the proverbial doting father against the long-lost adolescent son, whose demands for acceptance compel the father to do whatever must be done to win the son's approval. Apollo's better instincts are forsaken in this moment, neutralized by his emotional response as a father to demands that in any other circumstance would not be brooked.

Phaeton cannot be warned of his peril, nor is Apollo in the position to warn him. Rather than refuse Phaeton's request, Apollo takes up with a vengeance his new role as *pater,* offering all manner of (useless) advice to Phaeton as he proceeds to the chariot of the sun. But in assuming the identity he does, Apollo's words fail him, as they fail so many parents. Phaeton is hardened to his task. Only the dawn's intrusion shifts Apollo's attention to what must be done. Now Apollo's role as *pater* is delineated even further by Ovid. As the impending send-off approaches, Apollo takes to annointing Phaeton with sacred ointment, a salve to keep the burning flames of the sun from harming Phaeton's face (vv. 120 ff.). Then more talk occurs, pleas to reconsider one last time, warnings that Apollo is not quite ever up to the task of the chariot and its horses, as if more words could somehow save Phaeton. But time catches up with both father and son: "dewy night has reached her goal on the far western shore. We may no longer delay" (. . . Hesperio positas in litore metas / umida nox tetigit; non est mora libera nobis; *Met.* 2.142–143). With these words, Ovid closes the final moments of Phaeton's life, allowing Apollo to stand as the doting father who sanctions his own son's suicide, events recollected at the end of *Purgatorio* 4, where this moment is evoked through allusion.

In allusive space, the identities sought and achieved are rendered in the more specific context of *Purgatorio* 4. This canto begins with a discourse of the soul that has a direct bearing on identity in the context of Christian theology:

Quando per dilettanze o ver per doglie,
   che alcuna virtù nostra comprenda,
   l'anima bene ad essa si raccoglie,
par ch'a nulla potenza più intenda;
   e questo è contra quello error che crede
   ch'un'anima sovr' altra in noi s'accenda.
E però, quando s'ode cosa o vede
   che tegna forte a sé l'anima volta,
   vassene 'l tempo e l'uom non se n'avvede;
ch'altra potenza è quella che l'ascolta,
   e altra è quella c'ha l'anima intera:
   questa è quasi legata e quella è sciolta. (*Purg.* 4.1–12)

(When by pleasures or pains which one of our faculties receives the soul concentrates wholly on that, it seems to give heed to no other of its powers, and this is contrary to the error which maintains that one soul is kindled above another in us; and therefore, when a thing is heard or seen that keeps the soul strongly bent on it, the time passes and one is not aware, for the faculty that listens for it is one and that which holds the entire soul another, this as it were bound, the other free.)

Though Dante's Italian is compressed of meaning and philosophical in tone, he describes in these stern opening verses to *Purgatorio* 4 the myopia of perception that plagues all humans. Having lavished attention onto Manfred's story in the previous canto,[18] Dante has lost all track of time and uses his mental immersion as a foil to refute the theory of the plurality of souls. If there were more than one soul, Dante's practical experience teaches him, he would have known how much time had elapsed during Manfred's story and not been dead to the world during its telling. In other words, humans are victimized by their own inability to grasp the larger view of things, especially with respect to their own lives. Their perceptions, much like their search for self-knowledge, are often self-limited, proscribed by emotion, rendered without a full accounting of the situation in which they exist.

    This rumination on perceptual myopia serves as a foil to the Ovidian rendition of Phaeton and Apollo that resonates in allusive space. The play sanctioned there between the theological dictates of Dante's opening and the meditation on personality offered in Ovid's *Metamorphoses* reveals the fissure between spiritual necessity and personal choice. These two poles, the one ratified by God, the other operative in the fallen world of humans, are mediated in

18. On which see Freccero, "Manfred's Wounds and the Poetics of the *Purgatorio*."

Purgatorio 4 by the figure of Belacqua, who lingers in this canto as the human and Christian counterpart to Phaeton and Apollo.

Dante depicts Belacqua as a man trapped by what he was in life, doomed to suffer the consequences of his own identity. He sums up, by his own example, the discourse on the myopia of the soul's perception, but he also is a metaphor for humanity's often onesided search for selfhood, well symbolized by the history of Apollo and Phaeton. Belacqua's resigned lament, and the image of the sun drawn from the story of Apollo and Phaeton that follows that lament, frame Belacqua's unenviable position:

> Ed elli, "O frate, andar in sù che porta?
>   ché non mi lascerebbe ire a' martìri
>   l'angel di Dio che siede in su la porta.
> Prima convien che tanto il ciel m'aggiri
>   di fuor da essa, quanto fece in vita,
>   per ch'io 'ndugiai al fine i buon sospiri,
> se orazione in prima non m'aita
>   che surga sù di cuor che in grazia viva;
>   l'altra che val, che 'n ciel non è udita?" (*Purg.* 4.127–35)

(And he said: "O brother, what is the use of going up, for God's angel that sits in the gateway would not let me pass to the torments? The heavens must first wheel about me, waiting outside, as long as in my lifetime, because I put off good sighs to the last, unless prayer first helps me which rises from a heart that lives in grace. What avails the other that is not heard in Heaven?")

No prayers are forthcoming for Belacqua, only the swift injunction from Virgil, telling Dante that it is time to be on their collective way, reported in language that alludes to the story of Apollo and Phaeton. In their own imperfect and human steps up the mountain of purgation, therefore, Virgil and Dante themselves turn from a world of myopia, lost chances, stubborn grief, to a welcoming midday sun. It is this sun, with its Christian and Ovidian connotations, that confirms in the play of allusive space the inevitability of Belacqua's predicament no matter the intention, no matter the effort to move beyond the narrow limits imposed by the fall from grace or humanity's striving for selfhood and identity, the constant craving for the ladder to God.

Chapter 9 The Green World: Pound and Contemporary Allusion

Nacio
la palabra en la sangre,
creció en el cuerpo oscuro, palpitando,
y voló con los labios y la boca. . . .
Luego el sentido llena la palabra.
Quedó preñada y se llenó de vidas.
Todo fue nacimientos y sonidos:
la afirmación, la claridad, la fuerza,
la negación, la destrucción, la muerte:
el verbo asumió todos los poderes
y se fundió existencia con esencia
en la electricidad de su hermosura.
(The word was born in the blood, grew in the dark body, beating, and
flew through the lips and the mouth. . . . Later on, the word fills with
meaning. It remained pregnant and filled with lives. All was births and
sounds: affirmation, clarity, power, negation, destruction, death: the verb
assumed all the power and fused existence with essence in the electricity
of its beauty.)
—Pablo Neruda, *La Palabra*

Pablo Neruda conceives of the word, *la palabra*, not merely as a mental
construct nor simply as the purveyor of emotion formally concretized,

but as part of life itself, arising "in the blood" (en la sangre) and "beating" (palpitando), as if it were the heart, taking form from the lips and mouth that give shape to it ("voló con los labios y la boca").[1] It is also generative. When the word is full of meaning ("el sentido llena la palabra"), it gives rise to life and the progeny of word upon word harbors the plenitude of life's emotions. This unmediated plenitude, the fusion of existence with essence ("se fundió existencia con esencia"), leads to celebration, to a moment when words become a kind of redemptive potable of humanity's collective life.

The qualities that Neruda highlights in his description of the word—its semantic shadings, its manifold potentials, its unique and sometimes troubling autonomy, its connectedness to what is abiding for humans—ratify the difficulties of verbal communication and accentuate the ability of language to play beyond the control of its users. These difficulties have become in this century the touchstones of literary and critical activity, but the preceding chapters have suggested how old they are in the Western literary tradition and how allusion has consistently functioned by exploiting them.

Taking up where Dante and his successors left off, modern practitioners of allusion seem ever the more indebted to the power of the allusion's reader and, therefore, to the autonomy of the allusive word. Whereas Goethe turns to ancient material in a way strikingly similar to Catullus's allusive practice, allowing a single, prior model to inform the allusive play of his newer work of art, Baudelaire relies much more on the model of allusion bequeathed by Augustine and Dante, wherein multiple prior works inform an individual passage. Different from the habits of both Goethe and Baudelaire, however, is the allusive practice of Ezra Pound, who ratchets up the function of readerly power in his writing. To do this, Pound relies in the *Cantos* entirely on the power of the allusive reader to construct the interpretive contexts of his poems. It is no longer the case that discrete situations are imagined by the poet and embellished by allusion, whose interpretive bounties are reaped through readerly power. Instead, readerly power is required to construct the discrete situations themselves, and allusion becomes not an adornment to them but the very means by which they are constituted. In this way, the power of the reader and of the word coalesce, marking the apogee of allusive writing in the West. Thus, this final chapter, in addition to attending to modern versions of allusion, also brings the story of allusion down to a contemporary setting.

1. My text is P. Neruda, *Selected Poems,* trans. A. Kerrigan, W. S. Merwin, A. Reid, and N. Tarn (Boston, 1970), pp. 430, 432, whose translations have assisted me in making my own.

GOETHE AND TIBULLUS

Goethe was a wide and assiduous reader of the ancient literary tradition and he displays a variety of allusive approaches to that tradition.[2] In "Harzreise im Winter," for example, the poet evokes the verbal style of Pindar, lending to his poem attributes of form and theme that one more readily associates with Greek lyric: a belief in the rhetorical edificies of poetry, a vatic concern for the power of poetry to redeem, an insistence on the richness and the mysticism of language. By distinction, the glories of Catullus, Tibullus, and Horace are evoked in the *Römische Elegien* through allusion, sometimes directly through shared vocabulary, sometimes through more subtle verbal bows to qualities of syntax or patterns of prosody.

In the poems written in his earlier period, however, a style of allusion beholden to Catullus is more clearly evinced, wherein a single allusive model is brought forward verbally. "Ganymed," to take one example, evokes in its title the passions of Zeus for his cupbearer and establishes a situation of discourse in which Zeus pines after the young boy with whom he is smitten, linking allusively to the moment in Theognis where the passion of Zeus for Ganymede is described.[3] As it turns out, however, the poem gives shape to Ganymede's desires, concluding with the depiction of the cupbearer's frustrations at not being able fully to be with Zeus on account of the latter's divinity. The force of Goethe's title, therefore, which evokes in the play of allusion's space the ages-old history of this beautiful youth as more a passive victim than an active participant, renders to this poem an irony it otherwise would lack:

> Wie im Morgenglanze
> Du rings mich anglühst,
> Frühling, Geliebter!
> Mit tausendfacher Liebeswonne
> Sich an mein Herz drängt

2. The bibliography on Goethe's classicism is enormous; I have found useful W. J. Keller, *Goethe's Estimate of the Greek and Latin Writers as Revealed by His Works, Letters, Diaries, and Conversations* (Madison, 1916); K. D. Weisinger, *The Classical Facade: A Nonclassical Reading of Goethe's Classicism* (University Park, Pa., 1988); and, on the dramas, I. Wagner, *Critical Approaches to Goethe's Classical Dramas: "Iphigenie," "Torquato Tasso," and "Die natürliche Tochter"* (Columbia, S.C., 1995).

3. On Goethe's use of classical myth see H. G. Schmiz, *Kritische Gewaltenteilung: Mythenrezeption der Klassik im Spannungsfeld von Antike, Christentum und Aufklärung: Goethes "Iphigenie" und Hölderlins "Hyperion"* (Frankfurt and New York, 1988) and T. R. Wutrich, *Prometheus and Faust: The Promethean Revolt in Drama From Classical Antiquity to Goethe* (Westport, Ct., 1995).

Deiner ewigen Wärme
Heilig Gefühl,
Unendliche Schöne!
Daß ich dich fassen möcht
In diesen Arm!
Ach, an deinem Busen
Lieg ich, schmachte,
Und deine Blumen, dein Gras
Drängen sich an mein Herz.
Du kühlst den brennenden
Durst meines Busens,
Lieblicher Morgenwind!
Ruft drein die Nachtigall
Liebend nach mir aus dem Nebeltal.
Ich komm, ich komme!
Wohin? Ach, wohin?
Hinauf! Hinauf strebts.
Es schweben die Wolken
Abwärts, die Wolken
Neigen sich der sehnenden Liebe.
Mir! Mir!
In euerm Schoße
Aufwärts! Umfangend umfangen!
Aufwärts an deinen Busen,
Alliebender Vater![4]

(How you glow upon me, in the brightness of the morning, all round me, Spring, my lover! With thousandfold rapturous love the holy sense of your everlasting warmth presses against my heart, oh infinite beauty! That I might clasp you in these arms! Oh I lie at your breast, I languish, and your flowers and your grass press against my heart. You cool my bosom's burning thirst, dear wind of morning! Out of the misty valley the nightingale calls out to me in love. I come! I come! Whither, oh whither? Upward, upward I am driven. The clouds float down, the clouds descend to my love and my longing. To me! To me! Aloft, enveloped by you! embraced and embracing! Aloft, to lie at your breast, all-loving father.)

Here the evocations of love's perfection reflected in natural bounties and their infinite beauties (*unendliche Schöne*) imply that the youthful Ganymede is working his charms on Zeus. The personalization of the poem's voice at the end of the first stanza and the focus on the intimacies of love's desires do nothing to

4. My text is E. Staiger, ed., *Goethe*, 3 vols. (Zürich, 1952–1959). Translations are adapted from D. Luke, ed., *Goethe* (Harmondsworth, 1964).

counter this interpretation. The force of the poem's title leads readers to think that Zeus is the speaker who wishes that "I might clasp you in these arms" (Daß ich dich fassen möcht / in diesen Arm!). Of a sudden, however, the speaker is transported to some higher, ideal place (Hinauf! Hinauf strebts), and readerly doubts obtain at once, for Zeus ought not to suffer a transference of this sort. Not until the final line of the poem, however, do readers know for a fact that the speaker is Ganymede himself, smitten by the perfections of Zeus, the all-loving Father (Alliebender Vater). Yet the irony of Goethe's ending resonates only if the myth of Ganymede as given to the west by Theognis is recalled allusively. Without that link, Goethe's poem is just one more version of an ancient story. With the linkage, the powerful reversals of voice and position make the poem a much more complete, and therefore much more sinister, reflection on love's power.

"Das Tagebuch" functions in much the same way, evoking through an allusion to Tibullus the full play of a Latin poem against the more rarefied details offered in the newer German poem that calls it forward. The Latin allusion in question, a tag from Tibullus 1.5.39–40— ". . . aliam tenui, sed iam cum gaudia adirem, / Admonuit dominae deseruitque Venus"[5] (I have held another, but on the very brink of joy Venus admonished me of my mistress and abandoned me)—returns full-knowing readers to the exact midpoint of Tibullus's poem, where the speaker's present contemplations of an affair gone sour and his private dreams of time spent with his lover lead to a confrontation with insistent realities. The speaker declares that often he has tried to banish love's troubles by drinking, but pain turned the wine into tears (saepe ego temptavi curas depellere vino: / at dolor in lacrimas verterat omne merum; vv. 37–38). There follows the quotation that controls Goethe's poem.

This allusion focuses on the raw energy and passion of human sexuality: the tag, after all, leads full-knowing readers to a point in Tibullus's poem immediately preceding an orgasm that, as it turns out, is spoiled by memory and guilt. The function of guilt is ratified in Goethe's opening discussion of the human heart and its infinite ability to confound comprehension ("Das Menschenherz sei ewig unergründlich"), leading the poem's speaker to declare that both pagans and Christians are sinners ("So sei der Christe wie der Heide sündlich"). The situation of discourse in the Tibullan allusion, therefore, forms a foil to the emotions that resonate in Goethe's opening lines. The emotions imagined in the German poem take shape in the play of allusive space in

5. My text is G. Luck, ed., *Albii Tibulli aliorumque carmina* (Stuttgart, 1988).

Tibullus's latest spat with Delia, which has, as it turns out, important spiritual and psychological lessons to teach.

The German poem centers upon a chance sexual encounter at an inn, where the speaker has found himself holed up, unwillingly (at least at first), away from his beloved ("Von meiner Trauten lange Zeit entfernet") owing to a broken axle on his carriage. The feelings of remorse and longing, which assist the poet in an adroit construction of the subsequent seduction scene, quickly melt away when Goethe's speaker spies the mistress of the inn:

> So stand ich nun. Der Stern des nächsten Schildes
> Berief mich hin, die Wohnung schien erträglich.
> Ein Mädchen kam, des seltensten Gebildes,
> Das Licht erleuchtend. Mir ward gleich behäglich.
> Hausflur und Treppe sah ich als ein Mildes,
> Die Zimmerchen erfreuten mich unsäglich.
> Den sündigen Menschen, der im Freien schwebet—
> Die Schönheit spinnt, sie ists, die ihn umwebet.

(So there I stood. The star of the nearest inn sign spoke its summons. The lodging seemed decent enough. A girl came with the light; she was most rarely shaped, and at once I felt at ease. I found the hall and staircase very pleasing, and the little bedrooms absolutely delightful. When a sinful man is wandering abroad, it is beauty that spins a web to ensnare him).

Here the resonances of *sündlich* and *sündigen* confirm the growing force of guilt that is given full expression presently, for soon the girl comes to the speaker's room with supper and he can control himself no longer. He forces himself upon her, mildly but with authority. Her protests douse his passions momentarily, but those passions are ignited once again when, after explaining that she must get back to her grumpy aunt, she promises to return later, when her aunt and the rest of the guests will be sleeping.

The poem moves quickly to the central moment. Everything is perfect from the speaker's perspective. The girl is young, superbly formed and, most important of all, willing. Her willingness is perfect also, for she is, as Goethe makes certain to report, a virgin ("Du hast mich rein . . ."), heightening the eroticism of the poem's crux. Although the setting of this night and its amorous potential are as perfect in their scope, detail, and execution as any classical elegist could imagine, the night's wonder has an unfortunate side-effect, leading as it does immediately to an inability on the part of the speaker to perform sexually ("Weicht schülerhaft zurück und abgekühlet").

Goethe's poem now centers on the relationship of sexual performance and emotional consonance, and the play of allusion helps to confirm the necessary incongruity between the two. The poem's situation, with its perfect visions and teasing descriptions, leads to a moment of sterile disability. Yet that moment plays against the sentiments expressed by Tibullus in his poem, where a form of impotency owed to guilt frames the poet's ruminations on lost love. Those ruminations eventually confirm the poet's fidelity. After all, he has sought to banish love's troubles with Delia by taking another lover, yet the memory of Delia has disabled his performance. For the speaker of Goethe's poem, of course, the issue is not so straightforward because the event is too close to hand. The speaker spends a good deal of time reflecting on the fulfillment the girl would seem to have gained from their encounter. Thereupon he watches her sleep, feels like a traveler who, already withering of thirst, dies of a snakebite at the edge of a spring, condemns himself for his inabilities, grows smitten yet again with the perfections of her form, and dares not even move lest the low and beastly thing that he has become disturb the dreams of this fair and perfect creature:

> So lag sie himmlisch an bequemer Stelle,
> Als wenn das Lager ihr allein gehörte,
> Und an die Wand gedrückt, gequetscht zur Hölle,
> Ohnmächtig jener, dem sie nichts verwehrte.
> Vom Schlangenbisse fällt zunächst der Quelle
> Ein Wandrer so, den schon der Durst verzehrte.
> Sie atmet lieblich holdem Traum entgegen;
> Er hält den Atem, sie nicht aufzuregen

> (So thus the lovely creature lay, making herself comfortable as if the bed were all hers; and pushed against the wall, squashed like the very devil, he to whom she permitted everything lay and could do nothing. Thus a wayfarer, already parched with thirst, falls dead of a snakebite at the very edge of the spring. She breathed sweetly, dreaming a fair dream; and he held his breath lest he should disturb her.)

But almost at once the tone of the poem changes. The failures of this night lead to memories of earlier, more successful nights, mimicking in reverse the progression of the narration in Tibullus 1.5.[6] The recollection of those nights, in turn, leads to a vivid and fresh engram of the speaker's true love, who overpowered his senses so much that in front of the priest at their marriage the speaker

---

6. Who moves from dream (vv. 19–36) to reality (vv. 37 ff.).

was aroused (" . . . vor Priester und Altare, / Vor deinem Jammerkreuz, blutrünstiger Christe, / Verzeih mirs Gott, es regte sich der Iste"). With this humorous recollection, the speaker shifts his concentration to present dilemmas. He decides that there is not necessarily a connection between raw sexuality and emotion, that the passions that inform his physical needs are not necessarily the palliative that he requires or desires emotionally. Illness, he concludes, is the first test of health ("Die Krankheit erst bewähret den Gesunden"). His impotence and its remedy, in the event, are found in the love he feels for his wife, not in simple physical prowess fed by fantasies whose emotional quotient is nil but whose erotic potential is high indeed.

This would seem to be the lesson that Tibullus's speaker has learned— though too late. The reversal of roles in Tibullus's poem (Delia is bewitched by love, as the speaker in Goethe's poem was) heightens the loss implicit in its story. Delia is not like Goethe's speaker. She continues to have intimate nights with passionate lovers, living out the erotic fantasies that have haunted the mind of Goethe's diarist. Tibullus's speaker, by distinction, has learned the lesson that Goethe's poem spells out, that love's unending power ought to be respected. But the two positions cannot meet in the situation Tibullus creates: the two lovers, one informed by flights of erotic passion, the other hankering after a truer, purer love, remain apart, as they must. In Goethe's rendition, by distinction, the two positions, merged into the lone figure of the poem's speaker, can each have their articulation. The amelioration of both, however, means that the guilt and the impotency it causes in Tibullus's poem are sins expiated in allusive space, where Goethe gives shape to them under the sanitizing power of his speaker's love for his wife. Allusion's play thereby ratifies a broader and more profound notion of human love, a notion that accommodates both erotic fantasy and conjugal love. In so doing it also bears witness to the ways humans sometimes allow their emotions to tell them what they truly can or ought to know, as Goethe's speaker learns just in time, as Tibullus's speaker learns only after it is too late.

BAUDELAIRE AND VIRGIL

Unlike the linkage of Goethe's poem to Tibullus 1.5, Baudelaire's engagement of Virgil's *Aeneid* is much more divergent. The opening line of Baudelaire's "Le Cygne," for example—"Andromaque, je pense à vous" (Andromache, I think of you)—recalls the history of Andromache in her various classical guises, but especially the history articulated for her by Virgil in *Aeneid* 3, with its brooding emotions and deceived hopes.[7] Full-knowing readers who divert their attention to this book of Virgil's poem return to "Le Cygne" to find much that is familiar in this modern rendition of ennui, for the verbal linkage resident in the poem's opening line harbors other more specific connections.

More than any of its other books, the third book of Virgil's *Aeneid* imagines the horror of a kind of knowledge that paralyzes as it informs, leaving in its wake an overwhelming spiritual paralysis, an inability to act. The book advertises this posture in the ways it opens with haunting world-weariness:

> Postquam res Asiae Priamique evertere gentem
> immeritam visum superis, ceciditque superbum
> Ilium et omnis humo fumat Neptunia Troia,
> diversa exsilia et desertas quaerere terras
> auguriis agimur divum, classemque sub ipsa
> Antandro et Phrygiae molimur montibus Idae,
> incerti quo fata ferant, ubi sistere detur,
> contrahimusque viros. (3.1–8)[8]

(After it pleased the gods above to overthrow the power of Asia and Priam's guiltless race, after proud Ilium fell, and all Neptune's Troy smokes from the ground, we are driven by heaven's auguries to seek distant scenes of exile in waste lands. Just under Antandros and the mountains of Phrygian Ida we build a fleet, uncertain whither the Fates lead or where it is granted us to settle; and there we muster our men.)

The shifting trajectories of Aeneas's recollection, alternating between visions of hope and their invariable dashings, are given gruesome display at the start in Aeneas's discovery of the unburied Polydorus. The symbology of Polydorus

7. L. Nelson, Jr., "Baudelaire and Virgil: A Reading of 'Le Cygne,'" *Comparative Literature* 13 (1961), pp. 332–33 and n. 2, has argued cogently that Baudelaire intends for his readers to think only of Virgil's "Andromaque," not Racine's, but A. Feuillerat, "L'Architecture des *Fleurs du Mal*," *Yale Romanic Studies* 18 (1941), pp. 84–85, would argue for Racine's presence also. The point is moot. Since allusion empowers the reader, either position is tenable. The fact that Baudelaire added an epigraph—*falsi Simoentis ad undam*—taken from *Aeneid* 3 to the first publication of this poem, commends Virgil over Racine, but not, it seems to me, to the exclusion of Racine, as Nelson, p. 333, n. 2, would have it. Cf. K. Macfarlane, "'Le Cygne' de Baudelaire: *falsi Simoentis ad undam*,'" *L' Information littéraire* 27 (1975), pp. 139–44.

8. My text of Virgil is R. A. B. Mynors, ed., *P. Vergili Maronis Opera*, (Oxford, 1969). Translations are adapted from H. R. Fairclough, *Virgil*, 2 vols., Loeb Classical Library (Cambridge, Mass., and London, 1916).

only serves to heighten the sense of despair with which the book begins, evoking the kind of world Aeneas inhabits: empty, lost, devoid of certainty. There is a sense in which Aeneas empathizes with Polydorus, the Trojan lost to treachery. But in a larger sense Aeneas is himself lost to the knowledge of his own exile, whose details offer only spiritual and mental paralysis. The price of some kinds of wisdom, Aeneas would seem to learn as this book proceeds, is to be placed beyond the realm of action, in a harrowing and gray area, where reason subsists, but only to dull, by the very force of the visions it offers, a corresponding force of action. Here at the opening of book 3, therefore, Aeneas finds himself a living version of Polydorus. In burying him, Aeneas symbolically gropes for the means to put to an end the suffocating ennui suffused with the crystalline wisdom that world-weariness sanctions.

Aeneas's questions beginning at verse 88 are passionate in the ways they frame his spiritual situation in no uncertain terms. "Whom should we follow? Where do you order us to go? Where are we to build our home?" (quem sequimur? quove ire iubes? Ubi ponere sedes?). These are not the questions of the Aeneas who fought the impossible fight for Troy in book 2, nor of the man who scrambled for the hard truth about duty and life in declaring the sentiments that well summarize all of the *Aeneid:* "una salus victis nullam sperare salutem" (one salvation is there for the conquered, to hope for no salvation; 2.354). The Aeneas who acted upon the wisdom of this paradox was self-sufficient precisely because he believed in his ability to act. Now, however, though the wisdom of the paradox remains, the hard lesson of its truth has been refracted through the prism of defeat.

Only slowly are the struggles against defeat won. Later in book 3 one such struggle is imagined. There, Aeneas attempts, in the light of his own failures, to achieve a unity of individual purpose and of general history, bidding farewell to Andromache and Helenus, who come to represent all that must be abandoned for spiritual progress to obtain:

> Vivite felices, quibus est fortuna peracta
> iam sua: nos alia ex aliis in fata vocamur.
> vobis parta quies: nullum maris aequor arandum,
> arva neque Ausoniae semper cedentia retro
> quaerenda. effigiem Xanthi Troiamque videtis
> quam vestrae fecere manus, melioribus, opto,
> auspiciis, et quae fuerit minus obvia Grais.
> si quando Thybrim vicinaque Thybridis arva
> intraro gentique meae data moenia cernam,

cognatas urbes olim populosque propinquos,
Epiro Hesperiam (quibus idem Dardanus auctor
atque idem casus), unam faciemus utramque
Troiam animis: maneat nostros ea cura nepotes. (3.493–505)

(Farewell, you whose destiny is already achieved; we are still summoned from fate to
fate. Your rest is won. You needn't plow ocean plains, nor do you need to seek ever-
retreating Ausonian fields. A copy of Xanthus you see and of Troy, which your hands
built under happier omens and beyond the range of the Greeks. If ever I enter the
Tiber and Tiber's neighboring fields, and look on the walls granted to my people,
hereafter we will make our sister cities and allied peoples in Epirus and Hesperia, who
have the same Dardanus as their ancestor, and the same fall, we will make both one
Troy in spirit. Let those cares await our ancestors.)

The history of Andromache and Helenus situates the terrors of Aeneas's predicament more securely. Andromache and Helenus, for all their superficial happiness, are little more than specters, figures lost to time, characters beyond
conquering and salvation, who refuse the purifying rush of clarity that history's
memory and history's hope can bring. When Aeneas offers to these refugees
from Troy hope for the future, then, something for which they have no use
(vv. 502–3), he would seem to confirm more for himself than for them the
sanctifying power of that hope, even if he would seem not quite to possess it yet
on his own terms. The spirit that Aeneas summons here, therefore, is the spirit
of melancholic resolve to stand firmly in paradox: to refuse to leave the past, but
to know that such a refusal is the source of spiritual ruin. This realization proves
to be the foil against which Aeneas comes, if ever slowly, to terms with his own
spiritual dilemmas, posed so gravely at the core of this book's narrative.

Part of that realization inheres in the ways Aeneas gives shape to his memory
of Andromache beginning at verse 303, for she symbolizes in her quiet griefs
and pious acts of memorial a complete enslavement to the past. She is first
encountered offering libations "to the dust," (libabat cineri; v. 303) and calling
up the shade of Hector at his home-made tomb. She is crying. She is frightened
upon seeing Aeneas and his men and initially looses all color in her face,
becoming as white as bone before swooning (calor ossa reliquit; v. 308). When
she recovers, she is described as bending her head (deiecit vultum; v. 320) in
dejection before "whispering" a response to Aeneas's queries (et demissa voce
locuta est; v. 320). She tells Aeneas that she would rather have been Polyxena,
the daughter of Priam who was sacrificed on his tomb. Then her thoughts turn
to Ascanius, the son of Aeneas, but only in the context of the lost Creusa. After
the prophecies of her husband, Helenus, Andromache is the last to speak to

Aeneas, and her speech provides a final venue in which to confirm the glories and the perished consonances of the past as against the hope and potential of the future:

> accipe et haec, manuum tibi quae monimenta mearum
> sint, puer, et longum Andromachae testentur amorem,
> coniugis Hectoreae. cape dona extrema tuorum,
> o mihi sola mei super Astyanactis imago.
> sic oculos, sic ille manus, sic ora ferebat;
> et nunc aequali tecum pubesceret aevo (3.486–91)
>
> (Take these to be memorials of my hands and witnesses of the abiding love of Andromache, Hector's wife. Take these last gifts of your own kind, you who are the sole living image of my Astyanax. He was like you in eyes and hands and face; he would now be your age, his youth giving way to a maturer age.)

For Andromache, all is lost. There can be no new Troy, as there can be no hope for the future, only bitter recollection that leads to the oblivions of grief. The wisdom of Aeneas's earlier injunction that "the conquered have to them one salvation, hope for none," cannot function here, because hope, too, is a thing of the past. Hope is, in any case, a tenuous possession, not achieved in this book.

The tone of Aeneas's lament to his father well captures the world-weariness occasioned by the search for hope and the potentials of the future that it implies. Praising Anchises in no uncertain terms after his death later in this book, Aeneas nevertheless cannot suppress the bitter array of emotions that well up in his heart. When he declares, half in grief, half in anger, to his dead father that "you forsook me" (deseris, v. 711), this emotion resonates in the larger context of the third book of the *Aeneid*, endorsing the dilemmas of this book's narrative—the gloom of exile, the seeming abandonment of the gods, the need for direction, the accrual of knowledge that paralyzes as it informs.

Aeneas has little more to say after this appraisal of events. Virgil takes over the narrative and offers closure to this difficult book, but adds precious little to the book's finale: "finally he ceased and having made an end to his story, grew quiet" (conticuit tandem factoque hic fine quievit; v. 718). In a sense, the final word of the book well summarizes the spiritual lesson of its lines, whose thrust has been to assert the power of knowledge to abort one's ability to act. For Aeneas, the strength to act presumably has been found, for there is much more of his story to be told in the *Aeneid*, but at a price that can only be surmised and with a pain whose vigor cannot be fully or well articulated.

The spiritual dilemmas of *Aeneid* 3 are evoked in desperate earnest by the speaker of "Le Cygne," like Aeneas, an exile, who offers a modern vision of ennui:[9]

Andromaque, je pense à vous! Ce petit fleuve,
Pauvre et triste miroir où jadis resplendit
L'immense majesté de vos douleurs de veuve,
Ce Simoïs menteur qui par vos pleurs grandit,

A fécondé soudain ma mémoire fertile,
Comme je traversais le nouveau Carrousel.
Le vieux Paris n'est plus (la forme d'une ville
Change plus vite, hélas! que le coeur d'un mortel).

Je ne vois qu'en esprit tout ce camp de baraques,
Ces tas de chapiteaux ébauchés et de fûts,
Les herbes, les gros blocs verdis par l'eau des flaques,
Et brillant aux carreaux, le bric-à-brac confus.[10]

(Andromache, I think of you! This little river, a small and sad mirror through which once the immense majesty of your sad widowhood shone, the false Simois which is fed by your tears, has suddenly sparked my fertile memory, as I was crossing the new carousel. The old Paris is no more (the face of a city changes more quickly, alas, than the heart of a mortal); I see in spirit this whole colony of remains. The piles of rough-hewn capitals and their shafts, the grass, the large blocks greened by the water of puddles and, brilliant on this pavement, the confused bric-à-brac.)

The vision imagined in this poem is configured as if to invite the dynamics of allusive play by invoking them through description. The poem's speaker, after all, gives shape to his own mental play by offering that he "thinks" (je pense) of Andromache, which leads, in turn, to the admission that the body of water he spies, be it a puddle, a stream, or the Seine, forms a mirror (*miroir*) framing the grief of Andromache's widowhood that this scene has made him remember. The present, therefore, links directly in the speaker's mind to a prior textual

9. On Baudelaire's classicism, see K. H. Macfarlane, "Baudelaire's Revaluation of the Classical Allusion," *Studies in Romanticism* 15 (1976), pp. 423–44, a useful study hampered by its reliance on typologies. Useful also is F. W. Leakey, "The Originality of Baudelaire's 'Le Cygne': Genesis as Structure and Theme," in E. M. Beaumont, J. M. Cocking, J. Cruickshank, eds., *Order and Adventure in Post-Romantic French Poetry: Essays Presented to C. A. Hackett* (New York, 1973), pp. 38–55; V. Brombert, "'Le Cygne' de Baudelaire: Douleur, Souvenir, Travail," *Études Baudelairiennes* 3 (1973), pp. 254–61; and R. D. Burton, *The Context of Baudelaire's 'Le Cygne'* (Durham, 1980), esp. pp. 31–34, 56–57, 76–82.

10. My text is Y.-G. Le Dantec ed., *Oeuvres complètes de Charles Baudelaire* (Paris, 1954) pp. 157–59.

moment. This present is made to function in the context of a past story framed by Virgil.

The gloom and world-weariness of the third *Aeneid* infect the speaker's memory at once. The focus of lament initially is on the physical change of Paris, whose transformation is quicker than the heart that responds to the city's new forms ("Le vieux Paris n'est plus [la forme d'une ville / Change plus vite, hélas! que le coeur d'un mortel]"). Yet allusion's play frames the speaker's recollection in the context of impotence, for the memory of the heart of this particular mortal has been linked to the grief of Andromache, a figure, as we have seen, whose solace is entirely a function of past action. Memory here, then, offers no hope of future contentment, only the possibility of continual rumination and persistent grief.

Like Aeneas, who struggles throughout *Aeneid* 3 in order to escape the paralysis of a wisdom that becomes overpowering as the book progresses, the speaker in "Le Cygne" seems somehow caught in repose, once poised to act on the knowledge that inspired the exclamation of verse 1, but now lost to the desolation of the vision he beholds, a desolation mirrored in the activity of an exiled swan, out of its element, brave against the dusty, hard world:

Là s'étalait jadis une ménagerie,
Là je vis un matin, à l'heure où sous les cieux
Froids et clairs le Travail s'éveille, où la voirie
Pousse un sombre ouragan dans l'air silencieux,

Un cygne qui s'était évadé de sa cage,
Et, de ses pieds palmés frottant le pavé sec,
Sur le sol raboteux traînait son blanc plumage.
Près d'un ruisseau sans eau la bête ouvrant le bec

Baignait nerveusement ses ailes dans la poudre,
Et disait, le coeur plein de son beau lac natal:
"Eau, quand donc pleuvras-tu? quand tonneras-tu foudre?"
Je vois ce malheureux, mythe étrange et fatal,

Vers le ciel quelquefois, comme l'homme d'Ovide,
Vers le ciel ironique et cruellement bleu,
Sur son cou convulsif tendant sa tête avide,
Comme s'il adressait des reproches à Dieu!

(There once sprawled a menagerie; there I saw one morning, at that time when under skies cold and clear work arouses itself, where the street work throws a somber hurricane in the silent air, a swan that had escaped its cage and, rubbing its feet on the dry stone, under the rough sun displayed its white plumage, before a brook without water, the animal opening its mouth and bathing its wings nervously in the dust, as if saying, its heart full of his own beautiful natal lake: water, when will you rain? When will you crash thunder? I see this unfortunate creature, this strange and fatal myth, toward the heavens sometimes like the man of Ovid, toward the heavens, cruelly, ironically blue, on his quivering neck tends his avid head, as if he were addressing reproaches to God himself!)

The vision of the speaker is now specified further. He is not the swan he beholds, but its struggles, now perverse, now glorious, clarify the ways in which Andromache is a tragic figure, and render to his own predicament the soothing palliative of shared grief. Moreover, the swan is configured in terms that remind the full-knowing reader of Andromache. The first glimpse readers have of this exotic bird finds it rubbing its feet against the dry stone, much like Andromache, who, when Aeneas first sees her, is making libations to the dry earth. Too, the dominant color of the swan is white, just as the color Aeneas remembers of Andromache is the whiteness of her face. Questions frame the depictions of either figure: like Andromache, who asks of Aeneas if he is real or a phantom, so the swan asks of the heavens when they might rain and thunder. Much like the swan, attention is paid to the neck and head of Andromache, who is remembered by Aeneas as having downcast eyes and a neck bent forward.

But the swan is not the speaker, in the same way that Andromache is not Aeneas. The knowledge that paralyzes Andromache and the swan does not debilitate Aeneas or Baudelaire's speaker to the same extent:

Paris change! mais rien dans ma mélancolie
N'a bougé! palais neufs, échafaudages, blocs,
Vieux faubourgs, tout pour moi devient allégorie,
Et mes chers souvenirs sont plus lourds que des rocs.

Aussi devant ce Louvre une image m'opprime:
Je pense à mon grand cygne, avec ses gestes fous,
Comme les exilés, ridicule et sublime,
Et rongé d'un désir sans trêve! et puis à vous,

Andromaque, des bras d'un grand époux tombée,
Vil bétail, sous la main du superbe Pyrrhus,
Auprès d'un tombeau vide en extase courbée;
Veuve d'Hector, hélas! et femme d'Hélénus!

(Paris changes! but nothing in my melancholy has moved; new palaces, scaffolding, blocks, old neighborhoods all become for me allegory, and my dear memories are heavier than the rocks. In front of the Louvre an image oppresses me: I think of my great swan with its mad gestures as if it were an exile, ridiculous and sublime, consumed by a desire without truce! and I think of you, Andromache, fallen from the embrace of your great husband, the vile chattel under the control of haughty Pyrrhus, before an empty tomb, prostrated in ecstatic grief, widow of Hector, alas, and wife of Helenus!)

The speaker returns momentarily to the physical changes wrought on Paris, but this brings him round again to the struggles of the swan and the encumbering griefs of Andromache. Only then, with these analogues in place, does the speaker fashion a personal statement in the context of the scene he has created. That statement resonates against the backdrop of insufficient action and forsaken potential, against the images of the swan "consumed by a desire without truce" (rongé d'un désir sans trêve!), who seeks the power to act, yet lacks the ability to do so:

Je pense à la négresse, amaigrie et phthisique,
Piétinant dans la boue, et cherchant, l'oeil hagard,
Les cocotiers absents de la superbe Afrique
Derrière la muraille immense du brouillard.

A quiconque a perdu ce qui ne se retrouve
Jamais! jamais! à ceux qui s'abreuvent de pleurs
Et tettent la Douleur comme une bonne louve!
Aux maigres orphelins séchant comme des fleurs!

Ainsi dans la forêt où mon esprit s'exile
Un vieux Souvenir sonne à plein souffle du cor!
Je pense aux matelots oubliés dans une île,
Aux captifs, aux vaincus! . . . à bien d'autres encor!

(I think of the African girl, emaciated, tuberculous, traipsing through the mud and searching with haggard eyes in back of the immense wall of fog for the absent coconuts of her proud Africa. I think of all who have lost what they can find never, never again. I think of those who drink tears and suck grief as if it were the milk of a she-wolf, I think of sorry orphans withering like flowers. Thus, in the forest of my spirit's exile, an old memory runs the gamut of my heart and makes me think of sailors forgotten on an island, of captives, of the vanquished . . . I think of many others as well.)

Now he thinks of his lover, the African girl, who becomes a new version of the swan and of Andromache, now he thinks of all those who have lost what they can never have again, and, finally, he thinks of those who have lost themselves to all manner of debility. Only the saving grace of poetry keeps the speaker's memory from overpowering him, much as Aeneas's foray into the oblivions of Andromache's world is ended abruptly by Virgil's entry into the poem's narrative. Like Aeneas, the speaker of "Le Cygne" is an exile, but he is, at the end of this poem at least, an exile who seems poised to act on the knowledge his poem witnesses. Like Aeneas in the third *Aeneid,* we are not privy to that activity, but we surmise its consequences in the tone and spirit of the poem that articulates its potency. The speaker reposes, if nowhere else, with "many others," and by this phrase full-knowing readers understand him to mean Aeneas, Andromache, Virgil, and even Baudelaire himself, who bequeaths a sweet and pleasurable knowledge to them, but casts it in a strange and fatal context: "la doucuer qui fascine et la plasir qui tue."

POUND'S *CANTOS* AND THE FULL-KNOWING READER

In another of his demarcations of the world of poetry and of experience, Pablo Neruda seemingly banishes books and opts for the street (por las calles)—for life vividly lived and supremely felt:

Libro, déjame libre.
Yo no quiero ir vestido
de volumen,
yo no vengo de un tomo,
mis poemas
no han comido poemas,
devoran
apasionados acontecimientos,
se nutren de intemperie,
extraen alimento
de la tierra y los hombres.
Libro, déjame andar por los caminos
con polvo en los zapatos
y sin mitología:
vuelve a tu biblioteca,
yo me voy por las calles.

(Book, let me be free. I will not wear the clothes of books, and I do not come from a collection. My poems have not eaten other poems, but devour exciting happenings, feed on rough weather and dig their nourishment from the land and from men. Book, let me walk on the road with dust in my shoes, free of mythology. Get back to your library, books, I'm going for the streets).

The crux of Neruda's "Oda al Libro" centers upon the power of poetry to proffer life, as against the inability of a sterile collation of books to do much of anything, owing to the tenuous connection of books to life. Neruda does not here deny that he has read books, nor even that his learning has influenced what he has written and how he has written it. His purpose rather is to champion the essentialism of language and, in particular, of poetry, that is, to raise poetry above other forms of writing represented by books. In the process, Neruda becomes the mouthpiece for a poetry that is equivalent to life, for a poetry that not only reflects life but gives it in the reading.[11] The power of the poetic word, far from growing evanescent for its being written, becomes in the proper hands the apex of life itself.

This is perhaps a common notion in contemporary poetry, owing to the work of the French Symbolists,[12] all the more so in this century, where a great emphasis has been placed in literary art on the importance of somehow getting beyond old forms, such as realism, and well-worn models, such as the paradigm of mimetic copy and archetype. But it is a difficult thing to accomplish the implicit goal of Neruda's "Oda al Libro," that is, to make a poetry into experience, into life itself. Yet allusion, with its plenitude of meaning and its grant of power to the reader, well suits the project that would seek to proffer life through poetry. No Western writer would seem to have understood this better than Ezra Pound.

The full measure of Pound's *Cantos* inheres in the ways they exploit, in Plato's memorable phrase, writing's status as an orphan in search of a parent. To the extent that the *Cantos* invite their readers into their production, demanding of them nurturing and parenting, they succeed in bridging the gap between copy and original, proffering experience, not just vestiges of imitation. But Pound's allusiveness is different, because he allows the function of his narrative to subsist entirely within allusion's exploitation of writing's orphaned status, refusing to ground his allusions (or their full-knowing readers) in a discrete situation of discourse. To offer such a situation of discourse, to ground his poems in a contextual or even a rhetorical structure, would be to erect the sorts of barriers between copy and original that, in his view, deaden poetry and the experience it seeks to give. Pound forgoes the intrusion of his own voice in these poems, therefore, and leaves his readers to their own devices, allowing them to live his poetry as they read it. The *Cantos* exist, therefore, like an ongoing series of allusions linked only on the page on which they are printed, their meanings

11. Neruda writes of this in more detail in his essay "On Impure Poetry."
12. Or viewed, by negation, in the work of the so-called language poets, who, in opposition to symbolism and the "new American poetry," call for a poetics that rejects the notion that poetry somehow projects an objective status into the world.

entirely *in potentia*,[13] their words seeking always a reader to parent them to meaning.

When they read the *Cantos,* therefore, full-knowing readers confront the acme of allusive writing in the Western literary tradition, because they are asked to forgo entirely the normal constraints implied in reading and to draw entirely on the competencies of full-knowing reading to make these poems mean. Readers become, therefore, the authors of these complex poems, inventing (not reinventing) the experiences they imagine, creating (not recreating) them with fresh insight and voice. And because the *Cantos* are all allusion, because there is no situation of discourse imagined or constructed by which to ground the experience of the poems or to control allusive play, each reading of a canto, like each reading of an allusion, is a personal reading accomplished under the rubric of readerly power and rendered, depending on circumstance and historical accident, in manifold ways.

Many of the *Cantos* seem to consider the ways tradition and allusion conspire in the construction of the truly new creation. In canto 4, the potency and consonance of the materials of tradition are analyzed and then merged into a larger celebration of human intellect and passion:

Palace in smoky light,[14]
    Troy but a heap of smouldering boundary stones,
    ANAXIFORMINGES! Aurunculeia!
    Hear me. Cadmus of the Golden Prows!
The silver mirrors catch the bright stones and flare,
Dawn, to our waking, drifts in the green, cool light;
Dew-haze blurs, in the grass, pale ankles moving.
Beat, beat, whirr, thud, in the soft turf
    under the apple trees,
Choros nympharum, goat-foot, with the pale foot alternate;
Crescent of blue-shot waters, green-gold in the shallows,
A black cock crows in the sea-foam.

Canto 4 begins with *the* event of Western writing, the fall of Troy. But what does that fact, and this event, mean for modern readers of the Western literary tradition? The boundary stones and the burned city suggest that boundary and limit are fundamental to the process of writing within a tradition. But that is

13. M. J. Alexander, *The Poetic Achievement of Ezra Pound* (Berkeley, 1979), pp. 138–45, explores this issue.
14. My edition is *The Cantos of Ezra Pound* (London, 1986).

not all: "anaxiformiges, Aurunculeia!" Here the lyrical voices of the most formally perfect and the most intensely personal of antiquity's lyric poets sing out in praise of (and as a result of) the burning of Troy. The hymns of Pindar can sing of renewal, can offer wholeness from the smoldering stones and offer a means by which to rebuild the walls and the traditions from which they are shaped. In the same way, Catullus 61, an *epithalamium,* rejoices in the concord of nature and convention mediated through the act of marriage, the flaunting of which has caused the burning of Troy in the first place.

"Hear me": a personal voice intrudes upon the poem and reaches for the attention of Cadmus, suggestive of the struggle embodied in antique literature and mythology to find form and to rally against formlessness. Full-knowing readers are subsumed in this world, where the fight for wholeness is waged. The image of war subsists in the mirrors catching the flaring light and bright stones, as Troy fights the disintegration of its form, but immediately the reader transcends that moment and is transported to some calmer, more exotic realm. There, where cool lights and soft dews abide, pale ankles dominate the line of vision, whose beating and whirring evokes Sappho, reminding readers of Aphrodite's presence to this poet, a presence that links also to the line in Whitman ("beat, beat, whir, pound"). The apple mentioned here also recalls Aphrodite, since it is symbolic of the act of love Aphrodite sanctions. Sappho's chorus of nymphs follow close at hand seemingly for this reason, heralding the birth (or rebirth) of Aphrodite from the foam of the sea. From the awful raging into chaos and oblivion proffered by Cronus, we retrieve, and are retrieved by, Aphrodite, who offers through her powers the concord of love itself, the most potent rallying against formlessness possible:

> And by the curved, carved foot of the couch,
>   claw foot and lion-head, an old man seated
> Speaking in the low drone . . . :
>   Ityn!
> Et ter flebiliter, Ityn, Ityn!
> And she went toward the window and cast her down,
>   "All the while, the while, swallows crying:
> Ityn!
>   "It is Cabestan's heart in the dish."
>   "It is Cabestan's heart in the dish?
>   "No other taste shall change this."
> And she went toward the window,
>   the slim white stone bar

Making a double arch;
Firm even fingers held to the firm pale stone;
Swung for a moment,
    and the wind out of Rhodez
Caught in the full of her sleeve.
    . . . the swallows crying:
'Tis. 'Tis. Ytis!

The canto now worries the idea of form and the discords of humanity that are closely linked to it. Here, with Procne as symbol and speaker, the poem imagines the horror of her situation as a metaphor for the function of form itself. The crying swallows recall the fate of Procne and her son Itys, who was killed by her in order to be fed to her adulterous husband, Tereus (who had seduced Philomela, Procne's sister). Suddenly, another literary moment intrudes in allusive space. The mention of Cabestan brings full-knowing readers to a story of love and cannibalism not unlike Ovid's version of Procne and Tereus, but this newer (medieval) version of the story[15] is more harrowing because the moral and spiritual dilemmas that it broaches are not resolved: "no other taste shall change this." And the lone figure of Procne moving toward the window and smelling "the wind out of Rhodez" only heightens the sense of doom and moral lassitude that infects the poem. The low drone of the man speaking earlier is now shared by Procne, and also by the reader. The swallows cry, "Ityn." Indeed, " 'Tis. 'Tis. Ytis!" And there is nothing to be done about it except grieve (and pray).

    Actaeon . . .
    and a valley,
The valley is thick with leaves, with leaves, the trees,
The sunlight glitters, glitters a-top,
Like a fish-scale roof,
    Like the church roof in Poictiers
If it were gold.
    Beneath it, beneath it
Not a ray, not a slivver, not a spare disc of sunlight
Flaking the black, soft water;
Bathing the body of nymphs, of nymphs, and Diana,
Nymphs, white-gathered about her, and the air, air,

15. There are variants to the story in almost all of the European literatures, on which see C. F. Terrell, *A Companion to the Cantos of Ezra Pound* 2 vols. (Berkeley and Orono, Me., 1980–84), vol. 1, p. 12.

Shaking, air alight with the goddess,
    fanning their hair in the dark,
Lifting, lifting, and waffing:
Ivory dipping in silver,
    Shadow'd, o'ershadow'd
Ivory dipping in silver,
Not a splotch, not a lost shatter of sunlight.
Then Actaeon: Vidal,
Vidal. It is old Vidal speaking,
    stumbling along in the wood,
Not a patch, not a lost shimmer of sunlight,
    the pale hair of the goddess.

The dogs leap on Actaeon,
    "Hither, hither, Actaeon,"
Spotted stag of the wood;
Gold, gold, a sheaf of hair,
    Thick like a wheat swath,
Blaze, blaze in the sun,
    The dogs leap on Actaeon.
Stumbling, stumbling along in the wood,
Muttering, muttering Ovid:
    "Pergusa . . . pool . . . pool . . . Gargaphia,
"Pool . . . pool of Salmacis,"
    The empty armour shakes as the cygnet moves.

Of a sudden, the poem reverses its ostensible course. The images of the apple tree and the nymphs, symbolizing the possibility of concord in the cycles of love lost and love gained, now become countervailing symbols of the immutability of decline, disintegration, the withering of worlds and the fictions of those worlds. Procne, whose sleeve catches on the medieval breeze out of Rhodez, becomes Actaeon, wandering amid the leaves of trees, the glittering sun of antiquity or of any time and place, wandering into the sanctuary where he does not belong. Quickly, then, he is overtaken by the perfection of the place and, like Vidal—that is, Peire Vidals of Tolosa—metamorphosed.

"Not a patch, not a lost shimmer of sunlight." The perfected realm of concord and ideal vision cannot abide the unnatural and imperfect human contact imagined here; the human must suffer the consequences because humanity's curse is to know only too late the wisdom of its own victimization, the power of the cycles of time and of history that consume as easily as they exalt.

And so Actaeon is consumed. The perfect beauty of the golden hair of a goddess cannot give light, or anything, here, and not even the literary cry for help to the poet most expert at changing forms in this exotic and strange place (. . . Muttering, muttering, Ovid: . . .) can change the course of events imagined. The illusion of birth, regeneration, concord, is crashed to the ground with the false power of Cygnus, perhaps to return again, but never quite in the same way, or in the same form.

Thus the light rains, thus pours, *e lo soleills plovil*
The liquid and rushing crystal
   beneath the knees of the gods.
Ply over ply, thin glitter of water;
Brook film bearing white petals.
The pine at Takasago
   grows with the pine of Isé!
The water whirls up the bright pale sand in the spring's mouth
"Behold the Tree of the Visages!"
Forked branch-tips, flaming as if with lotus.
   Ply over ply
The shallow eddying fluid,
   beneath the knees of the gods.

Torches melt in the glare
   set flame of the corner cook-stall,
Blue agate casing the sky (as at Gourdon that time)
   the sputter of resin,
Saffron sandal so petals the narrow foot: Hymenaeus Io!
   Hymen, Io Hymenaee! Aurunculeia!
One scarlet flower is cast on the blanch-white stone.

Discord is imagined in the context of natural and historical cycles, confirmed in the circularity of this poem, and found in the repetition of "Aurunculeia," which links to the poem's opening lines. But there is more to the cycles of life than one's own culture can teach. Other patterns of habit, with their own monuments to form, exist, and the poem attempts to articulate them by alluding now to Eastern texts.[16] The linkage to other traditions confirms what would seem to be the poem's crux: that to be human is to share in the knowledge of decline and rebirth, is to participate in the immutability of nature and the dissonances of humanity and its whirling visions and forms:

16. For the particulars, see Terrell, *Companion*, vol. i, pp. 14–16.

And Sō-Gyoku, saying:
"This wind, sire, is the king's wind,
    This wind is wind of the palace,
Shaking imperial water-jets."
    And Hsiang, opening his collar:
"This wind roars in the earth's bag,
    it lays the water with rushes."
No wind is the king's wind.
    Let every cow keep her calf.
"This wind is held in gauze curtains . . . "
        No wind is the king's . . .

The camel drivers sit in the turn of the stairs,
    Look down on Ecbatan of plotted streets,
"Danaë! Danaë!
    What wind is the king's?"
Smoke hangs on the stream,
The peach-trees shed bright leaves in the water,
Sound drifts in the evening haze,
    The bark scrapes at the ford,
Gilt rafters above black water,
    Three steps in an open field,
Gray stone-posts leading . . .

Danaë represents the mergings and concords of nature and convention that have
been sundered in the canto's previous lines. It is Danaë's son, Perseus, the seed of
Zeus, who kills his grandfather Acrisius, but he is the product of a marriage of
earth and heaven, as his mother is the link between the two realms torn apart.

Père Henri Jacques would speak with the Sennin, on Rokku,
Mount Rokku between the rock and the cedars,
Polhonac,
As Gyges on Thracian platter set the feast,
Cabestan, Tereus,
    It is Cabestan's heart in the dish,
Vidal, or Ecbatan, upon the gilded tower in Ecbatan
Lay the god's bride, lay ever, waiting the golden rain.
By Garonne. "Saave!"
The Garonne is thick like paint,
Procession,—"Et sa'ave, sa'ave, sa'ave Regina!"—
Moves like a worm, in the crowd.
Adige, thin film of images,

Across the Adige, by Stefano, Madonna in hortulo,
As Cavalcanti had seen her.
   The Centaur's heel plants in the earth loam.
And we sit here . . .
   there in the arena . . .

Full-knowing readers are led from Danaë to an exotic place, where a priest talks to a Chinese mystic on a mountain in Japan; where Polhonac, the husband, helps a knight seduce his own wife; where a case of innocent voyeurism goes awry in Gyges; whence they return to Cabestan, Tereus, Vidal, Ecbatan, a whirling oblivion of images gleaned from the experiences of earlier moments in the poem. Then, ultimately, the maddening and paradoxical "rest" at the end: "And we sit here. . . ." Indeed we do, but this canto can never really end, because its readers are unable to accomplish closure for it. The play of allusive space subsumes the poem's texture and allows readers only the option of marveling at the good and bad in the world, of musing over the conflagration of literary tradition performed, like the burning of Troy, before their eyes. But how sweet is the summons to construct that tradition yet again with Euripides, Catullus, Ovid, and Pound himself[17] in allusive space, a summons well expressed by Wallace Stevens, another architect of literary and human form:

Total grandeur of a total edifice,
Chosen by an inquisitor of structures
For himself. He stops upon this threshold,
As if the design of all his words takes form
And frame from thinking and is realized.[18]

In another poem about form and order, Stevens once inveighed against the fictions of writing's ability to fix and modulate experience, preferring the pound of the ocean, the fresh vitality of life itself, to the " . . . Blessed rage for order . . . / The maker's rage to order words of the sea, / Words of the fragrant portals, dimly-starred, / And of ourselves and of our origins, / In ghostlier demarcations, keener sounds."[19] Here, the value of life is advanced at the expense of describing it or ordering it for others to see. The urge to delineate life's order comes up short and poetry can only lament what it cannot celebrate or offer. Yet Stevens would not denigrate the potential of poetry to become what he calls

17. On these complex relationships see G. Bornstein, ed., *Ezra Pound Among the Poets :
    Homer, Ovid, Li Po, Dante, Whitman, Browning, Yeats, Williams, Eliot* (Chicago, 1985).
18. Wallace Stevens, "To an Old Philosopher in Rome," vv. 76–80.
19. "The Idea of Order at Key West," vv. 51–55.

elsewhere "the poem of the act of the mind."[20] But Pound's assertion, articulated perhaps most compellingly in canto 81, is much firmer and radical in the power it would grant to the poem as a modulator of human experience, a modulation owed to the competencies of the poem's full-knowing reader.

Canto 81 is much later than canto 4.[21] Now the acclamation of voice is much clearer, the urge to forsake the poet's own identity as a means to empower his readers' identity more fundamental to the poetic project at hand.[22] In this sense, therefore, canto 81 is about the ways in which tradition is articulated, mastered, bequeathed in the literary firmament, as it is about the ways in which literary novelty and originality arise and survive. With its gropings for expression, its competitions of convoluted, withering and aspiring voices that rise and fail in allusion's play, canto 81 champions the dialogical quality of writing that is the acme of allusive function:

Yet
Ere the season died a-cold
Borne upon a zephyr's shoulder
I rose through the aureate sky. . . .
Hast 'ou fashioned so airy a mood
    To draw up leaf from the root?
Hast 'ou found a cloud so light
    As seemed neither mist nor shade?

        Then resolve me, tell me aright
        If Waller sang or Dowland played. . . .
Ed ascoltando al leggier mormorio
    there came new subtlety of eyes into my tent,
whether of spirit or hypostasis,
    but what the blindfold hides
or at carneval
            nor any pair showed anger
        Saw but the eyes and stance between the eyes,

20. In "Of Modern Poetry," v. 26.
21. Canto 4 was written in the 1920s, canto 81, part of the *Pisan Cantos,* in the 1940s.
22. The issue of voice in Pound is vexed. In "Homage to Sextus Propertius," Pound chose to hide under the voices of other poets. In the *Personae,* he began casting off "masks" of self which seemed to hide an inner, purer, self. See Ezra Pound, "Vorticism," in J. Sullivan, ed., *Ezra Pound: A Critical Anthology* (Harmondsworth, 1970), p. 50, as reported by W. R. Johnson, *The Idea of Lyric: Lyric Modes in Ancient and Modern Poetry* (Berkeley and London, 1982), p. 36. Critics will argue over the idea of voice in Pound as long as we possess his texts. A recent appraisal of Pound's epic voice that I have found useful is S. Sicari, *Pound's Epic Ambition: Dante and the Modern World* (Albany, 1991).

colour, diastasis,
    careless or unaware it had not the
   whole tent's room
nor was place for the full Ειδὼς
interpass, penetrate
   casting but shade beyond the other lights
      sky's clear
      night's sea
      green of the mountain pool
      shone from the unmasked eyes in half-mask's space.

The sense of this dense and difficult poem does not come easily to any reader. The words are beautiful to hear and they adumbrate, in their passion and compression, a unified meaning, but they would seem mostly to constitute a poetic Babel, a competition of voices, dialects, languages, vying for attention and comprehension, and affirming, in their jostlings, the ceaseless necessity, in Stevens's phrase, of humanity's "blessed rage for order."

Order is a hard thing to come by in canto 81. The poem would seem to fight for order, but it achieves it only provisionally, in the libretto, where the poem's speaker rages against a variety of topics and mostly against himself, singing to the music of Lawes and Jenkyns, to the music of tradition: "Hast 'ou fashioned so airy a mood / To draw up leaf from the root?" Where literary allusion and the engagement of tradition are concerned, the symbology of leaf and root is not new.[23] But images of nature's bounty give way to talk of separation and of knowing, to images of vision and blindness, pointing to an insight that joins the predilections of the poem's various speakers:

What thou lovest well remains,
     the rest is dross
What thou lov'st well shall not be reft from thee
What thou lov'st well is thy true heritage
Whose world, or mine or theirs
     or is it of none?
First came the seen, then thus the palpable
   Elysium, though it were in the halls of hell,
What thou lovest well is thy true heritage
What thou lov'st well shall not be reft from thee
The ant's a centaur in his dragon world.

23. It is a key image used by Pound in "A Pact," his own dialogue with Walt Whitman; it is used by W. H. Auden of Yeats; and it weaves a rich tapestry throughout the ancient and late antique evidence, as we have seen above.

Pull down thy vanity, it is not man
Made courage, or made order, or made grace,
   Pull down thy vanity, I say pull down.
Learn of the green world what can be thy place
In scaled invention or true artistry,
Pull down thy vanity,
      Paquin pull down!
The green casque has outdone your elegance.

Love, excellent and fair, resounds in the libretto, its simple power fusing the disintegration and rage of the previous lines of the poem. Here the vortex of allusive play obtains, and full-knowing readers find the mechanism by which this poem, and perhaps all of the *Cantos,* can be controlled with more authority. The clear voice of the libretto sings to full-knowing readers that there may be vanity in writing poetry (and, by implication, in reading it), but there is no vanity in loving strongly and deeply, in drinking in the rich experience of life's bounty. This drinking has an analogue in poetry (in writing) also, for love of experience fused into the texture of poetry will, in Neruda's phrase, "give life to life itself" (y dan vida a la vida). In this curious and potent literary confection, where author and reader exchange roles, where novelty of perspective is merged with tradition, where words linger with their manifold meanings, Pound's "green world" is found, the world where "scaled invention and true artistry" conspire to bequeath experience-in-the-making:

"Master thyself, then others shall thee beare"
   Pull down thy vanity
Thou art a beaten dog beneath the hail,
A swollen magpie in a fitful sun,
Half black half white
Nor knowst'ou wing from tail
Pull down thy vanity
   How mean thy hates
Fostered in falsity,
   Pull down thy vanity,
Rathe to destroy, niggard in charity,
Pull down thy vanity,
   I say pull down.

"Pull down thy vanity." The vanity admonished here would seem to be emblematic of the speaker's personal urge to dominate his poetry with his voice instead of luxuriating in the profound emotions and in the arrangement of imagined thoughts and feelings that recollect for readers the bounty of life's fullness. Fullness, this canto would seem to say, whether in reading or in meaning, is the end toward which all authentic writing, all authentic activity, tends, leading to the opulence of the "green world." But it can only be had through a merging of authorial and readerly voices. There can be no cause for censure on this score, only quiet and pure celebration of the fullness of play that is, in Schiller's words, the forging of human action that is entirely free and therefore, as we have seen, most completely human:[24]

> But to have done instead of not doing
>   this is not vanity
> To have, with decency, knocked
> That a Blunt should open
>   To have gathered from the air a live tradition
> or from a fine old eye the unconquered flame
> This is not vanity.
>   Here error is all in the not done,
> all in the diffidence that faltered . . .

Not to celebrate this epiphany of life's measure is nearly to forsake life itself, is to refuse the power of the green world on account of the moment's diffidence. Full-knowing readers ponder this celebration in allusive space by thinking now of other green worlds imagined by other writers: Virgil's allegorical forest of grafted trees, Varro's metaphor of the root as analogous to the mysticism of the word, Macrobius's pastoral resumé of allusive symbols. Even starker is Dante's creation, in *Inferno* 4, of the green world that represents Virgil's Elysium, which points, at the same time, to Dante's engagement with Ovid and the other classical poets. W. H. Auden relies on similar imagery in memorializing William Butler Yeats and alludes to the opening line of the *Inferno* in the process " . . . To find his happiness in another kind of wood . . . / The words of a dead man / Are modified in the guts of the living. . . . / . . . it survives, / A way of happening, a mouth."[25] And Pound himself, in thinking of the ways in which he might accomplish his engagement of tradition, reproaches Walt Whitman in similar terms as the father whose influence he cannot banish: "I make a pact with you Walt Whitman—/ I have detested you long enough. / I come to you

24. See especially *Letters on the Aesthetic Education of Man*, letters 12 and 15; and cf. W. Kaufmann, *Hegel: A Reinterpretation* (Notre Dame, IN, 1978), pp. 18–31, and esp. p. 28. On play itself, see V. Nemoianu and R. Royal, eds., *Play, Literature, Religion: Essays in Cultural Intertextuality* (Albany, NY, 1992) and V. Turner, *From Ritual to Theatre: The Human Seriousness of Play* (New York, 1982), among many recent works on this topic.

25. "In Memory of W.B. Yeats," vv. 19, 21–22, 40–41.

as a grown child / Who has had a pig-headed father; / I am old enough now to make friends. / It was you that broke the new wood, / Now is a time for carving. / We have one sap and one root—/ Let there be commerce between us."[26]

In imagining the pact's "new wood," Pound symbolizes more concretely the green world he imagines later in canto 81, which is the grand space in which allusion is made to play and to mean. Pound's pact with Whitman, symbolizing the acknowledgment and the advancement of literary tradition, also ratifies Pound's conception of what poetry must offer to its readers in order truly to be poetry. There must be, above all, in this green world, a dialogue, a "commerce," between author and reader, whereby the transcendence that writing seeks can be achieved by those readers open to the constant and manifold play of allusion.

Pound may be supremely bold in the ways he would center his poetry in allusion's space, but he is not unique in wanting to assist his readers in finding this world where writing gives way to dialogue, as he is not alone in seeking to ease their entry into it. William Carlos Williams attempts to render the glorious solitude and spiritual nourishment of the world of writing's dialogue by imagining again that he is sitting next to Ford Madox Ford in Provence or, perhaps, in heaven:

> Where is Heaven? But why
> do I ask that, since you showed the way?
>   I don't care a damn for it
> other than for that better part lives beside
>   me here so long as I
> live and remember you. Thank God you
>   were not delicate, you let the world in
> and lied! damn it you lied grossly
>   sometimes. But it was all, I
> see now, a carelessness, the part of a man
>   that is homeless here on earth.[27]

Now the dialogues of Ford and Williams are concretized in elegy, but the consonance of Ford's words remains "so long as I live and remember you." The

26. Ezra Pound, "The Pact." Cf. Hart Crane's depiction of Whitman's poetry in "Cape Hatteras," part of "The Bridge": " . . . in pure impulse inbred / To answer deepest soundings! O, upward from the dead / Thou bringest tally, and a pact, new bound, / Of living brotherhood."
27. William Carlos Williams, "To Ford Madox Ford in Heaven," vv. 34–44.

purity and heart-wholeness of writing, then, are akin to heaven's sustaining power, and both exist in Williams's rendition of Ford as an intellectual who used poetry to teach, preach, and criticize, not always honestly, but all the same in the only ways that he could.

Allen Ginsberg remembers his foray into the green world in a poem written upon learning of the death of Williams: "Williams is in the Big Dipper. He isn't dead / as the many pages of words arranged thrill / with his intonations the mouths of meek kids / becoming subtle even in Bengal. Thus / there's a life moving out of his pages."[28] The Big Dipper, or Heaven, forms the foil against which Ginsberg recalls Williams's "many pages of words" which give life to the living, becoming dialogue when read again and inspiring by their simple connectedness to life a celebration of humanity that moves beyond language.

Rilke fashions his remembrance of the green world in a recollection of Hölderlin:

. . . Du nur
ziehst wie der Mond. Und unten hellt und verdunkelt
deine nächtliche sich, die heilig erschrockene Landschaft,
die du in Abschieden fühlst. Keiner
gab sie erhabener hin, gab sie ans Ganze
heiler zurück, unbedürftiger. So auch
spieltest du heilig durch nicht mehr gerechnete Jahre
mit dem unendlichen Glück, als wär es nicht innen, läge
keinem gehörend im sanften
Rasen der Erde umher, von göttlichen Kindern verlassen.
Ach, was die Höchsten begehren, du legtest es wunschlos
Baustein auf Baustein: es stand. Doch selber sein Umsturz
irrte dich nicht.[29]

(Only you move like the moon. And underneath brightens and darkens the nocturnal landscape, the holy, the terrified landscape which you feel in departures. No one gave it away more sublimely, gave it back more fully to the universe, without any need to hold on. Thus for years that you no longer counted, holy, you played with infinite joy, as though it were not inside you, but lay, belonging to no one, all around on the gentle lawns of the earth, where the godlike children had left it. Ah, what the

28. Allen Ginsberg, "Death News," vv. 12–16.
29. Rainer Maria Rilke, "An Hölderlin," vv. 14–26; the German text and English translation are from *The Selected Poetry of Rainer Maria Rilke*, trans. S. Mitchell (New York, 1989) p. 140–41.

greatest have longed for: you built it, free of desire, stone upon stone, till it stood. And when it collapsed, even then you were not bewildered.)

Hölderlin embodies through his writing nature itself, holy, vast, a gift that, when given away, returns again with greater bounty. Hölderlin "plays," according to Rilke, with a joy that is equivalent to nature, to "the gentle lawns of the earth," beckoning others to follow. It was sweet when Hölderlin could share his perfected visions with the world, but when he could not, he was not bewildered, for the celebration of the green world was enough for him.

Nor is the celebration of this world limited to verbal art. The urge to celebrate the community of voices, the merging of the author's word and the reader's intent, is resident in other habitats of Western life, confirmation of the enormous place that allusion holds some fifteen centuries after its explicit introduction to the mainstream of Western literary culture. Modern experiments in music, for example, are a witness to the ways in which authorial intent can be challenged by, in this case, the intent of the performer. John Cage's "44," for example, a percussion quartet, consists of what Cage calls "time brackets" of seventy-five seconds' duration, during which musicians must begin playing during the first forty-five seconds and must end the passage between the thirtieth and the seventy-fifth second. Decisions about when to start and to stop and about what tempos and instruments to use are left to the performers.[30] In much the same way, Cage's celebration of human sound and voice, "Empty Words," was written using a procedure which allowed for the random collation of letters from the fourteen volumes of Thoreau's journals, thereby allowing for the "composition" of the words of the work letter by letter. The finished product is not "written" in a recognizable language, of course, but the point, as Cage admits, is not to communicate normally: "There is no meaning in the text, only sounds. It is a use of the voice that resembles music more than poetry."[31] It is an artistic procedure that well resembles the literary foray into allusive space, for there is little to distinguish Cage's practices from the one Pound recommends in the *Cantos*, where his readers, like Cage's musicians, are invited into the process of artistic construction.

There are less exalted instances of allusion that wend their way throughout popular culture, too, from the refrain in "Set Adrift on Memory Bliss," P. M. Dawn's musical allusion to the refrains of Spandou Ballet's "True" and Sam

30. My summary of "4⁴" is owed to A. Kozinn, "A Musical (a) Anarchist or (b) Liberator Is Turning 80," *New York Times*, July 2, 1992, p. C 13, col. 2.
31. Ibid., col. 3.

Cooke's "You Send Me," to the repetition of Gregorian chants in Enigma's "Sadeness," to the use of Sting's refrain from "Every Move You Make" in Puff Daddy's hip-hop tribute to Notorious B.I.G. Indeed laced throughout the rages and rhythms of hip-hop are a web of allusions to older songs from other popular traditions and to hip-hop's own artists and songs, the practice of which is called "sampling." To be a listener to contemporary music today is very much to be a full-knowing reader of that music and the traditions it implies.[32]

One can see the tendency to empower the reader at the expense of the author also in the rapidly expanding use of hypertext, a generic term coined two decades ago by Theodor H. Nelson to describe the writing done in the non-linear or nonsequential space made possible by a computer.[33] Now "literature" is being "published" on disk and as it is, the author grows evanescent and the reader gains strength. Michael Joyce's "Afternoon," for example, was brought out on disk in 1987 and Carolyn Guyer and Martha Petry recently produced their fiction piece "Izme Pass" on disk in the magazine *Writing on the Edge*.[34] They describe the process of reading hyperfiction in this way: "The form of the text is rhythmic, looping on itself in patterns and layers that gradually accrete meaning, just as the passage of time and events does in one's lifetime. Trying the textlinks embedded within the work will bring the narrative together in new configurations, fluid constellations formed by the path of your interest. The difference between reading hyperfiction and reading traditional printed fiction may be the difference between sailing the island and standing on the dock watching the sea. One is not necessarily better than the other."[35] Robert Coover, surveying the field of hypertextuality, concludes that "fluidity, contingency, indeterminacy, plurality, discontinuity are the hypertext buzzwords of the day, and they seem to be fast becoming principles."[36]

They are not new principles, however, nor are they the province of the computer generation. The assertion of the word's fluidity and plurality is the position staked out by Plato in the *Phaedrus*, as it is the position articulated in

---

32. On which see S. H. Fernando, Jr., *The New Beats: Exploring the Music, Culture, and Attitudes of Hip-Hop* (New York, 1994).

33. I use the summary of R. Coover, "The End of Books," in *New York Times Book Review*, June 21, 1992, p. 23, col. 1. Cf. Theodor H. Nelson, *Literary Machines* (Sausalito, Calif., 1992).

34. I follow here Coover, "The End of Books," p. 23, col. 2.

35. C. Guyer and M. Petry, directions to "Izme Pass," as reported in ibid., pp. 23–24.

36. Ibid., p. 25, col. 2. On hypertext in general see G. P. Landow, *Hypertext: The Convergence of Contemporary Critical Theory and Technology* (Baltimore, 1992).

Greek tragedy, in Roman comedy, in Christian rhetoric, in all of the writers of the Western tradition who have worked hard to communicate by setting words down—on wax, papyrus, vellum, paper, or disk. In making writing their medium, Western literary artists can scarcely have failed to notice, as much modern theorizing about literature would seem to assert, the wily, unpredictable, manifold ways in which language, and particularly writing, would seem to mean. In studying their responses to allusive language, it is clear that most of the writers of the Western tradition have been brave in the face of adversity. They have not succumbed, as many of their twentieth-century readers have, to nail-biting and nihilistic outrage at the indeterminacy of the word. Far from cowering in the corner at the sight of some Poststructural chimera, they have, like Aristophanes or Terence or Dante or Neruda, celebrated the difficulty of the word and in celebrating it, have managed to control for themselves some of the word's power in their own art.

Those who would bemoan language's ability to mean beyond the control of its author, who would worry over language's ludic quality, those who would reject the possibility of communicating something essential and abiding in language by virtue of its nature, cannot seriously advance their skepticism in the face of allusion's function, because allusion teaches those who study it that the surplus of meaning does not portend linguistic chaos—only the transference of meaning's authority from writer to reader. This transference does not mean that language that has forsaken those who would worry over its function, only that the worriers have forgotten the vast and exotic pleasures of writing, one of the more enduring being the luxuriant power of the reader to configure the text being read, to construct it, to nurture it. Allusion sets into high relief this power, but its function also ratifies the essence of writing as a communal project, metaphorized by Pound as the green world of his literary predecessors. To forsake that world because it is difficult or messy is not only to be foolish but, in Pound's words, to err for the sake of diffidence, or perhaps, as Pound himself suggests, to err on account of vanity. Vanity is not a good thing if it keeps us from the community of literature, if it disdains the plenitude of meaning as so much evidence of language's failure, if it allows us to forget, as we seem to have forgotten, in Schiller's words, that humans play only where they are human in the full meaning of the word, that they are wholly human only where they play.

Beyond the historical or aesthetic issues that touch on its function, therefore, allusion remains an abiding prescriptive against those who have forgotten that literature is not simply or merely language, that literature is about pleasure, and that the transcendence that literature always seeks and sometimes achieves is wrought most compellingly in that space where all of Western literature speaks in its various voices to its readers, who, like Walt Whitman, are "leaning late and reading there": " . . . I know I am solid and sound, / To me the converging objects of the universe perpetually flow, / All are written to me, and I must get what that writing means."

Index

Abelard, Peter, 179–198; and body, 179–181, 197–198; and castration, 179–181, 196–198; as reader, 196–198; *Historia calamitatum*, 181–198

Achilles, 172, 184

aemulatio, 86–87

Aeneas, 230–239

Aeschylus, 54, 89

Ajax, 184–185, 187, 194

allegory, xv, 9

alludere, 52

allusio, xvii, 51, 85

allusion: and the author, xvi, 6, 7, 10, 27, 51; and authorial intention, 5, 6, 21; as borrowing, 5, 6, 27, 29, 30–32; and connotative and denotative language, 17, 24, 37–38; as covert, 6, 27, 29, 38–40; and cultural power, 5; as cutting, xvii, 84, 100–106; as echo, 20; and essentialism, xv; as grafting, 100–106; as

implantation, xvii, 84, 99; new definition of, 47; and pragmatics and semantics, 17; and the powerful reader, xvi, xviii, 5, 26, 40–44, 84; and referentiality, 5–6, 21, 27, 29, 32–38; and signification, 6, 16, 28, 33, 51; as textual movement, xvii, 84, 99; and textual violence, xi; as trope, 24; and typologies, 30

allusive space, 43–44

Ambrose, 74

Anacreon, 114, 143; frags. *51* and *11*, 124–128

ancient rhetoric, xvi, 53, 55–63, 83, 86–88

ἀπέρχομαι, 91, 97

Aphrodite, 132–134, 138–140, 242

Andromache, 233–235

Anselm of Laon, 185–186

Apollo, 219–222

Apollonius Rhodius, 122–123